TRUTH

Truth

*Lectures from the 2025
Defend Apologetics Conference*

Tawa J. Anderson, editor

Truth: Lectures from the 2025 Defend Apologetics Conference
© 2025 by DeWard Publishing Company, Ltd.
P.O. Box 290696, Tampa, FL 33687
www.deward.com

All rights reserved. No portion of this book may be reproduced in any form without written permission from the publisher.

Cover design by Madelynn Duke.

Reasonable care has been taken to trace original sources for any excerpts and quotations appearing in this book and to document such information. For material not in the public domain, fair use standards and practices were followed. Should any attribution be found to be incorrect or incomplete, the publisher welcomes written documentation supporting correction for subsequent printing.

Printed in the United States of America.

ISBN: 978-1-947929-38-8

To Bob Stewart

Christian, Gentleman, and Scholar
Mentor, Exemplar, and Friend

Contents

Introduction: A Defense Worth Presenting ix
   Tawa J. Anderson

Part I – Epistemological Truth: Logic and Knowledge

1. "Your Truth, My Truth": Why Such Talk Is Wrong 3
   Richard Howe

2. The Art and Discipline of Identifying Logical Fallacies 19
   Eric Hernandez

3. Loving the Truth: A Profound Challenge 38
   Mary Jo Sharp

4. Permission to Doubt Your Faith 53
   Travis Dickinson

5. The Apologetics Matrix: The Purpose and Audience of
Christian Apologetics 69
   Tawa J. Anderson

Part II – Natural Truth: God and General Revelation

6. Life in a Finely-Tuned Cosmos 89
   Luke Barnes

7. Contemplating the Heavens: How the Beauty and Harmony of
Creation Gave Rise to Modern Science 103
   Melissa Cain Travis

8. What Christian Apologists Might Learn From Scientists 118
   Michael G. Strauss

9. Rhetoric and Reality: Biblical Literalism and a Christian View of Nature 135
   David H. Calhoun

10. If God is Good, Why is There Evil & Suffering?. 157
    Brett Kunkle

Part III – Scriptural Truth: God and Special Revelation

11. Discovering God's Goodness in the Hard Passages of Scripture . . .173
    Matthew Tingblad

12. Cleverly Devised Myths? The Historical Reliability of the Gospels and Acts. 188
    Nathan Ward

13. The Truth of the Deity of Christ 208
    Robert M. Bowman, Jr.

14. This World is Messed Up But God Raised Jesus from the Dead: Addressing the Pastoral Problem of Evil. 223
    Robert B. Stewart

15. Witnessing to Mormons with the Book of Mormon. 239
    James K. Walker

Part IV – Anthropological Truth: Human Nature and Communication

16. I Think, Therefore I'm Trans: A Closer Look at Transgenderism . . .259
    Alycia Wood

17. Sex Matters: Understanding the Differences Between Male and Female and Why It's Good 278
    Erin Kunkle

18. "Am I Not a Man and a Brother?" Scripture and Slavery in Ancient and Modern Contexts. 296
    Paul Copan

19. Straight to the Heart: Communicating the Gospel in an Emotionally Driven Culture. 314
    Mike Blackaby

20. Revelations of a Baptized Memory: Engaging Memory in
Spiritual Development 329
    Megan Rials

Conclusion: A Truth Worth Defending 347
    Tawa J. Anderson

Contributors 349

Introduction
A Defense Worth Presenting

Tawa J. Anderson

This humble book is a compilation of 20 keynote lectures from the Defend 2025 apologetics conference held at New Orleans Baptist Theological Seminary. Each year, Defend draws 400-500 attendees, mostly college students, for a full week of apologetics training and equipping. Defend 2025 had 17 plenary lectures and over 100 breakout sessions in 11 different 'tracks,' each with 11 time slots. Our conference speakers poured out their time and energy, eating meals with students, talking with attendees in between sessions and late into the night. Defend is a one-of-a-kind conference—in my estimation, the single best apologetics conference (bang-for-your-buck) on the planet.

In 2025, we began a three-year conference theme emphasizing the traditional Christian 'transcendentals'—truth, goodness (2026), and beauty (2027). Historically, Christians embrace Jesus as "the way, the truth, and the life," identify God as Truth (pure truth; full knowledge and honesty without admixture of error or deception), and promote Christianity as the true worldview. Furthermore, we embrace God as the Good (indeed, the Greatest Good, or *summum bonum*)—He from whom moral values and duties flow, identify Jesus as the incarnation of that Goodness which we are to emulate, and promote the Christian worldview as being unquestionably good for (i.e., contributing to the flourishing of) individuals and cultures. Finally, we embrace God as both Beauty and the source of all beauty, and promote the Christian worldview as the most beautiful story (metanarrative) on the planet—the story which we should all *want* to be true. The Triune God, then, is Truth, Goodness, and Beauty, and the Christian worldview, centered upon Him, is True, Good, and Beautiful. At Defend 2025, we focused upon that first transcendental—Truth—and these representative keynote lectures embody that Truth.

In contemporary culture, however, truth (let alone capital-T Truth) has fallen on hard times. The rise of aesthetic subjectivism in the 19th century gave birth to moral relativism in the 20th century, and eventually postmodernism questioned the existence of objective truth altogether. The historically-dominant correspondence theory of truth (roughly: truth is a matching relationship between our statements and the way things are in the real world) was replaced by either coherentism (true statements are those which fit with other true beliefs we hold), structuralism (truth is what we create with our mind-dependent language), or pragmatism (truth is what works for us, or 'what our peers will let us get away with'). Truth became a matter of personal perspective (subjectivism) or societal consensus (conventionalism). No longer is it a primary cultural value to pursue a life lived in accordance with objective truth; rather, we are told: "you do you;" "be yourself;" "live your truth;" "live your best life now;" "pursue authenticity."

A key marker of postmodern culture is a suspicion of metanarratives—'stories' that claim to be true for all people in all places at all times. If truth is personal or cultural rather than objective (universal/absolute), then naturally there cannot be an overarching story of the world (worldview) that is true for everyone. The problem, of course, is that Christianity is precisely such a universal story—a worldview which claims to be true for everyone, whether they believe it or not, whether they like it or not. In this volume, then, our twenty contributors defend the Truth of God and the Christian worldview. The book is divided into four thematic sections, each with five chapters.

Epistemological Truth: Logic and Knowledge

Epistemology is the study of knowledge, and involves questions like: What is truth? Does truth exist? What is knowledge? How can we know things? Can we know anything at all? Is there a difference between belief and knowledge? How is knowledge justified? What is the relationship between belief, doubt, and knowledge?

Richard Howe opens the section with a rigorous examination of contemporary relativism, pointing out a myriad of popular confusions regarding subjective and objective truth-claims. Eric Hernandez follows with an illustrated discussion of common logical fallacies, guiding us into avoiding poor reasoning ourselves and lovingly identifying fallacious arguments in others. Mary Jo Sharp discusses the difficulty of truly *loving* truth—a difficulty faced by Christians as much as non-Christians. Travis Dickinson then engages Christian deconstruction, encouraging readers to identify and articulate their questions, and providing concrete steps to faithfully resolve their doubts. To wrap up the section on epistemology, I (Tawa Anderson) outline the purpose and audience of Christian apologetics.

Natural Truth: God and General Revelation

Throughout church history, philosophers and theologians have held that God reveals Himself to humanity in two fashions: through His Word (the Book of Scripture) and through His World or His Works (the Book of Nature). Christians can thus discover divine truths via 'special revelation' (God speaking directly through His Word) and via 'general [or natural] revelation' (God speaking indirectly through His World). Many people wrongly believe that science and Christianity are at odds with one another, and that you have to choose between loving science and loving God; following scientific truth or following Christian faith. Historically, Christians have been at the forefront of encouraging and embracing scientific investigations, and science provides considerable empirical support for the Christian worldview.

Luke Barnes opens with a description of the fine-tuning of the universe at the level of particle physics, showing that the best current science demonstrates the need for an intelligent Creator to craft the parameters of a life-permitting cosmos. Melissa Cain Travis follows with a historical narrative of how the Christian worldview prompted early scientists to explore the beauty and harmony of the cosmos in order to better understand the Mind and Method of our Creator God. Mike Strauss pleads with Christian apologists to refrain from demeaning or demonizing science or scientists; instead, he argues, there is much to be learned from experimentalists and theorists in the hard sciences. David Calhoun explores the origin of 'Biblical literalism,' particularly vis-à-vis the doctrine of Creation in the early chapters of Genesis, advocating for a devout return to a nuanced literalism that avoids the rhetorical excesses seen in some contemporary circles. Brett Kunkle completes the section by responding to David Hume's objection against Natural Theology: if God is good and creates a good universe, then why is there so much dysfunctionality, defective design, evil, and suffering in the world?

Scriptural Truth: God and Special Revelation

While general revelation is sufficient (in my estimation) to arrive at the belief *that God exists*, Christians have traditionally held that salvific knowledge *of God* requires direct (special) revelation from God. Such knowledge God has communicated via the authors of the Old and New Testaments. The Bible communicates the story of God's redemptive-historical plan, first with Abraham and the patriarchs, then with the nation of Israel, and finally through Jesus with the Church. Along the way, Scripture reveals significant truths about God and His Creation.

If the Bible is God's Word, and God's ways are not our ways (Is 55.8–9), then we can expect that some of Scripture will be difficult for us to understand and/or accept. Matthew Tingblad walks us through several tough passages focused on God's law, divine judgment, and the doctrine of hell. If the New Testament does not provide an accurate picture of the person and work of Jesus Christ, then we cannot have any confidence in the central Christian truth-claims of the deity, atoning death, and bodily resurrection of Jesus. Nathan Ward provides a robust defense for the reliability of the historical books of the New Testament (Gospels and Acts). Rob Bowman follows up with a cumulative argument for Jesus's identity as God in the flesh. Bob Stewart then explores how the crucifixion and resurrection of Jesus provide the only compelling response to our tragedies, evils, and sufferings. James Walker concludes the section by interacting with Mormonism's alternative claim to divine inspiration, showing how we can utilize the *Book of Mormon* itself to effectively share the truth of Jesus Christ with Mormons.

Anthropological Truth: Human Nature and Communication

Anthropology is the study (*logos*) of human beings and cultures (*anthropos* = mankind). Both general revelation (God's World) and special revelation (God's Word) have a lot to say about humanity—we are, after all, made in the image of God and appointed stewards (caretakers) over His Good and Beautiful creation (Gen 1.26–30). Several truths about human beings have been misrepresented historically or are rejected today, and thus merit careful consideration.

Alycia Wood begins this section with a close look at transgender ideology, focusing particularly on clinical research and the testimonies of transgender transitioners and rueful de-transitioners. Erin Kunkle then explores the truth and goodness of God-given differences between the biological sexes. Paul Copan addresses the thorny question of slavery, illuminating biblical texts that have been misunderstood as promoting chattel slavery and highlighting the Scriptural trajectory toward the equal freedom of men and women of all races. Mike Blackaby switches gears and contemplates how people communicate: while humans are a combination of hands, head, and heart, he argues that we best respond to appeals to the heart; hence our apologetics and evangelism need to take emotions, not just rationality, into account. Finally, Megan Rials wraps up the entire volume with an exploration of the role of memory in discipleship, exegeting and building upon C.S. Lewis's ground-breaking work on 'baptized memory.'

In sum, these twenty chapters cover significant ground in epistemology, science, Scripture, and anthropology. The truth of the Christian worldview is worth defending, and as such, its defense is worth presenting. I trust that these chapters, individually and corporately, are an encouragement and a challenge as you seek to know and live the Truth in a post-truth society.

Acknowledgements

A project like this does not come together without the invaluable contribution of numerous individuals and teams. While some will inevitably be overlooked (please accept my sincere apologies), I would like to thank:

Nathan Ward, our editor and publisher with DeWard Publishing, for brainstorming together in summer 2024, and for seeing the value of the three-year project.

Our Defend 2025 speakers who have contributed not only to this volume, but to the success of the conference.

The Media Services and Communications teams at New Orleans Baptist Theological Seminary for not only ensuring that the Defend conference ran smoothly, but also for providing video, audio, and written transcripts of plenary sessions. Particular thanks to Thomas Johnson, Jeremy Montgomery, and Joseph and Madelynn Duke.

Brianna Oakley and Julie Ponder from NOBTS's Conferences Office for indomitable and flawless organizational work shepherding us apologists, academics, and speakers.

Emma Gregory, my administrative assistant at NOBTS's Institute for Christian Apologetics (ICA). She learned her job while I was learning mine, and was a God-sent gift with her attention to detail, excellence in communication, and eagerness to learn.

Marilyn Stewart and Emma Gregory, who did a tremendous amount of editing and polishing of individual chapters—you are both unsung heroes without whom this book would be far less beautiful (if it came together at all!).

The Administration and Trustees of NOBTS, for seeing the value of the Defend apologetics conference, and committing institutional resources and personnel toward its success.

My long-suffering wife, Vanessa, who endured yet another semester with an over-worked, too-often-absent husband. May we soon enjoy an empty nest accompanied by a less-demanding and less-stressful plate of commitments.

Finally, Dr. Robert (Bob) Stewart, my predecessor as Director of the ICA and the founding genius behind the Defend conference. For over a decade, Bob built the conference from the ground up. In addition, Bob has been a mentor, example, and friend to me. I am grateful for his confidence in nominating me to succeed him at the helm of Defend and the ICA. It is to 'Uncle Bob' that I dedicate this anthology.

PART ONE

Epistemological Truth
Logic and Knowledge

1

Your Truth, My Truth
Why Such Talk Is Wrong

Richard G. Howe

Introduction

As a student of Norman Geisler at Dallas Theological Seminary in the early 80s, I remember an episode he recounted about being approached by a coed after one of his presentations on a university campus. After the talk, she came up to him and remarked something to the effect, "That's very interesting, but that's your truth, not my truth." As Americans, Christians had been used to the specter of moral relativism that had been plaguing our country for decades. But this was Geisler's first encounter with a relativism about truth itself. Not very long before this incident, a Christian could make the claim in the marketplace of ideas that he held the Bible to be true with the rightful expectation that everyone would understand what he meant. To be sure, some would disagree with the claim but would undoubtedly know what the Christian was claiming when saying something was true. With the increasing influence of Postmodernism, a.k.a., relativism, it has only gotten worse since Geisler's encounter. No longer can we as Christians make a claim about the truth of Christianity and expect to always be understood.[1]

---

[1] In the Relativism course I teach at Southern Evangelical Seminary, we examine eight different types of relativism: relativism and truth; relativism and knowledge; relativism and faith/reason; relativism and history; relativism and morality; relativism and religion; relativism and the Bible; and relativism and the Gospel. In this chapter, I will have something to say only about relativism and truth and relativism and history.

Not All Relativism Is Bad

Before I unpack the elements of Postmodern Relativism, a few things need to be clarified. First, there are certain situations or experiences that can be true for one person and not true for another. Consider for example a father walking his toddler on the beach out into the ocean. It would take only a few steps before the water was "deep" to the toddler while still being "shallow" to the father. What constitutes 'deep' would be in relationship to—if you will, relative to—the height of the person. The same could be said about the categories of 'big' and 'little'. A spider the size of the hand would certainly seem big. But a baby elephant, though much bigger than the spider, will nevertheless seem small. The reason is because a spider as big as the hand is big *for a spider* while a baby elephant is small *for an elephant*. Further, everyone has experienced the differences of opinion about foods. I personally enjoy asparagus and loathe brussels sprouts. To be sure, if someone said to me, "Brussels sprouts taste good and asparagus tastes bad," I would not respond, "That's your truth, but not my truth." Instead, I would say that brussels sprouts taste bad *to me*. But the point remains that a given food can taste good to one person and taste bad to another.[2] Such examples show that my criticisms of relativism do not deny that things are relative in some sense.

Defining Some Terms

Subjective vs. Objective. An explanation of a few terms and categories is in order so as to make our examination and criticisms of Postmodern Relativism possible. First, we need to say something about the expressions 'subjective' (or 'subjective truth') and 'objective' (or 'objective truth').[3] Something is subjective when it can legitimately be true for one person and not true for another. Something is objective when it cannot legit-

---

[2] As will be made clear in due course, the statement "Brussels sprouts taste bad to Richard" is true for everyone even when the statement "Brussels sprouts taste bad to me" is true when I say it while it might be false when someone else says it. Such statements are known as token-reflexives or indexicals because the truth (or meaning) of a statement is "indexed" to the person saying the statement. For a treatment of the debates about token-reflexives and indexicals, see García-Carpintero, "Indexical."

[3] It should be noted that the contemporary definitions and usages of these terms 'subjective' and 'objective' that I give here are very nearly the reverse of the definitions and usages one will find in English translations of certain medieval philosophers. See, for example, Klima, "William Ockham."

imately be true for one person and not true for another. Of course, the operational term here is 'legitimately'.

Pressing things a little more, to be subjective means that the truth or falsity of a claim is with reference to the subject making the claim. It is dependent upon the subject's opinion or situation or some other factor that obtains with the subject. To be objective means that the truth or falsity of a claim is with reference to the object about which the claim is made. It is not dependent upon the subject's opinion or situation or some other factor that obtains with the subject. Thus, to say that "asparagus tastes good" is subjective in that it might be true for one person that it tastes good and false for another person that it tastes good. The "good taste" is dependent upon how the asparagus affects the taster. But consider the fact that asparagus is a vegetable. It would not make sense to say that asparagus is a vegetable to one person but not a vegetable to another person. The "vegetable-ness" of asparagus is something true of the asparagus itself and is not relative to any individual person.

Truth: Reality vs. Practicality. A third term that needs unpacking is 'truth'. Pontius Pilate famously asked Jesus, "What is truth?" (John 18.38).[4] The irony is that Pilate was asking the very one who said, "I am the way, the truth, and the life." (John 14.6) Elsewhere Jesus said, "And you shall know the truth, and the truth shall make you free." (John 8.32) The Geisler story shows the need to define the terms 'true' and 'truth'. A number of factors have led to confusion about truth. One factor that cannot entirely be blamed on the influences of Postmodern Relativism is the rise of competing definitions—what philosophers call theories—of truth. I contend that most people have what is known in philosophy as the correspondence theory of truth.[5] It says that a statement is true when it corresponds to reality.[6] Consider someone saying, "It is raining," after which someone asks, "Is that true?" only to have the first one answer, "Yes,

---

[4] Unless otherwise indicated, all Scripture quotations are from *The New King James Version* (1982).

[5] Other theories of truth include coherence, functional, power, and pragmatic. For explanations and examples of each, see Howe, "Truth about Truth."

[6] Aristotle succinctly put it this way. "To say of what is, that it is not, or of what is not, that it is, is false, while to say of what is, that it is and of what is not, that it is not, is true." [Aristotle, *Metaphysics*, IV, 7, 1011^{b}26-29].

it is." When the statement 'it is raining' is characterized as being true, this means that the statement "corresponds" to reality, which is to say that it is raining in reality. To be sure, there are different ways a true statement can correspond to reality. It could be raining now and not raining tomorrow or it could be raining here and not raining there and more.[7]

The practical significance of truth as correspondence to reality can easily be seen. No one would opt for an airplane pilot or physician who had a disregard for whether his instructions about flying or medicine corresponded to reality. We want the plane to *really* fly and the medicine to *really* cure. But while truth as correspondence can have tremendous pragmatic import, pragmatism itself—the idea that what "works" or is practical is true—is not a viable theory of truth. What is true might very well be pragmatic or practical. Indeed, in eternity the truth of God in one's life will lead to everlasting joy in communion with God. This side of eternity, however, what is true may or may not lead to personal practicality or flourishing. The testimony of Christian martyrs deftly demonstrates this. Thus, while being true may or may not translate into being pragmatic, it must be emphasized that just because something is pragmatic does not mean that it is true.[8]

Relativism and Religion: Religious Pluralism

The pragmatic theory of truth can lead to confusion. When the subject under consideration moves from the subjective to the objective, such a theory of truth will fail. As with the coed's comment to Geisler, there is likely no greater chance of encountering this failed theory of truth than with the subject of religion. With respect to religion, the relativism arising from the pragmatic theory of truth is more often called *religious*

---

[7] I have identified in the Bible at least eleven different ways that a true statement can correspond to reality, including literally, allegorically (allegory), metaphorically (metaphor), similarly (simile; technically, the noun 'simile' does not have an adverb form in English although 'similarly' seems to do the job.), analogically (analogy), symbolically (symbol), hyperbolically (hyperbole), phenomenologically, informally, synecdochically (synecdoche), and metonymically (metonymy). For biblical examples of each, see Howe, "Truth about Truth."

[8] Note in Jeremiah 44.16–18 how the Israelites defended their wickedness in burning incense to the queen of heaven and pouring out drink offerings to her by how beneficial the consequences were for them when they did so and how detrimental the consequences were for them when they did not.

pluralism. While the expression might refer to nothing more than the mere observation that there are many religions in the world, often the expression is referring to something more ominous. It can sometimes be an attempt—if only veiled—to claim that all religions are equally "valid" or "true." I suspect this is exactly what the coed was claiming. In this respect, it is likening religion to a hobby. One person may enjoy collecting coins while another may enjoy collecting stamps. It would be silly for the stamp collector to claim that coin collecting is a "false" hobby and insist that one should only collect stamps. The expression does not even make sense. A hobby correctly understood cannot be true or false because it does not make any claims about reality. What we are seeing is the increase of people who are understanding religions akin to hobbies. They are happy for someone who might prefer Christianity as his religion. But in the view of one who sees religion as one sees a hobby, it is unseemly if not outright offensive for the Christian to insist that others should embrace Christianity as well.

Religious pluralism poses several challenges to the evangelical Christian. Do religions even make claims about reality and human destiny or, like hobbies, are they merely designed to provide personal enjoyment and fulfillment? If religion is relevant to human destiny, could it be that all religions basically lead to the same destination? If religions are making claims about reality, are not all religions the same at the core and only differ in the peripherals? Or might it be the case that other religions are making claims that are incompatible with the claims of Christianity? If that is so, then how can the evangelical Christian maintain that only Christianity is true? Further, if it is the case that only Christianity is true, are the followers of those other religions eternally lost? This question then leads to the question that is likely the most commonly asked in this context, to wit, what about those who sincerely follow a false religion and never had a chance to hear the Gospel? A few comments are in order about these challenges.

Christianity and Truth. At the New Hampshire Writers' Project, Dan Brown, author of *The Da Vinci Code* commented, "I humbly submit that if all of us in this room had been born in Tibet, probably a lot of us would be Buddhist. I think the chance is pretty good. And I also think we'd hold on to that Buddhist philosophy with all the passion that some of us might hold on to our Christian ideals."[9] I think it is safe to assume that Dan Brown expected, rightly or wrongly, that many if not most in his audience self-identified as Christians. One should wonder exactly what Brown is implying with this comment, even if it was true. Let us grant it for the sake of argument. Even if it was true that most of the audience would be Buddhist instead of Christian if they had been born in Tibet, this has nothing to do with whether Buddhism is true or false and whether Christianity is true or false. What is more, Brown's claim is potentially self-refuting. One could respond to him by saying that the only reason Dan Brown believes what he said is because of where Dan Brown was born. In other words, maybe there is as much reason to dismiss Dan Brown's statement as he thinks there is to dismiss Christianity.

The problem here is that Brown is committing the genetic fallacy. This is the fallacy of suggesting that the origin of a belief is relevant to the issue of whether the belief is true or false. I suspect that if someone grew up in the Amazon jungle, he might very well believe that the Earth is stationary relative to the Sun and that the Sun is moving relative to the Earth (Geocentrism) instead of the reverse (Heliocentrism). With this, one can see how irrelevant Brown's comment is when cast this way. "I humbly submit that if all of us in this room had been born in the Amazon jungle, probably a lot of us would be Geocentrists. I think the chance is pretty good. And I also think we'd hold on to that Geocentric philosophy with all the passion that some of us might hold on to our Heliocentric ideals."

What would we say about someone who was born at a place or time in the world where they held such a view about the Earth and the Sun? Would we not say that if someone was in this situation, he would have been raised to believe something false about the Solar System? So, by parallel, the evangelical should not be shy in accepting the challenge for the sake of argument that if he was born in Tibet, he would have been a

---

[9] Whitcraft, "Meet the Real."

Buddhist. What this would mean, however, is that he would have been raised to believe a false religion.

Hopefully, this response would prompt Dan Brown to retort something to the effect, "How do you know your Christianity is true and the Buddhism is false?" With this, we would offer a hearty "thank you" to Dan Brown. This is the question he should have posed in the first place. To claim that if one had been born somewhere else, he would have believed something different is irrelevant to the question as to whether what he was raised to belief is true or not.

Now, in saying this, I am not suggesting that Brown's challenge is irrelevant on all counts. In fact, it is precisely what the evangelical Christian goes on to claim regarding Jesus as the only way to eternal life that gives rise to the additional challenges regarding the fate of someone who seemingly, through no fault of his own, had no opportunity to hear and believe the one message that would lead him to eternal life.

Christianity and Other Religions. One way some have sought to avoid the difficulty posed by Dan Brown's comment and show how it is that no one is at a disadvantage by being trapped, if you will, to believe what they do because of where they were born is by suggesting that perhaps all religions are the same at the core and only differ on the peripheral, less important, issues.[10] In this case, every religion will convey this essential core and no one will be in danger of missing those core truths due to the exigencies of his birth.

However, some might be quite surprised when looking at the world's religions. There, one will find the exact opposite. Many of the world's religions advocate moral duties like do not murder, do not steal, do not lie, be fair, honor your parents and elders, nurture children, and more.[11] These

---

[10] Jesus Seminar member Marcus Borg maintained, "[Religions] all affirm a way, a path; and the paths are all recognizable variants of the same path, the same way. ... The Way of the cross, the way of Lao Tzu, the way of the Buddha, the way of Islam, and the way of Judaism all speak of the same path: the path of dying to an old identity and way of being and being born into a new identity and way of being. All refer to the same transformation of the self." Borg, *Heart of Christianity*, 216.

[11] For example, Buddhism says, "Whoso in this world destroys life, tells lies, takes what is not given, goes to others' wives and is addicted to intoxicating drinks, such a one digs up his own root in the world." [*Dhammapada*, 246–247, 61]. Hinduism says, "He who commits adultery is punished both here and hereafter; for his days in this world are cut short and when dead he falls into hell." [*Vishnu*

will undoubtedly remind the Christian of the Ten Commandments. It is the same moral sense that motivated the writers of the Declaration of Independence where, when seeking to justify the States' right to declare independence from the British Crown, they appealed to the entitlement given by "the Laws of Nature and of Nature's God." To be sure, the expression 'laws of nature' include the familiar forces of nature like gravity or electromagnetism. But here it is specifically picking out moral laws. Just as it is that gravity and electromagnetism can be known and understood (at least to a certain extent) by human reason without reference to the Bible, the assumption on the part of the Founding Fathers maintained that there were certain moral truths that also could be known (again, at least to a certain extent) by human reason without reference to the Bible.[12] The presence of such moral duties in the world's religions that do not acknowledge the Bible corroborates this. This idea has come to be known as Natural Law Theory.[13]

The core beliefs would be those doctrines that define and distinguish each religion. These moral truths are not the defining core of these religions. Rather for some religions, these moral values are, in one way or another, implications of—which is to say peripheral to—their core. For others, they are deeply inconsistent with their core but nevertheless peripheral to it. Consider how a given religion will answer these basic questions: Does God Exist? What is God like? Who is Jesus? Is there life after death? How does one gain eternal life? The answers could not be more

---

Purana 3.11, 265]. Elsewhere, Hinduism says, "A man who commits violence [some translations have "murder"] should be regarded as the worst evil-doer." [*Laws of Manu*, 8.345, 188].

[12] Some argue that this is exactly what the Apostle Paul was referencing in Romans 2.14–15. "For when Gentiles, who do not have the law, by nature do the things in the law, these, although not having the law, are a law to themselves, who show the work of the law written in their hearts, their conscience also bearing witness, and between themselves their thoughts accusing or else excusing them."

[13] The American Founding Fathers were influenced by John Locke's *Two Treatises on Government*. The moral dimension of Locke's political philosophy is perhaps a vestige of Thomas Aquinas's thinking whose treatment of Natural Law is undoubtedly the zenith. It can be found in his *Summa Theologiae*, Ia-IIæ, QQ. 90–114 which has been separately published as *Treatise on Law*. For a treatment of Locke's view of Natural Law, including a treatment of the relationship between Aquinas's thinking and that of John Locke and how they differ, see Feser, *Locke*, 108–122. Feser expounds on Aquinas's Natural Law thinking in Feser, *Aquinas*, 174–192. For other treatments of Natural Law Theory, see Budziszewski, *Written*; Charles, *Retrieving*; Geisler and Turek, *Legislating*; Grabill, *Rediscovering*; Haines and Fulford, *Natural Law*; Richard G. Howe, "God and Morality" and "Moral Argument" and David VanDrunen, *Divine Covenants* and *Natural Law*.

diverse. Take, for example, the fact that Theravada Buddhism does not have a deity. Upanishadic Hinduism is pantheistic. Bhakti Hinduism is polytheistic. Judaism, Christianity, and Islam are monotheistic.[14] One will find such a spectrum in the answers to the other basic questions.

Perhaps the most illustrative of my point that not all religions are the same at the core is how they answer the question "Who is Jesus?" In my thirty years of teaching World Religions at Southern Evangelical Seminary, I have discovered that there is no other religion that says what we as evangelical Christians say in answer to this question. The absurdity of the claim that all religions are the same at the core is never more evident when one sees that no religion says what we say about the most important element of our religion, i.e., that Jesus is the unique Son of God, God in the flesh who died for the sins of the world and rose from the dead to offer eternal life and to give it to those and only those who trust in Him.

With this, it is manifest that I take religions to be saying something about reality whether explicitly or implicitly. Even if it is the case that for some people, religion functions like little more than a hobby, I know of no religion that fails to make claims about the human situation and offer a response—a solution, if you will—to remedy that situation. Where such claims conflict with each other, they cannot all be true. Since they are not all making the same claims about reality and offer radically different answers to the human condition and solution, it follows that they do not all lead to the same destination. The task, therefore, would be to adjudicate these claims to discover which, if any, of these religions are true at their core. This undertaking is precisely what Christian apologetics does in obedience to 1 Peter 3.15, "But sanctify the Lord God in your hearts, and always be ready to give a defense to everyone who asks you a reason for the hope that is in you, with meekness and fear." Christian apologetics deftly answers the challenge of how the Christian can say that Christianity is the only religion that has the truth about God and our relationship to Him. The task of apologetics shows the foundational principles that reality is knowable and that truth is objective. With that foundation, the

---

[14] Corduan, *Neighboring Faiths*.

Christian can demonstrate the existence and nature of God inasmuch as "since the creation of the world His invisible attributes are clearly seen, being understood by the things that are made, even His eternal power and Godhead" (Rom 1.20a).

The revelation of God in nature is known as General Revelation. The revelation of God in the Bible is Special Revelation. Demonstrating the existence of God establishes the possibility of miracles. Miracles, along with other data, play a role in establishing the historical evidence showing that Christianity is true. Given that God is known through His creation and through His Prophets, Apostles, and the Lord Jesus, the case can be made first, that no one, no matter where they are born, lacks full access to God's revelation of himself through creation; and second, to everyone who responds in faith to that revelation, God will get the gospel message and he will believe it.[15]

Relativism and History: Historicism and Situatedness

I should now like to take a look at another kind of relativism that plagues our culture and is an impediment to an objective understanding of God's truth in the Bible. This is the relativism of history. The notion of relativism with respect to history is sometimes called 'historicism'. Historicism maintains that one's place in history—his "situatedness"—unavoidably and inescapably prevents one from being able to acquire objective knowledge about reality. One can see the impact of historicism regarding making objective moral judgments about other cultures and objective judgments about biblical interpretation. If it is the case that one is inevitably influenced by one's own historical situatedness, then it would not be possible to objectively know the truth about events or writings that are situated in a different "history."

Canadian philosopher Jean Grondin puts it this way. "The basic doctrine [of historicism] is that every particular phenomenon must be conceptualized within the context of its age. The point is to avoid judging other times by the standards of our own, and instead to interpret historical

---

[15] Clearly, more needs to be said in defense of my claims here. See Howe, "What About Those," and Geivett, "A Particularist View."

events immanently, as expressive of their time."[16] But if "every particular phenomenon must be conceptualized within the context of its age," then how can one know what historicism is? Would not historicism as a model of interpretation itself have to be "conceptualized within the context of its age?" In which case, the very act of conceptualizing it would be within the context of the age of the one doing the conceptualizing. In this case, then, there would be no way to know whether, and to what extent, such a conceptualizing alters what historicism even is in the first place.

Australian philosopher C. Behan McCullagh maintains:

> First, scientists tell us that our perceptions are caused by things in the world stimulating our sense receptors ... This being so, our perceptions are best described as providing us with information about reality, but not necessarily mirroring it precisely. ... Second, our perceptions are influenced by our culture. ... So our perceptions of the world are not pure sense impressions of it. ... Finally, our perceptions are influenced by our needs, interests and desires. ... For these three reasons, at least, it is wrong to say that our perceptions simply correspond to the world.[17]

One must ask whether McCullagh's observation about perceptions mirrors them precisely. Are McCullagh's observations about perceptions influenced by his culture? Are his observations about perceptions influenced by his own needs, interests, and desires? Does McCullagh's conclusion about his own observations follow, to wit, that McCullagh is wrong to say that his observations "simply correspond to the world?" For McCullagh's comments to be consistent, the answer to each of these would have to be 'yes'. Given this, why should we believe that anything he says about perceptions is objectively true?

Such views on situatedness can be found among Christian theologians and biblical scholars. One can see how toxic the implications of historical relativism have been for principles of biblical interpretation. In every case, the foundation is laid that prevents in principle objective knowledge about what the written text of the Bible means. Philosopher Carl A. Raschke offers this observation in seeking to understand the Bi-

---

[16] Grondin, *Einführung*, 115.
[17] McCullagh, *Truth of History*, 17.

ble. "It is up to the interpreter to provide a new framework of discourse in which what was first written or spoken can be fleshed out. The 'truth' of a text can be discerned in its deployability within a particular set of life circumstances."[18] But, if "it is up to the interpreter to provide a new framework of discourse," then how are we to take the meaning Raschke is seeking to communicate through his own statement here? If the interpreter provides a new framework, then why should one take Raschke's statement to be objectively true?

Theologian Stanley J. Grenz argues, "In contrast to the modern ideal of the dispassionate observer, we affirm the postmodern discovery that no observer can stand outside the historical process. Nor can we gain universal, culturally neutral knowledge as unconditioned specialists. On the contrary, we are participants in our historical and cultural context, and all our intellectual endeavors are unavoidably conditioned by that participation."[19] But if what Grenz says is true, then his own statement itself does not come from an observer who stands "outside the historical process" and, thus, the statement is not itself "neutral knowledge" coming from an "unconditioned specialist." Since this is the case, why should one believe that Grenz's comments are objectively true?

Psychologist and essayist Dan McGee explains Postmodernism this way. "Postmodernism ... argues that all knowledge is mediated by an individual and that the experiences, biases, beliefs, and identity of that individual necessarily influence how they mediate any knowledge."[20] But if "all knowledge is mediated" and the individual has "biases" that "necessarily influence how they mediate *any* knowledge" (emphasis added), then this would be true of Dan McGee and the knowledge claim he is making here. But if this is true of Dan McGee's claim, why should one take his claim to be objectively true?

Theologian Robert E. Webber maintained, "In the twenty-first century world ... the new attitude ... is that the use of reason and science to prove or disprove a fact is questionable. ... This ... points ... to the postmodern

---

[18] Raschke, "Faith and Philosophy," 61.
[19] Grenz, *Primer*, 166.
[20] McGee, "Truth."

conclusion that we deal with 'interpreted facts.'"[21] But if we deal with "interpreted facts," then what does that say about Webber's statement itself? Is his claim here merely an "interpreted fact?" If so, then why should we take it as objectively true?

From these examples and many more we could give, it is evident how such a view of history and one's place in it can be detrimental to the notion that there is objective truth in the text of the Bible and that this truth can be known by the reader. To say that one's culture, language, upbringing, and other factors of his historical "situatedness" are unavoidable and will necessarily impact how he understands what he hears or reads is to abandon objectivity altogether. While it can at times happen that one's "situatedness" would obscure his understanding of what he hears and reads, it cannot be the case that it inevitably does so. As philosopher and language scholar Thomas Howe observes,

> If objective knowledge of history is out of reach, this is particularly problematic for Christianity that is based on the historical record of the Bible. Additionally, the problem of historicism poses a serious obstacle to the possibility of objective knowledge. The fact that every interpreter investigates history from his own historical situatedness raises the question of whether an interpreter's understanding of history is simply a view from his own place within history.[22]

Conclusion

Relativism is having an adverse impact on how some understand religion and history. The Christian needs to be steadfast in defending that Christianity is not merely a way of life but is making claims about reality that are objectively true. What is more, the Christian views the Bible as the written, inspired, and inerrant Word of God that gives us objective truth about reality, i.e., God and His creation. It is incumbent upon us to defend those claims in the marketplace of ideas. Part of that defense will at times need to show the error of religious relativism and historical relativism. To that end, we can show that, while some claims are relative to the individual, like the taste of certain foods, others are important

---

[21] Webber, *Younger Evangelicals*, 84.
[22] Howe, *Objectivity*, 55.

claims that are objectively true. Such claims include Christianity is true; religions are not all the same at the core; we can know objective truths from history, including from the Bible; and the methods of Postmodern Relativism are self-refuting.

Bibliography

Aquinas, Thomas. *Treatise on Law*. Cambridge: Hackett Publishing, Hackett Classics, 2000.

_____. *St. Thomas Aquinas Summa Theologica: Complete English Edition in Five Volumes*. Translation Fathers of the English Dominican Province. Westminster, MD: Christian Classics, 1981.

Aristotle. *Metaphysics*. Translation W. D. Ross. In Richard McKeon *The Basic Works of Aristotle*. New York: Random House, 1941.

Borg, Marcus. *The Heart of Christianity: Rediscovering a Life of Faith*. San Francisco: Harper Collins, 2003.

Buddhism. *Dhammapada* 246–247. Translation Acharya Buddharakkita. Kandy: Buddhist Publication Society, 1985.

Budziszewski, J. *Written on the Heart: The Case for Natural Law*. Downers Grove: InterVarsity Press, 1997.

Charles, J. Daryl. *Retrieving the Natural Law: A Return to Moral First Things*. Grand Rapids: William B. Eerdmans, 2008.

Corduan, Winfried. *Neighboring Faiths: A Christian Introduction to World Religions*. 2nd ed. Downers Grove: IVP Academic, 2012.

Ehrman, Bart. "Bart Ehrman—Are You a Postmodernist?" https://www.youtube.com/watch?v=uEc-MN2hTEA (2022), accessed 02/14/25.

Feser, Edward. *Locke*. Oxford: Oneworld, 2007.

_____. *Aquinas: A Beginner's Guide*. Oxford: Oneworld, 2009.

García-Carpintero, Manuel. "Indexical as Token-Reflexives," *Mind* 107 (July 1998): 529–563.

Geisler, Norman and Frank Turek. *Legislating Morality: Is It Wise? Is It Legal? Is It Possible?* Minneapolis: Bethany House, 1998. Republished *Legislating Morality*. Eugene: Wipf and Stock, 2003.

Geivett, R. Douglas. "A Particularist View: An Evidentialist Approach." In *Four Views on Salvation in a Pluralistic World*. Grand Rapids: Zondervan, 1996.

Grabill Stephen J. *Rediscovering the Natural Law in Reformed Theological Ethics*. Grand Rapids: William B. Eerdmans, 2006.

Grenz, Stanley J. *A Primer on Postmodernism*. Grand Rapids: William B. Eerdmans, 1996.

Grondin, Jean. *Einführung in die philosophische Hermeneutik*, 3d ed. Darmstadt: Wissenschaftliche Buchgesellshift, 2012.

Haines, David and Andrew A. Fulford. *Natural Law: A Brief Introduction and Biblical Defense*. Lincoln: Davenant, 2017.

Howe. Richard G. "God and Morality." http://richardghowe.com/index_htm_files/GodandMorality.pdf, 2015.

_____. "The Moral Argument for God's Existence: Some Thomistic Natural Law Musings," https://quodlibetalblog.wordpress.com/2018/04/17/the-moral-argument-for-gods-existence-some-thomistic-natural-law-musings/, 2018.

_____. "Truth about Truth." http://richardghowe.com/index_htm_files/TruthaboutTruth16x9.pdf, 2024.

_____. "What About Those Who Have Never Heard the Gospel? http://richardghowe.com/index_htm_files/WhatAboutThoseWhoHaveNeverHeard16x9.pdf, 2025.

Howe, Thomas A. *Objectivity in Biblical Interpretation*. Altamonte Springs: Advantage Books, 2004.

Kenneson, Philip D. "There's No Such Thing as Objective Truth, and It's a Good Thing, Too." In Timothy R. Phillips and Dennis L. Okholm *Christian Apologetics in the Postmodern World*. Downers Grove: IVP Academic, 1995.

Klima, Gyula. "William Ockham on Universals." In Gyula Klima, ed. *Medieval Philosophy: Essential Readings with Commentary*. Hoboken: Wiley-Blackwell, 2007), 71–78.

Laws of Manu. Translation Wendy Doniger and Brian K. Smith. London: Penguin, 1991.

Locke, John. *Two Treatises on Government*. Suffolk: The Chaucer Press, 1982.

McCullagh, C. Behan. *The Truth of History*. London: Routledge, 1997.

McGee, Dan. "Truth and Postmodernism." https://medium.com/@dddanmcgee/truth-and-postmodernism-816ea9b3007a, 2017.

The New King James Version. Nashville: Thomas Nelson, 1982.

Raschke. Carl A. "Faith and Philosophy in Tension." In Steve Wilkins, ed., *Faith and Philosophy: Three Views*. Downers Grove: IVP Academic, 2014.

Rorty. Richard. *Philosophy and the Mirror of Nature*. Princeton: Princeton University Press, 1981.

_____. "Solidarity or Objectivity," In *Objectivity, Relativism, and Truth: Philosophical Papers Vol. 1*. Cambridge: Cambridge University Press, 1991.

VanDrunen, David. *Divine Covenants and the Moral Order: A Biblical Theology of Natural Law*. Grand Rapids: William B. Eerdmans, 2014.

_____. *Natural Law: A Short Companion*. Brentwood: B&H Academic, 2023.

Vishnu Purana. Translation not indicated. Delhi: Motilal Banarsidass Publishers, 2002.

Webber, Robert E. *The Younger Evangelicals: Facing the Challenges of the New World*. Grand Rapids: Baker, 2002.

Whitcraft, Michael. "Meet the Real Dan Brown." https://www.tfp.org/meet-the-real-dan-brown/, 2006.

2

The Art and Discipline of Identifying Logical Fallacies

Eric Hernandez

Biblical Basis: Proverbs 26.4–5

Do not answer a fool according to his folly, or you yourself will be just like him. Answer a fool according to his folly, or he will be wise in his own eyes.

At first glance, these verses appear contradictory, leaving us to ask: should we answer a fool according to their folly or not? The key lies in understanding the reasons given for each instruction.

To begin with, the term "folly" entails the notion of foolishness or lacking good sense. When conversing with a nonbeliever, the first verse advises against responding to a fool in a manner that mirrors their irrationality—doing so makes us equally foolish. For example, responding to an insult with "I know you are, but what am I?" achieves nothing and lowers us to their level. We are instructed to avoid this "lest we become like him." In the second verse, we're instructed to answer a fool in a way that exposes and corrects their folly, preventing them from thinking their ideas are wise.

Two Rules for Conversing with Nonbelievers

With this biblical basis, we now have two "rules" for conversing with nonbelievers:

Rule #1: Avoid fallacious reasoning (lest you be like him).

Rule #2: Expose and correct their fallacious reasoning (lest he thinks he's right).

When defending Christianity, we must honor God as the foundation of reason and logic by presenting arguments that are consistent, rational, and biblically sound. Logical fallacies, incoherent reasoning, or unbiblical responses do not glorify Him. At the same time, when faced with flawed arguments, we must refute them with clarity and truth, offering corrections that reveal the flaws in their reasoning.

Identifying Logical Fallacies: The Example of Jesus

In the most basic sense, a **logical fallacy** is an error in logic or reason that either "breaks" a law of logic (a **formal logical fallacy**) or contains a fault in reasoning to a conclusion (an **informal logical fallacy**). Suffice it to say, Jesus was a master at this! Although you'll be hard-pressed to find the phrase "logical fallacy" or "false dichotomy" coming from the mouth of Jesus, we can examine one instance (among many) in which he employed this tool brilliantly.

Jesus Engages with the Sadducees. In Matthew 22.23–33, a group of Sadducees approach Jesus to question his belief in the resurrection. Before we look at their argument, some background context is needed.

To begin with, the Sadducees were a group of Jewish leaders and priests that followed God but denied commonly held theological beliefs, such as the existence of angels, the soul, and most notably, the resurrection of the dead (Acts 23.6–8). Hence, they're described as "those who say there is no resurrection of the dead." This further entailed a denial of two beliefs relevant to the situation: 1) the afterlife and 2) what is known in theology as the **intermediate state**—where a person continues to exist as a disembodied soul after death but prior to the final, bodily resurrection (which again, they denied).

For this reason, they'll present Jesus with a thought experiment with the intent of exposing His belief in the resurrection (and, by default, His belief in the afterlife and the intermediate state)[1] as a ***reductio ad absurdum*** fallacy. Their goal will be to show that if what Jesus believes is true, it'll ultimately lead to absurd conclusions.

The Argument From the Sadducees (verses 24–28). In a paraphrased fashion, their argument can be summarized as follows:

> Jesus, we don't believe in an afterlife, but you do, and here's the problem. Suppose a woman has seven husbands throughout her lifetime (marrying each one after the previous passes). When she dies and is resurrected, whose wife will she be in heaven? Because if what you believe is true, then it seems you only have two options—both of which lead to absurdity. If you say she's only married to the first, then she commits adultery against the other six. If you say she's married to all seven, then she commits polygamy. Either way, both options are prohibited by God, which is precisely the problem with your position. Your beliefs reduce to absurdity and, therefore, must be rejected.

Two Responses From Jesus. To understand the approach Jesus is about to take, two more things must be understood for context. First, the Sadducees were experts in Jewish law who *prided themselves in knowing and memorizing* Scripture. Second, Sadducees often had disciples that followed them around to sit under their teachings. Given that this was a premeditated attempt to publicly humiliate Jesus as ignorant and unbiblical (showing that their "intellect" was superior to His), there would've been a large group of their students with them.

Additionally, much like middle school students running to see a fight in the cafeteria, a sizable crowd would've gathered as they saw this group approaching Jesus. This was understandably a public challenge in this culture,[2] and the people were eager to see this fight happen. With this contextual picture in your mind, consider the two ways in which Jesus responds.

The Rebuttal (verses 29–30). In His first response, Jesus begins by publicly calling out their ignorance, telling them, "You are all wrong because you don't know the Scriptures." Given their pride in *devoting their lives* to

---

[1] "...future resurrection included affirmation of the intermediate state." Cooper, *Body, Soul, and Life Everlasting*, 136.

[2] O'Brien and Richards, *Misreading Scripture with Western Eyes*, 129, 135.

knowing and memorizing Scripture (and given the social context of the situation), this was *a public insult to* their perceived intelligence (again, think of the cafeteria scene). The crowd would've lost their minds!

Next, He points out how their argument rests entirely on the assumption that there's marriage in Heaven. Given that He rejects this false presupposition, their objection fails and is exposed as a false dichotomy. Hence, His rebuttal:

> You are all wrong because you do not know the Scriptures or the power of God. At the resurrection people will neither marry nor be given in marriage.

At this point, He's successfully demolished their argument. But consider the brilliance of His next response as He segues into a refutation.

The Refutation (verses 31–32). As before, He begins with an insult but adds a pinch of snark and sarcasm. "But about the resurrection of the dead—have you not read what God has said to you?" Again, the crowd goes wild! Now consider the reasoning behind this move. First, the foundation of Christianity rests entirely on the truth of the resurrection, which entails a belief in the afterlife and intermediate state of existence.[3] Hence, Saducean teaching was antithetical to the reception of the gospel, and this had a detrimental impact on their students.

Second, recall the large crowd that would've been present. Jesus was not only addressing the Sadducees, but wording His response in such a way as to reach the audience. Given that they looked up to the intellectual arrogance of the Sadducees, undermining their intelligence would've simultaneously undermined their authority.[4] While space does not permit further elaboration on this approach, suffice it to say that there's a time and place for this when foundational issues are on the table. Removing the intellectual authority of an influencer of such strongholds aided in shifting the plausibility structure within that culture.

Next, He begins His refutation by appealing to the authority of Scripture, quoting from Exodus 3.6, "I am the God of Abraham, and the God

---

[3] Cooper calls this a "two-stage eschatology." Cooper, "Scripture and Philosophy on the Unity of Body and Soul" in *The Ashgate Research Companion to Theological Anthropology*, 27–42.

[4] Strauss, *Jesus Behaving Badly*, 36, 45, 155.

of Isaac, and the God of Jacob." But note, this verse does nothing to prove an afterlife, much less a disembodied soul that will receive a final resurrection. Hence, He adds to the verse by stating, "He is not the God of the dead but of the living!" Nevertheless, this is an odd move to make. After all, if He wanted to appeal to the authority of Scripture for proving resurrection, there are far better verses to use, such as Isaiah 26.19 or Daniel 12.2. So, what gives? Did these verses slip His mind? Was Jesus having a bad day? Or was there, as they say, a "method behind the madness?" Indeed, there was.

For the Sadducees, only the Torah (the first five books of the Bible) was regarded as "God's authoritative word,"[5] and Jesus knew that quoting from Isaiah or Daniel would only devolve into a debate about the overall authority of Scripture. They didn't care what these other books had to say. For this reason, He quotes Exodus (a book they regarded as authoritative) and, note—*intentionally avoids the debate about biblical authority altogether*. Did you catch that? Because it bears repeating. In this instance, *Jesus chooses not to debate biblical reliability or the authority of Scripture*. To be clear, Jesus is not conceding what they believed about the rest of Scripture, but is conceding that *even if* what they believe about Scripture is true, His view would still be correct.

Thus, He quotes from Exodus 3.6, "I am the God of Abraham, and the God of Isaac, and the God of Jacob" (which was one of their favorite verses to quote![6]), and then adds, "He is not the God of the dead but of the living!" But what does that mean? Simply this; if God is the God of Abraham, Isaac, and Jacob, and He's not the God of the dead, but of the living, then *based on their own Scriptures*, it must follow that despite their physical death, Abraham, Isaac, and Jacob are still alive today— proving an intermediate state of continued existence that awaits a final resurrection. Hence, "He is not the God of the dead but the living!"

Summarizing the Response. With this background context in mind, we can now re-examine Jesus' response to the Sadducees and fully appre-

---

[5] Ibid, 44.
[6] This was a verse they would've all been familiar with (much like us quoting John 3.16), which adds a funny twist to his statement, "Have you not read?"

ciate how He identified, rebutted, and refuted their logical fallacies. In a "modern tone" fashion, consider the following paraphrase:

> Guys, look, I know you're trying to make my belief in the resurrection look like a *reductio ad absurdum* fallacy. But the problem is that *you just don't know the Scriptures.* Don't you know there's no marriage in Heaven? Which means your entire case is based on a false presupposition about marriage that has resulted in this false dichotomy. So, the fallacy isn't with my view but yours. But now that I've dismantled your argument, let's talk about the resurrection. *Haven't you guys read your own Scriptures?* I mean, come on; you've only got five books to memorize—and you're supposed to be the experts! Doesn't your favorite passage in Exodus say that God *is* the God of Abraham, Isaac, and Jacob, and don't you know that He's the God of the living, not the dead? But given your view, if Abraham, Isaac, and Jacob are dead and have ceased to exist, how can He be their God? Yet, if He's *still* their God—as the Scriptures imply—and is the God of the living, then it must follow that they continue to exist after death and are still alive today. Therefore, *even by your own standards of Scripture,* my view is still correct, your view cannot possibly be true, and thus, your rejection of the afterlife, the intermediate state, and the final resurrection must be false.

It's no wonder that Scripture states, "when the crowds heard this, they were astonished... Jesus had silenced the Sadducees... No one could say a word in reply, and from that day on no one dared to ask him any more questions" (Matthew 22.33–34, 46). This is the example and brilliance of Jesus, and we must strive to be like Him!

The Fool Has Committed a Logical Fallacy in His Heart: *Names, Definitions, And Examples*

With the two rules presented to us in the beginning of this chapter, let's examine the most common logical fallacies you'll encounter when witnessing to nonbelievers. This is because when the fool commits a logical fallacy in his heart (Psalms 14.1; 53.1), strongholds are birthed, and Scripture commands that we identify, expose, and destroy them (2 Corinthians 10.4–5). Again, we aim to destroy ideas, not people. We are to give a defense, but with gentleness and respect (1 Peter 3.15).

Unfortunately, most (if not all) of these fallacies are committed by believers as well. So, following the command of Matthew 7.5 (in a modified version), "we must first learn to take the logical fallacy out of our own eye so we can see clearly to remove the logical fallacy from another's." To do this, we'll learn what they are (names and definitions), how they're committed (by both believers and nonbelievers), and how to respond accordingly (while avoiding them ourselves).

A Self-defeating Statement: a statement that refutes itself by failing to meet its own standard. This is a *formal fallacy* (i.e., it breaks a law of logic) and occurs when a person has made a claim that proves itself false.

Examples: *"There is no absolute truth." "You shouldn't judge anyone." "No one should be intolerant of other beliefs." "Don't force your moral point of view on others."*

Responses: Is that absolutely true? Then why are you judging me for judging? Then why are you not tolerant of my beliefs? Then why are you forcing your moral point of view on me?

A Category Fallacy: Mistaking or attributing two categories that do not belong together. Given this does not break a law of logic, it's an *informal fallacy*.

Examples: *How many pounds does the taste of banana weigh? What does the color blue smell like? Show me scientific evidence for God.*

Responses: Although a banana is a physical object that has weight, the taste of a banana does not. While a blue flower may smell sweet, its color does not. Regarding the last example, this is *implicitly* a category fallacy. Science can only study the physical, and God is non-physical.

A Reductio Ad Absurdum: This occurs when a person holds a view that implicitly or holistically leads to irrational, illogical, and absurd conclusions.

Example: *If we don't allow women to have abortions, they'll do so illegally and be harmed in the process.*

Response: Correct me if I'm wrong, but are you essentially stating that if we don't allow women to *kill* their *innocent, unborn* children legally, then they might be harmed when trying to *kill* their *innocent, unborn* children illegally?

Note how my point here is to simply remove the "fluff" from the statement to expose the absurdity of the issue being discussed; the innocent life of the unborn.

A Logical Contradiction: A logical incompatibility or contradiction between two or more statements. There are two ways in which something can be logically contradictory: by *definition* or by *implication*.

Contradiction by Definition: *Who is the bachelor married to?*

Response: A married person is, by definition, not single, and a bachelor is, by definition, not married. Hence, a "married bachelor" is a logical contradiction. Note how asking this question also becomes a category fallacy. As you'll discover, some fallacies are often the result of others.

Contradiction by Implication (when taken together as a whole): *The existence of an immovable object and an unstoppable force.*

Response: Although an immovable object or an unstoppable force can exist independently, they cannot possibly exist simultaneously. This also becomes a *reductio ad absurdum*.

Example From Believers: *God Can Do the "Logically Impossible"*

To grasp why this statement is a logical contradiction, ask yourself, can God make a "married bachelor" come into existence? No. As we just learned, this is a logical contradiction by definition and, thus, cannot exist. Does this trouble you? If so, allow me to try a different approach. Ask yourself the following: Can God do *anything*? Is there anything I can do that God *cannot*?

Most believers respond by saying yes, God can do anything, and no, there's nothing I can do that God cannot. If this was your response, two more questions follow: Can God sin? Can God learn?

The obvious answer is "No," God can neither sin nor learn. However, we can sin and learn. Therefore, God cannot do anything, and we've established two things we can do that God cannot. But consider the reasons behind this.

Concerning the former, Hebrews 6.18 states that it's impossible for God to lie, and this sentiment is conveyed throughout Scripture (Numbers 23.19; Titus 1.2). This is because a God that is morally *perfect* cannot, by definition, do something morally *imperfect*. Thus, it's logically impossible for God to sin.

Concerning the latter, the same principle applies. Scripture teaches that His understanding is infinite and He knows all things (Psalms 147.5; 1 John 3.20). In philosophical, theological terminology, this means God is **omniscient**. Hence, if God knows all things, He lacks no knowledge, and if He lacks no knowledge, there's nothing left for Him to learn.

For this reason, when we say God *cannot* do the logically impossible, it's not due to a deficiency or lack of strength—as if God needed to lift more weights to gain the power to do these logically impossible acts. Rather, it's that logically impossible acts entail a contradiction in terms that cannot be done in the first place. Now consider the application.

God's "inability" to sin or learn becomes a reflection of His perfection, whereas our ability to do both is nothing to brag about. We can sin because we lack something, but God cannot because He lacks nothing. Additionally, our ability to learn demonstrates our ignorance, whereas God's "inability" to learn only demonstrates His omniscience. This should not trouble our faith but increase it. So, let's glorify God in knowing He cannot do the logically impossible!

Example From a Nonbeliever: *If God is omnipotent, can He create a rock so heavy He cannot lift?*

This popular question presents an alleged objection against the notion of God's omnipotence, attempting to show a logical contradiction by implication. However, the logical contradiction here isn't in God's nature but in the question. Historically, **omnipotence** has been defined as God's *ability to bring about a logically possible state of affairs.* As we saw above, this doesn't mean the ability to do the logically impossible.

Put differently, omnipotence is not the power to do anything, but is *the ability to do anything that power can do.* Hence, God cannot create a "married bachelor," a "squared circle," or "a rock so heavy He cannot lift." These are not logically possible states of affairs but contradictions, and no amount of power can make logical contradictions possible. So no, God cannot create a rock so heavy He cannot lift any more than He can beat Himself in a wrestling match. The question itself is a logically incoherent contradiction, which becomes an infringement, not against God, but logic.

Begging the Question: Implying, assuming, or presenting something as true without argument or justification. This always involves a **presupposition** (pre-supposing something is true beforehand).

Example: *Have you stopped beating your wife?*

The underlying presupposition here is that the person beats their spouse (and is married). With this fallacy, we've learned not to answer the question directly, but address the **false presupposition** by questioning the question: "Why would you assume I beat my wife?" or, "Why would you assume I'm married?"

Example From a Believer: *God exists because the Bible says so.*

This example has no *false* presupposition, but it's still question-begging. Note the underlying presupposition; whatever the Bible says is true. This isn't a question-begging fallacy because it's false, but because it erroneously assumes that the nonbeliever agrees with your view.

To illustrate, suppose that a Muslim wanted to convert you by quoting three verses from the Quran and declaring it as Allah's holy, authoritative word. Would you drop to your knees with tears of repentance and devote your life to Allah? No, because you disagree with his underlying presupposition—whatever the Qur'an says is true (and is God's holy, authoritative word). Hence, it commits the fallacy of begging the question. And if his approach didn't work for you, why expect it to work for the atheist when quoting the Bible?

Example From a Nonbeliever: *God doesn't exist because evolution is true.*

There are two question-begging assumptions within this statement. 1) Evolution is true, and 2) if evolution is true, God cannot exist. But note how with a rebuttal, we can focus on demonstrating how the overall argument (the second assumption) fails *even if* the first assumption (evolution) is true.

Response: *But if God exists, couldn't He use evolution to bring about our species?*

Given that the obvious answer is yes, their argument collapses. This is no different from the approach Jesus took with the Sadducees, demonstrating how their argument failed *even if* what they believed about Scripture was true.

Circular Reasoning: Using two or more reasons that assume each other to be true; I believe "X" because of "Y," and I believe "Y" because of "X." This often involves a question-begging assumption.

Example: *I'm the smartest person in the world because this book I wrote says so.*

In this example, the person believes they're the smartest person in the world, and this belief is based on a book they've written, making the belief (along with its justification) a fallacy of circular reasoning. However, this may not always be apparent, and the person may be unaware that their reasoning is circular. Using the same example, consider the following conversation:

John: I believe I'm the smartest person in the world.
Jane: How did you come to that conclusion?
John: Because this book says so right here.
Jane: I see. Who wrote the book?
John: I did!

Additionally, consider that when an *informal* fallacy is committed, it doesn't automatically mean the conclusion is false. The person may be "the smartest person in the world," but the way they've justified this conclusion is still fallaciously circular.

Example From a Believer:
Christian: I believe God exists.
Nonbeliever: Why?
Christian: Because the Bible says so.
Nonbeliever: I see. And who wrote the Bible?
Christian: God did!

Note that a logical fallacy doesn't become logical when we use spiritual language. Although we know the conclusion of this argument is true, we must present and defend it in non-fallacious ways.

Example From a Nonbeliever:
Nonbeliever: God doesn't exist.
Eric: Why?
Nonbeliever: Because He isn't real.
Eric: And why do you believe He isn't real?
Nonbeliever: Because He doesn't exist.

In this example, the fallacy now involves a **tautology**: repeating the same thing twice with different words that mean the same thing. With tautologies, no new information is provided to further the discussion. Consider a less obvious example.

Less Obvious Example: *We have no empirical method for testing supernatural claims, and we only discover natural explanations every time we study the physical world.*

This argument commits a handful of fallacies. (1) It *begs the question*—assuming we need "empirical methods" for testing supernatural claims. This is (2) a *category fallacy*. Additionally, the words "physical" and "natural" are being used as synonyms, which can be reworded as follows: "Every time we study the physical, we only discover the physical" or "studying the natural world only demonstrates something natural." This is (3) a *tautology*.

Given the tautology, we can now identify (4) the circular reasoning. This person implicitly believes that supernatural claims cannot be *empirically* validated because we can only study the natural world, but then believes we can only study the natural world because supernatural claims cannot be *empirically* validated (which, again, is a category fallacy). Hence, the entire argument is a tautological claim based on circular reasoning.

For the sake of space, we'll focus on how the nonbeliever commits the remaining fallacies and learn how to respond accordingly.

A Non-sequitur: This fallacy (Latin for "it does not follow") occurs when a person implies or directly states a conclusion that *does not logically follow* from what they've said.

Example: *She's wearing red shoes. Therefore, her favorite color must be red.*

Again, with informal fallacies, the conclusion *might* be true. Nevertheless, it *doesn't logically follow* that her favorite color is red *simply because* she's wearing red shoes. Hence, it's a *non-sequitur*.

Example From a Nonbeliever: *Belief in God is for people who don't understand science.*

A general rule for identifying this fallacy is determining where the word "therefore" should be placed in their statement. This is because the word "therefore" implies that something *must follow* based on what's been said. If their conclusion does not follow, it's a *non-sequitur*.

Response: *So, belief in God is for people who don't understand science. Therefore, what?*

At this point, the ball is back in their court. If they say, "therefore, God doesn't exist," you can point out how their conclusion doesn't logically follow from their claim. While it's true that *some* believers don't understand science, it's also true that some *unbelievers* don't understand science either. "So what?" Nothing relevant follows from the assertion.

The Genetic Fallacy: Attempting to falsify a belief by showing its origin.

Example #1: *People believe in God because of fear and ignorance.*

In this example, the person tries to falsify belief in God by showing (or more appropriately, assuming) where the belief came from. However, showing where a belief *may have* originated doesn't prove the belief is false. For instance, suppose a person believes everything they read in a fortune cookie. Their next fortune cookie reads "2+2=4," and on this basis, they come to believe it. Although they've arrived at this belief in an unusual way, it's nonetheless true. Similarly, *even if* we concede that belief in God is the product of "fear and ignorance," it doesn't prove that belief in God is false.

Example #2: *You're only a Christian because you were born in America. You'd be a Muslim if you were born in the Middle East!*

Again, even if we conceded the point, it wouldn't prove that Christianity is false. Arguing otherwise is not only a genetic fallacy but a *non-sequitur*. Hence, we could reply with a "therefore?," "go on," or "so what?" Additionally, we can take the principle of the claim and apply it to their position.

Eric: Are you an atheist simply because of where you were born?
Atheist: No, of course not!
Eric: So, why does your claim only apply to my position but not yours?

Appeal to Authority Fallacy: Attempting to prove something solely because an authoritative figure (especially one not in the relevant field) says so.

Examples: *No serious, respectable scientist believes in God. My doctor doesn't believe in prayer, only in medicine.*

It's important to understand that not every appeal to authority is an *appeal to authority fallacy*. For instance, if a person claimed that Christians shouldn't believe a historic Christian doctrine, then one could point to the authority of Scripture to show how they're factually incorrect. This is neither question-begging, circular, nor an appeal to authority fallacy. Why not? Because if the person is attacking a belief *within* the Christian worldview, then Scripture *is the appropriate authority* for settling the dispute.

By contrast, none of the authority figures in the examples above are the appropriate authorities to consult regarding the beliefs in question. Additionally, these examples are implicit category fallacies. Asking a scientist or doctor what they believe about God or prayer is like asking a plumber what he thinks about dentistry. This isn't an insult to either profession. It's simply pointing out how the nature of these professions isn't *directly relevant* to the belief in question.

Finally, note the caveat presented in the first example, "No *serious, respectable* scientist believes in God." This arbitrary standard is an example of a **No True Scotsman fallacy**. The name is derived from a Scotsman claiming that "no Scotsman puts sugar on his porridge!" only to hear a fellow Scotsman say, "But I'm a Scotsman, and I put sugar on my porridge." In raging disbelief, he pounds the table and shouts, "Well, <u>no true</u> Scotsman puts sugar on his porridge!"

Similarly, claiming that "no serious, respectable" scientist believes in God fails to recognize the history of science and, more pertinently, that many serious, respectable scientists believe in God today. Hence, we can ask what they mean by "serious" or "respectable." If they mean no *atheist* scientist, they've further committed the fallacies of begging the question (assuming only atheists can be "serious" scientists) and circular reasoning (believing that only atheists are "respectable" scientists because the only respectable scientists are atheists).

An **Ad Hominem** *Fallacy:* This fallacy (Latin for "against the man") occurs when a person attempts to falsify a belief by attacking the person's behavior or character.

Example: *Don't listen to that doctor. I hear he drinks and smokes!*

In this instance, the person wants to demean the doctor's advice, not by appealing to his authority but to his behavior. However, if a doctor told a person to refrain from drinking and smoking, the advice isn't invalidated if the doctor drank and smoked himself. At best, his advice is hypocritical but not false.

Example From a Nonbeliever: *"Your suit looks expensive."*

During the Q&A portion of a public debate, an atheist approached the microphone with a Bible to ask me a question. After reading a passage about frugality, he said:

> Your suit looks expensive, and while it's a nice suit, I could never afford something like that. So, how can you expect us to trust in God when clearly, you trust more in your money?

The audience, comprised of Christians and atheists, began to laugh at the question, but not for the same reason. Those who know me personally know I buy all my suits from thrift stores. So, with a smile on my face, I responded:

> Well, I genuinely appreciate the compliment because (examining my suit) I agree, it's a nice suit that *looks* expensive. However, I bought this for only $15 at a thrift store, and if you honestly feel you couldn't afford it, I'd be happy to buy one for you. Nevertheless, we should keep in mind that the topic of tonight's debate is "Does God Exist," and not "Is Eric's Suit too Expensive."

To be clear, not every assertion or complaint merits a response. However, given that his "objection" was attempting to muddy the waters against my character, not only did I refute his claim (the suit was only $15 from a thrift store) but offered a rebuttal that *even if* my suit were expensive, it wouldn't invalidate the truth of my arguments. Hence, the objection was an *ad hominem* fallacy and a *non-sequitur*.

A Red Herring Fallacy: This fallacy occurs when a person diverts the conversation by changing the subject to non-related, irrelevant issues. This phrase comes from the practice of escaped convicts who used the blood of fish to divert dogs away from their scent, leading the authorities to track the smell of the fish rather than him.

When conversing with nonbelievers, we want our conversations to "stay on track," keeping the focus on the existence of God and the truth of Christianity. If we take the bait, we allow the conversation to veer off into non-central issues. Hence, we must learn to avoid red herrings.

Atheist: Well, I don't believe in God *because* I don't believe in fairytales.
Eric: Great, me either.
[awkward silence]
Atheist: But you *do* believe in fairytales. Doesn't the Bible mention talking snakes? That's a fairytale!
Eric: If you're referring to Genesis, it says serpent. But we can go with "snake" if you prefer. Still, I don't see your point. If God exists, couldn't He allow a "snake" to talk?
Atheist: But I don't believe in God.
Eric: I understand. But follow me here. I'm simply asking *if* God existed, could He allow a snake to talk?
Atheist: Well, sure, but that's *only* if He existed.
Eric: Right. So, it seems that our central question shouldn't be whether snakes can talk but whether God exists. So, if you don't mind, let's address that question first, and maybe we can get to "talking snakes" later.

A Strawman Fallacy: A misrepresentation of a person's position or argument.

Suppose John puts a picture of Bill's face on a scarecrow, knocks it down, and claims victory. In this illustration, John didn't defeat Bill, but a *strawman* of Bill. Similarly, a nonbeliever may misrepresent certain beliefs within Christianity (or an argument you've just given in defense of Christianity) but note, when they "refute" the mischaracterization, they're not refuting Christianity but a *strawman* of it.

Example: *Christians believe in a magical sky daddy that grants them wishes, but no such being exists!*

Given that no doctrine within Christianity teaches such a thing, this is a strawman. Thus, we can respond by agreeing with the person that no such "magical sky daddy" exists.

As a side note, it may be possible to proactively prevent this fallacy at the beginning of the conversation by asking some questions. For example, if someone says they don't believe in God, you can ask them to describe the God they don't believe in. Chances are, they're denying a God the Bible doesn't describe.

Nevertheless, responding to this fallacy will depend on the strawman you are presented with, which may not be obvious. Consider these examples:

- If God exists, why doesn't He heal amputees?
- If Christianity is true, why did this person die of cancer?
- If God exists, why doesn't He remove all the evil in the world?

Note how these questions are implicit strawmen (that also beg the question) regarding *an assumed view* of God or Christianity. These implicit strawmen seem to be that:

A) God is some genie that must grant all prayer requests.
B) God's existence depends on how *we view* our quality of life.
C) We are like God's pets, and it's His job to keep us healthy and happy.
D) All of the above.

In response, we can begin uncovering these assumptions by turning their implicit accusations into questions. Using what the person has said to fill in the blanks, consider the following:

- Are you saying that if God existed, then He must _____?
- Are you implying that if God exists, then it's His job to _____?
- Are you under the impression that if Christianity were true, then _____?

- Are you arguing that the truth of Christianity depends entirely on _____?

Additionally, beliefs within a worldview must be considered holistically, and Christianity is no exception. In these instances, we use it to our advantage. For instance, if Christianity is true, then are not those in Heaven receiving the ultimate healing? Moreover, if Christianity is true, will God not one day rid the world of evil? And if Christianity is true, isn't it our job to feed the poor, visit the sick, and help those in need? Because not only does Christianity accurately predict these problems, but if true, adequately provides answers to them!

Conclusion

Knowing how to identify and respond to logical fallacies is an effective way to avoid unnecessary debates, diffuse potentially heated conversations, and bring the focus back to the heart of the issue. In Proverbs 26.4–5 we're given two rules for conversing with nonbelievers:

Rule #1: Do not engage in fallacious reasoning (don't be like him).

Rule #2: Point out and correct their fallacious reasoning (don't let him think he's right).

As an exercise, I encourage you to gather with a group, write down a list of questions, accusations, or objections you've heard from nonbelievers, and identify how they've committed one or more of the fallacies from this chapter. As you grow in this discipline, your conversations with nonbelievers will be more productive, less time-consuming, and make you a better ambassador for Christ.

Bibliography

Cooper, John W. "Scripture and Philosophy on the Unity of Body and Soul" in *The Ashgate Research Companion to Theological Anthropology*. United Kingdom: Ashgate Publishing Limited, 2015.

_____. *Body, Soul, and Life Everlasting: Biblical Anthropology and the Monism-dualism Debate*. United Kingdom: Leicester, 2000.

O'Brien, Brandon J., Richards, Randolph E. *Misreading Scripture with Western Eyes: Removing Cultural Blinders to Better Understand the Bible*. United States: InterVarsity Press, 2012.

Strauss, Mark L. *Jesus Behaving Badly: The Puzzling Paradoxes of the Man from Galilee*. United States: InterVarsity Press, 2015.

Additional Resources

Craig, William Lane, Moreland, J.P.. *Philosophical Foundations for a Christian-Worldview*. United States: InterVarsity Press, 2017.

DeWeese, G. J., Moreland, J. P.. *Philosophy Made Slightly Less Difficult: A Beginner's Guide to Life's Big Questions*. United Kingdom: InterVarsity Press, 2021.

Hernandez, Eric. *The Lazy Approach to Evangelism: A Simple Guide for Conversing with Nonbelievers*. United States: GC2 Press, 2023.

Moreland, J.P.. *Love Your God with All Your Mind: The Role of Reason in the Life of the Soul*. United Kingdom: The Navigators, 2014.

3

Loving the Truth
A Profound Challenge

Mary Jo Sharp

The Challenge of Truth

To love truth is to embrace its entirety—the beautiful and the brutal, the comforting and the confronting. This requires relentless pursuit, a willingness to grapple with uncomfortable realities, and the courage to reject convenient falsehoods. Crucially, this pursuit involves a relationship with Jesus, the King of Truth. Jesus frequently encountered those claiming commitment to truth, yet their understanding often fell short. One such encounter occurred in Mark 10 after a period in Capernaum, as Jesus and his disciples journeyed through Judea, beyond the Jordan. While he was teaching, Jesus was posed a question that would shape our understanding of the difficulty in genuinely loving the truth.

> And as he was setting out on his journey, a man ran up to him and knelt before him and asked, 'Good Teacher, what must I do to inherit eternal life?' And Jesus said to him, 'Why do you call me good? No one is good except God alone. You know the commandments: Do not murder, Do not commit adultery, Do not steal, Do not bear false witness, Do not defraud, Honor your father and mother.' And he said to him, 'Teacher, all these things I have kept from my youth.' And Jesus, looking at him, loved him, and said to him, 'You lack one thing: go sell all that you have and give to the poor, and you will have treasure in heaven; and come, follow me.' (Mark 10.17–21 ESV)

Naturally, the man quickly realized the truth of what Jesus said, sold all his possessions, and followed Jesus. Well, no, that is not what happened. As the Scripture reads, "Disheartened by the saying, he went away sorrowful, for he had great possessions." (Mark 10.22 ESV) Yet another translation says, "But he was stunned at this demand, and he went away grieving because he had many possessions." (Mark 10.22, HCSB)

Isn't it curious? This deeply religious man, who seemed to earnestly seek guidance on salvation, was given an answer from Jesus—only to find himself grieved by it. The truth, stark and uncompromising, was precisely what he refused to embrace, a reality he wouldn't integrate into his existence. This man's question—and the grief that followed—weighs on me.

As I've reflected on this encounter with Jesus, I've realized it reveals a difficult conflict: the man believed he wanted truth—until that truth demanded an honest look at himself. Suddenly, accepting it became much harder. But this tension between seeking truth and resisting it isn't just an ancient struggle—it's a perpetually human one, still unfolding in our own time.

Oxford Dictionaries' 2016 word of the year was "post-truth," an adjective defined as "relating to, or denoting circumstances in which objective facts are less influential in shaping public opinion than appeals to emotion and personal belief, or privatized, internalized belief."[1] In that one word, we can see our Western societies' succumbing to their own battle with hard truths. In fact, this word of the year highlights how culturally acceptable it has become to dismiss truths that are emotionally uncomfortable, challenge our sense of identity, or fail to reinforce our existing beliefs. Giving voice to this cultural phenomenon, American comedian Stephen Colbert popularized a related word he coined as "truthiness," which he describes as "the quality of seeming or being felt to be true, even if not necessarily true."[2] *Truthiness.* Though he uses it humorously, the best comedy often lands because it holds a kernel of truth.

---

[1] Oxford Languages, "Word of the Year 2016."
[2] Oxford Languages, "The American comedian Stephen Colbert popularized a related word, truthiness, as 'the quality of seeming or being felt to be true, even if not necessarily true'."

The same issue of "truthiness" has become a challenge for the church, both in America and around the world. For example, in my Christian university classes, I noticed that students increasingly shaped truth by personal experience, ignoring a mind-independent reality. When tasked with writing an academic paper that required exegeting a passage of Scripture or engaging with a philosophical argument, I often found that instead of presenting a well-reasoned analysis supported by evidence, students would submit papers focused largely on personal anecdotes. The 'proof' offered in these papers was based almost entirely on personal narrative, rather than on careful textual analysis, logical argumentation, or scholarly critique.

In my daily conversations with Christians about theology and philosophy, I've noticed a growing tendency toward an expressive individualism—where people seek God's affirmation of their beliefs rather than the hard truths that might challenge them. Expressive individualism is the idea that "the highest good is individual freedom, happiness, self-definition, and self-expression…"[3] In this view, "the existence of an objective reality external to an individual would pose a perceived threat to personal authenticity and individual freedom, since the ability to fashion reality as one pleases is vital to ultimate autonomy."[4] Further, in "The State of the Great Commission Report" for the Lausanne Movement's Fourth International Congress on World Evangelization 2024, scholars in Kenya and China report similarly concerning challenges to objective truth.[5]

As I wrestled with this issue of loving truth, and the worldwide movement away from objective truth, I turned to Scripture and saw the man in Mark's gospel, grieving when confronted with truth. It struck me that truly loving truth is a far greater and more difficult challenge than we often realize—including for those who study apologetics. Making a case for what we believe is valuable, but even more important is genuinely loving truth.

In this chapter, we'll explore how to deepen our love for truth and become better seekers of it—a pursuit that becomes especially challenging when the truth is difficult to accept. We'll consider three steps: acknowl-

---

[3] Loke, Ndereba, and Sharp, "Challenges to Objective Truth."
[4] Ibid.
[5] Ibid.

edging our fallibility, renewing our minds, and pursuing a deeper relationship with God. We'll examine relevant scriptures illustrating how truth is handled throughout the Bible.

Step One: Accept My Fallibility

John 18.33–38 depicts a pivotal encounter between Jesus and Pontius Pilate. This passage, though somewhat lengthy, presents a deeply significant exchange about Jesus' identity and the nature of His kingdom. The narrative unfolds as follows:

> So Pilate entered his headquarters again and called Jesus and said to him, 'Are you the King of the Jews?' Jesus answered, 'Do you say this of your own accord, or did others say it to you about me?' Pilate answered, 'Am I a Jew? Your own nation and the chief priests have delivered you over to me. What have you done?' And Jesus answered, 'My kingdom is not of this world. If my kingdom were of this world, my servants would have been fighting that I may not be delivered over to the Jews. But my kingdom is not of this world.' Then Pilate said to him, 'So you are a king.' And Jesus answered, 'You say that I am a king. For this purpose I was born, and for this purpose I have come into the world to bear witness to the truth. Everyone who is of the truth listens to my voice.' (John 18.33–38 ESV)

Pilate then responds with a famous skeptical question: "What is truth?"

Our discussion of the passage will focus on two significant details concerning Jesus's ministry. First, Jesus explicitly declared that His purpose on earth was "to bear witness to the truth." He then connects this mission to His kingship in His response to Pilate's statement, "So you are a king." Instead of outright denying the claim, Jesus replies, "You say that I am a king," while clarifying that His kingdom is not of this world. By linking His testimony to the truth with His discussion of kingship, Jesus reveals Himself as the King of Truth. It is important to note, though, that the term, 'King of Truth,' is not a direct biblical quote. Rather, it's a descriptive term I'm using to encapsulate the essence of Jesus's self-understanding as revealed throughout his discourse. We will now explore this concept in more detail.

The title 'King of Truth' requires careful unpacking. The very term "king" implies a relationship; one cannot be a king without subjects. Traditionally, kingship signifies authority over a specific lineage or people in a certain time in history. However, Jesus's claim to be King of Truth transcends this traditional understanding. His authority isn't limited to a particular group, as he noted, "If my kingdom were of this world, my servants would have been fighting… But my kingdom is not of this world." He asserts his expansive authority by stating, "Everyone who is of the truth hears my voice." This "kingship" extends to *all humanity*. Unlike earthly rulers who merely teach or proclaim their wisdom, Jesus, as the King of Truth, speaks with ultimate authority, bearing witness to truth itself.

One insightful commentary clarifies the distinction between earthly authorities and Jesus's authority over truth. In the context of John 18, "truth" is not merely a collection of teachings about God or about Jesus functioning as an earthly leader; rather, it is God's very reality revealed in Christ Himself.[6] Therefore, the statement, "Jesus is King of Truth," carries two profound implications. First, it affirms that God's divine reality is fully manifested in Jesus. Second, it establishes a kind of lineage of truth itself—truth originates from Jesus, is embodied in Him, and is made known through Him. His claim to kingship, then, is not merely symbolic or political but deeply tied to His very nature as the embodiment of truth. But this claim is not meant to remain at the level of intellectual assent; it demands more than just mere acknowledgment.

Jesus declares, "Everyone who is of the truth listens to my voice." In this passage, "listening" extends beyond passive hearing—it implies trust, obedience, and the active pursuit of truth in one's life. Commentaries emphasize this engagement, describing those in Jesus's kingdom as "doing the truth"—a way of living that unites perception with action.[7] True discipleship is not merely speaking about Jesus or affirming His teachings; it is about integrating His truth, love, and way of life into our own. To acknowledge Jesus as the King of Truth means to follow Him, not just in thought but in practice, aligning our lives with the reality He reveals.

---

[6] Morris, *The Gospel according to John*, 260–261.
[7] Exell, *The Biblical Illustrator: St. John*, 254.

One part of 'listening' to Jesus's voice, *the obedience part*, can present quite a challenge for us. The very idea of it can feel heavy, stirring resistance and a deep desire for autonomy. My own struggles reflect this tension—I argued with my father so often that he once said I should be a lawyer. I remember telling him, "I'll do what you ask as long as you tell me why I'm doing it." Yet, I often want to do what I want to do in the way I want to do it. I want to think about things in the way I want to think about them. Further still, I desire to be affirmed in what I already believe, rather than looking to Jesus for what is actually true. This struggle is not unique; it reflects a deeper human tendency to resist surrendering personal autonomy, especially when it challenges deeply held beliefs.

Resistance to fully embracing Jesus's authority is often rooted in a reluctance to confront personal imperfections. Christianity's central teaching—that humans are inherently sinful and in need of a Savior—is widely acknowledged. It is important to note that this doctrine of the fallen nature also affects our ability to reason well. Nevertheless, many people have a strong tendency to believe they are always right, a mindset I frequently observe in myself and within the broader Christian community. This deep-seated self-assurance can hinder true submission to Jesus's authority—not just in the comfortable aspects of faith or moments of deep study, but in every area of life. I find that acknowledging His superior knowledge and authority is one thing, but living in daily obedience to Him is another. To understand why this struggle is so common, let's briefly highlight two challenges of living as though Jesus is the King of Truth.

First, Paul tells us we are at war with ourselves. He says, "For I do not understand my own actions. For I do not do what I want, but I do the very thing I hate," revealing an internal conflict with which we all struggle. (Romans 7.15 ESV) How many times have we told ourselves that we know what to do, and yet we find ourselves not doing those things? So even when we gain knowledge about God, we still wrestle to enact that knowledge. This inner struggle, coupled with Jeremiah's warning that "the heart is deceitful above all things," (Jeremiah 17.9 NIV) emphasizes the complexity beyond simple intellectual assent to propositional truths. Our desires, motives, and emotions deeply intertwine, making self-understanding a difficult task.

A second common issue within the church is the underappreciation of Jesus as the greatest thinker who ever lived. Despite His unparalleled influence, Jesus is often sidelined in discussions of great thinkers, even though His words have shaped entire civilizations, legal systems, and moral frameworks for centuries. Many Christians focus on Jesus primarily as a divine Savior, emphasizing His role in redemption while neglecting His intellectual depth. While His spiritual authority is central, this focus sometimes leads to an underappreciation of His intellectual contributions as a teacher, debater, and philosopher. Failure to recognize, or truly embrace, Jesus's intellectual authority can make it difficult to admit when we're wrong. For we may tend to overestimate our own intellect while neglecting the unmatched wisdom and reasoning of Jesus. Consequently, we often wrestle with epistemic humility—the recognition that our knowledge falls far short of God's—and this resistance to admitting error makes teaching Christians, or any human, a challenge.

Saint Augustine, in his *Confessions*, keenly observes our flawed relationship with truth: we humans tend to love truth when it supports what we want to be true, but we hate it when it shows us up as being wrong.[8] Scripture, however, demands a different approach—to be *lovers of truth*. For example, many know 1 Corinthians 13 for its wedding-appropriate verses stating that love is patient and kind (and so forth), but in verse 6, Paul emphasizes a crucial element of love: delighting and rejoicing in the truth. This is explicitly contrasted with loving evil, highlighting the imperative to delight in truth rather than falsehood.

Let's be honest, facing the truth head-on is one of life's toughest challenges. It means surrendering to the refining fire of truth—a process that can be intensely painful as it burns away the layers of deception we've carefully built around our hearts. It hurts, but it's essential. We humans are incredibly skilled at justifying nearly anything we want to be true. That's why Paul's call to embrace truth directly counters our tendency to

---

[8] Adapted from: "They love the truth because it brings light to them; they hate it in as much as it reproves them." Saint Augustine. *The Confessions of Saint Augustine*, 217.

love evil. When we think we're always right, we become unteachable, content in our comfortable lies, and that leads to ruin—in small and big ways.

C.S. Lewis's *Voyage of the Dawn Treader* exemplifies our wrong-headedness in the character of Eustace. The young boy, Eustace, is described as a particularly unpleasant know-it-all. He views the other children in the story as untrustworthy and is constantly skeptical of, well, almost everything except himself. There's a particularly poignant part of the story in which Eustace unintentionally transforms into a dragon. Lewis describes the transformation as a consequence of Eustace's greedy, dragonish thoughts. It's a vivid depiction of what happens when one rejects the authority of the King of Truth and resists His life-changing teachings.

For Eustace to be restored to his true self, a boy, his dragon layers—his layers of falsehood—must be scraped away. In a heart-wrenching scene, Eustace attempts to peel off the dragon layers only to continue finding more dragon underneath. There was only one way to return him back to his true nature; the Great Lion, Aslan, had to use his claws to tear off the false dragon on him. It's a striking illustration of what happens when you do not set Jesus as the King of Truth in your life, recognizing his authority *and* your own shortcomings. A first step towards becoming a lover of truth is that we must acknowledge our own fallibility, that we are often wrong about things.

Step Two: Repair the Mind

The next step engages the transformative power of renewing the mind, a concept central to Paul's teachings in Romans 12. We'll delve into the implications of his exhortation to resist conformity to the world and embrace transformation, examining the practical application of this principle within the context of discerning God's will.

Paul's words in Romans 12.2 offer a compelling challenge: "Do not be conformed to this world, but be transformed by the renewal of your mind, so that by testing you may discern what is the will of God—what is good, acceptable, and perfect." This isn't merely a passive suggestion; it's a powerful warning against adopting the deceptive philosophies, trends, and cultural norms—even within religious circles—of a fallen world. Paul repeatedly emphasizes the need for testing and rigorous discernment, underscoring the importance of critical evaluation—even within the Church. Rather than conformity, he calls for transformation—a deep change in character and perspective—achieved through the continual renewal of our minds.

Intrigued by the term "renewal," I sought to clarify its meaning in relation to a love of truth. Exploring various definitions and synonyms, I found "repairing" to be particularly relevant and insightful. Our minds are often marred by the falsehoods prevalent in the world. Renewing our mind is akin to repairing damage inflicted by these falsehoods, enabling us to discern God's will—to distinguish good from evil. This "repair" isn't merely metaphorical; it reflects a very real transformation. Our minds are profoundly shaped—even wounded—by worldly influences and need this restoration.

J.B. Phillips' translation captures this idea beautifully, saying, "Don't let the world around you squeeze you into its own mold." (Romans 12.2, *Phillips*) Imagine what happens when you try to squeeze something into a mold for which it's not intended; for example, trying to force a square peg into a round hole or shoving together puzzle pieces that don't fit. You're going to typically damage those items. Now think about your mind being damaged when you try to conform it to worldly ideas. The inference from this passage is that it becomes harder and harder to discern God's will, to discern what is good and what is evil. While this idea may seem obvious, it's a bit more complex.

Conforming to worldly ideals often manifests subtly, even within religious communities. I've witnessed firsthand how the worldly belief that "the end justifies the means" can be used to rationalize abusive behavior among church members. I remember a lay leader who was put in charge of an outreach event for our church. Because the work he was doing was for a noble cause (the end), he felt empowered to act confrontationally toward others to get the results he wanted (justifying the means). This is sadly not an isolated incident in my experience with Christians. I have too often seen the body of Christ marginalizing and dehumanizing others while rationalizing that their actions are merited. These persons assume that because their work is "for Jesus," they can disregard unethical conduct, damaging relationships and undermining the church's witness to the world. In the process, they not only cause harm to others, but also further erode their own ability to discern good from evil.

Our minds, created with intention and purpose, are designed to connect us to our Creator. They are instruments of communication and relationship, integral to our humanity and our journey toward salvation. This journey involves rational belief, confession, communication, and heartfelt trust—all processes that function best with a healthy mind. However, to break free from destructive mental patterns, we must actively engage in daily restorative practices.

Circling back to the writings of C.S. Lewis, in *Mere Christianity*, he rightly emphasizes the active nature of faith:

> If you have once accepted Christianity, then some of its main doctrines shall be deliberately held before your mind for some time everyday. That is why daily praying and religious reading and churchgoing are necessary parts of the Christian life. We have to be continually reminded of what we believe. Neither this belief, nor any other will automatically remain alive in the mind. As a matter of fact, if you examined a hundred people who had lost their faith in Christianity, I wonder how many of them would turn out to have been reasoned out of it by honest argument? Do not most people simple drift away?[9]

Christian beliefs, like any others, require consistent nurturing. Church attendance, prayer, and Bible study aren't mere rituals; they're vital for renewing our minds and sustaining our faith. Paul's warning against spiritual neglect underscores our need for mental repair, a process encompassing psychology, philosophy, and theology, all contributing to a deeper relationship with God. Active maintenance—essential for all, regardless of intellectual background—requires acknowledging our fallibility and committing to ongoing mental repairs.

---

[9] C.S. Lewis, *Mere Christianity*, 125.

Step 3: Pursue the Person

The pursuit of truth is often framed as a purely intellectual endeavor—a cold, impersonal accumulation of facts and theories. But what if truth itself was incarnated in a person? This radical proposition, central to the Christian faith, is illuminated in John 14.6. In context, Jesus is comforting his disciples with some knowledge of the afterlife. He tells them that where he's going, they will be also. He's trying to give them a glimpse of heaven. Then Thomas speaks out, saying that the disciples don't know where Jesus is going. Thomas, voicing the disciples' uncertainty, asks, "How can we know the way?" His question is met not with a map to heaven, but with a profound declaration: "I am the way, the truth, and the life. No one comes to the Father except through me" (John 14.6 ESV).

This seemingly simple statement brings a shift in perspective. While we often view "truth" as impersonal—facts, theories, or data—Jesus identifies Himself as the truth, personalizing it in a way that deeply resonates within the Christian worldview but may feel foreign in modern conceptions of knowledge. Typically, we approach knowledge as the scientific gathering of facts and information. However, John 14 presents a fundamental shift: the pursuit of truth leads to a person—Jesus. This redefines learning, where knowledge becomes a relational journey toward understanding and connecting with Him. Jesus reiterates this truth in His interaction with Pontius Pilate, emphasizing that at the heart of knowledge is not merely data, but a relationship with the truth Himself.

If Jesus is the truth, my pursuit of knowledge becomes a deeply personal quest—seeking not just facts, but a relationship with a Creator, an Artist, a Designer. The relational aspect of truth in the Christian worldview is crucial because trusting in a person, especially one defined as truth, requires more than analyzing impersonal data. It demands personal revelation. While I can gather information about someone, that will never lead to true intimacy. Such intimacy is built through relationship, and naturally, in that relationship, I have less control than I do in my relationship with theories or facts.

I believe many, both within and outside the church, miss God because they treat Him as a set of doctrines or a philosophical theory rather than as a Person. We must shift our perspective of God to align more with how we relate to others as individuals. Trust in a person isn't built on the demand for 100% certainty; it's developed through time, observation, and the recognition of consistent character. For example, I trust my husband's love for me, not by calculating probabilities, but by observing his consistent actions and character, reasonably concluding his love is genuine. While not precisely the same, we can translate this idea to our relationship with God. His revelation of unconditional love—sending His Son to die for us while we were His enemies—proves His reliability and trustworthiness. This act of ultimate sacrifice forms the foundation for a trust that surpasses the limitations of mere theoretical understanding.

In C.S. Lewis's *The World's Last Night*, he succinctly articulates this understanding of our relationship with God:

> To believe that God, at least this God exists, is to believe that you as a person now stand in the presence of God as a person. What would a moment before have been variations in opinion now become variations in your personal attitude to a person. You are no longer faced with an argument which demands your assent, but with a person who demands your confidence.[10]

C.S. Lewis highlights a crucial shift in our understanding from intellectual assent to personal relationship. As an apologist, his ideas resonate with me as to the true goal of apologetics: to cultivate a personal relationship with God. Knowledge of God, in this sense, isn't just about mentally acknowledging truths or accepting doctrines; it's about entering into an intimate connection with the divine. Apologetics, therefore, isn't a battle of wits or a contest to win debates; it's a pathway to opening one's heart and mind to the presence of God, allowing the intellectual journey to lead toward genuine encounter and transformation.

Consider how apologetics arguments can have a profound influence on our spiritual formation. The Kalam cosmological argument points to a necessary being, a Creator who intentionally designed the universe, including each one of us. We can infer, then, that we were individually created with intention and purpose. Similarly, wrestling with the prob-

---

[10] Lewis, *The World's Last Night and Other Essays*, 26–27.

lem of evil and its various solutions not only acknowledges the reality of suffering but also offers a way forward in a world filled with evil. In such circumstances, Jesus commands us to "love your enemies, do good to those who hate you" (Luke 6.27 ESV) and to treat others as we wish to be treated, saying, "as you wish that others would do to you, do so to them" (Luke 6.31 ESV). Apologetics, therefore, is not just about imparting information; it's a formative process that shapes our relationship with God, carrying deep relational and personal significance.

This idea is reflected in Lewis's quote, which underscores that the pursuit of truth about God is ultimately a pursuit of a Person. As we deepen our understanding of Him, we are not merely accumulating facts but are invited to honor and relate to Him in a personal, meaningful way—just as we would with any other person we come to know. God is not merely the source of truth; He *is* the Person from whom all truth flows.

Conclusion

To be lovers of truth demands acknowledging our inherent fallibility. We are frequently wrong, a truth deeply rooted in Christian doctrine and reflected in our fallen human nature, which includes our minds. Our status necessitates a constant vigilance, a diligent repair of the mind, actively combating the influences that lead us astray, distorting the distinction between good and evil. Ultimately, however, the pursuit of truth culminates in a relationship with Jesus Christ, profoundly impacting every aspect of our lives. The critical question then becomes: do we genuinely desire truth, even if it causes grief or pain, challenges societal norms, and demands fundamental change? Or, like the young man who walked away from Jesus, will we choose comfort over conviction?

In today's culture, I've seen Christians unknowingly retreat from truth. We live in a time where reason is increasingly sidelined, and emotions, biases, and desires are often elevated to the highest authority. This shift has created a crisis of irrationality, where the concept of truth has become increasingly subjective. In this landscape, individual intuitions and subjective experiences are treated as the ultimate arbiters, overshadowing objective truth and leading to widespread confusion about what is real and reliable.

Consequently, when hearts clash, the discourse descends into vitriol and name-calling—the inevitable endpoint of reason's abandonment. We've effectively excised the very organ of truth from our collective consciousness yet simultaneously demand truthful behavior in public life. This hypocrisy is hardly surprising; as the prophet Isaiah laments, "Justice is turned back, and righteousness stands far away; for truth has stumbled in the public squares, and uprightness cannot enter. Truth is lacking, and he who departs from evil makes himself a prey." (Isaiah 59.14–15 ESV)

As Christians, embracing the command to love truth cannot be taken lightly. The battle for truth begins within our own minds. God's invitation is clear: "Come now, let us reason together." (Isaiah 1.18 ESV) He desires to engage with our questions, to purge falsehoods, and to renew our minds, reversing the dehumanizing effects of flawed thinking and restoring our humanity. He offers himself as Truth, the source of life, redemption, and true fulfillment.

The path forward begins with a single step: acknowledging even one area where we are wrong. This small act initiates a transformative journey towards a relationship with the King of Truth.

Christians, we cannot take the command of to be lovers of truth lightly, because the battle of truth begins here and now in your own mind. God is calling me and you to reason together. He wants to wrestle with you in your questions. He wants to strip away falsehoods and renew your mind, allowing you to heal the dehumanizing effects of a damaged mindset. He wants to be Truth in your life to save your life, to redeem your life, and for you to have anything that looks like life at all. So which step will you take first? If it's just recognizing one area in which you've been wrong, then you're stepping towards that relationship with the King of truth.

Bibliography

Augustine, Saint. *The Confessions of Saint Augustine.* Image Classics. New York: The Crown Publishing Group, Kindle Edition.

Exell, J. S. *The Biblical Illustrator: St. John.* Vol. 3. London: James Nisbet & Co., n.d.

Lewis, C. S. *Mere Christianity.* New York: Macmillan, 1943.

Lewis, C. S. *The World's Last Night and Other Essays.* HarperCollins. Kindle Edition.

Loke, Andrew, Kevin Muriithi Ndereba, and Mary Jo Sharp. "Challenges to Objective Truth." Lausanne Movement Website. Accessed February 28, 2025. https://lausanne.org/report/trust/challenges-to-objective-truth.

Morris, Leon. *The Gospel According to John.* Wm. B. Eerdmans Publishing Co., 1995.

"Word of the Year 2016." Oxford Languages. Accessed February 28, 2025. https://languages.oup.com/word-of-the-year/2016/.

4

Permission to Doubt Your Faith

Travis Dickinson

I. Introduction

There was a time where I found myself doubting my Christian faith. I was in seminary, at the time. I was meant to be preparing for ministry and was sitting among a roomful of others preparing for ministry, and yet I was doubting whether Christianity was even true. This was a big moment. To understand the significance here, it's worth knowing I grew up in a *very* Christian household. My folks were in the ministry, a ministry started by my great-great-grandfather, literally in the 1800s!

We were also very committed to church. If the church doors were open, we were there. I have no memory of ever missing church except for severe sickness. It pretty much had to be a safety issue for us to miss church! And I experienced everything that the church had to offer. I experienced a weekly church service, Sunday school, camps, youth group, youth retreats, and mission trips. I even went to Bible college and worked on a church staff. I got all the way to seminary without ever asking an important question: Is Christianity really true? Now, I probably asked some questions along the way, but I never asked those questions genuinely open to the possibility of Christianity's being false.

That's what happened in that seminary classroom. For the first time, I had some questions I couldn't answer and I was genuinely open to the possibility that it was indeed false. For the first time in my life, I questioned whether it was *really* true. In short, I doubted my faith.[1]

---
[1] See Dickinson. *Wandering Toward God.*

Exiting the Church

We face a pretty big challenge in the church today. The problem that we face is that a majority of our Christian youth are walking away from the church, at least for a time. According to a prominent Barna study, the rate of Christian youth who drop out of church is 64%.[2]

Now, it's important to understand this statistic. Some are not rejecting Christian spirituality—they are rejecting the church. They might, for example, still see themselves as Christians but reject "organized religion" preferring to pursue their spiritual lives disconnected from the church as an institution. And some return to church after a time, especially when they get married and have kids. But these will often live very nominal Christian lives because Christianity has only played a nostalgic role in their lives rather than being central to their worldview. But of course, some of these leave the church rejecting Christianity never to return.

The question to ask is why. Why are so many people walking away from the church? While I think the answer is likely quite complex and varied, I want to suggest that part of the answer is that the church is not always a safe place to ask deep and difficult questions. The church is not always a safe place to doubt faith. Far too often our kids have not been encouraged to question and they, at some point, find themselves struggling with doubts, and they can't find any help.

Two Claims

I have two claims to make. One is that asking the deep and difficult questions is a crucial part of Christian discipleship. It is important to genuinely question your faith, genuinely ask: is this really true? It's finding answers to those sorts of questions that causes our faith to go down deep.

My second claim is that asking questions is often going to involve some doubts, and that's okay. That should just be seen as the normal process as you ask the deep and difficult questions. Their being deep and their being difficult should alone make this obvious. There just will be some struggles along the way. And that's okay. I hereby give you permission to doubt your faith. If you are doubting your faith right now, I want

---

[2] Kinnaman and Matlock, *Faith For Exiles*, 15.

you to hear this: you are normal!! Struggling with how to answer the deep and difficult questions often means that you are taking an honest look and willing to admit that you're still working it out. If that's you, I applaud you! Keep going, because I think you'll find answers and your faith will grow as a result.

II. Asking Questions

Let's first think about *questioning*. Is it okay to question Christianity?

In the Gospels, there's a very unique story about Jesus when he is an adolescent. In Luke 2.41–50, Luke tells us that, when Jesus was 12 years old, he and his family went up to Jerusalem for the Passover festival. Having stayed for the whole festival, showing they're a devout family, they depart Jerusalem assuming 12-year-old Jesus is with the group. Once they realize Jesus is not with them, it takes them three days to find him. Where do they find him? In the temple. Luke says, "After three days, they found him in the temple sitting among the teachers, listening to them and asking them questions. And all those who heard him were astounded at his understanding and his answers."

Not being where you are supposed to be is pretty typical 12-year-old behavior. But what he's doing in the temple is far from typical. They found him in the temple sitting *among* the temple teachers. Now that detail seems important. He's sitting with them. He's not sitting at their feet simply absorbing what they say. He's sitting among them and engaging them. Luke 2 says that he's "listening to them and asking them questions" (v. 46). The divine Son of God, at 12 years old, is sitting among the religious elites, listening and asking questions. And these religious elites were "astounded at his understanding and his answers" (v. 47).

Now, lest one thinks I'm making too much of this reference, what frames this story are two statements about the wisdom of Jesus. Luke 2.40 says that Jesus as a boy was growing strong and was "filled with wisdom." And then after the story of Jesus being found in the temple engaging the teachers, Luke 2.52 says that Jesus "increased in wisdom and stature, and in favor with God and with people." How does 12-year-old Jesus increase in wisdom? The story seems intended to answer that question. Jesus was in the habit of pursuing answers to his questions.

What Jesus models for us is a pattern for how we may grow in wisdom as well. We need to be pursuing the truth and this is going to involve both listening (perhaps the harder task!) and asking questions. This is, in a very real sense, Christ-like behavior.

As Jesus began his ministry and throughout the gospels, he is pictured as a rabbi. Jewish rabbis were often itinerant teachers that would travel around and teach the people. They typically traveled with a group of disciples, just as Jesus did. The disciples were essentially rabbis-in-training. So, they would listen in when the rabbi taught his lessons to the people. But then disciples would have access to the rabbi in a way the people didn't. They would eat their meals with the rabbi, walk along the roads with the rabbi, and sit around with him at the fire at night. This was part of the training. The disciple was meant to ask questions in order to understand and become like the rabbi. It wasn't to be a nuisance or to make the rabbi's life more difficult. It was wrestling and struggling through the deep and difficult questions in order to master those issues so that the disciples could become rabbis themselves and, one day, teach and disciple others.

We are of course called to be Jesus's disciples. If you are a Christian, as a follower of Jesus, you are meant to be his disciple. You are meant to ask the deep and difficult questions of your rabbi so that you can learn his ways.

Sometimes people don't like the idea of questioning God because it sounds as if the idea is to be a troublemaker shaking a fist at God, saying "why God? why?" But this is not the picture at all. In fact, our questions should flow from a place of honor and respect for Jesus, our rabbi.

At one point, Jesus offers the most important command of all. What's extraordinary about this is that part of the command is that we should intellectually pursue God out of love. In Matthew 22.37, Jesus identifies as the greatest command to "Love the Lord your God with all your heart, with all your soul, and with all your mind." Notice that Jesus, as part of this command, calls us to love God with all our minds! This just is, I suggest, the intellectual pursuit of God. This is not meant to be troublemaking or an intellectual shaking of the fist but, rather, a pursuit of love in seeking to know God fully and deeply. When we love someone, we want to know that person and know them deeply. How else can this happen other than asking questions? We ought to love God by asking questions in the pursuit of knowledge.

What is doubt?

We turn now to my second claim: that it is permissible and normal to doubt one's faith. The simple fact is that when we ask the deep and difficult questions, it's not always easy. It can be a struggle to see our way clear of the intellectual hurdles that come our way. We are often in the process of wrestling with challenges, and they are going to bother us to some degree. This is all it is to doubt. Doubt is the struggle of intellectual tension when we encounter an objection or a hurdle to believing. To put it another way, it's when one of our beliefs seems like it might be false and this bothers us.

Objections can come when we are least expecting it. We may be talking with someone, or reading something, or encountering something online, and all of a sudden we are faced with an objection, and you feel its pull. Objections have a bit of a zing to them, a little electricity. You feel the force of the objection and it gives you a moment. Why? Because this is a contrary claim to one of your beliefs and it may seem a bit plausible. And that's going to create some tension.

But this is normal for any big intellectual pursuit. We ask the deep and difficult questions and it's their depth and difficulty that creates the struggle. In 1 Corinthians 13.12, Paul characterizes our knowing God and the deep things of the world as one of seeing in a mirror dimly. The reality is that mirrors in those days produced an extremely obscured image. You might be looking straight at it, but it only returned, at best, an obscure or dim image. That's what our knowledge is like in a fallen world. Paul looks forward to a time in which we will know in full (just as we are fully known), but, for now, we only know in part. So of course we are going to have questions we must struggle through. Of course, we will sometimes have intellectual tension and doubts. This is just part of our human situation.

III. The Value of Doubt

Now, as I said, if you doubt—if you've ever doubted or you're doubting right now—I do want you to hear this: you are normal. This is just a normal part of the journey. But I also want to be really clear that doubt is not the goal. Doubt is like doing push-ups. Nobody does push-ups for their own sake. Or at least no one *should* do pushups for their own sake! Normal people don't do them for the sheer joy of it given that they are typically quite unpleasant. Why do pushups then? We do them to get something else—strength and health. Exercises, such as pushups, are what are known as instrumental goods. They are good, but their good is in what they bring us. Doubt is a good in this sense. It's good, but it's only an instrumental good. Despite the fact that there are some, even some pastors, who seem to think that doubt is a good in itself, my claim is that there is a tremendous value to doubt, but it's only valuable for what it may lead to. It's not the destination in that it's not good for its own sake.

What is the value of doubt? Doubts function much like warning lights. When a warning light comes on your dash in your automobile, it's not good—certainly not in itself. But it is good for letting you know that there's something amiss. Likewise, with doubts, they let you know there's a problem or a gap in your beliefs that needs to be addressed, and we ignore this warning at our own peril. When you doubt, it's time to lean in. What is the good to which doubts lead? Doubt, when handled well, leads us to truth and knowledge. And truth and knowledge leads us to greater confidence and a greater faith.

Now, I say this as a Christian who has been wrestling with the biggest questions and the hardest objections to Christianity for well over twenty years and who has found that Christianity holds up to life's biggest questions. Is it possible that somebody leans into their doubts, and it leads them away from Christianity? Sure, but ignoring a person's doubts, I suggest, leads to far worse consequences. And all I can do is give my own testimony of finding Christianity to be eminently reasonable and many of the most brilliant minds throughout history agree. I've asked these questions as honestly as I know how and I've found good and compelling answers to life's biggest questions. But how we lean in is vitally important. We turn now to how to doubt well. We'll look at seven strategies for handling doubt well with the aim to find truth.

IV. 7 Strategies for Doubting Well

1. Doubt in the Posture of a Seeker

The first strategy for doubting well is to approach your questions and doubts in the posture of a seeker of truth. Now, this might seem obvious, but you'd be surprised how often people ask questions but are not actually looking for answers to those questions. The person typically has his or her mind made up about an issue and is attempting to raise issues and problems for the opposing view. So it may look like a question, but really it's a rhetorical move. It's being a troublemaker. And unfortunately these rhetorical moves are not uncommon with those who are questioning their faith. They seem to have their minds made up already that Christianity is false or deeply problematic and are just making a show of asking questions. In this situation, they are not really looking for evidence or trying to discover truth because everything is already decided.

But it's always a bad idea to be closed off from the truth. Even if our minds are made up, to some degree, we should be seeking the truth. If we're to be followers of Christ, if we're going to apprentice under rabbi Jesus, then we should never stop seeking the truth. We should ruthlessly pursue the truth.

This contrast between troublemakers, on one hand, and genuine truth seekers can be seen in Jesus's ministry. At one point, John the Baptist sends his disciples to Jesus to ask a question, saying, "Are you the one who is to come? Or should we expect someone else?" (Mt 11.3). Now, this is pretty extraordinary because this is John the Baptist, the forerunner of the Christ. If anybody should be clear on this, in a sense, it should be John the Baptist. When John sees Jesus at the beginning of his ministry, he says, "Look, the Lamb of God, who takes away the sin of the world! This is *the one* I told you about..." (Jn 1.29-30a, emphasis added). John identifies Jesus as "the one."

But something's happened from that point to here, where he sends his disciples to Jesus and says, are you really him? Are you really the Messiah? And of course, what's happened is that John is in jail. Now, I'm speculating here, but I suspect that this result was not how John thought things would go. I suspect he didn't think he'd end up languishing in jail for standing up to king Herod facing execution. Having some doubts about the situation is pretty reasonable when we understand the context. John is just honestly asking Jesus, "Are you really the one or is there someone else?"

What's really extraordinary is how Jesus answers. He tells them to report to John what they see happening: miracles. The blind see, the lame walk, people are being healed, the deaf hear, and even the dead are being raised! He points to evidence. The answer is borne out in the evidence of Jesus's works.

We have another story of a questioner in Matthew 22.15–22 where one of the Pharisees asks: "Is it lawful to pay taxes to Caesar or not?" Here, it's made clear the Pharisees are asking this question in order to trap him. Now, Jesus knows what they are up to, but he says, "Give me a coin." They give him a coin, and he says, "Whose face is on this coin?" And they say, "Caesar's." And he says, "Pay to Caesar what is Caesar's and to God what is God's." Now, they ask a question, but they're not seeking. In fact, Matthew 22 says, "they left him and went away." Notice they didn't want the answer. They weren't seeking truth. They just wanted to trap Jesus, but Jesus was of course up to the challenge.

We can also contrast truth seeking to the extremes of fundamentalism and skepticism. These can be seen as ditches on either side of the road that should be avoided. There's the ditch of, what's sometimes called, fundamentalism, where someone is not open to any questions at all about their faith. You just believe it, and that settles it. The fundamentalist might have some true beliefs but they are not *seeking* the truth and will therefore not be well grounded in those beliefs. And if they *don't* have true beliefs, there's little hope they'll find truth if their beliefs can't even be questioned. There's also the ditch of skepticism, where no answer will do. For any answer that's given, the skeptic, as I'm using the term, says, "but why?" And then if an answer to that question is offered, the skeptic says, "but why?" And on and on it goes without ever being satisfied. Neither the fundamentalist nor the skeptic is actually interested in the truth. The fundamentalist is unwilling to even ask the questions and the skeptic is unwilling to accept any answer. Neither of these postures is truth seeking. We need to steer clear of these ditches and seek the middle way of asking questions in the pursuit of truth.

We also need to avoid emotional reasoning. Emotions are very good and God-given. We are designed to have emotions. But they're not always good at pointing us to truth. They tend to point us to what we *want* to be true, to that in which we are emotionally invested. But of course what we want to be true is sometimes different from what is actually true (such as how healthy our bank accounts are!). I suspect this is what's happening today with so many Christian youth walking away from the church. They're bored by their church experience, or they've had a bad church experience, maybe even some kind of religious abuse. And there are a lot of emotions driving those doubts. If this has been your experience, I'm so very sorry. We don't want to ignore the emotions connected to our past experiences, and we very well may need someone to help us sort out and walk through those emotions. But I'd also suggest we don't want to put our emotions into the driver's seat for making decisions about our worldview. It's just so hard to find the truth in navigating the deep and difficult questions of life when it's an emotional charged situation. We of course can't be completely non-emotional. But as we are able to, we should put our emotions in check as we pursue truth in the posture of a seeker.

2. Go Slow

The second strategy for doubting well is to go slow. Take your time with this. Hang on, because again, in the moment of crisis, it can be difficult to think rationally. The first thing I say to someone who is in the place of doubt is just to hang on. When we're struggling with something, we often need a little emotional distance to really evaluate it. One of the most important and helpful things to understand is that you can be in a place of doubt and a place of faith all at the same time. You're not going to explode. You can have doubts about Christianity while placing 100% faith in the truth of Christianity.

Consider getting on an airplane. Even though I get on them regularly, I really don't know much about how an airplane works. Now this is a good illustration of faith because we really entrust ourselves fully to the airplane when we get on board. What if we begin to have some doubts about the airplane we are about to get on? Suppose we find out that our airplane weighs about 1 million pounds. We notice that it is mostly made of metal. We are told that we'll be cruising at 30,000 feet, which is about 6 miles off the planet. All kinds of things can go wrong from mechanical failure, human error, issues with the computer systems, etc. Pondering these things, suppose we are genuinely doubting that getting on the airplane is a good idea.

Here's the question: could we get on board? Sure, we can (especially if we are going somewhere sunny with a beach!). We might be struggling with it, but we can get on board the airplane and entrust ourselves despite the doubts we are experiencing. We can even be on the airplane, flying through the air, asking questions about how this is even possible.

I think this is a beautiful picture of the Christian journey. I'll be honest with you. I've got questions about Christianity. I don't have it all figured out. But I'm on board and committed to the journey. I'm going to keep pressing in to find answers. The point is that we can have unanswered questions and even be struggling with the big questions and completely on board and committed to the journey. And for this reason, we should take out time and exercise due care.

Os Guinness has said it this way, he said, "Doubt is not the opposite of faith, unbelief is."[3] When we are doubting, we still believe. If we weren't believing, there'd be nothing there to doubt. So there's no inconsistency with being in a place of doubt and still maintaining our faith. So we should hang on and go very slowly as we lean in to our doubts.

3. Don't Doubt Alone

Third, don't doubt alone. Doubt makes you feel lonely, and it makes you feel isolated. It makes you feel as if you've just found the smoking gun

---

[3] Guinness, *God in the Dark*, 29.

of Christianity—the error that shows the whole thing to be false. It's an amazing thing to just go talk to someone about it, especially folks who are further down the road than us, and ask our questions. Sometimes just articulating the question or the doubt is all it really takes. We find that maybe the issue is not as problematic as I thought it was. Now, this is why our churches should be the very first place that we run to when we are in a place of doubt, because we need the community of like-minded believers to help us through our questions.

You need community, but you also need guides. The best option is to have someone in your life who's a bit further down the road than you, who's asked these questions already that can lead you through it. Unfortunately, that's sometimes hard to find. But what you absolutely have at your fingertips, especially in today's digital world, is a tremendous amount of resources. Some of my most beloved mentors are people I've never met, and they maybe didn't even live in this century. But they've recorded their thoughts in books that can be like a cool drink of water for one dying of thirst. Reading C. S. Lewis or St. Augustine, who both wrestled a lot with doubts about Christianity, can be invaluable guides for us as we wrestle. And today, as they say, is the golden age of apologetics. We have books being written at every level, from the scholarly to children's books. We have numerous apologetics websites and YouTube channels aimed at walking through the tough questions. There's never been a point in history where more apologetics content is being produced and is available to anyone who's willing to pursue. You *can* find answers.

So don't go at it alone. Find community where you can explore the big questions and with whom you can share your doubts. Also find helpful guides. Find those, both in person and in resources, who can help lead you through your doubts.

4. Aim at Confidence Not Certainty

The fourth strategy for doubting well is not to aim at absolute certainty in our Christian journey. Now I realize that may sound a little controversial, but the basic reason for this is that we just won't ever achieve absolute certainty in this life. Again, according to 1 Corinthians 13.12, we see in a mirror dimly in that our knowledge will always be partial and obscured in this life. The problem is that absolute certainty is all or nothing. And if we think we need absolute certainty, then our faith can actually become quite fragile. It becomes something of a house of cards. A house of cards is when someone takes playing cards and balances them on their edges together to build a whole structure. The problem is that this structure is necessarily fragile. If you take one card out, the whole thing comes toppling down. If you think we must have absolute certainty about Christianity, what happens if a difficult question comes along? Again, certainty is all or nothing. If you have a question you can't answer, then you don't have certainty and faith can come toppling down.

Don't aim at 100% certainty, aim at confidence instead. Aim at being confident that Christianity is true because confidence can tolerate our unanswered questions. Confidence can tolerate doubts in a way that certainty cannot. Take the airplane example again. If we need absolute certainty to get on an airplane, we'll never get on board. You can't ever have absolute certainty that the airplane will get you where you want to go without issue. But you can have rational confidence in getting on an airplane. And I'm convinced you can have rational confidence in the truth of Christianity as well..

5. Don't Simply Deconstruct

Fifth, don't deconstruct. At least don't deconstruct *only*. If you do, I want to suggest it will be an incomplete project. Now, deconstruction has become a contemporary buzzword with innumerable videos and social media posts about dismantling religious commitments in whole or in part. I have some deep concerns about those who aim to deconstruct their faith.

The first concern is that the term 'deconstruction' far too often just means "on the way to deconversion." It's not just taking things apart in evaluating one's beliefs. It just is the process of rejecting those beliefs. So if this is what is meant by deconstruction, then, of course, I don't think we should be on the way to deconversion. We need to be on the journey of evaluation and investigation to find the truth, but let's not decide the case before we've evaluated.

But even if someone doesn't mean that they are simply on the way to deconvert, deconstruction as a concept, is incomplete. It is a fundamentally negative project. It's taking something apart. And sometimes we need to take things apart. When we lean into asking questions about the faith, some dismantling may have to happen. But it's necessarily incomplete if all we do is deconstruct. It's no good to us when we just simply take things apart. Let's say we, as a project, take a car apart. We remove each of its parts and we set those out on the garage floor. The problem is how we are going to get anywhere now. We've got to get those parts back together or replace them. The same goes with our worldviews. When we deconstruct our Christian faith, that's an incomplete project. You may be able to get along in life without a car, but you can't not have a worldview. We will put something in its place. You will have beliefs about the world.

What too many people who are deconstructing do is they deconstruct their Christianity, and they will do it with an extremely high requirement of evidence. If it doesn't reach this almost unattainable standard of evidence, then it's no good, and they reject it. But, again, you can't not have a worldview. People will so often embrace, almost uncritically, some other view that's more acceptable by those around them. But this is glaringly inconsistent.

In some ways, the most important thing here is not so much what we deconstruct. Sure, take things apart and question everything! This might get messy and that might just be how it goes. It's not easy to do this in a neat and clean way. It can feel like your faith has been taken apart. But what's so important is to put things back together in reasonable ways. So don't just deconstruct. Spend most of your time evaluating what you should in fact believe, what you have good reason to take as truth.

6. Doubt Your Doubts

Sixth, and this is crucial, we need to doubt our doubts. The idea here is that doubts show up and they beat us up a bit, but they should not win out against our beliefs just because they're there. Yes, we need to evaluate our beliefs. But, just as much, we need to evaluate our doubts. Just because somebody raises an objection doesn't mean it's a good objection. We have to do the work of investigation.

Now this is really my story. So going back to my seminary days where I'm sitting in a seminary classroom doubting my faith. It really bothered me. I suddenly didn't know that Christianity was true and, for the first time in my life, I was open to the possibility that it wasn't. But here's the thing: *I also didn't know it was false.* I just didn't have confidence either way. A lot of people walk away from Christianity right here. But this is entirely too soon. For me, it would have been completely irresponsible for me to walk away given that Christianity, for all I knew, could still be true. I just didn't know. What I needed to do is investigate. I was doubting my Christian beliefs, but I needed to also doubt my doubts.

And here's what happened. I leaned in. I pursued truth. I tried to be as brutally honest as I possibly could. And I found a lot of compelling answers. I of course didn't get everything figured out, but I did find a few really important answers that solved a good deal of the tension. I found that the questions that I had, that were beating me up, were actually questions that Christians have been asking for a very long time and have provided compelling answers for us. I came out of the other side of that with a great value. I found truth and knowledge, and an even greater confidence in Christianity. The doubts, quite ironically, led to a greater faith.

Now, I will say this too: I want you to know that my seminary degree was a degree in apologetics. I had read books like this one prior to my doubts. I knew a lot in my head, but I had never genuinely investigated Christianity in a completely honest way open to let the evidence lead. So you're reading this thinking that you are not susceptible to doubt. Well, I might have thought the same thing until those doubts crashed the party. This is why we need to be asking genuine questions. But, just in case doubts come crashing in for you, just know that your task is to investigate and doubt your doubts.

7. *Abide in Christ*

Finally, as a seventh strategy for doubting well, I suggest there's a real need to abide in Christ as we face down these struggles and questions.

Now, some people may be on the brink of walking away and the last thing they want to be told is to be nourished in their souls by Christ. But the reminder here is that we are not mere logic machines. Our doubts are almost never purely intellectual struggles. It's important to be reflective about what all is going on in our hearts as well as minds and there's no better way than bringing our struggles before the Lord in all their mess and with all honesty we can muster.

Jesus invites and even calls us to abide in him, make our home or abode in him (John 15.4–5). He uses the analogy of a vine and its branches, saying that if we don't abide in him as the vine, then we won't be able produce fruit. The thought is that without abiding in Christ we are cut off from the true source of life. It can be very difficult to make any progress with our doubts when we are not abiding in Christ. And when we are abiding in Christ, it helps put our doubts into perspective.

So we should ask our questions and struggle through our doubts. But I do think there's a need for us, as we're asking the questions, to commune with Christ as we abide in him. That word "abide" can be translated as "remain, to stay, to lodge with, and to wait for." It's a rich biblical term that points to our pursuit of not just intellectual answers but of Christ himself. We shouldn't just be pursuing truth and knowledge, but pursuing Christ.

And here's the promise: "Ask and it will be given to you. Seek and you will find. Knock and the door will be open to you. For everyone who asks receives, and the one who seeks finds, and to the one who knocks, the door will be opened" (Matthew 7.7–8). The invitation is to ask, seek and knock; and Jesus promises success. That's a big promise. Now, if you haven't found, I say keep going. Do it as honestly as you possibly can. It's worth it. That's my promise to you!

As Christians, we are meant to be asking our questions, leaning into our doubts in pursuit of Christ out of love for him. And I trust that when we do so with honesty, courage and persistence, we'll find answers and life in his name.

Bibliography

Dickinson, Travis. *Wandering Toward God: Finding Faith amid Doubts and Big Questions.* Downers Grove, IL: IVP, 2022.

Guinness, Os. *God in the Dark: The Assurance of Faith Beyond a Shadow of Doubt.* Wheaton, IL: Crossway, 1996.

Kinnaman, David, and Mark Matlock. *Faith For Exiles: 5 Ways for a New Generation to Follow Jesus in Digital Babylon.* Grand Rapids, MI: Baker, 2019.

5

The Apologetics Matrix
The Purpose and Audience of Christian Apologetics

Tawa J. Anderson

I. What Is Apologetics?

The term apologetics comes from the Greek απολογια *(apologia)*. The Greek term denotes a courtroom scene and suggests presenting one's defense in the face of prosecution, or providing the reasoning for one's legal position. After Socrates is arrested on charges of atheism and corrupting the youth of Athens, he presents a defense for his philosophical ministry to the Athenian court, which comes down to us as *The Apology of Socrates*.[1]

Apologetics is a giving of reasons for what one believes or practices. As such, one can be an apologist for Donald Trump, the sport of hockey, a vegan diet, Christmas carols, or Communism. Christian apologetics has been defined as "the art of persuasion, the discipline which considers ways to commend and defend the living God to those without faith."[2] Doug Groothuis defines apologetics as "the rational defense of the Christian worldview as objectively true, rationally compelling and existentially or subjectively engaging."[3] Together, these definitions bring out the heart of apologetics: the defense and explanation of the Christian faith.

In some Christian circles, however, apologetics is a dirty word. Lay Christians and popular teachers question whether Jesus or the Apostle

---

[1] Plato, *Five Dialogues*.
[2] *New Dictionary of Christian Apologetics*, 3.
[3] Groothuis, *Christian Apologetics*, 24.

Paul would be bothered to engage in modernistic reasoning, trying to persuade people to embrace the reasonability of Christian discipleship. Others insist that apologetic arguments only ever convince the already-convinced, and are hence an exercise in evangelistic futility. So, the first question I want to address is not *can* apologetics be done, but rather, *should* apologetics be done? For Christians, the Word of God is, or at least should be, authoritative. What the Bible says and shows about apologetics, then, ought to determine how we approach providing reasons for our faith.

II. Apologetics in the Bible

So what *does* the Bible say about apologetics? In short, the Bible commands all believers everywhere to always be ready to engage in apologetics and includes numerous examples of apologetic encounters. The key apologetic mandate comes from 1 Peter 3.13–17.[4]

> Who is going to harm you if you are eager to do good? But even if you should suffer for what is right, you are blessed. "Do not fear their threats; do not be frightened." But in your hearts revere Christ as Lord. Always be prepared to give an answer to everyone who asks you to give the reason for the hope that you have. But do this with gentleness and respect, keeping a clear conscience, so that those who speak maliciously against your good behavior in Christ may be ashamed of their slander. For it is better, if it is God's will, to suffer for doing good than for doing evil.

In verse 15, Peter commands his listeners to *be prepared*. Be prepared for *what*? To give *an answer*. What *kind* of answer? An answer for the reason for the hope that you have. In other words, God commands all Christians to be ready to answer questions that people have concerning our faith. It is not the apologetic *suggestion*, where God gives us the option, if we are so inclined and if we have the right abilities, to try to answer people's questions. Instead, God delivers the apologetic *mandate*, commanding all believers everywhere to always be prepared to give an answer to everyone who asks you to give the reason for the hope that you have. That one passage is sufficient to establish a mandate for apol-

---

[4] All Biblical references are to the New International Version (NIV), unless otherwise noted.

ogetics, but there are numerous other biblical passages that demonstrate and demand apologetic involvement.

Luke begins his Gospel by stating his intent and process:

> Many have undertaken to draw up an account of the things that have been fulfilled among us, just as they were handed down to us by those who from the first were eyewitnesses and servants of the word. Therefore, since I myself have carefully investigated everything from the beginning, it seemed good also to be to write an orderly account for you, most excellent Theophilus, so that you may know the certainty of the things you have been taught. (Lk 1.1–4)

Luke is not just conveying interesting stories he has heard. Instead, he has *carefully investigated* the life of Jesus, interviewing eyewitnesses and communicating their stories about Jesus. He provides a researched account of Jesus's life and ministry. Why? He desires for his readers to *know with certainty* the things they have been taught about Jesus.

Elsewhere, the Hebrew poet, King David, invites his hearer to behold the works of nature, and consider what they imply about nature's Creator:

> The heavens declare the glory of God; the skies proclaim the work of his hands. Day after day they pour forth speech; night after night they display knowledge. There is no speech or language where their voice is not heard. Their voice goes out into all the earth, their words to the ends of the world. (Ps 19.1–4)

Along with passages like Job 38–41, Psalm 19 serves as a prototype of later arguments for God from design and/or beauty. We are called to see the grandeur and majesty of God through the wondrous Creation He has wrought.

In Jeremiah 10, the 'weeping prophet' builds an argument from Creation to the existence of Yahweh, the God of Israel, to the exclusion of the gods of other nations.

> Hear what the Lord says to you, O house of Israel. ... Do not learn the ways of the nations ... For the customs of the peoples are worthless; they cut a tree out of the forest, and a craftsman shapes it with his chisel. They adorn it with silver and gold; they fasten it with hammer and nails so it will not totter. Like

> a scarecrow in a melon patch, their idols cannot speak; they must be carried because they cannot walk. Do not fear them; they can do no harm nor can they do any good. (Jer 10.1–5)

Jeremiah reminds the people of how idols (statues of gods) are fashioned, and how those idols are incapable of moving or acting, let alone creating all that exists. Jeremiah then points to the creative work evident throughout the earth and points to Yahweh as the source of all that is.

> These gods, who did not make the heavens and the earth, will perish from the earth and from under the heavens. But God made the earth by his power; he founded the world by his wisdom and stretched out the heavens by his understanding. When he thunders, the waters in the heavens roar; he makes clouds rise from the ends of the earth. He sends lightning with the rain and brings out the wind from his storehouses. (Jer 10.11–13)

Jeremiah is providing a rational argument for abandoning idol worship and returning to Yahweh-worship—an apologetic against the ways of the nations and for the God of Israel.

The book of Acts is full of apologetic reasoning. For example, Peter's sermon on the Day of Pentecost, recorded in Acts 2.14–36, argues for the divinity of Jesus based upon Old Testament prophecy and his own eyewitness testimony of the resurrection:

> Men of Israel, listen to this: Jesus of Nazareth was a man accredited by God to you by miracles, wonders, and signs, which God did among you through him, as you yourselves know. ... God has raised this Jesus to life, and we are all witnesses of the fact. (Acts 2.22, 32)

Peter further explains that the Psalmist David had declared (Psalm 16.8–11) that God would not abandon the body of God's "Holy One" to decay in the grave. But given that all good Jews knew not only that David had died, but also where his very tomb could be found (Acts 2.29), Peter argues that David, under the inspiration of the Holy Spirit, was speaking of the future resurrection of God's Christ (Acts 2.30–31). In other words, Peter gives the reasons for the hope that he has in the crucified and risen Savior.

In my estimation, the pre-eminent apologist in the New Testament is the Apostle Paul. Let's look at Acts 17 to see how Paul operates in two different settings.

> When Paul and his companions had passed through Amphipolis and Apollonia, they came to Thessalonica, where there was a Jewish synagogue. As was his custom, Paul went into the synagogue, and on three Sabbath days he reasoned with them from the Scriptures, explaining and proving that the Messiah had to suffer and rise from the dead. "This Jesus I am proclaiming to you is the Messiah," he said. Some of the Jews were persuaded and joined Paul and Silas, as did a large number of God-fearing Greeks and quite a few prominent women. (Acts 17.1–4)

Note how Paul acts here. He *reasons* with Jews in Thessalonica, *explaining and proving* the death and resurrection of Jesus. The result? Many were *persuaded*. Paul does not just appeal to their hearts—he appeals to their reasoning capacities, showing how belief in Jesus as the risen Messiah made sense. The terminology emphasizes that Paul is presenting rational arguments in support of his Christian faith.

While speaking to the Jews in Thessalonica, Paul begins with Old Testament Scripture. Why? His Jewish audience accepts Scripture as authoritative, and so citing the Old Testament provides common ground upon which both parties can stand and reason. Paul uses Scripture as a springboard to the reasons for the hope that he has. Later in Acts 17, Paul is ministering in Athens, and the different context requires a different apologetic approach.

In Athens, Paul first notes points of commonality with the people of the city, and even *commends* their religiosity despite their pagan idolatry (Acts 17.22–23). The people of Athens are religious, and even have an altar inscribed *To an unknown God*—Paul proposes to show them who that God is. Paul continues with natural revelation—evidence for God's existence that can be discerned from the world around us—noting the divine Being who created heaven and earth cannot be contained by human-built temples. Paul then quotes from two Greek poets to drive his point home (Acts 17.28).[5] Why does Paul quote Greek poets rather than Old Testament

---

[5] Acts 17.28: 'For in him we live and move and have our being.' As some of your own poets have said, 'We are his offspring.'

Scriptures? Paul desires to reach the Athenian people where they are, using whatever common ground he can, to share the reason for the hope that he has. After establishing common ground and providing a basic argument for God from Creation, Paul closes with a uniquely Christian apologetic surrounding the resurrection of Jesus (Acts 17.29–31). The result? Some scoffed; some wondered; while "some of the people became followers of Paul and believed." (Acts 17.34)

We could multiply examples, pointing to passages like Exodus 3–4, John 21.24–25, Acts 9.1–19, and 1 Corinthians 15.3–8, as biblical examples and exhortations toward apologetics. But I trust the point is clear: throughout Scripture, God encourages His people to think, to reason to their faith, to reason for their faith, and to give reasons why others ought to believe. We see examples in the Old Testament and New Testament of the people of God engaged in robust apologetics. There are, therefore, powerful Scriptural reasons to engage in apologetic ministry to share the Gospel with those who do not believe. Put simply, God commands it, the Bible demonstrates it, and Christians ought to be doing it.

III. The Apologetics Matrix

A. Existing Apologetic Schools and Approaches

There are various schools, or methods, of apologetics. Steve Cowan's edited volume, *Five Views of Apologetics*, presents five schools: classical; evidential; cumulative case; presuppositional; and Reformed epistemological.[6] Kenneth Boa and Robert Bowman's classic work, *Faith Has Its Reasons*, identifies four schools: classical, evidential, Reformed, and fideist, plus a fifth approach which they term 'integrative.'[7]

In addition to these traditional apologetic schools or methods, apologists talk about different *approaches* to the apologetic enterprise. *Narrative* apologetics focuses on the use of story and imagery; *relational* apologetics seeks to understand and build bridges to the apologetic partner; *scientific* apologetics brings the methods and data of contemporary science to the table; *rational* apologetics identifies logical arguments which support the

---
[6] Cowan, *Five Views on Apologetics*.
[7] Boa and Bowman, *Faith Has Its Reasons*, 2nd ed.

faith; *cultural* apologetics employs cultural artefacts to defend Christian faith. Such approaches can easily be multiplied.

For the purposes of this chapter, I wish to emphasize that each apologetic school and approach finds a home within the apologetics matrix. The apologetics matrix is not specific to a particular type of apologetics; rather, it is an overarching theoretical framework which can readily incorporate all the various methods as we seek to engage others apologetically.

B. Outlining the Apologetics Matrix

The apologetics matrix has four cells, governed by two columns and two rows.

The Focus (Audience) of Apologetics: Evangelistic (Outward) vs. Devotional (Inward)

The columns of the apologetics matrix describe the focus or audience of apologetics. Apologetics can be either **evangelistic** or **devotional**; that is, our apologetics ministry can be oriented to those who are already Christians, or to those who are not yet Christians.

Apologists sometimes assume that apologetics is primarily about demolishing the pretentious arguments of atheists and giving a reasonable defense of Christianity. This is certainly a crucial aspect of the apologetic enterprise, but it is not all there is. Christian apologetics has two distinct audiences—those outside the church, *and* those *within* the church. Consider why many young Christians abandon their faith. Sometimes it is moral rebellion; sometimes it is pride and arrogance. Sometimes, however, they have serious questions and doubts as young believers, but nobody provides them with reasonable, thoughtful responses to those questions. A crucial aspect of apologetics is presenting reasons to continue believing to those who are already within the flock of God. Given the current condition of the North American church, and the rapid pace at which young adults are deconstructing their faith, I even hazard to say that devotional apologetics is *more important*, more essential, than evangelistic apologetics.

To summarize, there are two audiences for apologetics ministry—those outside the church (evangelistic apologetics) and those inside the church (devotional apologetics). The former are given reasons to *become* followers of Christ (or alternatively, reasons to give up their opposition to Christianity); the latter are given reasons to *remain* followers of Christ (or alternatively, reasons not to give up their commitment to Christianity).

The Purpose (Goal) of Apologetics: Offensive (Positive) vs. Defensive (Negative)

The rows of the matrix are governed by the *purpose* of apologetics. There are two fundamental goals or purposes of apologetics ministry. First, **offensive apologetics** (or **positive apologetics**) gives people positive reasons why we believe (and why they ought to believe) that Christianity is true. It provides historical, evidential, and logical arguments to support the truth of our faith.

Second, **defensive apologetics** (or **negative apologetics**) gives people reasons not to disbelieve Christianity. It responds to objections or attacks against our faith by providing historical, evidential, and logical arguments to support the truth of our faith.

In a sense, defensive apologetics is clearing away the intellectual brush that obscures the path to faith in Christ, and positive apologetics seeks to replace the intellectual brush with a paved intellectual path that leads to faith in Christ. No one is under any illusions—apologetics on its own, as a purely human enterprise, will not bring anyone to saving faith in Jesus Christ. Rather, it is only the conviction and illumination of the Holy Spirit working within a person's heart that can work salvation. Nonetheless, we also know that the Holy Spirit can and does empower our divinely-dependent apologetic endeavors as part of the process of bringing someone (heart, soul, mind, and strength) to the foot of the Cross.

So apologetics can have two different purposes—offensive (positive) and defensive (negative). Apologetics presents reasons *to believe* (or alternatively, reasons to continue believing), or reasons *not to disbelieve* (or alternatively, reasons not be begin disbelieving). With that groundwork laid, let's flesh out the 4 cells of the Apologetics Matrix.

1. Apologetics for Outspoken Opponents (Defensive Evangelistic Apologetics)
Defensive evangelistic apologetics responds to arguments or objections made by non-Christians to clear the brush away, to remove obstacles to them believing in Jesus Christ. I call this apologetics to "outspoken opponents." My friend Peter[8] led a small group Bible study at a little Baptist church in Saskatchewan. In time, one of the church members began bringing a couple of friends from work. These friends came to Bible study happily and regularly, but they did not believe anything that was taught. When Peter led a study on the parable of the sower in Matthew 13, one of the newcomers asked, "Why should I believe that? I don't think Jesus even said that. Matthew made that up, and there's no reason for us to accept it as being true for us today." The following week, Peter's Bible study focused on the majesty and glory of God. One of the atheist friends protested: "But how do you even know that God exists? I think we just project God out of our desire for an Almighty power that we can trust and rely upon."

Peter desired to guide his Bible study group, but he also desired to minister to the atheists. He gently responded to a key objection or doubt that they expressed. For example, after they professed disbelief in God, and insisted that God was a product of human wishful thinking, Peter noted that the professed origins of a belief do not indicate the truth or falsity of that belief. Furthermore, contrary to their claims, there are good rational and evidential arguments that strongly point toward the existence of God. Peter shared in brief form the argument from objective morality and the argument from religious experience. Finally, he noted that the assertion that belief in God is the product of wish-fulfillment can easily be turned around on its author. Contemporary atheists may put forth the non-existence of God as a wish-fulfillment: they do not want to be held morally accountable to any higher power, so they imaginatively project the non-existence of God to exempt themselves from His moral judgment. Peter engaged in defensive evangelistic apologetics—giving non-Christians reasons to not disbelieve.

---

[8] I have changed names and descriptions of ministry contexts slightly in order to mask the identity of people described in this section. Nonetheless, each individual is a colleague in ministry.

There are two sides to the apologetic task to outspoken opponents: first, demonstrating the ability of Christianity theism to respond to potential *defeaters*[9] or attacks; and second, demonstrating the irrationality and inconsistency of the other person's worldview. The non-Christian is often smug in their non-Christian worldview, confident that it is coherent, consistent, and superior to Christianity. The role of the apologist is to gently 'take the roof off,' demonstrating that their worldview, in fact, does not hold together. The goal is to make the opponent discontented with his existing worldview, such that he is open to considering the truth of the Christian worldview. Thus, the atheists in Peter's Bible study needed to be given reasons *not to disbelieve*.

Sadly, when unbelievers visit our churches or converse with Christians, they often find their objections and doubts dismissed. What is the atheist's natural logical conclusion when a Bible study leader, Sunday school teacher, youth pastor, or preacher is either unable or unwilling to engage their questions? 'I ask these questions; they don't answer them. There must not be rational, legitimate responses to the issues that I raise.' Atheists become more strongly entrenched in their opposition to the Christian faith due to the inability or unwillingness of Christian leaders to thoughtfully respond to intellectual objections against Christianity. Worse yet, when Christians within the church witness the inability of Christian leaders to respond to these objections, it can raise doubts within them as well. The intellectual credibility of Christianity within our contemporary culture suffers immeasurable harm when Christians (particularly Christian leaders) fail to live up to God's apologetic mandate.

In the book of Acts, the early church in Jerusalem faced outspoken opposition from the Jewish leaders. In chapters 4 through 7, we see the apostles engage apologetically and evangelistically with their Jewish opponents. Their apologetic often focuses upon Jesus' resurrection. When Peter and John are hauled before the Sanhedrin to account for their healing of a crippled beggar, Peter proclaims:

---

[9] I.e., objections launched against the rationality, evidentiality, and/or intelligibility of Christian theism. Such defeaters rationally compel us to abandon our belief in God *unless* they are themselves defeated. Hence, defensive evangelistic apologetics is engaged in *defeating defeaters*.

> Rulers and elders of the people! If we are being called to account today for an act of kindness shown to a cripple and are asked how he was healed, then know this, you and all the people of Israel: It is by the name of Jesus Christ of Nazareth, whom you crucified but whom God raised from the dead, that this man stands before you healed. He is 'the stone you builders rejected, which has become the capstone.' Salvation is found in no one else, for there is no other name under heaven given to men by which we must be saved. (Acts 4.8–12)

Peter provides the ruling elders with reasons to cease their persecution of the infant Church, and instead to become followers of the Messiah—God raised the crucified Jesus back to life, and continues to work miraculous healings through Jesus' name. Jesus is the Messiah, the capstone, the foundation block for Israel; and there is no salvation outside of Christ.

2. Apologetics for Seeking Skeptics (Offensive Evangelistic Apologetics)
Both types of evangelistic apologetics are geared to people who are not (yet) Christian. The difference, more in degree than in type, is that the first group is actively opposed to the Christian faith; the group we are considering now is at least minimally open to considering Christianity. Offensive evangelistic apologetics presents positive reasons for non-Christians to embrace the truth of the Christian faith. This is apologetics to "seeking skeptics." My friend John was a pastor to youth and young adults in a university town. John had regular contact with non-Christians through a local college ministry. A number of foreign students were spiritually seeking and open to the Gospel of Christ, but they would not consider Christianity without seeing and hearing compelling reasons to believe that it was true. They wanted to be convinced that Christianity made sense and was rationally defensible before they would dive in. John had always known Christianity to be true; but he had not been forced to present a defense for its rationality before. Now he had seekers who asked him how it made sense. John's students were open to God; but they needed to be shown that Christianity is a rational, well-founded faith before they would consider embracing Jesus as Savior and Lord. They needed *reasons to believe*.

The Apostle Paul engaged in apologetics to seeking skeptics throughout his ministry. One uncommon example is his 'trial' before Festus and

King Agrippa in Acts 25 and 26. Agrippa is knowledgeable of the Jewish Scriptures and curious about the new Christian Church. Paul concludes his appeal to Agrippa in 26.23–29:

> "The Christ would suffer and, as the first to rise from the dead, would proclaim light to his own people and to the Gentiles."
>
> At this point Festus interrupted Paul's defense. "You are out of your mind, Paul!" he shouted. "Your great learning is driving you insane."
>
> "I am not insane, most excellent Festus," Paul replied. "What I am saying is true and reasonable. The king is familiar with these things, and I can speak freely to him. I am convinced that none of this has escaped his notice, because it was not done in a corner. King Agrippa, do you believe the prophets? I know you do."
>
> Then Agrippa said to Paul, "Do you think that in such a short time you can persuade me to be a Christian?"
>
> Paul replied, "Short time or long—I pray God that not only you but all who are listening to me today may become what I am, except for these chains."

Paul's appeal to Agrippa is not just evangelism, it is evangelistic apologetics. He speaks what is 'true and reasonable.' He defends the reasonability of his faith to someone he hopes is seeking after the truth. Seeking Skeptics will ask us why we believe what we believe; apologetics provides them with reasons that they too ought to believe as we believe. Then we pray that God will empower our words with His Holy Spirit to bring our apologetic conversation partner to knowledge of Himself.

Pastor John engaged in positive evangelistic apologetics by seeking to lay out evidential and existential reasons for immigrant students to embrace the truth of the Gospel. First, he argued for the historical reliability of the New Testament Gospels, looking at internal and external evidence that demonstrates their eyewitness content. Second, he utilized an updated version of C. S. Lewis' trilemma, sharing the claims the historical Jesus made for Himself—that He was the divine Son of Man, the anointed Messiah (Savior) of Israel, the unique Son of God; that He possessed the unique divine authority to teach God's truth in His own name, to heal people directly, to forgive sins, even to determine people's eternal destiny. John led students through Mark 14.62 and John 8.58 to show that, given the reliability of the Gospels, one cannot help but conclude that Jesus believed He was God incarnate. Third, John turned to the historical evidence for the resurrection of Jesus, seeking to show that the most probable conclusion is that God raised Jesus from the dead, resulting in the transformation of the disciples, the conversion of Paul and James, and the birth of the early Christian Church. Finally, John shared his own personal testimony, beginning with his atheistic upbringing, moving through his gradual conversion, and talking about the newfound purpose, fulfillment, and joy that he had found as a servant of Christ. John insisted that these students too could find completeness through faith in Christ, and that such faith was not a blind leap in the dark, but rather a reasonable step of faith illuminated by the evidence and arguments that God sets before us. God used John's offensive evangelistic apologetics to draw numerous students to a saving faith in Jesus.

3. Apologetics for Doubting Disciples (Offensive Devotional Apologetics)

We move now from the left-hand column of the apologetics matrix to the right-hand column. In doing so, we move from evangelistic to devotional apologetics; from apologetics for those outside the church, to apologetics for those inside the church. Offensive devotional apologetics provides 'doubting disciples' with *reasons to continue believing*. My friend Greg grew up in a strong Christian family. He accepted Jesus as his Savior and Lord when he was nine years old, and was active in Sunday school and youth group throughout middle school and high school. When Greg was finishing high school and entering college, he began to have doubts about the truth of Christianity. He noticed that some things in the Gospels did not seem to add up. Matthew and Luke had different genealogies for Jesus. The details surrounding who visited Jesus' empty tomb were different—how many women were there? Were there angels or men at the tomb? How many of them? He also questioned the character of the God presented in parts of the Old Testament. Why did God hate Esau? How could a loving God order the annihilation and extermination of entire people groups in the Promised Land? And how can God be both three and one? Greg is typical of millions of young Christians throughout North America—he believed in Jesus, but he had questions and doubts about his faith. Positive devotional apologetics, apologetics to doubting disciples, seeks to demonstrate the truth of the core historical claims of biblical Christianity or to establish the logical coherence of difficult Christian doctrines.

The paradigmatic biblical example of apologetics to a doubting disciple comes in John 20.19–29, where the risen Jesus appears to 'doubting Thomas.' When the other disciples proclaimed that the risen Jesus had appeared to them, Thomas refused to believe them until he saw the risen Christ with his own eyes. In verse 26, we read:

> A week later his disciples were in the house again, and Thomas was with them. Though the doors were locked, Jesus came and stood among them and said, 'Peace be with you.' Then he said to Thomas, 'Put your finger here; see my hands. Reach out your hand and put it into my side. Stop doubting and believe.' Then Thomas said to him, 'My Lord and my God!'

Thomas doubts the resurrection of Jesus; Jesus comes to him and provides evidence that He is indeed risen from the dead. Incidentally, note that Thomas' response to Jesus' apologetic appearance is the clearest, most explicit and emphatic declaration of Jesus' divinity in the New Testament. Thomas is not mocked or belittled as a perennial or despised doubter; rather, he is an example of one who doubts, but whose faith is reconfirmed and deepened by positive devotional apologetics. The goal of apologetics to doubting disciples is to resolve their doubts, that they would, like Thomas, 'stop doubting and believe.'

4. Apologetics for Besieged Believers (Defensive Devotional Apologetics)
Defensive devotional apologetics also responds to questions that Christians have, but with a different nuance. Here, Christians are drawn by external forces to question their faith and even to replace their Christianity with some other worldview. It seems to me that most contemporary deconstructors fall into this category. They hear skeptics insist that belief in Christianity is irrational. They hear cultural despisers accuse Christianity of suppressing science, promoting slavery, and oppressing women and minorities. They hear Hindu or Buddhist teachers proclaim the superi-

ority of Eastern meditation and thought and they wonder whether their Christianity is simply the product of western bias and prejudice.

Consider the experience of an 18-year-old Southern Baptist boy as he heads off for his first year of college. He sits down in his first philosophy class, only to hear the professor boldly declare that philosophy has roundly rejected the possibility of God's existence: traditional theistic proofs fail, there are no good reasons to believe that God is real, and plenty of good reasons to believe that God is *not* real. He then goes to his first biology class, only to hear the professor confidently declare that Darwin not only established the truthfulness of macro-evolution, but also demonstrated that life emerged and evolved strictly according to natural selection and random mutation. Darwin, declares the biology professor, demonstrated that God is not needed in the process, and thus is an unnecessary hypothesis. Our Southern Baptist boy then proceeds to his first religious studies class, only to hear the professor insist, in no uncertain terms, that the flow of human thought has 'progressed' from animism, through polytheism, to monotheism (including Christianity); from monotheism, human religious thought continued to evolve and progress, through deism to mechanical naturalism, to a contemporary pluralism that embraces the equality of all religious beliefs and encourages all humans to tolerate the beliefs of one another in perfect peace and harmony. L'il Joe Baptist finds his young and intellectually immature faith under attack at every corner, and is tempted to embrace either scientism, nihilism, or pluralism. He truly is a 'besieged believer.'

The difference between apologetics to doubting disciples and besieged believers is one of degree, not type. The primary difference between them is the source or origin of the questions they have, the precipitating cause of the need for apologetic ministry in their lives. Doubting disciples have questions or doubts that arise through their own reflection, reading, or observations. Besieged believers, on the other hand, have questions or doubts raised within them by the reflection, observations, or attacks of others. Hence, it can be helpful to identify the source of the questions and doubts that Christians are expressing. A simple preliminary response: "That's a really great question, or a thoughtful objection—I'm curious, where does that question come from?" can help direct your apologetic response.

Scripture provides examples of apologetics to besieged believers. I suggest that the entire book of Revelation is an apologetic treatise designed to reassure Christians of the truth of their faith in the midst of the intense persecution they are facing under Emperor Diocletian. First John contains apologetic affirmation for believers facing objections and attacks from proto-Gnostics. At the beginning of the letter, John writes:

> That which was from the beginning, which we have heard, which we have seen with our eyes, which we have looked at and our hands have touched—this we proclaim concerning the Word of life. The life appeared; we have seen it and testify to it, and we proclaim to you the eternal life, which was with the Father and has appeared to us. We proclaim to you what we have seen and heard, so that you also may have fellowship with us. And our fellowship is with the Father and with his Son, Jesus Christ. We write this to make our joy complete. (1 John 1.1–4)

John emphasizes that he (and the other apostles) truly *saw* and *touched* and *heard* what they proclaim about Jesus Christ. Though Gnostic opponents and others might question the physicality and corporeality of Jesus, particularly the risen Jesus, John assures them that Jesus was truly in the flesh. As fellow believers, apologists are called to share the burden borne by besieged believers. When they feel under attack on account of their faith, it is incumbent upon us to walk alongside them. Defensive devotional apologetics, geared toward besieged believers, completes our apologetics matrix (see opposite page).

IV. Conclusion

The apologetics matrix is a (hopefully) helpful little tool which illustrates the purpose and focus of apologetics. The *focus* (audience) of apologetics can be either devotional (aimed at those within the Church) or evangelistic (aimed at those outside the Church). The *purpose* (goal) of apologetics can be either offensive (giving reasons *to believe*) or defensive (giving reasons *to not disbelieve*). Defensive evangelistic apologetics provides outspoken opponents reasons to not disbelieve. Offensive evangelistic apologetics provides seeking skeptics reasons to begin believing. Offensive devotional apologetics provides doubting disciples reasons to continue believing. Defensive devotional apologetics provides besieged brethren reasons not to start disbelieving. The apologetics matrix can be utilized by practitioners of traditional apologetic schools and approaches. Rather than prescribing a particular method to apologetics, the apologetics matrix supplies a theoretical framework within which to understand and engage in the apologetic enterprise.

God commissions His children to always be prepared to give an answer to those who ask us the reason for the hope that is within us. Whether our conversation partner is an outspoken opponent, a seeking skeptic, a doubting disciple, or a besieged brother, I pray that we would always be prepared to respond to the questions and doubts that come our way. God has commanded it; His Word exemplifies it; our contemporary context demands it.

THE APOLOGETICS MATRIX

		Evangelistic (Non-Christian)	Devotional (Christian)
The Purpose of Apologetics	Offensive (Positive)	**Seeking Skeptics** *Reasons to Believe* Acts 25.13–26.32	**Doubting Disciples** *Reasons to Continue Believing* John 20.19–29
	Defensive (Negative)	**Outspoken Opponents** *Reasons to Not Disbelieve* Acts 4.4–12	**Besieged Believers** *Reasons to Not Start Disbelieving* 1 John 1.1–4

The Focus (Audience) of Apologetics

Bibliography

Boa, Kenneth D., and Robert M. Bowman, Jr. *Faith Has Its Reasons: An Integrative Approach to Defending Christianity*. 2nd edition. Waynesboro, GA: Paternoster, 2005.

Campbell-Jack, W. C., and Gavin McGrath, eds. *New Dictionary of Christian Apologetics*. Downers Grove: InterVarsity, 2006.

Cowan, Steven B., ed. *Five Views on Apologetics*. Grand Rapids, MI: Zondervan, 2000.

Groothuis, Douglas. *Christian Apologetics: A Comprehensive Case for Biblical Faith*. Downers Grove: IVP Academic, 2011.

Plato. *Five Dialogues: Euthyphro, Apology, Crito, Meno, Phaedo*, 2nd edition. Translated by G. M. A. Grube, Edited by John M. Cooper. Indianapolis: Hackett, 2002.

PART TWO

Natural Truth

God and General Revelation

6

Life in a Finely-Tuned Cosmos

Luke Barnes

I. Introductory Remarks

One of the great things about my job comes at our weekly astronomy meeting at Western Sydney University. We go through the news to find what's happened recently in astronomy. A pretty picture always stops the room. The beauty of our universe never gets old. When we look deep into the universe, the view is breath-taking. It's a wonderful thing.

Please: go online and find high-resolution pictures from the Hubble Space Telescope, or the James Webb Space Telescope. Find a picture of a supernova remnant: when stars get old and run out of fuel, they blow up. Find a picture of a star-forming region, where dust and gas are collapsing towards ignition. These pictures always stop the room.

My job is to try to understand what's going out there, which isn't always straightforward. But if you're into mathematics, it's an awful lot of fun. (There is no mathematics in this article.) What we see in the universe shows its forces, matter and energy playing out, crafting the astounding spectacle of the night sky.

II. How Physics Explains

As a physicist, there's a way we want to do things. There's a way we want to *explain*. Roughly speaking, it boils down to the following three things.

First of all, there are the laws of nature, things like gravity. Gravity has a certain mathematical form. We can use it to predict the way things will move when gravity has hold of them. We need an explanation in terms of the general way that the universe works, not particular laws but general laws.

Second, initial conditions. The laws aren't enough. For example, no matter how much mathematics you do, starting from the law of gravity you can't tell me where Mars will be in the night sky tomorrow. The extra information that you need is where everything is arranged and what it's doing *tonight*. Given that information, you can solve the equations and work out where Mars will be tomorrow. We call this extra information an *initial condition* (or a boundary condition). The laws of nature don't tell you how the universe is; they tell you how the universe changes.

Third, the fundamental constants. There's another ingredient, the one that's going to be of a lot of interest to us for most of this talk. If you remember any of your high school physics, you might remember Newton's Law of Gravity, which includes a number represented by a capital G. This is called Newton's gravitational constant. It's just a number, in a certain set of units. It has a certain value. We can measure it. The important thing is it's not a number that comes *out* of the equations as a prediction. It's a number that goes *into* the equations. We have to put it in there by hand. We don't have a deeper reason why it is what it is.

The fundamental constants are going to be rather important to us because starting about 40 or 50 years ago, thanks to these constants, scientists began accidentally asking the right question.

What do these constants actually do? Let me give an example. As best we know, you are made of three types of particles: electrons, the up quark, and the down quark. The "LEGO set" of the universe has three pieces in it. It's doing wonderful things with those three pieces.

Imagine a production line in a factory, beginning with a supply of the three types of particles. From these, what can you make?

The first step along the production line sees the up quark and the down quark make the proton and the neutron. The bits then can stick together, as the pieces do in a LEGO set. We can take another step along the production line: the protons and neutrons stick together in the nuclei of atoms, and the electrons go around the outside: there are atoms. There are plenty of different ways that protons and neutrons can be placed in a nucleus. The periodic table demonstrates this: each entry in the table is characterized by how many protons are in a given nucleus. For example, hydrogen has one proton, helium two. (I'm an astronomer, not a chemist, so that's where my knowledge of the periodic table ends.)

Stepping further down the line, if you put nuclei close to each other, so that their electron's orbits overlap, the electrons will follow a more complicated path around the whole thing. This is how nuclei bind together to make molecules. The water molecule, for example, is held together by the electrons going around the outside.

This production line is working beautifully, but it's barely got started. In DNA, molecules are chained together so that, when the electrons follow their path through the structure to hold it together, it can literally code information. You can write instructions. At this point, we're a long way outside of my expertise, but I'm told the thing that's coded for in DNA is a type of versatile molecule called a protein. If you put enough of those together, you can make a living cell. And if you put enough cells together, you can make people. Please consult your nearest biologist for more details.

Remember that we were talking about the fundamental constants. Why do they matter? Because they're all the way back at the start of the production line. Let's retrace our steps, but more briefly. We started with the simplest particles of the universe: electrons, up quarks, and down quarks. Then: protons and neutrons, nuclei, atoms, chemical molecules, long molecular chains that can store information, proteins, small biological things, big biological things, and people. All of that wonderful structure builds up from the bottom.

So, if we messed with the fundamental particles, all the way back at the start, what would happen? Let's give it a try. A basic property of these particles is their mass: how heavy are they? Their masses are extremely small in any human-sized units, but we know what the numbers are. However, we don't know why.

Starting in earnest about 50 years ago, as the details of this picture were falling into place, physicists started asking the right question, 'What if the constants of nature had been different? What would happen?' This is a perfectly normal thing for a physicist to do. In fact, any scientist should do this when they have a mathematical model with what are called *free parameters*, i.e. numbers that you have to put *into* your model. Scientists need to understand what would happen in their model—what would happen to its predictions—if we messed around with the model's assumptions. As I said: a perfectly expected thing to do.

III. The Fine-Tuning of the Universe for Life

Physicists did this with the fundamental constants of nature, and something weird happened. Let me give you a tour of what happens when you change three numbers: the masses of the electron, up quark, and down quark. You can find all the details and a series of diagrams in my book with Geraint Lewis, *A Fortunate Universe*;[1] here I'll just describe it in words.

If you choose three numbers, you can represent your choice by a point in a three-dimensional space. Think of an ordinary chunk of the world, like the inside of a big room. We can treat the room as menu of universes: choose a point in the room—anywhere you like, including mid-air—and that will select these three numbers: the mass of the electron, the mass of the up quark, and the mass of the down quark. Our own universe is somewhere in the middle. (The walls of the room represent the limits to which we can push our models—see *A Fortunate Universe* for more details.)

So, choose yourself a universe. Once you have, we go to the equations and ask, 'What would have happened in that universe? What would have happened if a universe were born with the same laws as ours, but with the new set of those numbers that you've chosen?'

Now, I'm going to help you out with your choice from the menu. I'll exclude parts of the room that you probably don't want to order from.

---

[1] Lewis and Barnes, *A Fortunate Universe: Life in a Finely Tuned Cosmos*, Chapter 7.

Why? Because of what would happen to the production line. For a big chunk of the room, while you still have up quarks, down quarks, and electrons, they won't make protons and neutrons. They will form into another type of particle, either the "Delta-plus-plus" or "Delta minus". The details don't matter; all you need to know is that the production line is over.

These particles will not attach to anything. They will not stick to themselves. They won't make structure. Consider LEGO again: imagine a LEGO set that had pieces that could attach to exactly one other piece. What could you make? Almost nothing. A pile, maybe. All of the complexity of the later stages of the production line evaporates. The story of the universe's complexity ends too early.

Once we exclude these kinds of universes—where there will be no more than one element in the periodic table, where nothing can stick to anything else at all, or where the contents of the universe aren't able to generate stable energy—we leave an extraordinarily small slice of parameter space, a sliver of the menu. Hit that this target, and interesting things might happen. But miss, and you'll get a really boring universe.

This was not what was expected. If our universe is nothing special, then some other combination of constants would surely just result in some heavier nuclei, or some different chemicals, or life based on other proteins. But what physicists instead found was that unless the constants are in a very small region, nothing complex happens at all.

These calculations were done in professional physics journals. This was not the work of apologists or philosophers, or anyone else trying to stir up trouble. Physicists discovered this *fine-tuning of the universe for life*.

IV. The Cosmological Constant and How Galaxies Form

Here's another example, one that relates to my research. I study how galaxies form. Thanks to the cosmic microwave background, we have an idea about how smooth the universe was initially. And the answer is: quite smooth, but not completely smooth. A lump of matter in the universe, thanks to the attractive pull of gravity, can draw in more matter, and grow.

The idea is simple, but the details are messy. In practice, we teach a computer to solve this problem for us. Break the universe up into pieces (mathematically!). Program into the supercomputer the laws of the little pieces. Follow all of those little pieces, and see what happens. This is called a simulation.

The Eagle Project at Durham University, for example, has simulated the universe in remarkable detail. On a typical laptop, their simulations would take 500 years to complete. So, they use a supercomputer instead: a network of linked computers.

What we see is a universe that starts simple—almost smooth—and develops structure as it expands. Gravity is the hero of the story: any part of the universe that is more dense than average will pull on its surroundings. It will collect matter around it, and become even more massive.

But gravity isn't the only thing. We also see gas being pushed out of galaxies as well, thanks (mostly) to the combined effect of supernovae. This creates a cosmic ecosystem: galaxies form by collapsing. Inside galaxies, stars form. Stars, as they explode, push gas into interstellar space, and sometimes push the gas right out of the galaxy. Some of this gas is pulled back in by gravity. And around it goes.

The large-scale structure of the universe is called the cosmic web. There are very dense bits of the universe, where galaxies and clusters of galaxies form. There are almost empty bits of the universe called cosmic voids, which lost their matter to the lumpy bit nearest to them. And some matter is in filaments, which haven't quite decided which way they want to fall yet. That's a rough summary of how we think galaxies form in our universe.

My colleagues and I wanted to change the numbers. Working with the team who produced the Eagle Simulation, we took the same computer code and ran it with one of the numbers changed: appropriately, it is called the cosmological constant. I don't need to go too much into details here. It's a number that accounts for the fact that the expansion of our universe is accelerating.

We've known since the 1920s that if you look at a galaxy out there in the night sky, it's moving away from us. We've known since 1998 that not only is that galaxy out there moving away from us; it's moving *faster* today than it was yesterday. It's accelerating away from us. To account for this, there's a number in our models. Cosmologists thought, for the longest time, that it was zero. But we've now managed, thanks to these discoveries, to measure that number. And it's not zero. But what if it had been different?

We ran a bunch of simulations to work this out. You can find a video of the simulations at www.youtube.com/watch?v=2Fp_VK-xuKE, but I'll describe it here. The first panel shows (roughly) our universe. It will do all that wonderful stuff I explained above. It's going to make structure on a range of scales, from stars to galaxies and beyond.

The second panel shows what would happen if we made the cosmological constant ten times larger than it is in our universe. That might sound like a large change, but compared to what could have been, it's a very, very small change. In this simulated universe, the early stages look roughly the same as in our universe. However, thanks to the cosmological constant, everything starts accelerating away from everything else. Gravity isn't as effective at pulling matter together to make galaxies and stars and planets.

The third panel shows what would happen if we made that cosmological constant a hundred times larger than it is in our universe. Now, we see a universe where maybe a few stars could have formed, just before everything in the universe was blown away from everything else. This is a picture of the way things can go wrong in the universe. Not much happens at all.

I stress again: a factor of a hundred *relative to our universe* is a very small change relative to the total range that this number could have in our equations: one part in 10^{90}. In other words, if you want a universe which does anything interesting at all, the chance of hitting the target at random is one in a number with about 90 digits in it. This is the fine-tuning of the universe for life. Of all the possible values of the fundamental constants of nature, the subset that permits the existence of life is very small.

V. The Implications of a Fine-tuned Universe

Here's my favourite summary of fine-tuning (though I can't find the source, unfortunately):

"I'm not religious, but something weird is going on here."

Some of the physicists who worked all this out, who first glimpsed the fine-tuning of the universe for life, were honest enough to blurt out what they thought that meant. In 1971, an article by physicist Freeman Dyson contains the following words,

> As we look out into the universe and identify the many accidents of physics and astronomy that have worked together to our benefit, it almost seems as if the universe must in some sense have known that we were coming.[2]

The astrophysicist Fred Hoyle wrote in 1981,

> A common sense interpretation of the facts suggests that a superintellect has monkeyed with physics, as well as with chemistry and biology, and that there are no blind forces worth speaking about in nature. The numbers one calculates from the facts seem to me so over-whelming as to put this conclusion almost beyond question.[3]

We know what fine-tuning looks like. It looks like foresight.

If you want more details about the physics of fine-tuning, see the book that I co-authored with Prof. Geraint Lewis, an astrophysicist colleague at the University of Sydney.[4] Geraint is an atheist. We wrote the first seven chapters of the book together. And apart from one footnote, we agreed on all of the science. Fine-tuning is all there in the physics literature. We just read the papers, checked some calculations, and explained it to the layperson.

What was disagreed about came in chapter eight, which takes the form of a dialogue. But note well: the fine-tuning of the universe for life is a topic on which an atheist and a Christian can sit down together, write a book, and agree on almost all the science.

---

[2] Dyson, "Energy in the universe," *Scientific American vol. 225*, 51.
[3] Hoyle, "The Universe: Past and Present Reflections," *Annual Review of Astronomy and Astrophysics vol. 20.1*, 1–36.
[4] Lewis and Barnes, 2016. See also, Barnes, "A Reasonable Little Question: A Formulation of the Fine-Tuning Argument," *Ergo vol 6*, 42.

Let me give my interpretation of what all this means. Richard Dawkins, atheist and evolutionary biologist, wrote on the opening page of *The Blind Watchmaker*, "Biology is the study of complicated things that give the appearance of having been designed for a purpose. Physics is the study of simple things that do not tempt us to invoke design."[5]

Dawkins *defines* biology as the study of things that looked designed. But, says Dawkins, don't worry. Thanks to biological evolution, the processes that shape biology are all blind and mindless. It's just physics down there. And physics, Dawkins assures us, will not tempt us to invoke design.

But Dawkins is not a physicist; he's a biologist. Is he sure? Shouldn't he check very carefully, to make sure that he's right? Does physics tempt us to invoke design? How can we answer this crucial question?

In his book, in the same chapter, Dawkins gives us a method.

> It is true that there are quite a number of ways of making a living - flying, swimming, swinging through the trees, and so on. But, however many ways there may be of being alive, it is certain that there are vastly more ways of being dead, or rather not alive. You may throw cells together at random, over and over again for a billion years, and not once will you get a conglomeration that flies or swims or burrows or runs, or does anything, even badly, that could remotely be construed as working to keep itself alive.[6]

Why does the hummingbird appear to be designed? In a slightly macabre thought experiment, Dawkins imagines a process in which the cells of a disassembled hummingbird are thrown together at random. You wouldn't get something that flies, even if you had billions of years of attempts. That's a way to show that something is designed.

Here's Dawkins' method. The question from biology is, 'Why do we think that biological things look designed?' One answer—certainly not the only one, but the answer that Dawkins himself has offered—is to ask the question, 'What happens if you throw the pieces together at random?' There is something to explain about the hummingbird because randomly arranged cells don't fly.

---

[5] Dawkins, *The Blind Watchmaker*. 1.
[6] Ibid, 11–12.

We can apply that method more broadly. Dawkins has invited us to look at physics. How will we know whether physics tempts us to invoke design? We can use the same criteria: 'What happens if you throw a universe together at random?'

How can we answer that question? We can't do the experiment, sure, but we didn't actually liquify a hummingbird, either. Do I just imagine all the bits of a universe being thrown together? But the bits obey laws. How do I throw some laws together at random?

Here is a reasonable approach. We don't just imagine universes. We use the best physical theories that we have available today. Within the deepest laws of nature that we know, there are the fundamental constants. They are just numbers. So, we can vary them and work out what would happen. I can work out what would happen because I can do my job as a theoretical physicist.

Indeed, let's be kind to the atheist. Let's grant the laws of our universe, which we already know are capable of producing life. All that the godless universe has to do is hit on the right set of constants. To address the question "What happens if you throw a universe together at random?", we do what physicists do: we create a model. We ask, 'What would happen in a universe with our laws, but with constants chosen at random?'

The answer that comes back from the fine-tuning of the universe for life is overwhelming: the universe doesn't fly. It won't stick anything to anything. It won't make any structure. It won't make the most basic building blocks of our universe, let alone the astonishing complexity we see around us. So, according to Dawkins' method, physics tempts us to invoke design in exactly the same way that biology does. The design goes all the way to the bottom.

VI. The Multiverse

Let me anticipate one objection: the multiverse. This year marked my first visit to New Orleans. I walked around with songs about New Orleans in my head: "Way Down Yonder in New Orleans"; "Do You know what it means to Miss New Orleans?"; "Basin Street Blues," and so on.

If you ever visit my home state in Australia, you're probably not going to walk around with songs in your head about New South Wales, because there aren't that many. There is, however, at least one. It's from a band called *The Whitlams*, whose song "Up Against the Wall" goes like this:

"Some say love it only comes once in a lifetime,

Well once is enough for me.

She was one in a million,

So there's five more just in New South Wales."

(Bonus mathematical problem: work out the population of New South Wales in 1997.) That's the central idea of the multiverse. Even a one in a million girl is out there, as long as your home state is large enough.

Here's another example, to highlight exactly what's needed. Why is there a winner of the lottery on the front page of the newspaper? Well, because lots of people buy different tickets, and because a lottery loser isn't news. We need all of those parts. You need lots of players, because if only three people buy tickets, the most likely outcome is that no one wins. You need them to buy different tickets, because if a million people buy the same ticket (with the same numbers), then that doesn't improve the odds of a winner at all. And we need the winner to be more likely to be observed, otherwise the lottery player most likely to appear on the newspaper is a lottery loser.

Applied to the fine-tuning of the universe for life, the multiverse has the following requirements. First, lots of other universes. Otherwise, if you have only three other universes and you choose their properties at random, you'll probably end up with three dead universes. Second, they have to be different. There's no point just making copies of the one (probably) dead universe. Third, we need fine-tuned universes to be more likely to be observed, which is why it is relevant that life-forms are observers.

How should we respond? Here's one way. Remember the logic of our argument. The world is amazing. We look at hummingbirds, and we instinctively think that the world seems to be well-put-together. This is one of the oldest arguments for the existence of God, probably at least as early as Socrates. As even Dawkins admits, the living world looks designed.

But wait! There is more to nature. The hummingbird doesn't just exist on its own. Zooming out, it exists as part of an ecosystem. Does that mean it's not designed? No! The ecosystem looks designed as well. But, zooming out even more, what if our universe is a kind of factory that makes hummingbirds? Well, a hummingbird factory sounds even more amazing than a hummingbird, even if it takes a billion years.

Dawkins hoped that when we got to the bottom of the hummingbird factory, to the physics of our universe, we'd find something that looked boring and unexceptional and typical. He hoped that it wouldn't tempt us to invoke design. And that failed spectacularly. Instead, we got the fine-tuning of the universe for life, and the whole show looks more designed than ever.

The multiverse is trying to add another factory. Its proposing a hummingbird factory factory. (Read that slowly.) But someone proposes this new level below physics, we don't just ask whether it exists. We also have to ask: what happens if you throw a multiverse together at random?

Remember, this was Dawkins' point. It's not enough that physics *exists*; it mustn't tempt us to invoke design. The appearance of design kept following us because we kept asking the right question. The question isn't simply "can this level be explained by a lower level?" The question is, "can this level be explained by a lower level *that doesn't look designed*?" Keep your eye on the right question. So, again: what happens if you throw a multiverse together at random?

Here's the problem: we don't have the slightest clue what the answer to that question is. We don't have a standard theory of the multiverse. We don't know what its constants are. We can't use the strategy to check out all the alternatives. You might as well appeal to the Spider-Man multiverse. And so, the multiverse is the equivalent of taking your bat and ball and going home. (You're thinking of baseball, I'm thinking of cricket: it works either way.) It avoids losing by appealing to rules of a game that we don't have and can't play.

Here's the situation with the multiverse. The biological realm looks designed. When we ask the right question down at the level of physics, it looks designed as well. The multiverse advocate hopes that when we can get a chance to look even lower, it won't look designed. But we have no clue about that. It might look just as designed as the one above it. The multiverse wants a rematch where it won't tell us the rules.

VII. How Fine-Tuning Vindicates the Design Intuition

How do you defend the fine-tuning argument? You might think that you've got to memorize a bunch of really technical stuff about physics that you don't understand, so that you can regurgitate it to someone who won't have a clue what you're talking about.

I want to suggest it's precisely the opposite. The fine-tuning argument is powerful and useful because you are going *with* the weight of the scientific evidence, not *against* it. At no point do you need to argue that a scientific theory is wrong. It is no part of this argument to point out a tension between a scientific theory and empirical data. That's not what this is. A book written by a Christian and an atheist agrees on all the relevant science. You can simply appeal to the science as it stands in the scientific literature. (I would love for you to learn the science, of course, but to each their own.)

What we're *not* doing is trying to make an apologetic case by first knocking down a scientific theory. We are not arguing about what follows from the *failure* of a scientific theory. We are asking what follows from the *success* of the deepest theories we know about the way the universe works. We are not arguing that science is wrong about something. In particular, we're not arguing that a certain set of natural causes are incapable of producing some natural effect.

The fine-tuning argument agrees with (indeed, it rejoices in) the fact that the natural world we see around us can do wonderful things. We add the crucial detail: it does these things because there is design all the way down.

The important thing about fine-tuning is this: by seeing design at the deepest level, it vindicates our instinct for design all the way back up to biology. It vindicates design at *every* scale.

You may have felt, as I did at one point in my life, that if you start to say, 'the hummingbird looks designed', the next thing you have to do is prove biological evolution wrong. You don't. Evolution can only happen in a universe that is designed. That deserves to be said again: *evolution can only happen in a universe that is designed.* Whether biological evolution actually happened is a separate issue, but it could *only* happen in a universe that is designed. You have to get the physics right before you get any biology at all, and it takes design to get the physics right.

When you see design in the hummingbird, the question of whether it evolved or not is irrelevant. If it didn't, then it's designed. If it did, then it's designed, because the design goes all the way to the bottom, to the deepest laws of nature that we know about.

The fine-tuning argument, far from sinking us into technical details of modern physics, returns us to our first impression of nature, to our amazement at how well this whole thing is put together. It justifies that feeling you get when you see a sunset, or a hummingbird, or an ecosystem, or Saturn's rings. (Go read a book about the way your body is put together. It is astounding.) If you see design at any level, *you're right*. If you experience God in nature, the full weight of science is behind you, down to the deepest physics. That is what the fine-tuning argument is telling us.

Go look at the stars.

Bibliography

Barnes, Luke A. (2019). "A Reasonable Little Question: A Formulation of the Fine-Tuning Argument." In *Ergo*, 6 (2019).

Dawkins, Richard. *The Blind Watchmaker*. London, Penguin Books, 1996.

Dyson, F. J. "Energy in the universe." In *Scientific American, 225* (1971).

Hoyle, Fred. "The Universe: Past and Present Reflections." In *Annual Review of Astronomy and Astrophysics, 20.1* (1981).

Lewis, Geraint, and Luke A. Barnes, *A Fortunate Universe: Life in a Finely Tuned Cosmos*. Cambridge: Cambridge University Press, 2016.

7

Contemplating the Heavens
How the Beauty and Harmony of Creation Gave Rise to Modern Science

Melissa Cain Travis

Then God said, "Let there be lights in the expanse of the sky to separate the day from the night. They will serve as signs for festivals and for days and years. They will be lights in the expanse of the sky to provide light on the earth." And it was so. God made the two great lights—the greater light to have dominion over the day and the lesser light to have dominion over the night—as well as the stars. God placed them in the expanse of the sky to provide light on the earth, to dominate the day and the night, and to separate light from darkness. And God saw that it was good.

Perhaps you have been fortunate enough to visit one of the International Dark Sky Places, nature preserves protected from light pollution so that celestial objects appear their brightest to terrestrial observers. If the weather was favorable, I imagine it was a profound experience of the sublime. Consider the fact that even ancient humans, who lived long before the rise of modern science, before anyone knew anything about the material qualities of the brilliant lights in the night sky, also beheld their majestic beauty. It is no wonder that human curiosity about the heavens has inspired observation, astronomical record-keeping, and spiritual contemplation since the earliest civilizations.

Ancient Mesopotamia was established sometime between 4000 and 3500 BC in the region often referred to as the fertile crescent (modern day Iraq, Syria, Turkey, Israel, Lebanon, Palestine, and a small portion of Egypt). By the early third millennium, BC, these ancient people began constructing enormous ziggurats, which are believed to have been predominantly used for religious ceremonial purposes. These breathtaking structures were built for many centuries, and the latest of them were probably completed under the reign of King Nebuchadnezzar (~600 BC).[1] To be sure, the religious beliefs of these ancient pagans were connected to natural phenomena, such as the movements of the stars and visible planets, so it is not surprising that some of these structures stand in places where ancient scribes invented the mathematical art of astronomy. Surviving cuneiform star catalogs and records of astronomical calculations, the earliest of which date back to the 16th century BC, tell us that these scribes were intellectually sophisticated, especially for their technologically primitive era. It's amazing to consider the fact that, without telescopes or computers, they were able to predict the positions of the known planets hundreds of years into the future. The quantitative methods they developed for their studies gave rise to early Egyptian, Indian, and Greek mathematical astronomy. All of this strongly suggests that in addition to their ceremonial use, these ziggurats served as the earliest proto-scientific observatories. Perhaps the most well-known is the Great Ziggurat of Ur, construction of which began in 2100 BC. The city of Ur is in modern day Iraq, about 100 miles northwest of the Persian Gulf. It was the birthplace of Abraham about 150 years later, so it is fascinating to consider the fact that this architectural marvel would have been a very familiar site to him.

There are various surviving artifacts that offer intriguing clues to the earliest astronomy, such as the beautiful Nebra Sky Disk, discovered in Mittelberg, Germany. Dating to about 1600 BC, the 12-inch disk is made of bronze and is the earliest known realistic representation of the night sky. This is why it is considered one of the most important archaeological finds of the 20th century. The disk depicts a full moon (or possibly the sun), a crescent moon, horizons on opposite edges (one has fallen off), and at the bottom is a boat, which is a symbolic reference to ancient mythology. A seven-star grouping near the top represents the Pleiades, a star

---

[1] Recall that in the second chapter of Daniel, King Nebuchadnezzar summons the court magicians and astrologers to interpret a troubling dream.

cluster that is mentioned a few times in Scripture (Amos 5.8, Job 9.9, and Job 38.31, for example).

Many artifacts reveal the ancient Egyptians' impressive breadth of astronomical knowledge. Consider the ceiling of the tomb of Senenmut, a high official and architect who served in the court of Egypt's most successful female pharaoh, Hatshepsut. This ceiling mural, if you will, was created sometime between 1479 and 1458 BC. The figures represent constellations or protective gods; the columns of text in the upper section list planets and star configurations known as the decans. The twelve circles in the lower part, each labeled with the Egyptian names for the months of the year, are divided into twenty-four segments that represent the hours of the day and night. By scholarly estimates, this inscription would have been created during the lifetime of Moses, while he was living as a shepherd in the land of Midian. As a male member of the Pharaoh's family, his education would have been world class; it would have included disciplines such as mathematics, geometry, and astronomy. Remember this the next time you hear someone make that popular allegation that the Pentateuch is just a bunch of legends made up by uneducated nomads!

The British Museum houses many artifacts related to astronomy, including a celestial planisphere discovered in Nineveh, in the library of the Assyrian king, Ashurbanipal, who reigned from 668 to 627 BC. This circular clay tablet is fourteen centimeters in diameter and is divided into eight sections, each containing cuneiform inscriptions. The principal constellations are positioned in eight sectors, with the constellation Gemini near the top. Thanks to sophisticated astronomical calculation software, we know that the planisphere represents the night sky over Nineveh on either the third or fourth of January, 650 BC. Fun fact: this would have been during the prophetic ministry of Nahum, who foretold the fall of that very city! (Remember that Nineveh indeed fell, just a few decades later.)

Various other clay cuneiform tablets, also housed in the British Museum, provide valuable data about the history of astronomy. One particular tablet, created in Babylonia sometime between 350 and 50 BC, was deciphered in late 2015. It turned out to be an astronomical procedure text for tracking the path of Jupiter over a period of sixty days, starting with its first appearance in the night sky right before dawn. It exhibits a rudimentary form of integral calculus, which involves mathematical concepts that were (prior to the deciphering of this tablet) believed to have arisen in Europe many centuries later.

Wisdom of the Ancients

Now that we've seen a sampling of evidence from the world's earliest civilizations that demonstrates humankind's perennial fascination with the night sky, we'll move to the region surrounding the Aegean Sea (the birthplace of Homer's famous epics) to see how natural philosophy (i.e., the study of nature) developed within the Western tradition. What we shall see is that the idea of beauty—both visual and intellectual—facilitated discovery and played a major role in the rise of modern science. We'll begin with Pythagoras of Samos (c. 570–490 BC), the best-known of the pre-Socratics (philosophers who predated Socrates). It is believed (but not completely certain) that Pythagoras himself coined the term *philosophy* (meaning, the love of wisdom). He was an oral teacher who left behind no writings, but his enthusiastic disciples, the so-called Pythagoreans, went on to establish schools of philosophy in various locales. Surviving histories that scholars deem largely reliable indicate that the Pythagorean schools, led by a diverse assortment of philosophers, developed in unique ways. Consequently, it is notoriously difficult to determine which doctrines go back to Pythagoras himself and which were later accretions. The one that is most likely to be an original teaching is the idea that number is the essence of the sensible realm. In other words, the rational order of nature, to which number can be applied, and the human ability to discern this order, are indicative of reality's fundamentally mathematical structure. The Pythagoreans were fascinated with the concept of *harmonia*—different parts fitting together in symmetry and beauty—and believed that the world itself is an orderly, harmonious *kosmos*. When they discovered that harmonic musical tones can be expressed in exact numerical ratios of whole numbers, they concluded that beauty and rationality are deeply intertwined such that our aesthetic sensibilities play a role in the pursuit of truth. The Pythagoreans are believed to be the originators of the "music of the spheres" concept—the belief that a musical harmony generated by the movements of the invisible spheres that carry the heavenly bodies in their cycles pervades the cosmos. Humans cannot discern it because their ears have never experienced its absence.

Plato (c. 429–347 BC) was largely responsible for the endurance of Pythagorean ideas in the Western tradition. His dialogue *Timaeus*, which was the only Platonic work available to the early medievals and thus very influential, features a Pythagorean character named Timaeus who describes the creation of the world. He says that a Divine Craftsman formed the sensible realm based upon an eternal, mathematical, and harmonious model. As human beings, we are part of this created order, thus our senses and intellect reflect these same properties. This enables us to perceive the exquisite beauty and rationality of the heavens. According to Timaeus, the fundamental elements have unique geometries, each taking the form of one of the five Platonic solids (convex polyhedra with all congruent faces and the same number of faces meeting at the vertices). Plato's philosophical influence is incalculable; the adage is well deserved: all of Western philosophy ever since has been a series of footnotes to Plato.[2]

Plato's most famous pupil, Aristotle (385–323 BC), should be mentioned at this juncture, not merely because of his influence on Western Christian thought, but also because he was responsible for elaborating a geocentric cosmology that dominated astronomy up until the scientific revolution. In the Aristotelian model, the earth rested at the center and the moon, sun, and five known planets revolved around it in perfectly circular orbits against the backdrop of the fixed stars (the outermost cosmic sphere). The cosmos was divided into two main regions: the sublunar and the supralunar. From the orbit of the moon inward was the realm of mutability and decay, where the heavy elements—earth and water (water being somewhat lighter)—sank. Air, being lighter, hovered in the region

---

[2] This is a paraphrase of Alfred North Whitehead's famous remark that "the safest general characterization of the European philosophical tradition is that it consists in a series of footnotes to Plato." Alfred North Whitehead, *Process and Reality: An Essay in Cosmology* (New York: Free Press, 1985), 39.

above water's natural resting place. Fire, the lightest of all, had an upward tendency and encircled the rest. The supralunar region was the perfect, aether-filled realm of the divine celestial bodies with their eternal circular motion.[3] In addition to geocentrism, the philosophical idea that circular motion signified perfection went on to play a major role in later cosmological discourse, as shall be seen.

Our geographical focus will now shift southward to ancient Alexandria, a city on the Mediterranean coast of Egypt that served as a major intellectual center of the ancient world. Popularly known for its mythic library, we know for sure that the city included important Greek, Roman, Egyptian, and Jewish scholarly communities. As a side note, Christian tradition tells us that sometime in the mid-first century, the apostle Mark established the first Christian church in Alexandria, and several prominent church fathers were from there, notably Clement, Origen, and Athanasius. There was a populous Jewish colony, and it was within this cultural context that the Old Testament was translated from Hebrew to Greek (the Septuagint). A key Jewish intellectual leader, Philo of Alexandria (c. 20 BC–50 AD), who is hailed as the most important literary phenomenon of the Hellenistic world, is relevant to the present discussion. Although he was a devout Jew, he was also an adherent of Middle Platonism, a school of philosophy steeped in the Pythagorean-Platonic philosophical tradition. Part of his life's work was integrating the compatible treasures of that tradition with his monotheistic faith. For example, he identified the Greek concept of the *Logos* with the divine rationality that is (in a finite respect) made manifest in creation, including the mind of man. This is why humans can discern the order and harmony of nature and from it infer a transcendent mind. Notice how this idea hearkens back to Pythagoras and Plato yet also fits perfectly with the Genesis creation narrative. Philo believed that through mathematical arts such as astronomy, one "is allowed to see that which is second best [to seeing God himself], namely, the heaven which is perceptible by the external senses, and the harmonious arrangement of

---

[3] Aether was the postulated quintessence of the celestial realm and considered the fifth element.

the stars therein, and their truly musical and well-regulated motion."[4] Through the creation the creator is perceived.

The following century, Aristotelian cosmology was geometrically formalized by Claudius Ptolemy of Alexandria (born c. 100). Ptolemy retained the idealized circular motions of the celestial bodies, but to better account for observed phenomena (such as retrograde motion of the visible planets), he added smaller circular paths called epicycles. This Aristotelian-Ptolemaic cosmology, as it came to be called, was published in Ptolemy's treatise, *The Almagest*, around 150. It was the reigning model of the universe for about fifteen centuries thereafter. The church readily embraced it, in part because it supported their literalistic reading of various passages of Scripture. They understood certain verses (such as Joshua 10.12–13, Habakkuk 3.11, Ecclesiastes 1.5, 1 Chronicles 16.30, Psalms 93.1, and Psalms 96.10) as suggesting either a stationary earth or moving sun. Thus, the Aristotelian-Ptolemaic view became entrenched in both academic and ecclesial circles (between which there was major overlap anyway).

Intellectual Aesthetics and the Scientific Revolution

Nicolaus Copernicus is known for launching the scientific revolution, but contrary to popular belief, did not *discover* heliocentrism. Rather, his famous treatise (published when he was on his deathbed), *On the Revolutions of the Heavenly Spheres*, merely presented a sun-centric mathematical model of the known universe. There was no new empirical data that had weakened the case for the Aristotelian-Ptolemaic cosmology, and the Copernican model was ultimately not conceptually simpler. For one thing, it retained many Ptolemaic epicycles to account for observable phenomena (contrary to the historical myth that is still perpetuated by science writers and celebrities such as Neil de Grasse Tyson), and for another, its geometric maneuverings were otherwise similarly (if not more) complex.[5] What motivated Copernicus was a deep-seated aesthetic sensibility about the harmony and elegance of a heliocentric model, and the theological belief

---

[4] Philo of Alexandria, *On Mating with the Preliminary Studies*, X.51.
[5] Owen Gingerich has elucidated this fact in multiple places, including his outstanding book, *The Eye of Heaven: Ptolemy, Copernicus, Kepler*, 198–199.

that beauty and harmony, grounded in the nature of God, are indicative of truth about his creation. In the Copernican model, the orbits of the known planets were geometrically harmonized such that changing the diameter of one proportionally changed the diameter of all the rest. Regarding this mathematical fine-tuning, Copernicus remarked, "This correlation binds together so closely the order and magnitudes of all the planets and of their spheres or orbital circles and the heavens themselves that nothing can be shifted around in any part of them without disrupting the remaining parts and the universe as a whole."[6] About the Creator's beautiful arrangement of this "temple" (i.e., the universe), he writes:

> In the center of all rests the sun. For who would place this lamp of a very beautiful temple in another or better place than this where from it can illuminate everything at the same time? As a matter of fact, not unhappily do some call it the lantern; others, the mind; and still others, the pilot of the world… And so the sun, as if resting on a kingly throne, governs the family of stars which wheel around.[7]

Renowned astronomer and historian of astronomy Owen Gingerich calls the Copernican system a "striking unification" that was, despite its geometrical complexity, a "profound simplification" conceptually.[8] Copernicus was undoubtedly enamored with the harmony and elegance of heliocentrism; intellectual beauty was lighting the path of discovery.

Copernican cosmology held a powerful attraction for the young Johannes Kepler (1571–1630) beginning in his university years.[9] As a mathematical prodigy obsessed with astronomy, he appreciated the elegance of the heliocentric model's geometry and shared Copernicus' belief that beauty and harmony are indicative of God's rational plan for creation. While heliocentrism was not officially taught at his university in Tübingen, his favorite professor was a Copernican who gave private seminars on the topic. A devout Lutheran, Kepler's original objective was a career

---
[6] Copernicus, *On the Revolutions of the Heavenly Spheres*, 6.
[7] Ibid., 24-25.
[8] Gingerich, 199.
[9] For an in-depth treatment of Kepler's natural theology and extensive biographical details, see Melissa Cain Travis, *Thinking God's Thoughts: Johannes Kepler and the Miracle of Cosmic Comprehensibility* (Moscow, ID: Roman Roads Press, 2022).

as a theologian; his path changed when he was recommended to fill a mathematics teaching post at an elite upper school that catered to sons of aristocrats.[10] One day, while giving a lecture, it dawned on Kepler that the [known] planets were five in number, which is the same number of polyhedra in the set known as the Platonic solids.[11] Struck with inspiration, he came up with a thoroughly Pythagorean-Platonic model in which each circular planetary orbit (represented by nested concentric spheres) was separated from the next by the geometric dimensions of a Platonic solid.[12] This explained (in Kepler's estimation) the divine reason for the number of planets and the distances between their orbits. The intellectual beauty, the unifying harmony of the arrangement beguiled him, and this was related to his conviction that God desires us to see his power and ingenuity in the creation (Romans 1.20) and thus specially designed us with the cognitive capacity to perceive the mathematical structure of the universe. To quote his most famous and frequently paraphrased words, which appear in a letter he wrote to one of his patrons: "there are, in the whole material world, material laws, figures and relations of special excellency and of the most appropriate order…Those laws are within the grasp of the human mind; God wanted us to recognize them by creating us after his own image so that we could share in his own thoughts."[13]

Today, Kepler is most widely remembered for his three laws of planetary motion, and even the basic idea of each one heightens appreciation for his mathematical prowess (remember, all of this was done without an electronic calculator!). The first law says that the orbits of planets are elliptical with the sun off-center (at one focus), rather than a perfect circle as Aristotle, Ptolemy, and Copernicus had believed. The second is that even though planets move faster when they're in the part of their orbit that brings them closer to the sun, no matter where they are in their elliptical

---

[10] Kepler was decidedly Protestant and studied at Lutheran institutions, but he struggled with certain tenets of the Formula of Concord.

[11] These five polyhedra are convex, have congruent faces, and the same number of faces meet at each vertex. They include the cube, tetrahedron, octahedron, icosahedron, and dodecahedron.

[12] For a helpful illustration that Kepler sketched himself, see https://commons.wikimedia.org/wiki/File:Kepler-solar-system-1.png.

[13] Kepler, Letter to Herwart von Hohenburg dated April 10th, 1599.

path, they will "sweep out" the same size area of the ellipse given the same amount of travel time.[14] These first two laws were published in his 1608 treatise, *The New Astronomy*. The third law is significantly more complex and was the one that sent Kepler into intellectual ecstasy: the Harmonic Law, published in his 1618 magnum opus, *Harmony of the World*. Stated simply, it says that the square of the orbital period of any planet (the time it takes that planet to revolve around the sun one time) is proportional to the cube of its semi-major axis (its mean distance from the sun). Remarkably, when the earth's orbital period and semi-major axis are used as the standard units (1 year and 1 Astronomical Unit [AU], respectively), then the equation yields a one to one ratio for every planet in the solar system. Consider, for example, Jupiter:

Orbital Period (T) = 11.86 years

Semi-major Axis (a) = 5.2 AU

T^2 = 140.66

a^3 = 140.61

$T^2 = a^3$

Kepler delighted in this mathematical harmony of the planets, this *true* music of the spheres:

> I have brought [the Harmonic Law] into the light, and have most truly grasped beyond what I could have ever hoped: that the whole nature of harmony, in its full extent, with all its parts…is to be discovered among the celestial motions. It is to be discovered indeed not in the way which I had mentally conceived (and this is not the least part of my joy), but in a totally different way, and also at the same time a quite outstanding and perfect way.[15]

As hard as he had worked to make his beautiful polyhedral model fit the observational data (even attempting to modify it with the ratios of Pythagorean harmonic theory), he was overjoyed by the discovery that his

---

[14] A good analogy here is when the intersection of the cuts made in a pie is off-center; it is possible for a wider but shorter slice to have the same amount of pie as a narrower but longer slice. See the diagram provided by Encyclopedia Britannica: https://cdn.britannica.com/42/196742-050-C74B43FA/law-Kepler-motion-radius-vector-planet-lengths.jpg.

[15] Kepler, *Harmony of the World* (1618), Book V.

first model had been incorrect. It is one of the remarkable facts of scientific history that Kepler's circuitous pursuit of intellectual beauty brought him to the truth sooner than any other method could have at that time, all things considered.[16]

Several decades after Kepler's discoveries, Sir Isaac Newton published his *Principia Mathematica*, which presented his universal theory of gravitation. Technically, it contained all three of Kepler's laws of planetary motion (without crediting Kepler, mind you) and demonstrated that the laws governing terrestrial and planetary motion were the same. In the General Scholium of the third edition of the *Principia*, he remarked: "This most beautiful System of the Sun, Planets, and Comets, could only proceed from the counsel and dominion of an intelligent and powerful being."[17] Like Kepler, Newton saw the intellectual beauty of the cosmos as a signal of a transcendent mind.[18] At that time, natural philosophers freely integrated their theological convictions with their investigations of the natural world. Had anyone told them this was bad scholarly practice, they would have thought that absurd. After all, if there is one divine source of all things, then of course truths about the world are interrelated.

Mathematical Beauty Continues to Guide

Over the past hundred years or so, we have learned much more about the mathematics of the universe, but not just at the macro scale. The development of particle physics, the field concerned with the dynamics of subatomic particles, has been a revolution of its own. It has revealed astonishing facts about the deep structure of nature and is another field in which intellectual beauty has served as a signpost to scientific truth. Consider the following example. In the 1960s, physicist Peter Higgs and several of his colleagues were working on the problem of how subatomic

---

[16] See Ferguson, *Pythagoras: His Lives and the Legacy of a Rational Universe*, 275. Some would use the word "mystical," but this is misleading; Kepler was pursuing mathematical harmony for theological reasons, as explained earlier.

[17] Sir Isaac Newton, General Scholium to the *Principia Mathematica* (1726).

[18] Newton considered himself a Christian, but he definitely held some unorthodox views on doctrines such as the Trinity.

particles (specifically, the quarks that make up protons and neutrons) get their mass. At the time, the standard model of particle physics suggested that particles have no mass—a counterintuitive notion to say the least; how would macro-scale objects have mass if their tiniest constituent parts have none? Assigning numerical masses to subatomic particles destroyed the mathematical symmetries that made the standard model wonderfully elegant and intellectually satisfying. Convinced that physical reality did include these symmetries but having no empirical proof, Higgs hypothesized that mass must be an *emergent* property of some kind. He suggested that empty space is permeated with an invisible energy field from which particles glean energy and thus mass (recall Einstein's famous equation that demonstrated the equivalence of mass and energy). This theoretical field came to be known as the "Higgs field" and, despite the total lack of empirical support, it was gradually (and sometimes begrudgingly) accepted by many in the physics community as a viable solution. The benefit was that it allowed physicists to keep their aesthetically satisfying, consistent system of mathematical equations while accounting for particle mass.

Half a century later, CERN (the European Organization for Nuclear Research in Geneva) was finally able to test Higgs field theory using the multi-billion-dollar Large Hadron Collider (LHC), a 17-mile-long underground particle accelerator outfitted with a system of high tech particle detectors. Calculations based upon Higgs field theory indicated that particle collisions inside of the LHC should result in reverberations that force the hypothesized field to fling off a signature particle—the Higgs boson. On the fourth of July, 2012 physicists at CERN announced that a particle fitting the Higgs boson profile had been detected, and the final piece of the standard model fell into place. Essentially, Peter Higgs' *mathematical* theory had accurately predicted the existence of an unobserved *physical* entity (Max Tegmark of MIT has often quipped that the Higgs field was predicted with a pencil). Forty-nine years after their initial prediction, Peter Higgs and his colleague Francois Englert shared the 2013 Nobel Prize in physics. Stephen Hawking, who did not believe this would ever happen, joked about the "personal cost" of the prize: his $100 bet with an associate that the Higgs boson would never be found.[19]

In an article for *The Guardian*, Dr. Jeff Forshaw of University of Manchester's School of Physics and Astronomy wrote the following about the Higgs' achievement: "Faith in the idea that nature's laws should be elegant and compelling has, yet again, delivered insight. The Higgs discovery is the jewel in the crown of particle physics and a worthy testament to nature's astonishing beauty."[20] Dr. Forshaw is not a religious believer, and neither was Peter Higgs. The same is true of some of the most famous science personalities of our day—Brian Greene, Sean Carroll, and Neil deGrasse Tyson. Their materialism is difficult to comprehend considering how astonishingly mathematical nature shows herself to be; one may be reminded of the skeptical and villainous Uncle Andrew from C.S. Lewis' book, *The Magician's Nephew*, which describes Narnia's creation. Aslan sings a beautiful, other-worldly song that brings all things into existence, but Uncle Andrew doesn't hear the music for what it is. Rather, he convinces himself that all he hears is the roar of an ordinary lion. In a similar way, scientific materialists are often enraptured by the grandeur and deep rationality of nature, but they fail (or perhaps in some cases simply refuse) to recognize the ultimate source of beauty and truth. Ironically, science itself would be impossible without the existence of a transcendent mind and the Keplerian cosmic harmony of mathematics, matter, and mind. Science is essentially the substitute religion of the materialist.

Coda

In a 1956 lecture, Lewis reflected on the music of the spheres as a concept the medievals were right to embrace:

> This is the only sound which has never for one split second ceased in any part of the universe…Presumably if (*per impossibile*) it ever did stop, then with

---

[19] Pallab Ghosh interview's Hawking: "Stephen Hawking on Higgs: 'Discovery has lost me $100,'" BBC News (4 July 2012), accessed at https://www.bbc.com/news/av/science-environment-18708626.

[20] Jeff Forshaw, "The beauty of the Higgs boson: The discovery of the Higgs boson is the jewel in the crown of particle physics," The Guardian (August 4, 2012). Accessed at https://www.theguardian.com/science/2012/aug/05/jeff-forshaw-higgs-boson-discovery.

terror and dismay, with a dislocation of our whole auditory life, we should feel that the bottom had dropped out of our lives. But it never does. The music which is too familiar to be heard enfolds us day and night and in all the ages.[21]

Indeed, should the Creator cease upholding the cosmos, all would dissolve. As Hebrews 1.3 says, "The Son is the radiance of God's glory and the exact expression of His nature, sustaining all things by his powerful word" (HCSB). It is fitting to end an essay on the beauty and harmony of the cosmos with a poem, and it just so happens that a rather obscure poet by the name of Charles N. Holmes wrote one that is extraordinarily apropos:

The Music of the Spheres
How angelic is the music
From an organ's mighty throat,
Or a song by human voices,
Or a harp's harmonic note;
How melodious the music
In the wide world out of door,
Of a skylark or a brooklet,
Or the surf upon the shore.

And philosophers once told us,
In an epoch long gone by,
Of sublime celestial music
From the spheres within the sky;
Though our firmament is silent
Over land and over sea,
Suns and worlds unite together
In symphonic harmony.

Were our ears attuned to hear it,
Ah! What music would arise
From the stars amid Orion
To the universal skies!
Underneath God's spangled heavens,

---

[21] Lewis, *Studies in Medieval and Renaissance Literature*, 52.

Which have neither depth nor years,
We might hearken, soul enchanted,
To the chorus of the spheres.[22]

Bibliography

Copernicus, Nicolaus. *On the Revolutions of the Heavenly Spheres*. New York: Prometheus, 1995.

Ferguson, Kitty. *Pythagoras: His Lives and the Legacy of a Rational Universe*. New York: Icon Books, 2008.

Forshaw, Jeff. "The beauty of the Higgs boson: The discovery of the Higgs boson is the jewel in the crown of particle physics," The Guardian (August 4, 2012). Accessed at https://www.theguardian.com/science/2012/aug/05/jeff-forshaw-higgs-boson-discovery.

Ghosh, Pallab (interviewer). "Stephen Hawking on Higgs: 'Discovery has lost me $100.'" BBC News (4 July 2012).

Gingerich, Owen. *The Eye of Heaven: Ptolemy, Copernicus, Kepler*. New York: The American Institute of Physics, 1993.

Holmes, Charles N. "The Music of the Spheres." *Popular Astronomy*, Vol. 31 (1922), 463.

Kepler, Johannes. *Harmony of the World* (1618).

Kepler, Johannes. Letter to Herwart von Hohenburg dated April 10th, 1599.

Lewis, C.S. *Studies in Medieval and Renaissance Literature*. New York: Cambridge University Press, 2013.

Newton, Sir Issac. General Scholium to the *Principia Mathematica* (1726).

Philo of Alexandria. *On Mating with the Preliminary Studies.*

---

[22] Charles N. Holmes, "The Music of the Spheres," *Popular Astronomy*, Vol. 31 (1922), 463.

8

What Christian Apologists Might Learn From Scientists

Michael G. Strauss

I. Science and Christianity

As an experimental particle physicist, I study the structure of matter, the fundamental particles and forces in the universe. How are we able to probe into the structure of matter? How do we know what a proton is made of? Suppose, instead, you wanted to know how your car was put together. If you are a particle physicist, you might get the car going very fast and smash it against another car going very fast and see what parts come flying out.

We do something like that to explore the structure of the universe. At CERN laboratory near Geneva, Switzerland there is a circular tunnel about 100 meters underground and 27 kilometers in circumference, housing a machine that accelerates protons to nearly the speed of light and smashes them against other protons moving in the opposite direction. We build huge detectors to see the debris from these collisions. I do research with the ATLAS detector at CERN, which is the height of a ten-story building and half as long as a football field. It is used to examine the fundamental structure of the universe by observing the debris from forty million proton collisions per second.

Not only am I a scientist, but I'm also a Christian. There is a perception among some people that science and Christianity are at war with each other. This war narrative is sometimes perpetuated by both scientists and Christians.

For instance, Jerry Coyne, a biologist, says "In the end, it's irrational to decide what's true in your daily life using empirical evidence but then rely on wishful thinking and ancient superstitions to judge the 'truths' undergirding your faith."[1] He is implying that you cannot be someone who is rational, like a scientist, and also believe any religious ideas.

Some Christians also maintain the idea that Christianity and science are at war. Ken Ham says, "The sad aspect of this is that Christians are taking the words of fallible men who use fallible methods who were not there in the past and therefore don't know everything about the past as a basis for interpreting Scripture."[2] Ham seems to be saying that you cannot trust scientists because they are fallible and have their presuppositions and biases. The supposed war between science and Christianity is perpetuated by scientists who think that faith is a vice, and by Christians who think that science cannot be trusted.

In contrast, the biblical idea is that science and Christianity are in accord. Science is the study of the natural world and Scripture proclaims that by looking at the natural world we should see God's character. Psalm 19.1 says, "The heavens declare the glory of God. The skies proclaim the work of his hands" (NIV), and Romans 1.20 claims, "For since the creation of the world, God's invisible qualities—his eternal power and divine nature—have been clearly seen, being understood from what has been made, so that people are without excuse" (NIV). We should not just see some vague idea of God when we look at nature, but we should see his actual character, including his eternal power and divine nature.

As a Christian scientist, and based on what the Bible says and what I learn through scientific inquiry, I am convinced that there is a great harmony between science and Christianity. They have the same Author. The Author of Creation is the Author of the biblical text, and the Author should speak with one voice and with one truth. The truth that we find

---

[1] *Newsweek*, "The War Between Science and Religion," December 26, 2018. See https://www.newsweek.com/war-between-science-and-religion-opinion-1271062.

[2] "Do the Days Really Matter," September 1, 1990, See https://www.icr.org/article/689.

in nature by studying God's creation should agree with the truth we find in Scripture by reading his Word. Consequently, I think there are things scientists could learn from a Christian worldview and Christians could learn from scientists. Since I'm talking to an audience that is primarily Christian, I will focus on some things Christians could learn from how scientists approach their discipline.

II. Be Curious and Pursue Truth

The first thing Christians could learn from scientists is to be curious and pursue truth. Irving Langmuir says, "The scientist is motivated primarily by curiosity and a desire for truth."[3] Like children who continually ask "why," scientists ask the "why" questions and are curious about the world. We, as Christians, should be curious as we search to discover truth.

The theoretical physicist Sean Carroll writes, "Science should be interested in determining the truth, whatever that truth may be, natural, supernatural or otherwise."[4] My personal definition of science is, "Science is a search for truth by observing the natural world." As Christians, it should be obvious that we are to be curious and search for truth. After all, we serve the God of all truth. Isaiah writes, "I, the Lord, speak the truth."[5] Jesus said, "But when He, the Spirit of truth, comes, He will guide you into all truth."[6] Because we are followers of the God of truth, finding truth should be an overriding principle.

When I was a postdoctoral researcher, I took some time to think about what motivates me in life, not just in my spiritual life or my professional life, but in general. I realized that a primary motivational factor for me was a desire to understand truth. There are some Christians who are afraid to explore various truths because they think that some "truths" might lead them away from God. But if God is God of all truth, we should never be afraid to search for and find truth. No matter where that truth leads, it should ultimately lead back to the God of truth. That

---

[3] Irving Langmuir, Nobel Prize Speech, December 10, 1932, See https://www.nobelprize.org/prizes/chemistry/1932/langmuir/speech/.
[4] Sean Carroll, *The Big Picture*, Dutton, 2016 (p 133).
[5] Isaiah 45.19a (NIV)
[6] John 16.13 (NIV)

shouldn't be surprising because Jesus said He is the truth: "I am the way, the truth, and the life."[7] In my life, every time I've had a crisis of faith, or a desire to probe something deeper because I didn't understand it, or I had doubts about my faith, searching for and finding truth has ultimately led me back to Jesus.

But truth has another consequence. Jesus said, "If you hold my teaching, you are really my disciples, and you will know the truth, and the truth will set you free."[8] The idea that truth will set you free has broad applications. I know Christians who feel a tension between science and the biblical text, and it causes them to sometimes experience a deep inner conflict. But finding the truth sets us free. It gives us freedom to love and trust God more deeply. It gives us freedom to be bold as we evangelize because we have a stronger faith in God and the truth that He gives. Truth sets us free, and Christians should be avid truth seekers, just as scientists are. When scientists come to conclusions, it's not because they are trying to destroy faith or theistic beliefs. It's because they are trying to find truth.

III. Be Skeptical and Test Everything

The second thing Christians could learn from scientists is to be skeptical and test everything. This is both a scientific and a biblical idea. The apostle Paul writes, "examine everything carefully; hold fast to that which is good."[9] Christianity should be critically examined and tested. Paul praised the Bereans in Acts 17 because when he told them about Christ, they didn't just accept it. They searched the Scriptures to see if it was true. This is what we should do: we should test everything. However, encouraging Christians to test everything does bring up additional questions. I would like to address three of them.

If you are going to test everything, you need some level skepticism. The first question then is "How is skepticism compatible with faith?" One reason that question comes up is because of a misunderstanding of faith. Richard Dawkins gives a poor definition of faith when he says, "Faith is

---
[7] John 14.6 (NIV)
[8] John 8.31b-32 (NIV)
[9] I Thessalonians 5.21 (NASB1995).

the great cop out, the great excuse to evade the need to think and the need to evaluate evidence. Faith is the belief in spite of, even perhaps because of, the lack of evidence."[10] This is an incorrect idea about faith. If you believe something without evidence, that's not faith; that's stupidity. If you get an email from a Nigerian prince who wants you to send him money, and you have no evidence that he is trustworthy, and you send him money, that's not faith; that's stupidity. Believing something without evidence is not the definition of biblical faith.

Instead, biblical faith is always based on evidence. A lawyer came to Jesus and asked Him what was the greatest commandment. As Christians we believe Jesus was God. If you can ask God one question a pretty good one would be what this lawyer asked, "God, out of everything you have said, what's the most important?" Jesus answered him, "Love the Lord your God with all your heart and with all your soul and with all your mind and with all your strength."[11] As Christians we are to use our minds.

Thomas was a disciple of Jesus who needed to test things. He wanted evidence that Jesus rose from the dead. He is sometimes called "doubting Thomas" but I prefer to call Thomas the "patron saint of scientists," because he needed evidence to believe. Thomas said, "Unless I see the nail marks in his hands, and put my finger where the nails were, and put my hand into his side, I will not believe."[12] The response of Jesus to Thomas was not, "Don't you know that faith is believing without evidence?" Instead, Jesus showed him the evidence and only then did Jesus ask Thomas to believe.

John Lennox, an Oxford mathematician, gives a much better definition of faith than Richard Dawkins does. He says, "Faith is not a leap in the dark. It is the exact opposite. It's a commitment based on evidence."[13]

---

[10] From a speech at the Edinburgh International Science Festival, April 15, 1992. Quoted in "EDITORIAL: A scientist's case against God". *The Independent* (London): p. 17. 20 April 1992. and Paul Gomberg (27 May 2011). *What Should I Believe?: Philosophical Essays for Critical Thinking.* Broadview Press. p. 146. ISBN 9781554810130

[11] Mark 12.30 (NIV)

[12] John 20.25 (NIV).

[13] Lennox, John. The original source of this quote is uncertain, but it is attributed to Lennox and repeated on numerous web sites such as https://amillennialsdivinedefense.com/meet-an-apologist-professor-john-lennox/. A similar confirmed quote from Lennox is from a radio debate with

Perhaps a better word for faith would be trust. We have evidence that God is trustworthy, so we are willing to trust ourselves, our very lives, to Him.

The next question I want to address that comes up when we are encouraged to test everything is, "What do we do if the data contradicts our beliefs?" We may think that if the data seems to contradict our core believes then we are in trouble. But there are good options on how to proceed.

We should first note that it is a biblical idea that if what we believe is not true, then we shouldn't believe it. Paul writes, "If Christ has not been raised, our preaching is useless and so is your faith. And if Christ has not been raised, your faith is futile."[14] If the resurrection did not really happen, then we shouldn't believe it because we serve a God of truth.

So, what should we do when a new idea seems to contradict our currently held beliefs? First, don't discard your faith; instead start by digging deeper. We live in a society in which many things are presented to us in a superficial manner. We have thirty second sound bites, and TikTok messages that take fifteen seconds. But complex issues are complex. For instance, in my research, I study quantum mechanics, how the universe works at very small distances. Quantum mechanics is complex. We live in a complex world. You are not going to get insight on something challenging with a thirty second video. Dig deeper and embrace that complexity. This is how you resolve difficult issues, issues that at first seem to contradict core beliefs.

There have been things I have learned in science or studied in Scripture that may seem to contradict each other. Instead of assuming the conflict is irreconcilable and walking away from my faith, I first choose to dig deeper. There are good answers to resolve these conflicts, but they are usually not found on the surface. Every time I have come to a crisis where at first something I learned doesn't seem to correlate with Christian beliefs, as I have dug deeper I've gotten to know God better. I've gained new

---

Michael Ruse and can be found at https://premierchristian.news/en/news/article/video-exclusive-faith-is-not-a-leap-into-the-unknown-but-an-evidence-based-commitment-claims-oxford-professor where Lennox says, "Christian faith consists, not in faith as a leap into the unknown, it is evidence-based commitment."

[14] 1 Corinthians 15.14 (NIV).

insight into God and aspects of His creation and His character. I walk away loving God more and trusting Him more because I took that apparent contradiction as a challenge to learn more and see what I was missing. God is always trying to show me that He is much bigger than the little box I put Him in, and these are opportunities to do that.

Let's look at two biblical examples of things I have concluded are true because of the advice to "test everything." The first is that I believe the Bible is historically reliable. I can't go into much detail, but let me give a few reasons why I believe the Bible is accurate. First, the New Testament contains eyewitness testimony. John writes, "That which was from the beginning, which we have heard, which we have seen with our eyes, which we have looked at and our hands have touched."[15] John claims Jesus rose from the dead and he knows it because he saw and touched the risen Jesus. Peter writes, "We did not follow cleverly devised stories when we told you about the coming of our Lord Jesus Christ in power, but we were eyewitnesses of his majesty."[16] The New Testament was written within decades after Jesus lived, and the authors of the New Testament were eyewitnesses and knew it was true.

Other accounts of Jesus that were not from eyewitnesses were from those who carefully examined the life of Jesus. Luke, who was an educated physician, wrote, "Since I myself have carefully investigated everything from the beginning, I too decided to write an orderly account for you, most excellent Theophilus."[17] Luke carefully investigated what happened and Luke's account contains details about Jesus' birth and life that no other account does. For instance, he tells us what Mary is thinking at times and that "she thought about them over and over."[18] How did Luke know what Mary was thinking? My best guess is because he sat down with Mary and interviewed her. He carefully investigated the life of Jesus.

Another reason I believe the New Testament is true is because it is confirmed by archaeology. At times, skeptics have proclaimed that certain

---

[15] 1 John 1.1 (NIV).
[16] 2 Peter 1.16 (NIV)
[17] Luke 1.3 (NIV)
[18] Luke 2.19 (NIRV)

details in the New Testament were false, but then archeological evidence is found that corroborates the biblical record. For instance, at one time people claimed that those who were crucified were always thrown into a common grave, and nobody was ever put into a private tomb, so the account of Jesus' burial must be false. But then, the ankle bone of someone who had been crucified with the nail still in the bone was found in a private tomb. Now we have archeological evidence that people who were crucified could be buried in private tombs. Other archeological finds that validate the veracity of the New Testament include the "Pilate Stone," describing Pontius Pilate as the prefect of Judea, and the discovery of the Pool of Siloam mentioned in the Gospel of John. The Bible talks about many historical people, places, and events that have been validated by archaeology. I believe the New Testament is valid because it has been tested through eyewitness accounts, and it has been confirmed by archaeology.

There is one particular event in the New Testament that I have tested and concluded is true: the resurrection of Jesus. In the early first century, the disciples of Jesus made two important claims: that the tomb of Jesus was empty, and they saw Jesus alive. Although there are many alternative theories about what might have happened that first Easter day, none of them can explain the facts. None of them can adequately explain these two things that the disciples said convinced them that Jesus rose from the dead.

Additionally, we have evidence today that Jesus rose from the dead. We have the written and oral history of the Christian church which can be traced back to about 32 AD, beginning in Jerusalem with people who claimed that Jesus rose from the dead. Another powerful evidence we have today of the resurrection is that Christians worship on Sunday. The first Christians were Jewish, and the Jewish day of worship is Saturday, yet by the early to mid-first century, Christians were worshipping on Sunday. These devout Jews changed their day of worship to Sunday because something remarkable happened on Sunday.

Finally, we have the New Testament documents themselves. There are six independent testimonies that Jesus rose from the dead that can be dated to the first century, three of them from eyewitnesses, with accurate accounts of the resurrection of Jesus. Only an actual resurrection explains all the facts.

Be skeptical and test everything. It is because I have tested my beliefs that I believe the Bible is accurate and that Jesus rose from the dead. It isn't because of some blind faith. The world is full of truth claims. How are you going to know which ones are true? You test them as Paul encouraged us to do. Ultimately, testing things will lead us to the God of all truth.

IV. Be a Critical Thinker

The third thing that Christians could learn from scientists is to be a critical thinker and consider all the data. Pay particular attention to the things that may at first seem to contradict what you believe.

Let me give you an example from science where truth could only be discovered by considering all the data including things that seemed to be contrary to accepted ideas. In the mid 20th century, scientists thought they understood how the sun worked through nuclear fusion, and that the process of fusion should produce particles called electron neutrinos. But when scientists measured the number of electron neutrinos coming to Earth from the Sun, there were only a third of what was expected. The scientists realized that to discover the truth they had to dig deeper and consider various options and all the data. One unconventional idea was that maybe neutrinos are weird and, although they start out as electron neutrinos from the Sun, somehow in the process of coming to Earth, they change to other types of neutrinos called muon neutrinos and tau neutrinos. Scientists realized that to be critical thinkers and consider all the data they had to test this idea of "neutrino oscillations." When the idea was tested it was shown to be true. Neutrinos from the Sun start out as electron neutrinos, and on their trip to Earth they change to muon neutrinos and tau neutrinos. When all the types of neutrinos are measured, we find exactly what is expected from our models of how the Sun works. If scientists had said, "Even though things don't make sense, let's not look at other options; let's just give up," they might have never learned that neutrinos can change their type.

At times, Christians are unwilling to consider all the data, particularly data that may be problematic to their current beliefs. For instance, Christians have different views on how God created the universe. Consider three questions. (1) Is God the Creator? (2) Did the Big Bang happen? In other words, did the universe come into existence about 14 billion years ago? And (3) has macroscopic evolution occurred? In other words, is all life related to each other and has it evolved over time so that through many minor changes, big changes have occurred?

Various Christians who believe the Bible is true answer these questions differently. Some Christians, young earth creationists, would say God created the universe, but that the universe did not start with a Big Bang, and macroscopic evolution did not happen. Most young earth creationists believe the universe is about 6000 years old. Some Christians, old earth creationists, believe that God is the Creator and that God used the Big Bang to create the universe 14 billion years ago, but that God didn't primarily use evolution to create the diversity of life on Earth. Finally, some Christians, evolutionary creationists, believe that God is the creator, and that God used both the Big Bang and macroscopic evolution to accomplish his creative work. These various groups would agree that the Bible is true and accurate in its account of creation but may have different ways of interpreting the text.

There are some questions that any person should ask themselves when trying to determine which of these views may be true. Do you know why Christians who differ from you in their belief about creation hold to their view? Do you know what their biblical and scientific claims are? Do you know the data that may contradict your view? Have you read, not just the people who agree with you, but others who disagree with you? Do you know why evolutionary creationists believe that God used evolution, or why naturalistic evolutionists don't believe God is necessary to describe the history of our universe? How can you know the truth if you haven't looked critically at the other views?

If you want to know the truth, you must know what other people think and why. In my searches for truth, I have investigated many different ideas to try to consider all the data. I have read many books by atheists trying to support their view, so that I have a good understanding of the best arguments for atheism. Reading their "best" arguments has only strengthened my faith because I believe the arguments for Christian theism are so much stronger than the arguments for atheism. To know the truth, you must be a critical thinker, consider all the data, and pay attention to contradictory information.

V. Have an Open Mind

The next thing that Christians could learn from scientists flows logically from what has been developed to this point: have an open mind and be willing to change your mind and accept what the evidence reveals. If you want to know and follow the truth, you are going to have to change your mind at times. Surely, there are some things you or I now believe that are not correct, and if we want to find the truth, we must be willing to change our minds.

This happened in science at the beginning of the 20th century. Scientists thought they had the universe pretty much figured out, and that they just needed to do a few more minor mathematical calculations. But then, two unexpected discoveries were made: Einstein's theories of relativity, and quantum mechanical principles. Those discoveries radically changed our understanding of the universe. If scientists had said, "We already have it figured out. Don't give us any more information. We're not going to change our minds," then scientists may have never discovered two of the most revolutionary concepts in physics.

As an application of this principle for Christians, consider in more detail the question, "How do science and the Bible fit together?" To investigate this question, I first considered what the Bible said about *when* the universe was created. I had grown up in a culture in which many people believed the universe was created about 6000 years ago, so that was my default belief. But I wanted to know the truth, and I wanted to explore what the Bible actually said to see if it suggested that the universe was only thousands of years old. To answer this question, I knew I had to try to understand the ancient Hebrew text in which the Genesis account of creation was written. My dad was a pastor, so I went into his office, which had thousands of books, to help understand the original language and culture of the Bible. There I consulted volumes that were unbiased, including interlinear Bibles that have the English words linked to the original Hebrew words, Hebrew dictionaries that indicate what words mean, and Hebrew concordances and commentaries. I asked the question, "Does the Bible tell us when the universe was created?" In some sense the answer is "yes." The first statement in the Bible in Genesis 1.1 is, "In the beginning, God created the heavens and the earth." I thought, "That makes sense. But when was the beginning?"

To investigate when the beginning was, I looked at the indications of the passage of time in the Bible. I found that people infer when the universe was created from the timeline presented. First, there is a creation event, then there are six "days" that pass, and finally, there are genealogies that trace the history of humanity from Adam to Jesus. In 1650, Bishop Ussher had made some assumptions about this timeline, that the "days" of creation were each 24 hours and that the genealogies were a complete record, and he concluded that the beginning was in 4004 BC. But he made assumptions that were not necessarily justified. To really investigate when the beginning of the universe occurred there were three questions that had to be addressed. The first question is, "Is there any passage of time between the creation of the 'heavens and the earth' and the beginning of the six days?" The second question is, "Are the 'days' of Genesis meant to be 24 hours long?" And the third question is, "Are the biblical genealogies complete?"

As I researched these questions, the answers became clear. Regarding the first question, is there any passage of time before the six days begin, the answer is certainly "Yes." The first two verses in the Bible say "In the beginning, God created the heavens and the earth. The earth was formless and void, and darkness was over the surface of the deep."[19] Then the next verse says, "Then God said, let there be light."[20] Because every "day" of

---

[19] Genesis 1.1-2a (NASB1995)
[20] Genesis 1.3 (NASB1995)

creation starts with the phrase, "Then God said" it is obvious that the first day starts after God had already created the heavens and the earth. There is clearly a length of time between when God created the heavens and the earth and the beginning of day one. Although the Bible does not tell us the length of that time, scientific observations fill in the gap and make it clear that the time from the origin of the universe in the Big Bang until when the earth first formed was about 9 billion years.

When I investigated the second question, what do Hebrew scholars think is the length of each "day," I found a variety of opinions. There are at least 11 different ideas that I encountered, including that each day is 24 hours, that the days have no length of time associated with them but simply form an outline or framework for the story, that the days are analogical days, that is they are God's days which are analogous to our days but not of the same length, and that each day is an extended period of time, an epoch or an era. Before I studied this for myself, I was usually told that each day was 24 hours, but I found that the best scholars of ancient Hebrew did not agree with that assertion.

So I investigated the various meanings of the Hebrew word *yom*, which we translate "day." Like the English word "day," *yom* can have many meanings. It can mean the period of daylight, a period of 24 hours, or an unspecified long period of time, as well as other meanings. To know what the word means, you must look at its literary context. If you take the literal meaning of the word, outside of context, you may misunderstand the word. For instance, if you are listening to a baseball game on the radio, and the announcer says, "The base runner is hugging the base," and you think that the base runner is laying on the ground embracing the base, then you would be incorrect.[21] If you take something literally, and it's not supposed to be taken literally, you are wrong. In the sentence, "In George Washington's day, the colonists fought the Revolutionary War," the context indicates that "day" means an extended period of time.

Since I don't speak ancient Hebrew, I looked to other scholars to determine the meaning of the word *yom* in the context of Genesis. Gleason

---

[21] This baseball illustration is from *How to Study the Bible for Yourself* by Tim LaHaye, Harvest House Publishers, Eugene Oregon, 1982.

Archer was one of the best scholars of ancient Hebrew in the 20th century. He writes, "On the basis of internal evidence, it is this writer's conviction that *yom* in Genesis one could not have been intended by the Hebrew author to mean a literal 24 hour day."[22] So although a cursory reading of the creation account in English may imply that each "day" of creation is 24 hours, that is not the case when one understands the original language. According to Archer, each "day" cannot be 24 hours. Consequently, each "day" of creation could be a long period of time. I also learned that ancient Hebrew has no word that means epoch, era, or extended period of time. If the author wanted to indicate that there were six epochs of creation, the only word he could use would be the Hebrew word *yom*.

Because there is time between the creation of the heavens and the earth and the first "day" of creation and because and each "day" could be considered as an epoch of creation, there is no indication in the Bible when the beginning of the universe occurred or how old the universe is.

Finally, regarding the third question of whether the genealogies are complete, the answer is "no." There are often gaps in Hebrew genealogies. For instance, the Gospel of Matthew lists fourteen generations from David to the Babylonian exile and explicitly states there are fourteen generations during that time. Yet, the comparable genealogy in Chronicles lists seventeen generations. Matthew does what is common in Jewish genealogies; he skips generations and even counts them differently. But since the purpose of the genealogies is not to give a complete record but an overall list of ancestries, this is not a problem.

Given that there are gaps of unknown length in the genealogy from Adam to Christ, we do not know when Adam lived. After investigating these three questions I came to the same conclusion as that found in the notes of my Scofield Reference Bible which says, "Scripture gives no data for determining how long ago the universe was created."[23] The Bible only tells us that in the beginning, whenever that was, God created the heavens and the earth. Consequently, I changed my mind. Before I had investigated all the data, I had accepted the naïve conclusion that the universe

---

[22] Archer, "*A Survey of Old Testament Introduction*," 199.
[23] Scofield, C.I., New Scofield Reference Bible, New York, Oxford University Press, 1967, p. 1.

was only thousands of years old. But by studying Scripture, by looking at the data and digging deeper, by following these principles, I became an old earth creationist, believing that God created the universe though the process of the Big Bang about 14 billion years ago. This conclusion wasn't because I had some scientific bias, but because I studied the Bible for myself and consulted good biblical scholars that changed my mind.

I should add one important point. When I've changed my mind about something within the Christian realm, it hasn't changed the foundations of my faith. The essential elements of the Christian faith are so well grounded in evidence that it is unlikely that anything discovered would be so overwhelming as to shake that firm foundation.

VI. Effectively Communicate Your Passion

The final thing Christians could learn from scientists is to effectively communicate your passion. In science, it is important to publish a paper describing the results of our research. Until we've communicated our passion to others, the work is not done.

We also need to do this as Christians: effectively communicate our passion. Peter writes, "But make sure that in your hearts you honor Christ as Lord. Always be ready to give an answer to anyone who asks you about the hope you have. Be ready to give the reason for it. But do it gently and with respect."[24] Notice that the foremost principle is to make Christ Lord, to put Him first. We are also instructed to speak gently and with respect. Remember, the purpose of these dialogues is not to win arguments, but to lead others to Christ. In this talk and during this conference, we are not providing you apologetic evidence so you can win arguments. We are giving you apologetic evidence so you can introduce people to Jesus. This is our passion.

My passion is not the evidence for the resurrection, although that's why I believe Jesus is who He claimed to be. My passion is not the evidence for the reliability of the New Testament documents, although that's why I believe the New Testament is trustworthy. My passion is Jesus. This

---

[24] 1 Peter 3.15 (NIRV)

is because the heart of the Christian message is God's passion for me. The God of the universe left heaven to become a human, only to have nails driven into his hands, a spear stuck in his side, and a crown of huge thorns pounded into his head because He loved us. Paul tells us this amazing truth, "But God demonstrates his own love toward us, in that while we were still sinners, Christ died for us."[25] Is Jesus your passion? Is that what you communicate first and foremost to others?

Not only did Jesus come to earth and die because He loved you and me, He also conquered death. Because of that, because He is alive, you and I can have a personal relationship with Him. You cannot have a personal relationship with a dead person. My father died in 1993. I wish I could talk to him, but I can't, and he can't talk back. But I can talk to Jesus, and He can talk back because He is alive.

I learned the lesson to effectively communicate my passion in a profound way when I was a graduate student. I lived in an apartment with two other guys. Jeff was a non-believer and Scott was a believer. Jeff and I would talk about Christianity and I would share reasons why I believe in Jesus and discuss some of the evidence for Christianity. Scott would get up in the morning, read his Bible and pray, and then sing hymns. Often early in the morning, Jeff and I would be awakened by Scott singing hymns. The three of us eventually went our separate ways. Jeff later became a Christian and he and I discussed some of the reasons that convinced him to follow Jesus. Jeff said, "Remember when we lived in the apartment and we would discuss Christianity. Back then, you taught me a lot about Christianity. You answered a lot of my questions, but Scott showed me how much he loved God." That pierced my heart because I had never shared with Jeff how grateful I am for what God had done for me on the cross, and why I love Him so deeply. I never really shared my passion for Jesus. I learned a lesson that day.

Later, I was talking to another friend about the message of Christianity. After many conversations, I asked him if I could share some personal things. I shared my passion; what God has done for me, and how

---

[25] Romans 5.8 (NASB).

much I love Him, and how much He loves me. Later that evening, my friend became a Christian.

We, as Christians, need to effectively share our passion. We need to remember what our passion really is. It isn't just apologetics. It isn't just the reasons we believe. It's Jesus Christ who died for us as a demonstration of God's great love and grace, even when we were still sinners.

Let me summarize some things that Christians can learn from scientists. Be curious and pursue the truth. Be skeptical and test everything. Be a critical thinker and consider all the data. Be willing to look at different ideas and understand why other people believe them. Have an open mind. If you want to find truth, you're going to have to change your mind sometimes. And finally, effectively communicate your passion, the Lord and Savior Jesus Christ who loved us and gave Himself for us so that we might know God and have an eternal relationship with Him.

Bibliography

Archer, Gleason. *A Survey of Old Testament Introduction.* Chicago: Moody, 1994.

Carroll, Sean. *The Big Picture.* New York: Dutton, 2016.

Newsweek, "The War Between Science and Religion," December 26, 2018.

Scofield, C.I. *New Scofield Reference Bible.* New York: Oxford University Press, 1967.

9

Rhetoric and Reality
Biblical Literalism and a Christian View of Nature

David H. Calhoun

The Enigma of Biblical Literalism

Biblical literalism is in many ways a puzzling phenomenon. A statistically declining though still common view, literalism is widely criticized and even reviled, not only by critics and opponents but also by theologically traditional Christians one might expect to be sympathetic allies. And yet, over the last century, traditional Christians, including many evangelicals and fundamentalists, have settled on and continue to maintain the language of literalism to defend a robust view of the truth and authority of the Bible. What should we think about literalism? Is it effective as an evangelistic or apologetic strategy? Is it a necessary component of faithful Christian witness?

Even though biblical literalism is something of an enigma, I want to try to make it *intelligible*, that is, to describe the logic by which it can be understood to make sense. At the same time, I want to show how it is *problematic*, especially with respect to biblical claims about nature. While literalism and the historical and cultural springs that have motivated it involve a complex mix of theological, cultural, and historical themes, I hope to shed some light on what biblical literalism is, what role it plays in American culture and religion, the historical and cultural conditions that spurred its rise, and the problematic way it positions Christianity with respect to science.

Literalism is inherently linked to fundamentalism, which is in turn connected to questions about the compatibility of Christianity and modern science.[1] Biblical literalism significantly underwrites the Christianity-science "war narrative," the idea that Christianity inherently conflicts with science. While I think the war narrative is false,[2] I want to explore how literalism complicates current (and future) pathways for showing the compatibility of Christianity and science.

I want to make three related claims: (1) emphatic public assertions of biblical literalism, while technically false, serve an important rhetorical function, namely, to defend the authority and relevance of the Bible against dismissive attack; (2) the rhetorical value of literalism has high costs in clarity and accuracy; and (3) more precise public rhetoric about the truth and authority of the Bible can promote apologetic efforts to demonstrate the compatibility of Christianity and science.

Biblical Literalism in the Public Sphere

A prominent public exchange twenty years ago provides a vivid point of reference for understanding the nature and motivation of biblical literalism. As part of the lead-up publicity for the release of his film *The Passion of the Christ* (2004), Mel Gibson was interviewed by Diane Sawyer on ABC News Primetime.[3] Sawyer framed the controversy of Gibson's film in part by contrasting "the tension between those who see the Bible as literal history and the scholars who say it's one interpretation of historical events":

> SAWYER NARRATION: Gibson believes as do 60% of Americans according to an ABC News poll that the Bible is historical fact.
>
> SAWYER: Do you have a literal belief of the Bible, every sentence in it?
>
> GIBSON: Yes. Yes. You either accept the whole thing or don't accept it at all.

---

[1] Fundamentalism as an outlook is closely associated with a literalist view of scripture. At the same time, fundamentalism features multivalent related commitments, including biblical inerrancy, sufficiency, and transparency; on this see Brasher, *Encyclopedia of Fundamentalism*, xvi, 282-84; Criswell, *Why I Preach*, 119.

[2] Calhoun, "Christianity and Science."

[3] Mel Gibson, "Mel Gibson's *Passion*." Quotations taken from audio soundtrack.

SAWYER NARRATION: So what about the historians who say that the gospels were written long after Jesus died and are not entirely fact but political points of view and metaphor?

SAWYER: Historians you know have argued that in fact it was not written at the time; these were not eyewitnesses . . .

GIBSON: [crosstalk] Oh, they were . . .

SAWYER: . . . in the New Testament—Matthew Mark Luke and John—but historians have said they don't think so . . .

GIBSON: They may have written a little afterwards but they were the people that were there who saw it could relate these stories.

Sawyer shows her ignorance of the Bible and of Christian culture by offering an oversimplified dichotomy of historical fact on the one hand and "political points of view and metaphor" on the other, effectively proposing a stark contrast: is scripture simple fact or manufactured partisan fantasy? While Gibson's response emphasizes forceful assertion over nuance, he embraces the language of literalism to affirm the authority and reliability of the scriptures, particularly the grounding of the gospel accounts in near contemporaneous eyewitness reports.

ABC News' polling placed Gibson in good, or at least plentiful, company on the question of literalism. Gallup has been surveying Americans on attitudes about the Bible for years, offering a more fine-grained analysis that distinguishes the literal (or "historical fact") view from another position supportive of the Bible (that it is "inspired by God, not to be taken literally"), and contrasting both of those stances with a dismissive view (that the Bible is "a collection of fables, history, and moral precepts recorded by man"). Gallup's survey data suggests that the ABC statistic of 60% was about double actual American support for biblical literalism at that time.[4] The most striking aspect of the Gallup survey, however, is its revelation that biblical literalism is in slow but steady decline. The view that the Bible is the "actual word of God, and is to be

---

[4] Newport, "Fewer in U.S." A 2002 poll yielded a result of 30% support for biblical literalism, while another two years later reported 34%.

taken literally, word for word" has dropped nearly by half in just under a half a century, from 38% of the US population in 1976 to 20% in 2022.[5] All Christians preferred the inspiration view to the literalist view 54% to 30% in 2017 versus 58% to 25% in 2022, a slight shift away from literalism. While Gallup's survey has not asked respondents to specifically self-identify as evangelical / born again until their 2022 survey, in that year even evangelicals favored the inspiration view over the literalist view 51% to 40%.

As one might expect, the view of human creation most naturally associated with biblical literalism, that "God created human beings pretty much in their present form at one time within the last 10,000 years or so"—the Young Earth special creation (YESC) view—partially correlates with polling views about the Bible. In 1982, when Gallup first began to survey creation-evolution opinions, 44% of Americans supported the YESC, while biblical literalism garnered about 37% support. The most recent data, for 2024, shows 37% support for YESC while those committed to literalism had dropped to 20% by 2022. In other words, support for both YESC and biblical literalism have declined, but support for a non-developmental creationist view tends to show more steadiness than support for literalism.[6]

Is the Bible Literally True?

What does it mean to say that one interprets something literally? The primary meaning of "literally" is "in a literal, exact, or actual sense; not

---

[5] Saad, "Record Few Americans"; Newport, "Fewer in U.S." In the same time period the inspiration view has held steady in the high 40s and low 50s, from 45% in 1976 to 49% in 2022. Aggregated together, the literalist view and the inspiration view have moved from 83% in 1976 to 69% in 2022, a modest but undeniable drop. On the other hand, the dismissive "human fable" view has more than doubled from 13% to 29%. It would seem that critics of the Bible are winning the day.

[6] Brenan, "Majority Still Credits God for Humankind." Gallup's data on creation and evolution goes back to 1982, with the Young Earth special creationist response shifting from 44% in 1982 to 37% in 2024. Aggregation of the two creation views, Young Earth and divinely guided development, total 71% in 2024, very close to the total of the American population that agrees that the Bible is a source of truth (compare to "Public's Views on Human Evolution"). There is some evidence that Americans express different views about creation depending on how questions are asked ("Evolution of Pew Research Questions").

figuratively, allegorically, etc."⁷ The adverbial form, dating to the 1400s, derives from the adjective "literal," which similarly specifies direct meanings that are contrasted to the figurative or allegorical. An important variant sense of "literal" originates from theological concerns involving interpretation of scripture, and specifies the "primary concrete meaning" of a term, as opposed to figurative meanings, including the metaphorical, anagogical, moral, mystical, or tropological.⁸ So biblical literalism is reading the Bible in a straightforward or direct way, as the Gallup survey question captures.

Understood in these terms, is the Bible *literally* true? Those who take the Bible to be an authoritative source of truth will insist that many claims not only can, but should be, read literally, as true in the plain, nonfigurative sense. Historical narratives such as Exodus or Kings present chronicles of events in the life of the people of Israel. The Gospels, as records of the person, actions, and sayings of Jesus, purport to be an accurate account of Jesus' earthly ministry. Particular historical and theological claims the scripture makes are, according to Christians generally, truthfully asserted: that the physical universe is the creative product of God's agency (Genesis 1.1; John 1.1–3), that God established and maintained a covenant with a particular people (Genesis 12.1–3, 17.1–22), that God entered history in human form, as the man Jesus of Nazareth (John 1.10, 14; Hebrews 1.1–3), and having done so, died a painful and gruesome death on a Roman cross (Matthew 27.32–50; John 19.17–29). Paul communicates in 1 Corinthians 15 what is of most importance (*en protoi*, 15.3), namely the Good News of Jesus, that Jesus died for human sin, was buried, and was witnessed by many people to have been raised again to life (15.3–8). Paul emphatically argues that a follower of Jesus must regard the resurrection as a real event, because "if

---

⁷ *Oxford English Dictionary* s.v. "literally," meaning I.1.a.

⁸ *Oxford English Dictionary* s.v. "literal," meaning II.5.a. The various figurative forms of biblical interpretation have been employed since the beginning of Christianity (Walter C. Kaiser and Moisés Silva, *Introduction to Biblical Hermeneutics*, 23–62; Criswell, 190–96). The Roman Catholic Church, while granting the value of non-literal interpretive approaches, insists on the *primacy* of the literal sense in biblical interpretation, that which concerns the meaning "intended and expressed by the sacred writer" (Pope Pius XII, *Divino Afflante Spiritu*, §26; see also §§23, 54; Brown, "Hermeneutics," 606–10).

there is no resurrection of the dead, then Christ has not been raised either. And if Christ has not been raised, then all our preaching is useless, and your faith is useless" (1 Corinthians 15.13–14 NLT).[9]

However, if the question "Is the Bible literally true?" concerns the scripture *taken as a whole*, the obvious answer is "no." Many biblical passages make poetic, symbolic, parabolic, metaphoric, and allegorical assertions—figurative claims, in other words—that should not be taken literally, because taken literally they either would be nonsense or would conflict with other claims in scripture. For example, the Psalmist describes God as an avenging sky god, riding an angelic being down from heaven, concealing his attack by clouds, blowing smoke out of his nose and breathing flames out of his mouth (Psalm 18.7–11). Given that God is spirit, however, not an anthropomorphic physical being (John 4.24), Psalm 18 must be understood as poetry describing God's powerful rescue in dramatic figurative terms. When Jesus says "I am the door of the sheep" (John 10.7 NASB), does he mean that he believes himself to be an opening in a rock wall? No. This metaphor is part of a series of figurative images that Jesus uses to describe himself—living water (4.10), bread (6.35), shepherd / sheepfold door (10.1–16), and vine (15.1–8). These metaphors are part of Jesus' use of what the Gospel author notes is figurative expression (*paroimia*, 16.25), which includes parable, fictional narrative, and hyperbole, none of which should be read literally.

While dreams and visions convey particular content that is communicated straightforwardly, which is to say *literally*, those contents convey a nonliteral context that requires interpretive elaboration (Genesis 40.1–8, 17–32; Acts 10.9–38; Revelation 1.10–20; Revelation 4). Imprecatory psalms certainly may be understood as conveying the attitude of the Psalmist, but cannot be taken as grounds for theological conclusions. Psalm 137 vividly communicates the Psalmist's grief and anger over the conquest and sack of Jerusalem by the Babylonians, but 137.8–9 cannot

---

[9] N.T. Wright's monumental *The Resurrection of the Son of God* seeks to show that the biblical authors and the early church did not mean for their claims about the resurrection to be read in metaphorical or spiritualizing—that is, merely figurative—terms. The fact that Wright thought it valuable to write the book demonstrates that there are some who would defend a metaphorical meaning to the claim "Jesus rose from the dead."

be adduced as grounds for the claim that God is happy, or that people in general should be happy, when infants are slaughtered.

There are doubtless many difficult passages that pose thorny interpretive problems for the literalist. It will discomfit many evangelicals to point out that if you are a radically consistent literalist, you should accept the real presence of the blood and flesh of Jesus in the Lord's Supper. After all, Jesus insists that "unless you eat the flesh of the Son of Man and drink His blood, you have no life in yourselves" (John 6.53 NASB). This hard case is amplified by the fact that Jesus' contemporary audience understood him to be speaking in literal terms amounting to something like cannibalism, so much so that many putative followers abandoned him (John 6.66).

However, Christians who emphatically defend literalism concede that the scripture is not universally susceptible to a straightforward or literal interpretation. Prominent Southern Baptist conservative pastor and two-time Convention president W.A. Criswell wrote a book defending literalism, *Why I Preach that the Bible Is Literally True*. He concedes that interpretation of scripture is necessary and denies that literalism commits him to patently false claims, such as taking as literal what the scripture clearly presents as figurative.[10] Similarly, the International Council on Biblical Inerrancy, a distinguished group of evangelical leaders formed in the 1970s-80s, produced a series of public statements and related publications defending the truth and authority of the scriptures. They assert that faithful interpretation of the scripture requires flexible consideration of genre and context.[11] This flexible approach is nonetheless properly *literal*, specified by the biblical author's intention:

> Interpretation should adhere to the *literal* sense, that is, the single literary meaning which each passage carries. The initial quest is always for what God's penman meant by what he wrote. The discipline of interpretation excludes all attempts to go behind the text, just as it excludes all reading into passages of meanings which cannot be read out of them and all pursuit of ideas sparked off in us by the text which do not arise as part of the au-

---

[10] Criswell, *Why I Preach*, 194–95.
[11] See especially International Council on Biblical Inerrancy, "Chicago Statement on Biblical Inerrancy," Articles XIII and XVIII and 9; "Chicago Statement on Biblical Hermeneutics," Articles X-XV.

thor's own expressed flow of thought. Symbols and figures of speech must be recognized for what they are, and arbitrary allegorizing (as distinct from the drawing out of typology which was demonstrably in the writer's mind) must be avoided.[12]

Both Criswell and the International Council identify their version of literalism as the "grammatical-historical method," roughly equivalent to standard traditional biblical interpretation prior to the hermeneutic revolution of the 1800s, which the Council describes as "the linguistically natural way to understand the text in its historical setting."[13] This approach emphasizes the intention of the author as embedded in a particular historical context (the "historical") and literary genre (the "grammatical"). It marks a method that can reasonably be called literal, even if it allows for figurative readings, because it takes as foundational the immediate common-sense meaning of the text. Further, it can be regarded as literal in the theological sense, avoiding figurative approaches that read a text in allegorical or figurative ways.[14] Through this approach, preachers and scholars insist that apparent confusions and potential contradictions of the biblical text can be resolved satisfactorily.[15]

The caution of scholars and pastors advocating for biblical literalism reveals an important point. The biblical literalism of hermeneutically sophisticated pastors and scholars is literal in the theological sense, that is, in the sense of generally eschewing allegorizing spiritual interpretations of the text. While practitioners of the historical-grammatical method of interpretation acknowledge that the scriptures often—perhaps even frequently—use figurative language, their view is that responsible interpreters will take as figurative *only* those passages of scripture that signal by their content or context that they are or must be read figuratively.

---

[12] "Chicago Statement on Biblical Hermeneutics," 7.

[13] "Chicago Statement on Biblical Hermeneutics," 7; Criswell, 190–96; see also Walter C. Kaiser and Moisés Silva, *Introduction to Biblical Hermeneutics*, 34–35, 193–94.

[14] See *Oxford English Dictionary* s.v. "literal," meaning II.5.a. The figurative interpretive approaches that emerged by the early church period and were codified in the medieval era included allegorical, moral, and anagogical as primary, though the general understanding was that figurative interpretations were dependent upon the literal (see Klein, Blomberg, and Hubbard, *Biblical Interpretation*, 23–45).

[15] For example, Criswell argues that the contexts of Jesus' remarks about the Lord's Supper rule out a literalist reading of the presence of his body and blood in the elements (*Why I Preach*, 122–23).

However, the caution of hermeneutically informed pastors and scholars exposes a related important point. Biblical literalism in its *literal* sense, the claim that the Bible can and should be read, word for word, in a simple nonfigurative sense, is *false*. That brings us to a thorny problem. Surely, only a small percentage of respondents to Gallup's surveys about biblical interpretation are professional pastors or theologians. That forces us to a disagreeable inference: many Americans emphatically hold a view of the Bible that is false. Put another way, our analysis of literalism yields two competing senses of "literal": a cautious, theologically informed and historically traditional reading that avoids taking scripture in allegorical ways versus a popular or unsophisticated literalism.

These two forms of biblical literalism are dramatically illustrated by the two primary antagonists of the famous Scopes "Monkey Trial," skeptic lawyer Clarence Darrow and evangelical politician William Jennings Bryan. Darrow observed of the Bible, "there isn't a human being on earth believes it literally." Strikingly enough, Bryan agreed with Darrow on this point, affirming only a qualified literalism: "I believe everything in the Bible should be accepted as it is given there; some of the Bible is given illustratively. For instance: 'Ye are the salt of the earth.' I would not insist that man was actually salt, or that he had flesh of salt, but it is used in the sense of salt as saving God's people."[16] Bryan's literalism is informed and cautious. By contrast, Darrow's target is unsophisticated literalism, which he dismisses abruptly. Darrow attacks the *rhetoric* of literalism as untenable, while Bryan clarifies that the *reality* of literalism is more nuanced.

Gallup's survey data shows that unsophisticated "rhetorical" literalism is in decline. At the same time, the Gibson-Sawyer exchange, and countless instances like it, illustrate that rhetorical literalism is stubbornly resilient. Why, we might ask, has the language of biblical literalism become so prevalent among Christian traditionalists, generally characteristic of a significant minority of evangelicals, and nearly universally associated with fundamentalists? Why have these commitments persisted as much as they have in the face of relentless public criticism and ridicule?

---

[16] *The World's Most Famous Court Trial*, 146, 285.

How and Why Did the Rhetoric of Biblical Literalism Arise?

The story of the rise of biblical literalism in modern America is essentially the story of the rise of fundamentalism, since biblical literalism is a key feature of Christian fundamentalism.[17] The primary catalyst for the rise of fundamentalism is the sense that Christianity's essential truth claims, practices, and moral commitments are being subjected to hostile assault or abandonment or experiencing widespread collapse. The century from the mid-nineteenth to the mid-twentieth centuries was a time of enormous cultural, social, political, and intellectual upheaval across the world that prompted many American Protestant Christians to believe that such a restoration of tradition was necessary.

The stage for the cultural and intellectual shifts of the late 1800s and early 1900s was set in early nineteenth century Europe with rationalist, romantic, and antisupernaturalist thinkers such as G.W.F. Hegel and Friedrich Schleiermacher and theologians such as David Strauss who emphasized historical and developmental processes in human culture, intellectual life, and theology. First, the developmental conception of human intellectual culture *historicized* truth, heightening the idea that truth could only be discerned by examining the dynamic processes of human social, cultural, and intellectual life. Second, this approach *naturalized* truth by undermining the distinction between empirical and contingent claims known through the senses and eternal transcendent truths apprehended through logic, philosophy, or revelation. At the popular level, these philosophical concepts manifested as a general notion of progress across all spheres of culture and society.[18]

Another critical factor in the intellectual culture of the 1800s was an increasing theological skepticism. A hallmark of the Enlightenment was a willingness to subject traditional theism to analysis, criticism, and even ridicule. While Hegel himself understood the apex of human spiritual evolution in terms of philosophically articulated German Protestant

---

[17] To be fair, Beale notes that fundamentalism is not *merely* literalism, but is rather marked by "the *unqualified acceptance of and obedience to the Scriptures*" (*In Pursuit of Purity*, 3). Such a characterization entails commitment to literalism.

[18] See Beale, *In Pursuit of Purity*, 78–80.

Christianity, philosophers and theologians after him took the notion of historicist developmentalism in different directions, arguing, for example, for an economic-social-political historical dialectic of humans toward communism (Marx) or for the idea that human ethical "values" were part of a long historical process that had descended into decadence and needed to be reversed or "transvalued" (Nietzsche). This contributed to a trend of intellectual secularization, what Nietzsche called the "death of God," that increasingly took a variety of forms: freethinking, theological innovation, agnosticism, and even militant atheism.[19]

A final intellectual development that radically altered intellectual life in the United States was the restructuring of colleges and universities as professional research institutions on the German model.[20] The older model of higher education in the United States was a liberal arts college focused on moral and theological formation, offering generalized training for non-academic professions or preparation for theological or legal studies. A series of reformers in the post-Civil War period introduced incremental changes to the older model that cumulatively amounted to a radical transformation, replacing focus on theological and character formation with emphasis on academic disciplines, the practice of scholarship, and the notion of the academic life as a profession. Their efforts were reinforced by a flood of American students who attended German universities in the late 1800s, received training in the German educational approach, and returned to the United States as professors and administrators in higher education.[21]

These general intellectual and academic changes generated ripple effects in academic theology. The historicist framework of Hegelian philosophy reoriented the study of biblical texts toward historical-critical hermeneutics, which stressed examination of the social and cultural processes at work in the production, assembly, and editing of the scriptures. This had the effect of naturalizing the scriptures, that is, treating the Bible

---

[19] Charles Taylor's monumental *A Secular Age* attempts to unravel the threads of this complex story. The idea of the "death of God" is scattered throughout Nietzsche's works, appearing most vividly in the parable of the Madman (*The Gay Science*, §125).

[20] This theme is a central claim of Marsden, *Soul of the American University*.

[21] See Marsden, *Soul of the American University*, 104.

just like any other book.²² At the same time, application of historicist assumptions to the New Testament Gospels sparked the search for the historical Jesus, the concrete historical figure stripped of the mythological and theological innovations supposedly introduced by the Gospel authors and the early church.

These currents together promoted the emergence of what we would now call theological liberalism, which was marked most significantly by a willingness to "spiritualize" or take as figurative key doctrinal claims of Christianity. Just as Hegel argued that the representations of art and religion could be transcended and made conceptually explicit by philosophy, liberal theologians reinterpreted such doctrines as the virgin birth, miracles, and the divinity of Christ as symbols or metaphors. Further, aspects of Christianity regarded as morally or scientifically questionable, such as the doctrine of eternal damnation or supposedly fantastic instances of miraculous divine intervention in nature, were reinterpreted or abandoned outright. Most significantly, theologians in this tradition promoted what we might call "social justice reductionism," in which the theological core of Christianity was gradually reinterpreted in social and ethical terms, yielding a reformulated Christianity that emphasized the "social gospel": social and ethical imperatives extracted from the Christian narrative.²³

Significantly, while changing scientific views were part of the cultural milieu in the late nineteenth century—Darwin's *Origin of Species* was published in 1859 and the *Descent of Man* in 1871—they do not seem to be primary catalyst for the emergence of fundamentalism. For most of the four decades after the publication of the *Origin* there was a wide range of Christian views about biological change that included both theologically liberal opponents of Darwin and theologically traditionalist Darwinians.²⁴ When statements of Christian "fundamentals" that needed defense from sustained attack began to emerge, they focused

---

[22] Beale, *In Pursuit of Purity*, 82–84; Marsden, *Soul of the American University*, 207.

[23] Beale, *In Pursuit of Purity*, 69–86; Marsden, *Soul of the American University*, 173–75, 207–8.

[24] Calhoun, "Christianity and Science," 61; Numbers, *The Creationists*, 16. Moore, *Post-Darwinian Controversies*, surveys the range of thinkers in this time; see also Beale, *In Pursuit of Purity*, 80–81.

on theological doctrines and principles of biblical interpretation. Perhaps the earliest known such statement, the 1898 Niagara Creed promulgated by the Niagara Bible Conference, affirmed fundamental theological commitments such as the inspiration and authority of the scriptures, human sin and redemption, the Christian's pursuit of holiness, heaven and hell, and millennial hope—precisely the sort of theological and doctrinal claims subject to liberal criticisms and reinterpretations. No threats from the scientific quarter are even mentioned.[25]

When in 1910 the Presbyterian General Assembly set out "Five Fundamentals," their list championed biblical inerrancy, key theological doctrines, and affirmation of miracles against antisupernaturalist skepticism.[26] Similarly, the set of ninety essays collected in twelve volumes and published from 1910–1915 called *The Fundamentals: A Testimony to Truth*, widely distributed to pastors and ministry leaders across the United States, targeted modernist patterns of biblical interpretation, including German-style higher criticism of the Bible and central Christian doctrines.[27] Articles in the collection aggressively defend the truth, authority, and inspiration of the scriptures, but they rarely employ the language of literalism except to call for literalist readings of specific biblical passages. Still more surprising, the collection features attacks on evolution, but also includes essays defending theistic evolution.[28] This fundamentalism did not emphasize the rhetoric of biblical literalism.

However, by the 1920s, especially in the United States, the cumulative force of challenges to orthodox traditional Christianity reached a breaking point. Ecclesiastically, traditionalists in mainline denominations lost ground to theological liberals, with the routing of traditionalist Presbyte-

---

[25] Beale, *In Pursuit of Purity*, Appendix A (375–79); see also 23–33. While the statement affirms the Divine inspiration of "every smallest word, and inflection of a word" (376), it does not use the word "literal."

[26] The Fundamentals were: "(1) the inerrancy of Scripture, (2) the Virgin Birth of Christ, (3) his substitutionary atonement, (4) his bodily resurrection, and (5) the authenticity of the miracles" (Marsden, *Fundamentalism* 147).

[27] Marsden notes, "The crucial issue seems rather to have been perceived as that of the authority of God in Scripture in relation to the authority of modern science, particularly science in the form of higher criticism of Scripture itself" (Fundamentalism, 151).

[28] Orr, "Science and the Christian Faith" and Wright, "The Passing of Evolution"; see also Moore, *Post-Darwinian Controversies* 70–73; Marsden, *Fundamentalism*, 153–54.

rians first in the overall governance of the denomination and then in the administrative control of Princeton University a particularly bitter set of blows.[29] J. Gresham Machen's *Christianity and Liberalism* (1923) sounded a clear battle cry, contrasting as "two totally diverse religions" traditional Christianity on the one hand and on the other the "religion of liberalism" that redefined and reconceptualized the central doctrinal claims of historic Christian orthodoxy as spiritual and moral principles.[30] While the contrasting words "literal" and "figurative" do not appear in Machen's book, he means to distinguish religion based on Jesus as the embodied agent of historical events with a symbolized spirituality: "the liberal theologian seeks to rescue certain of the general principles of religion, of which these particularities are thought to be mere temporary symbols, and these general principles he regards as constituting 'the essence of Christianity.'"[31] In Machen's view, the concrete and historical dimension of Christian orthodoxy is transformed by liberalism into something abstract, symbolic, diffused, and weak. However, that poor imitation was besting the original in the American religious mainstream. The end result of this process was a consensus of many scholars and pastors that Jesus did not rise from the dead and that the resurrection accounts in the scripture could, and indeed *should*, be interpreted in metaphorical and spiritualizing terms as a description of the hopeful fantasies of Paul and early Christians concerning the glorification of Jesus and the continued spiritual influence of Jesus over the church.

At roughly the same time, the natural sciences both in universities and U.S. government agencies were increasingly professionalized in a way that hardened the willingness to scientists to challenge public religiousness. While very hard to date precisely, at some point in the 1920s-30s Darwinian evolution and Mendelian genetics were unified in what eventually came to be known as the Evolutionary Synthesis, which reconceived biology as mechanistic, materialistic, deterministic, and therefore atheistic, thereby eliminating progressive and spiritual conceptions of

---

[29] Beale, *In Pursuit of Purity*, 153–64; Marsden, *Fundamentalism*, 1–3.
[30] Machen, *Christianity and Liberalism*, 109.
[31] Machen, *Christianity and Liberalism*, 6.

biological change.[32] Perhaps most importantly for public perception of Bible-science issues, the controversy burst into public attention with the Scopes "Monkey Trial" in 1925.

These changes gave traditionalist American Christians the undeniable sense that religiousness faced a polarizing dichotomy: orthodoxy or heresy, faithful or liberal theology, supernatural religion or naturalized mythology. The result was a hardened and more militant Fundamentalism that increasingly resorted to martial language to describe itself as embattled and under siege.[33] An important weapon in their arsenal was the rhetoric of biblical literalism, an emphatic way to affirm the truth of the concrete and historical aspects of Jesus' Incarnation and mission in the context of the whole counsel of the scripture.

Modes of Literalism, Intensive and Otherwise

The standard explanation for the hyperliteralism of fundamentalist and traditionalist Christians is defiant ignorance of the sort mocked by Darrow and Mencken. According to that story, only unlettered superstitious rubes would describe themselves as committed to the view that the Bible is the "actual word of God, and is to be taken literally, word for word." Is there an alternate reasonable explanation? Why have traditionalist Christians used the language of literalism when it is transparently clear that that the Bible is not literally true?

We might find a clue in the fact that the word "literally" is often itself *not* used literally. Consider these examples:

"I literally laughed my head off."

"After the long day's hike, they fell asleep literally dead to the world."

"The president and Congress were literally trading horses as they tried to work out a compromise."

As these examples demonstrate, "literally" has a well-attested use meaning "figuratively." The venerable *Oxford English Dictionary* ac-

---

[32] Provine, "Progress in Evolution;" Calhoun, "Christianity and Science," 61–65.
[33] Moore, *Post-Darwinian Controversies*, 70–76.

knowledges this shift, tracing this paradoxical use back as far as 1769.[34] Modern American grammarians and dictionaries note and sometimes decry this usage as controversial, since it reverses the primary meaning of "literally"—"truly," "actually," *not* figuratively—to mean "figuratively," its mirror opposite. Nonetheless, it is easy to see the appeal of this usage. In passages like these, the word "literal" functions as an *intensifier*, to emphasize what is being said. It is no surprise that this use has a long history, because it offers an important *rhetorical* tool for a speaker to emphatically affirm a claim.

Awareness of modernist challenges to Christianity in the early 1900s was largely confined to universities, seminaries, and academically trained pastors. Even if resources like *The Fundamentals* were distributed widely to Christian leaders, and even if there were debates about innovations in biblical interpretation among educated Christians, most "pew" Christians were unaware of developments like higher criticism, denial of miracles, or skepticism about the Resurrection.[35] Dramatic public events such as the 1925 Scopes trial along with more subtle shifts like control of denominations ended this period of innocence. As ordinary Christians became aware of liberal dismissals of Christian theological distinctives or were confronted with a supposed binary option between scientific innovations and the old-time religion of their forbearers, the rhetoric of literalism offered an attractive way to emphatically affirm the truth and authority of the Bible. Even now, dramas like the exchange between Mel Gibson and Diane Sawyer occur repeatedly in our culture. Ordinary Christians, when offered stark dichotomies of Bible or science, fable or fact, history or fantasy, affirm what is important to their lives as authoritative. Further, to the extent that they believe that the alternatives offered to them are misleading or distorted, they are likely to respond more and more emphatically.

While it is true that the rhetoric of biblical literalism can devolve into a wooden literalism, people who use the language of biblical literal-

---

[34] *Oxford English Dictionary* s.v. "literally" includes meaning I.1.c: "*colloquial.* Used to indicate that some (frequently conventional) metaphorical or hyperbolical expression is to be taken in the strongest admissible sense: 'virtually, as good as'; (also) 'completely, utterly, absolutely.'"

[35] See Newman, "Recent Changes in Theology of Baptists," esp. 608; Marsden, *Fundamentalism*, 134.

ism are no more committed to the belief that Jesus was asserting himself to be a literal door in John 10.7 than the person who laughs her head off risks suffering actual decapitation. Biblical literalists mean to affirm the truth and reliability of the Bible, not to assert that God rides cherubs or that Jesus thought Nicodemus could repeat his physical birth. The problem, however, is that *rhetorical* literalism easily transmutes into *selective* literalism. Even though I might recognize that Jesus' parables do not generally make factual claims, I might be tempted to think that Jesus' description of the mustard seed as "the smallest of all seeds" (Matthew 13.31–32 NLT) can or should be taken as literal, perhaps even *scientific*.[36] The problem is that selective literalism is, in the end, arbitrary, because it is motivated by proof-texting distortion of the scripture. Rather than scouring the scripture for passages that can be read as prefiguring modern scientific claims, we should, as principled literalists, carefully interpret the scripture in the light of its genre and historical contexts. Should Genesis 1–11 be read as historical narrative, as Young Earth Creationists advocate? Or should we heed William Lane Craig's argument to read it as "mytho-history"?[37] I won't try to resolve that question here, but we should acknowledge that arbitrary literalism underwritten by rhetorical literalism alone cannot answer the question.

The Bible, Literalism, Cosmology, and Science: A Cautionary Tale

Jews and Christians have held versions of at least three cosmologies from antiquity to the modern period: (1) the ancient near eastern cosmology of a flat disc earth covered by a heavenly dome; (2) the geocentric planetary model codified by the Alexandrian astronomer Ptolemy; and (3) the early modern heliocentric planetary model developed and defended by Copernicus, Galileo, and Kepler.[38] While the transition from the first

---

[36] The problem with this assertion, of course, is that the mustard seed is *not* the smallest of all seeds. However, this does not mean that Jesus makes false assertions in the parable. The parable is not a scientific description of nature, but is spiritual instruction about the nature of the kingdom. Selective literalists want to interpret the parable as literal or protoscientific, even if they know that doing so is problematic.

[37] Craig, *In Quest of the Historical Adam*, Parts 1–2, pp. 3–242.

[38] I say "at least" three cosmologies because it is not at all clear that (1), the Ancient Near East cosmology assumed in many of the biblical texts, constitutes a unitary shared view. On this point

to the second is obscured by history, an extensive documentary record exists for the move from the second to the third. As it turns out, biblical literalism played a significant role in resistance to adoption of Copernican heliocentrism.

Roman Catholic church leaders and many of the early Reformers were disinclined to embrace the new heliocentric cosmology when it was proposed by Copernicus in his book *On the Revolutions of the Heavenly Spheres* (1543). Some of the resistance was scientific: until Copernicus' theory was modified and adapted, most importantly by Kepler's proposal of elliptical orbits, the old Ptolemaic model provided more accurate predictions of planetary motion. But a significant part of the hostility to heliocentrism was motivated by the apparent conflict between heliocentrism and the fact that the scriptures seem to assume geocentrism, not only in the commonsense way that modern references to sunrise and sunset do (Ecclesiastes 1.5), but in specific claims that the sun moves about the earth, such as in the story of the battle of Gibeon (Joshua 10.12–13), or in claims that the earth is stable and motionless (Psalm 93.1; 119.90). Despite mounting scientific evidence for geokinesis from Galileo's telescopic observations, the intuitiveness of geostasis buttressed by the authority of the literalist interpretations by the Church Fathers led to formal rejection of heliocentrism by an Inquisition trial of Copernicus' book in 1616 and years later of Galileo for defense of heliocentrism in his book *Dialogue on the Two Chief World Systems* (1632).[39]

Biblical literalists in Galileo's day believed they were protecting the authority of the scripture against illegitimate assertions of ungrounded human wisdom. The Roman Catholic Church eventually acknowledged that Galileo was right and that prosecution of him was wrong.[40] While biblically motivated geocentrists can still be found lurking on the internet, modern

---

Pennington and McDonough observe: "the New Testament texts do not offer enough information to reconstruct a uniform 'early Christian view' of the physical universe" (*Cosmology*, 189); see Greenwood, *Scripture and Cosmology*; Adams, "Graeco-Roman and Ancient Jewish Cosmology"; Oden, "Cosmogony, Cosmology"; and Crouser, "Cosmology," for details regarding biblical cosmology.

[39] Galileo, *The Essential Galileo*, esp. 8–11, 103–178; Greenwood, *Scripture and Cosmology*, 169–81; Calhoun, "Christianity and Science," 55–58.

[40] John Paul II, "Address to the Plenary Session," §§5–12.

Christians overwhelmingly accept heliocentric cosmology both because they accept that the evidence for its truth is compelling and because they see that scripture can be reasonably interpreted to accommodate it.

We must be vigilant to ensure that our commitment to defend the authority and truth of the scripture does not entangle us in futile rejection of true claims about nature. That caution can help us see the limits of biblical literalism as we emphatically affirm the truth and authority of the scripture. Cosmologies come and go, but the word of God endures forever.

Bibliography

Adams, Edward. "Graeco-Roman and Ancient Jewish Cosmology." In Pennington, Jonathan T., and Sean M. McDonough, eds. *Cosmology and New Testament Theology*. London: T&T Clark, 2008.

Bartkowski, John. "Beyond Biblical Literalism and Inerrancy: Conservative Protestants and the Hermeneutic Interpretation of Scripture." *Sociology of Religion* 57, no. 3 (1996): 259–272.

Beale, David O. *In Pursuit of Purity: American Fundamentalism Since 1850*. Greenville, SC: Unusual Publications, 1986.

Brasher, Brenda E., ed. *Encyclopedia of Fundamentalism*. New York: Routledge, 2001.

Brenan, Megan. "Majority Still Credits God for Humankind, but Not Creationism." Gallup Politics, July 22, 2024. https://news.gallup.com/poll/647594/majority-credits-god-humankind-not-creationism.aspx.

Brown, Raymond E. "Hermeneutics." In *The Jerome Bible Commentary*, 2 vols. Ed. Raymond E. Brown, Joseph A. Fitzmeyer, and Roland E. Murphy. Englewood Cliffs, NJ: Prentice-Hall, 1968, vol. 2.605–23.

Calhoun, David H. "Are Christianity and Science at War with One Another?" *Journal for Baptist Theology & Ministry* 21, no. 1 (Spring 2024): 39–69.

Craig, William Lane. *In Quest of the Historical Adam: A Biblical and Scientific Exploration*. Grand Rapids, MI: William B. Eerdmans, 2021.

Criswell, W. A. *Why I Preach that the Bible Is Literally True*. Nashville, TN: Broadman Press, 1969.

Crouser, Wesley. "Cosmology." *Lexham Bible Dictionary*. Ed. John D. Barry. Bellingham, WA: Lexham, 2016.

"The Evolution of Pew Research Center's Survey Questions About the Origins and Development of Life on Earth." Pew Research Center, February 6, 2019. https://www.pewresearch.org/religion/2019/02/06/the-evolution-of-pew-research-centers-survey-questions-about-the-origins-and-development-of-life-on-earth/.

The Fundamentals: A Testimony to Truth. 12 vols. Chicago, IL: Testimony Publishing, 1910–1915. https://digitalcommons.biola.edu/the-fundamentals/.

Galilei, Galileo. *The Essential Galileo*. Ed. Maurice A. Finocchiaro. Indianapolis, IN: Hackett, 2008.

Gibson, Mel. "Mel Gibson's *Passion*. Interview by Diane Sawyer. ABC News Primetime, February 16, 2004.

Greenwood, Kyle. *Scripture and Cosmology: Reading the Bible between the Ancient World and Modern Science*. Downers Grove, IL: IVP Academic, 2015.

International Council on Biblical Inerrancy. "Chicago Statement on Biblical Hermeneutics." Dallas Theological Seminary, Special Collections, November 13, 1982. https://library.dts.edu/Pages/TL/Special/ICBI_2.pdf.

International Council on Biblical Inerrancy. "Chicago Statement on Biblical Inerrancy." Dallas Theological Seminary, Special Collections, November 7, 1978. https://library.dts.edu/Pages/TL/Special/ICBI-1978-11-07.pdf.

John Paul II, Pope. "Address to the Plenary Session on 'The Emergence of Complexity in Mathematics, Physics, Chemistry and Biology.'" Pontifical Academy of Sciences, October 31, 1992. https://www.pas.va/en/magisterium/saint-john-paul-ii/1992-31-october.html.

Kaiser, Walter C., and Moisés Silva. *Introduction to Biblical Hermeneutics: The Search for Meaning*, rev. ed. Grand Rapids, MI: Zondervan, 2007.

Klein, William W., Craig L. Blomberg, and Robert L. Hubbard, Jr. *Introduction to Biblical Interpretation*, rev. ed. Nashville, TN: Thomas Nelson, 2004.

Machen, J. Gresham. *Christianity and Liberalism*. New York: Macmillan, 1923.

Marsden, George M. *Fundamentalism and American Culture*, 3rd ed. New York: Oxford University Press, 2022.

———. *The Soul of the American University: From Protestant Establishment to Established Nonbelief.* New York: Oxford University Press, 1994.

Moore, James R. *The Post-Darwinian Controversies: A Study of the Protestant Struggle to Come to Terms with Darwin in Great Britain and America 1870–1900.* Cambridge: Cambridge University Press, 1979.

Newman, Albert H. "Recent Changes in Theology of Baptists." *American Journal of Theology* 10 (October, 1906), 587–609. https://www.jstor.org/stable/3154427.

Newport, Frank. "Fewer in U.S. Now See Bible as Literal Word of God." Gallup Religion, July 6, 2022. https://news.gallup.com/poll/394262/fewer-bible-literal-word-god.aspx.

Numbers, Ronald L. *The Creationists: From Scientific Creation to Intelligent Design,* expanded ed. Cambridge, MA: Harvard University, 2006.

Oden, Robert A. "Cosmogony, Cosmology." *The Anchor Bible Dictionary*, vol. 1. Ed. David Noel Freedman. New York: Doubleday, 1992. 1162–71.

Orr, James. "Science and the Christian Faith." In *The Fundamentals*, vol. IV, 91–104. https://digitalcommons.biola.edu/the-fundamentals/2/.

Pennington, Jonathan T. and Sean M. McDonough. *Cosmology and New Testament Theology.* London: T&T Clark, 2008.

Pius XII, Pope. *Divino Afflante Spiritu.* Vatican, September 30, 1943. https://www.vatican.va/content/pius-xii/en/encyclicals/documents/hf_p-xii_enc_30091943_divino-afflante-spiritu.html.

Provine, William B. "Progress in Evolution and Meaning in Life." In *Evolutionary Progress.* Ed. Matthew H. Nitecki. Chicago: University of Chicago Press, 1988, 49–74.

"Public's Views on Human Evolution." Pew Research Center, December 30, 2013. https://www.pewresearch.org/religion/2013/12/30/publics-views-on-human-evolution/.

Saad, Lydia. "Record Few Americans Believe Bible Is Literal Word of God." Gallup Social & Policy Issues, May 15, 2017. https://news.gallup.com/poll/210704/record-few-americans-believe-bible-literal-word-god.aspx.

The World's Most Famous Court Trial: Tennessee Evolution Case, 3rd. ed. Cincinnati: National Book Company. University of Minnesota Law Library: Clarence Darrow Digital Collection. https://librarycollections.law.umn.edu/darrow/trials_details.php?id=7

Wright, George Frederick. "The Passing of Evolution." In *The Fundamentals*, vol. VII, 5–20. https://online.flippingbook.com/view/409726/5/.

Wright, N.T. *The Resurrection of the Son of God*. Christian Origins and the Question of God, vol. 3. Minneapolis, MN: Fortress Press, 2003.

10

If God is Good, Why is There Evil and Suffering?

Brett Kunkle

I. The Question of Suffering

The reality of evil and suffering may pose the greatest single challenge to Christian theism: If God is good and all powerful, how is evil and suffering compatible with His existence? This objection certainly poses an intellectual obstacle to belief in God. But oftentimes, we're forced to confront this question when we experience evil and suffering *personally*. This was the case in my own life.

I was raised in a Christian home. I had a good upbringing by loving parents who were always active in the local church. At five years of age, I put my faith in Christ. After moving from the East Coast when I was in junior high, our family joined a fantastic church in Southern California, and that's where I met the Vasquez family.

Pastor Dan Vasquez was our pastor, and his son Danny was my best friend throughout junior high, high school, and college. Danny and I did everything together. We attended our church's weekly youth group programs, monthly youth events, and were student leaders together. Outside of church we would hang out all the time, hitting the beach to go surf, playing sports, and spending the night at each other's houses. In fact, we were born on the same day, so even birthday celebrations were done together. As a result, I was at the Vasquez home all the time, and this provided a "backstage" glimpse of the Vasquez family and of the personal life of my pastor, Pastor Dan. Far from the general cries of Christian hypocrisy, I was in a unique position to see that my pastor was the same man "off stage" that he was "on stage." And that's why Pastor Dan was beloved by our entire congregation.

Tragedy hit the Vasquez home our freshman year in college, as Pastor Dan was diagnosed with melanoma cancer. For the next year, our church watched Pastor Dan and his family battle cancer. Through the endless hospital visits, chemotherapy treatments, and radiation, the "ups" began to dwindle and the "downs" increased. The cancer was taking a tremendous toll on Pastor Dan's body.

I'll never forget the day we received an early afternoon phone call from the church secretary, informing us Pastor Dan had stopped breathing. The paramedics had resuscitated him and he was being rushed to the ICU. At this news we hurried to the hospital and soon thereafter, the visitor room began filling up with people from our church as word spread. All we could do was pray and wait.

Later that evening, I remember sitting just outside of the double-doors of the ICU, within earshot of Pastor Dan's room. I could hear the steady beeping of his heart monitor. And I remember, while sitting on the cold tile floor of the hospital, the piercing tone of his heart monitor as it flatlined. Pastor Dan had died. Immediately after, there was another sound, one I had never heard before. It was the sound of human wailing. His wife Bev, his daughters Jenny and Jody, and my best friend Danny were all in the room when Pastor Dan breathed his last. Overcome with grief, they cried, wept, and wailed.

At that moment, the problem of evil and suffering became more real to me than ever before. "God, if you are good, if you are loving, if you are all powerful and all knowing, why would you let this happen? Pastor Dan wasn't one of the bad guys. He was one of the good guys." My thoughts overwhelmed me. Here was a man who dedicated his life to God's work through the church. He sacrificed. He served. He was faithful. And yet,

God allowed Pastor Dan, his wife, his daughters, and my best friend to suffer through a painful, protracted, year-long battle with cancer.

The problem of evil and suffering was now deeply personal.

II. The Emotional Problem of Evil

C.S. Lewis wrote, "I believe in Christianity as I believe that the sun has risen, not only because I see it, but because by it I see everything else."[1] The parallel he draws between the sun and the Christian faith would eventually be of great help to me as I wrestled with the problem of evil. How do you know the "sun has risen"? Walk outside, look into the sky, and you will have direct evidence when your eyes meet the sun. However, I'm guessing that's not your regular routine. Instead, how do you most often come to know the sun is out? It lights up the world around you. You "see everything else." In the same way, if you look for it, you can discover direct evidence for the truth of Christianity. But there's another way we can know the truth of the Christian faith—it "lights up the world around us." It makes sense of reality. It has what philosophers call explanatory power. It provides coherent explanations that makes sense of the features of our world, including evil and suffering. And when it comes to these issues, Lewis was no stranger.

In 1940, he wrote a book entitled *The Problem of Pain*, in which he attempts to reconcile God's existence with the reality of evil. I think Lewis provides us with a powerful intellectual answer. However, if you're familiar with the details of his life, you know that later in life, Lewis married Joy Davidman. Their marriage was short lived as she passed away from cancer about four years later. Afterward, Lewis wrote a second book on the problem of evil entitled *A Grief Observed*. Same topic, very different book. In *The Problem of Pain*, Lewis dealt with the intellectual question. In *A Grief Observed*, we have a collection of his reflections, as he journals his way through the pain and grief of losing his wife. Here is a sample of his raw and unfettered thoughts: "But go to him. Go to God when your need is desperate. When all other help is vain. And what do you find? A door

---
[1] Lewis, *Is Theology Poetry?*, 165.

slammed in your face, and the sound of bolting and double bolting on the inside. After that silence."[2] In this second book, Lewis wrestles with his personal experience of evil and suffering.

These two books reveal two distinct problems when it comes to evil. The first, represented by *A Grief Observed*, can be called the emotional or existential problem of evil. This is the experience of evil itself. When evil touches our lives, it ceases to be a mere intellectual dilemma and thus, a different response is required.

As my best friend Danny was in the midst of losing his dad to cancer, I did *not* attempt to explain to him how God's existence was compatible with his suffering. I did *not* offer rational explanations for why God had allowed his dad to suffer and then die. I didn't quote Romans 8.28, assuring him God had a plan. I didn't offer an apologetic in response. Instead, I stopped talking. I listened. I cried with Danny. I hugged him. I mourned with him. The emotional problem of evil requires a relational response, where we walk with our friends and family through the valleys with gentleness, humility, and care.

III. The Intellectual Problem of Evil

The second problem is the intellectual problem of evil. There are two aspects: the logical problem and the evidential problem (sometimes called the probabilistic problem). For our purposes, we will not address the logical version but instead point you to the work of philosopher Alvin Plantinga in his book *God, Freedom and Evil*, where he provides a successful defense. As a result of Plantinga's work, much of the action has shifted to the evidential problem.

To understand this version, think about scales. One side of the balance represents the evidence for God, and the other is the evidence against Him. The skeptic will attempt to stack instances of evil—human suffering, child abuse, rape, war, slavery—to tip the scales against God's existence, concluding that given the amount of evil and suffering in our world, it is probably or most likely the case that God does not exist. In response,

---

[2] Lewis, *A Grief Observed*, 6.

the theist must stack evidence on the "for God" side of the scale to show that even in the face of real evil, it is more probable that God exists.

IV. Defining Evil

Sometimes the skeptic will raise the problem of evil this way: "Theists believe God created all things. Therefore, God created evil, as well. If this is true, then God is responsible for evil." This informal formulation of the problem surfaces an important question that must be answered first: what is evil? Here, analogies may prove useful in understanding the nature of evil.

Think about a donut hole. Have you ever eaten one? No, because in contrast to the round sugar ball of dough you may be envisioning at this moment, a donut hole properly defined is the absence of donut in the middle of one. It's the place in the donut where there is *no* donut!

What is a shadow? Can you pick up your shadow and show it to us? Obviously not because a shadow is not some *thing*, it's the absence of something. A shadow is the absence of light in a particular place. Or, what is blindness? Blindness is the absence of sight. Notice what we're referring to with these terms. They are all references to the *absence* of something.

In the same way, evil is not some *thing*. It's the absence of something. Evil is the absence of good. Evil is like a parasite; it is parasitic on goodness. You can have good without evil, but you cannot have evil without goodness. Evil is the absence of goodness. It is not something created or made. Therefore, God did not create evil. Evil is a corruption of the goodness He brought into existence. So, where does evil come from? Humanity.

V. The Free Will Defense

Our first response, the Free Will Defense, rightly recognizes that God creates human beings with genuine moral freedom. However, free will entails the possibility of evil. C.S. Lewis puts it this way: "God created things which had free will. That means creatures which can go wrong or right. Some people think they can imagine a creature which was free but had no possibility of going wrong, but I can't. If a thing is free to be good it's also free to be bad. And free will is what has made evil possible." God created human beings with moral freedom and their abuse of it brought evil into existence. Thus, God did not bring evil into existence, we did.

Lewis anticipates a follow up question:

> Why, then, did God give them free will? Because free will, though it makes evil possible, is also the only thing that makes possible any love or goodness or joy worth having. A world of automata—of creatures that worked like machines—would hardly be worth creating. The happiness which God designs for His higher creatures is the happiness of being freely, voluntarily united to Him and to each other in an ecstasy of love and delight compared with which the most rapturous love between a man and a woman on this earth is mere milk and water. And for that they must be free … If God thinks this state of war in the universe a price worth paying for free will—that is, for making a live world in which creatures can do real good or harm and something of real importance can happen, instead of a toy world which only moves when He pulls the strings—then we may take it it is worth paying.[3]

There are certain moral goods that can only be secured in a world of genuine human freedom. For example, a donation to charity is good if it is not coerced. If I hold a gun to your head and force you to give money against your will, your donation would not be morally praiseworthy. Why? Proper moral action is incompatible with coercion.

This brief summary of the Free Will Defense demonstrates that God is not responsible for evil. Proper blame belongs to human creatures who misuse their moral freedom. Thus, it provides us with a first response we can stack on the scales in God's favor.

VI. Morally Sufficient Reasons for Evil

Even if the skeptic is satisfied by our explanation concerning human freedom, he may raise a separate yet related objection: "God may not be the cause of evil, but if He is sovereign—in charge of the universe in some sense—at the very least, He has permitted it. Why would God *allow* evil?" Let me illustrate an answer to this challenge.

---

[3] Lewis, *Mere Christianity*, 52–53.

I'm the dad of five children. As a result, I've made numerous trips to the doctor's office with my kids. Sometimes, those visits can be painful ... for my kids. I recall taking my first son, Micah, to his doctor for his first checkup since his birth. He was just four months old at the time. The nurse took us to our room, and had us undress Micah down to his diaper and lay him on the doctor's table. She then proceeded to roll out a tray holding four syringes. Without hesitation, she plunged the first needle into Micah's chubby little thigh. He howled with pain. Three additional shots ensued, as well as more crying and screaming.

Now, if you were watching this scene unfold in the doctor's office, what would be your assessment? Would you conclude that I was an evil dad for allowing pain and suffering into my child's life? Of course not. You understand there are times it is morally permissible for a parent to allow some pain (getting stuck with a needle) to secure some greater good (protection from disease). In such cases, the parent has morally sufficient reasons to allow their child to experience pain and suffering.

In the same way, God may have morally sufficient reasons for permitting evil. Furthermore, since our human perspective is finite and extremely limited, we could never justifiably claim that God does *not* have good reasons for His allowance of evil in our world. Think of that four-month-old baby receiving a painful shot. Is the baby in any position to judge the moral status of the parent's action? No. Why? Because he doesn't have the requisite knowledge to make a proper judgment. If there is such a gap in knowledge between a child and a parent, imagine the gap between a finite human being and an omniscient God who sees and knows all things. As a result, we are in no position to determine whether God is justified or not in what He permits.

Furthermore, just because God permits pain and suffering, it does not follow that He is not morally good. C.S. Lewis puts it this way: "What do people mean when they say, I'm not afraid of God because I know he is good? Have they never even been to a dentist?"[4] A dentist may have morally sufficient reasons to cause you pain, which is not in-

---

[4] Lewis, *A Grief Observed*, 38.

compatible with him being a good man. Likewise, God may have good reasons for allowing evil and thus, this objection does not count against His good moral nature. Hence, we add an additional response to the side of the scales *for* God.

VII. The Problem of Good

I've played soccer all my life—in rec leagues since I was five, for my high school team, in competitive intramurals during college, and in men's and co-ed leagues since. I've always loved competing on the soccer pitch.

Imagine the following scenario at my next men's league game. I show up to the soccer field, but I'm running late and arrive just a few minutes before the game is supposed to start. While I'm sitting on our team's bench quickly trying to put on my socks, shin guards, and cleats, the referee gathers all players from both squads at the center circle for some opening instructions, which I miss. By the time I make it onto the field, the ref blows his whistle to signal the start of the match. A teammate passes me the ball, which I collect, and then start dribbling. An opposing player challenges me with a slide tackle. However, his cleats don't touch the ball. Instead, they proceed directly into the back of my calf, and I go down hard.

Lying there in pain, it dawns on me there was no whistle blown to signal a foul. I stand myself up and look around for a single person, the referee, and yell out, "Ref, why didn't you blow your whistle? Why didn't you call a foul?" The referee responds, "Oh, you were the player who missed the opening instructions at the center circle. Let me clarify. Both teams decided that they wanted to play tonight's soccer game with *no* rules."

Pause and consider the consequences of what the ref has just told me. In a soccer game where there are no rules, what happens to my appeal for a foul? It becomes irrelevant. Why? Well, in any game with no rules, there are no fouls. Take this illustration and apply it to the universe. In a universe where there are no rules, there are no "fouls." In other words, in a universe where there is no objective standard of morality—no moral values, laws or duties—there is no evil.

Yet, the problem of evil is generally the atheist's most prominent objection to God. In his book *The God Delusion*, Richard Dawkins, arguably the most well-known atheist in the world, writes this infamous line:

> The God of the Old Testament is arguably the most unpleasant character in all fiction. Jealous and proud of it. A petty, unjust, unforgiving control freak, a vindictive, bloodthirsty ethnic cleanser, a misogynistic, homophobic, racist, infanticidal, genocidal, filicidal, pestilential, megalomaniacal, sadomasochistic, capriciously malevolent bully.[5]

What is Dawkins essentially saying? God is evil. Or, using our sports analogy, God has committed foul after foul after foul. However, for this claim to be coherent, Dawkins must also believe there are objective rules. Remember, in a game with no rules, there are no fouls.

Thankfully, Dawkins has provided his view on these matters elsewhere. In his book *River Out of Eden*, he explains the implications of his evolutionary views regarding the universe. He writes,

> In a universe of electrons and selfish genes, blind physical forces and genetic replication, some people are going to get hurt, other people are going to get lucky, and you won't find any rhyme or reason in it, nor any justice. The universe we observe has precisely the properties we should expect if there is at bottom no design, no purpose, no evil and no good, nothing but blind, pitiless indifference.[6]

Do you see the contradiction? Here, Dawkins claims there is *no* good or evil. Instead, all we're left with is the "blind, pitiless indifference" of an impersonal universe. But in *The God Delusion*, he claims the God depicted in the Old Testament is evil. Those two views are incompatible. His own atheistic views about the nature of morality undermine his objection to God and therefore, Dawkins has a dilemma: (1) deny evil and discard his claim that God is evil or (2) affirm objective moral good and discard his evolutionary implications. Most skeptics will not choose (1) and deny the existence of evil. In doing so, they would lose one of their stronger arguments against God's existence. However, belief in the reality of evil raises an additional problem for the skeptic—the problem of good.

---

[5] Dawkins, *The God Delusion*, 31.
[6] Dawkins, *River Out of Eden*, 132–133.

Anyone attempting to identify particular examples of evil must first have a standard of goodness in place by which to measure whether any action is evil. C.S. Lewis, an atheist before his conversion, described this dilemma: "My argument against God was that the universe seemed to be cruel and unjust. But how had I got this idea of just and unjust? A man does not call a line crooked unless he has some idea of a straight line. What was I comparing this universe with when I called it unjust?"[7]

Evil is a departure from the way things ought to be. However, if there is a way things ought to be, then there is an objective moral law. But if there is an objective moral law, what best explains the existence of such a thing? Laws come from lawgivers. A Moral Law points to a Moral Lawgiver as the best explanation. Therefore, we can turn the objection of evil on its head, arguing that evil is powerful evidence *for* God's existence and not against it. And we have yet another reply to the problem of evil that favors God.

VIII. Additional Evidence

There's more we can say. We could employ the Soul-making Defense. Building on the argument that God has morally sufficient reasons for permitting evil, this response highlights one of those potential reasons: character development. God is not simply interested in human happiness defined along the lines of pleasurable satisfaction. He's more interested in the kind of people we are becoming and often, God uses evil and suffering, and the difficult circumstances that result, to form our character. Scripture makes this clear: "Consider it pure joy, my brothers, whenever you face trials of many kinds, because you know that the testing of your faith develops perseverance. Perseverance must finish its work so that you may be mature and complete, not lacking anything" (James 1.2–4 NIV). Romans 5.3–5 exhorts us to "…exult in our tribulation, knowing that tribulation brings about perseverance, and perseverance, proven character, and proven character, hope. And hope does not disappoint." Even though God is not responsible for bringing about evil, He's able to use evil in our lives for the greater purpose of shaping character.

---

[7] Lewis, *Mere Christianity*, 45.

We can say even more. Having an eternal perspective puts the moments of suffering into a different light. For those of us who have put our faith in Christ, an eternity of heavenly bliss awaits. But doesn't this perspective inform how we see individual instances of evil and our ability to endure them? This seems to be the Apostle Paul's argument in 2 Corinthians 4.17–18:

> For momentary, light affliction is producing for us an eternal weight of glory far beyond all comparison, while we look not at the things which are seen, but at the things which are not seen. For the things which are seen are temporal, but the things which are not seen are eternal.

In addition to all the specific answers to the problem of evil offered here, we have at least a dozen powerful arguments *for* God's existence. The arguments of natural theology—the cosmological argument, various design arguments, the fine-tuning argument, the moral argument—can be stacked on the scales, for God.

IX. The Problem of Evil is Everyone's Problem

Evil is not a problem for Christians alone. Every view out there must give an account of the reality of evil and suffering. You don't find the responses that I've provided satisfying? No problem. Provide us with your own superior explanations. Yes, even our atheist friends, who most often raise this problem for theism, need to explain to us how they account for evil in an atheistic universe.

Bertrand Russell, a famous British atheist philosopher and towering individual in the history of philosophy, is often quoted as saying, "No one can believe in a good God if they've sat at the bedside of a dying child." Russell tugs on the heartstrings with this example, attempting to make us feel the force of the objection. However, understanding this is a challenge for every worldview, I have been able to turn it on its head. Indeed, in a conversation with my atheist friend Ricardo, who lives in the Bay area, I directed Russell's question at atheism. I said, "Ricardo, as an atheist, what would you say at the bedside of a dying child?" I added a caveat, "And it has to be consistent with your atheistic worldview."

Ricardo is thoughtful, so he stopped and paused. He thought a while longer, before he offered his explanation: "Well, I guess I would have to say that crap happens." Yes, that was the heart of his explanation for evil.

I looked at him and said, "Ricardo, thank you." I thanked him sincerely because he offered me an intellectually honest answer, an answer consistent with his worldview. On atheism, where there "is no design, no purpose, no evil and no good," crap happens. And the universe doesn't care. Remember how Richard Dawkins put it? There's nothing but "blind, pitiless indifference." Our impersonal universe is entirely indifferent to your pain and suffering.

Now, after hearing the various accounts of evil and suffering, we must examine each one and determine which to be most satisfying, intellectually *and* emotionally; and the "crap happens" account is neither. The atheist's alternative is not better than the Christian's. Indeed, it is far inferior.

But not only does Christian theism provide a robust explanation of evil, it also provides a solution to the problem. What is the solution to evil and suffering? Jesus. Oftentimes, when we raise the problem of evil, we often refer to things that occur "out there" in the world. But Christianity tells us the primary source of evil is "in here." It's in my heart. It's in your heart. Evil lurks in every human heart. Jeremiah 17.9 describes our hearts this way: "The heart is deceitful above all things and desperately sick. Who can understand it?"

And only Christianity provides a solution to the problem: "To this you were called because Christ suffered for you, leaving you an example that you should follow in his steps. He committed no sin. He committed no evil, and no deceit was found in his mouth. When they hurled their insults at him, he did not retaliate. When he suffered, he made no threats. Instead, he entrusted himself to him who judges justly. He himself bore our sins in his body on the tree, so that we might die to sin and live for righteousness. By his wounds you have been healed" (1 Pet 2.21–24). The solution to your personal evil and mine is the cross of Christ, where God poured out his mercy on sinners by taking our punishment. And the final restoration is secured by Jesus' resurrection.

Following Pastor Dan's death, I remember the kind of conversations that Danny and I would have. Danny's faith in Jesus meant that while he certainly grieved the loss of his dad, he did so as one "not without hope" (1 Thess 4.13), because he knew one day we would see Pastor Dan again. He held fast to the hope of the resurrection.

In that incredible fifteenth chapter in the book of 1 Corinthians, Paul highlights the eyewitness testimony to Jesus' resurrection, addresses the implications, and speaks to the final resurrection. Regarding the latter, he writes:

> Now I say this, brethren, that flesh and blood cannot inherit the kingdom of God, nor does the perishable inherit the imperishable. Behold, I tell you a mystery. We will not all sleep, but we will all be changed in a moment, in the twinkling of an eye, at the last trumpet. For the trumpet will sound, and the dead will be raised imperishable, and we will be changed. But when this perishable will have put on the imperishable, and this mortal will have put on immortality, then will come about the saying that is written, Death is swallowed up in victory. O death, where is your victory? O death, where is your sting? The sting of death is sin, and the power of sin is the law, but thanks be to God, who gives us the victory through our Lord Jesus Christ. (1 Cor 15.50–57)

Pastor Dan's story did not end with his death to cancer. No, his death was "swallowed up in victory," because at the final resurrection, Dan's "perishable" earthly body will be replaced with an "imperishable" resurrected one, no longer bound and broken by sin. This future story is only made possible "through our Lord Jesus Christ." And that is why only the Christian account of evil and suffering can end with, "Amen."

Bibliography

Dawkins, Richard. *River Out of Eden: A Darwinian View of Life.* New York: Harper Collins, 1995.

Dawkins, Richard. *The God Delusion.* Boston: Houghton Mifflin Harcourt, 2006.

Lewis, C.S. *A Grief Observed.* New York: Harper & Row, 1961.

———. *Is Theology Poetry?* London: Geoffrey Bless, 1962.

———. *Mere Christianity.* New York: Simon & Schuster, 1996.

PART THREE

Scriptural Truth

God and Special Revelation

11

Discovering God's Goodness in the Hard Passages of Scripture

Matthew Tingblad

Several years ago, a young woman called me up to confess that she didn't believe God was real. This change of mind was really difficult, and she was hoping I could talk her back into belief.

Immediately, I started rehearsing apologetic arguments for God's existence in my head such as the Kalam Cosmological Argument, the Fine-Tuning Argument, and others. I reminded myself of the arguments against God's existence, like the problem of pain and suffering, and how Christians can respond. While these are excellent arguments to be familiar with, none of them prepared me for the conversation I was about to have.

I asked this woman, "What's holding you back from believing in God?" In a somewhat sheepish and sad tone, she responded, "Ah! Well, I want to believe in God… but… I just can't accept that God would command Joshua to destroy the Canaanites, or that he would send plagues over Egypt. Or what about hell? And what about all the confusing laws in the Old Testament?"

"Hold up," I interrupted. "You told me that you're struggling to believe in God, right?" "Yeah."

"Well, based on what you shared, it doesn't sound like the existence of God is your problem."

"What?"

"I'm serious!" I said. "It sounds to me like what's really bugging you, creating doubt and pulling you away from accepting God, is not that you don't think God is real. It's that you don't like God."

Silence. She hadn't thought about it that way before, yet this was exactly her issue. In fact, whenever I hear a struggling Christian or a skeptic explain themselves, almost always, the goodness of God is one of their most challenging barriers to the Gospel.

Indeed, if God is not good, then we have no way to relate to God in a meaningful way. Christianity would be incomprehensible and completely fall apart. As the famous 20th-century author Isaac Asimov once said, "Properly read, [the Bible] is the most potent force for atheism ever conceived."[1] He understood that many Christians open the Bible and see difficult stories of judgment and warfare. They see difficult teachings, such as the doctrine of hell or all the strict laws for the death penalty in the Old Testament. For many Christian readers, it's like we must turn off our conscience in order to make it through these hard passages of the Bible. If we take this approach, we will never be prepared to answer the tough questions people (like this young woman on the phone) are asking, nor are we reading God's Word as God intended.

It's time we look at these difficult passages and stories of the Bible square in the eye. In doing so, our goal cannot be to simply show that God is not as bad as it seems. God is good. Always good. Anything less than that is not the God of Scripture.

Space does not permit us to cover every bible difficulty, but we will explore three of the biggest challenges people encounter in the Scripture: the Law of God, the judgment of God, and the doctrine of hell. For a more thorough discussion of the challenging parts in Scripture, check out my larger work, *Why Did God Do That?*, published by Harvest House, available at store.josh.org and elsewhere.

---

[1] Cited in Jeppson, *Notes for a Memoir*, 58.

The Law of God

I remember when I set out to read through the Bible cover-to-cover as a young Christian. Things were going well for a while. I encountered familiar characters I learned in church, like Abraham, Noah, and Moses. Then I hit Exodus 20. This is where we find laws, and lots of them! Apart from a few stories sprinkled throughout, the Laws of God carry on all the way through the end of Exodus, and the next book, and the next book, *and* the next book! Many who set out to read the Bible give up in the law portion of Scripture because they grow tired of reading them all. But even if they have the endurance to push through, some of the laws come across as weird or offensive. For many, it seems as though God is a cosmic control freak, a micromanager, and a killjoy. How should Christians think about the laws (or "Law") of God?

Let's put the Law of God in context. The story of the Bible begins in the Garden of Eden, where the first humans, Adam and Eve, experience fullness of life in the presence of God. Everything is the way it's supposed to be. But then, Adam and Eve sin by eating the forbidden fruit. Because of sin, they are expelled from the Garden and expelled from life in the presence of God. From that point forward, the world is broken, and we still feel its effects today.

The great tragedy of the Garden was that Adam and Eve lost the presence of God. However, the story doesn't end there. In Exodus 19—one chapter before all the laws begin— something significant happens. God says to Moses, "I will come to you" (v. 9), and Moses leads the Israelites out to meet with God (v. 17). For the first time since the Garden, God is preparing to reestablish himself with his people. But there's a problem: people still sin, and God is still holy. So, what does God do? He gives laws for how Israel is to behave as a nation hosting his presence. God's act of lawgiving, therefore, is an act of God's goodness because his laws enabled a way for his people to live in his presence. It's as if the Garden of Eden is being restored!

True, many of the laws about how to build God's house, how the priesthood is to dress, how to make a suitable sacrifice, etc., don't make much sense to our ears. We could look at some good commentaries which help to show the sensibility behind many of them. But for our purposes, I don't think that is necessary. Suffice it to say that even if many of the laws don't make sense to us, they made sense to the Israelites, and they saw the Law as a wonderful thing. In fact, the longest song of praise recorded in the Bible (Psalm 119) is all about praising God who graciously gave us his commandments.

One reason the laws of God are so numerous is not because God is a control freak. It is because God is establishing a nation. We must remember where these laws appear in the context of Israel's history. God's people just came out of Egypt as former slaves. They had no government, they needed one, and governments need a lot of laws. Consider this: How many laws exist to govern the nation you live in? Quite a lot! Moreover, if our government has problems, most of us would say that our country needs *better* laws, not fewer laws. We believe this because we know that good laws are good things, and society is all the better with them.

If you take the time to read these laws, you will quickly discover that a great deal of God's concern was for the weak, the oppressed, and the marginalized. For example, Deuteronomy 24 shows God's love for widows and foreigners. Exodus 23 displays God's heart for justice and the needy. Deuteronomy 15 brings out the importance of generosity. Leviticus 19 offers protection for the elderly and the handicapped, as well as regulations for honest business.

Consider the 10 commandments (Honor God, honor your parents, don't murder, don't steal, don't lie, don't cheat on your spouse, don't be jealous of your neighbor's stuff, etc.) Ask yourself: would our world be better off if everyone obeyed these commandments? Absolutely! As Jesus rightly pointed out, the Law of God boils down to the commandment to love God and love your neighbor (Mt 22.34–40). God is not trying to be a cosmic killjoy. He's trying to show us the way of life! The laws of God, then, do not tarnish the goodness of God; they magnify it.

Even still, some laws of God appear to be offensive or inappropriate. For many, the problem of slavery in God's law is a strong hurdle. The issue is already covered extensively by Paul Copan in this volume, so we will look briefly at a different matter: the death penalty.

While some people (particularly in America) believe that the death penalty is appropriate in some circumstances, few would think it is appropriate for all the circumstances discussed in the Law of God. Cases that call for the death penalty include practicing sorcery (Ex 22.18), adultery (Lev 20.10), having sex with an animal (Ex 22.19), and unauthorized touching of holy things (Num 4.15). Seems a bit harsh, don't you think?

It helps to realize that the Law of God may not be as rigid as we tend to think. In our modern world, the idea of *law* is strict and absolute. In the Old Testament, the Hebrew word for law, *Torah*, is usually better translated as *instruction* or *teaching*. Back then, such "law" writings were not interpreted the same way as we interpret today's legal systems. The Old Testament Scholar John Goldingay points out that, in the Old Testament world,

> When a king lays down a set of statutes, it doesn't mean they become the basis of legal practice. They are rather a collection of indications of the kind of moral and social norms that the king claims to be committed to. The Old Testament operates on a parallel basis. "Laws" that prescribe execution for murder, adultery, idolatry, and a long list of other acts are markers of the kind of religious, moral, and social commitments that God expects his people to accept. They are indications of how serious these offenses are.[2]

Curiously, the death penalty applies to about 15 offenses in God's law, but for one of these offenses—premeditated murder—we are told that no ransom or substitute would be allowed (Num 35.31). This implies that, for the other cases of the death penalty, death could be averted with a ransom or a different penalty. If this was indeed possible, you can expect it would have happened virtually every time!

Even still, we can't pretend that the death penalty was never actually executed. (Just ask Jesus!) For many, it remains a problem. If we are to understand the issue completely, we need to spend time on the next big Bible difficulty to be discussed in this chapter—the judgment of God.

---

[2] Goldingay, *Old Testament Ethics:* 5.

The Judgment of God

You may have felt that God in the Bible, especially in the Old Testament, doesn't make sense. Sometimes God presents himself as loving and compassionate (Ex 34.6–8). Other times, God appears as a cruel, hot-tempered overlord sending plagues, killing people, and commanding other people to kill people. These are stories of God's judgment. They include the plagues of Egypt, the destruction of Sodom and Gomorrah, the Canaan wars, and the flood of Noah. (Let's be real. Genesis 6–8 is not a happy story of an old man with a beard on a floating petting zoo!)

Most of us understand that judgment can be a good thing if it's done properly. If I stole money from an orphanage, there is a deep longing inside of us that something must be done. This "something" is a proper judgment. In court, we want a *fair trial* because we want a *fair judgment.* So, the problem is not that God issues judgment but that we think his judgment is way too severe. Too overkill. (Literally!)

What if you were fined $350 for slapping someone? You might say that the punishment was too severe. But what if the person you slapped was the king of England? That changes things! You might even wonder if $350 was severe enough. The example helps to show that the severity of one's judgment is not just determined by the offensive act. It is also determined by the *offended.* If I assaulted a 46-year-old businessman, I would deserve a certain kind of punishment. If I assaulted a 46-year-old uniformed navy officer, I would deserve a different kind of punishment. *What if our problem with the severity of God's judgment is not that God overestimates the offense, but because we underestimate who God is and what it means when we sin against him?*

As readers of the Bible, we encounter difficult stories of judgment from God. This same text, however, gives greater context for how we are to understand judgment because it tells us something important about God, whom we offend with our sins. We are told that God is *holy* (Ex 15.11, Lev 10.3, Ps 22.3).

In Isaiah 6, the prophet Isaiah encounters God in his holiness. What did Isaiah do here? Did he take the opportunity to complain to God about all the terrible things happening in his day? (There were many!) No. To the contrary, Isaiah cried out, "Woe is me! For I am lost; for I am a man of unclean lips, and I dwell in the midst of a people of unclean lips; for my eyes have seen the King, the LORD of hosts!" (Is 6.5, ESV). When Isaiah encounters the holiness of God, it's as if he is suddenly stripped naked and sees a fuller picture of his sin.

God's holiness is difficult to define, but it's the kind of thing that makes *whatever that was* come out of Isaiah. You might say that to call God holy is to speak of God as infinitely sacred and utterly set apart from all things impure—far more than we could possibly comprehend. So, when people commit an offense against God by their sin, their offense is far more severe than we could possibly comprehend. When God issues judgment, then, we can say that God's judgments are rightly given. They are not too severe. That's exactly what we would want for a good judge, and that is a *good thing*!

Yes, God's judgment puts us in a bad spot, but that's our problem, not God's. Think of it this way: If we placed a good judge to render judgment over a deeply immoral society, and if this judge was uncompromising to the perfect standard of rightness, the people of that society wouldn't like it. They might mistakenly think that this good judge is bad because their standard of goodness is so low. Likewise, we may think God to be a bad judge, but that's because his holiness is far purer than we can stomach.

If we can wrap our heads around the severity of sin and God's holiness, everything changes. No longer are we surprised to see God acting according to his holiness. That's expected. Because of sin, we are not even entitled to the very air we breathe! What surprises us is when God acts according to his mercy. The only reason we don't see this is because we underestimate the holiness of God, and we take his mercy so much for granted!

For example, 2 Kings 25 speaks about the exile of Israel. The Bible is clear that this was a judgment from God. Everything about it was horrible. The people were starving and trapped by the terrifying armies of Babylon. They breached the walls, stormed inside, ripped families apart, and dragged out many Jews who would live the rest of their lives as captives in a foreign land. Decades later, a small group of surviving Jews are finally set free to return to their city, still in ruins. After they return, the prophet Ezra prays to God, saying, "What has happened to us is a result of our evil deeds and our great guilt, and yet, our God, you have punished us *less than our sins deserved* and have given us a remnant like this" (Ez 9.13, NIV, emphasis mine). Ezra sees mercy because he knows who God is and he knows the severity of our sin committed against Him. If the Bible is true with all its challenging stories of judgment, then this passage is also true. God was merciful because God is good.

In speaking of God's judgment, we must not forget a crucial point: just as a good judge does not delight in sentencing criminals to prison, neither does God enjoy executing judgment. According to Ezekiel 33.11, "Say to them, 'As surely as I live, declares the Sovereign LORD, I take no pleasure in the death of the wicked, but rather that they turn from their ways and live. Turn! Turn from your evil ways! Why will you die, people of Israel?'" (NIV). Likewise, Lamentations 3.32–33 says, "Though [God] brings grief, he also shows compassion because of the greatness of his unfailing love. For he does not enjoy hurting people or causing them sorrow" (NLT). That last sentence, more literally, says in Hebrew that God does not afflict "from his heart." We must take these verses with us whenever we encounter difficult stories of judgment in the Bible.

Think back to the Canaan wars in the book of Joshua, arguably the prime example of judgment and bloodshed in the Bible sanctioned by God. The Canaanites were cruel, vicious people who sacrificed children. Yet, in mercy, God waited four hundred years before he commanded Joshua to destroy them (Gen 15.13–16). Even then, the first story in the Canaan wars was not a story of judgment. It was a story of mercy, the story of Rahab in Joshua 2. Her story informs the reader that the Canaanites knew about Israel's God, they heard the stories of God's power, they knew God's army was coming to destroy them, and (most importantly) even a prostitute could receive mercy.

Does it surprise you that the story of Rahab comes first? Maybe the real tragedy of the Canaan wars is that they didn't want mercy.

Jonah's story is another example of God's heart concerning judgment. By God's command, Jonah prophesied judgment over Ninevah, but the people repented. No judgment. Evidently, these judgments were delivered as a warning so the people would have a chance to repent.

As we have seen, our sin makes it so that God's judgment can't possibly be overly severe. Anything less than maximum severity is mercy. Moreover, whenever judgment looms in the Bible, mercy reaches out. We'll never see the extent of God's goodness in judgment unless we approach the Bible holistically, taking all the theological framework into account. That's when we start to realize that even in judgment, God reveals himself as good.

The Doctrine of Hell

If any subject in the Bible is to be crowned the most difficult of them all, my bets go to the doctrine of hell. The traditional view of hell, the view which I find to be most convincing from Scripture, is that those who die having rejected God will go to a place of eternal conscious punishment.

For many, eternal conscious punishment in hell is painful even to think about. Most of us know loved ones who have passed away, and we don't know if they received Christ in the final moments of their lives. It's hard to imagine that any of them could ever wind up in a place like hell. However, as we venture into this difficult arena, take heart. I find that our challenge with hell is not the doctrine itself, but how it has been misunderstood.

What comes to mind when you think of hell? For many, we imagine something like those medieval paintings of a fiery, underground torture chamber where Satan and his demons plunder the souls of their victims, screaming in agony. Now that they know God is real, they say they're sorry, and they want to get out. But alas, it's too late for them! We might even imagine God sitting on a cloud, looking down in pleasure like some sort of vengeful monster as they writhe in agony.

This view of hell, this view of God, even, is about as horrifying as it is wrong.

Hell is not a pleasant place by any stretch of the imagination. But when the Bible discusses the eternal destiny of the unsaved, it doesn't speak that way. In fact, it might surprise you to know that, as much as we ponder what hell might be like, the Bible tends to focus on a different issue: *where is hell located?* As you will soon see, by understanding *where* hell is, we will be in a better position to understand what hell is like, and how God could possibly be good because of it.

Some people like to point out that hell never appears in the Old Testament. While the word for hell is not in the Old Testament,[3] the concept certainly is. At the end of Isaiah, we are told of the final destinies of humanity. There's a city where God and his people dwell, but when people go outside that place, they see dead, burning bodies eaten by worms that never die (Is 66.24). You guessed it—that's hell.

Fast forward to the New Testament. When Jesus talks about hell, he often uses the word Gehenna. Gehenna was an actual area with a physical location just outside the city of Jerusalem. It was an awful place where people did tremendously evil things, and it served as the dumping ground for burning garbage and dead bodies of criminals.[4] So, once again, we have this illustration where there's a city of God, Jerusalem, and outside that city is where we find hell.

Fast forward some more to Revelation 20 and 21. Jesus returns. All the dead are raised. The heavenly city of God descends and is established here on Earth, but only those saved by God's grace can enter the city. The others are said to be cast into a lake of fire, outside the city.

So, where is hell located? It's located *outside the city*. Hell is banishment! That's its defining feature. If the Garden of Eden is to be understood as life in the presence of God, we might say that hell is precisely *not that*. Hell is horrible because it is death and separation from relationship with God. As Paul told the Thessalonians, "They will be punished with eternal destruction, forever separated from the Lord and from his glorious power" (2 Thess 1.9, NLT).

If hell is understood as banishment, as I am arguing for, we are ready to ask how the doctrine of hell displays the goodness of God. I'll mention two reasons.

---

[3] The KJV often translates the Hebrew word "Sheol" as hell, but Sheol and hell are not the same thing.
[4] Elwell and Beitzel, "Gehenna," in *Baker Encyclopedia of the Bible*.

First, if the agony of hell is the loss of God's presence, then hell only makes sense if there is something good and beautiful about God that is lost. So, hell, *by definition*, requires that God is good. God is so good that life without God is living hell. Second, when we understand hell as separation from God, it becomes apparent that hell is the ultimate end of what people had already chosen on earth. If they don't want God, God respects their wish, but he also respects their life and grants them a place where they can spend the rest of their existence elsewhere.

Don't misunderstand me: hell is still a punishment! But it is the kind of punishment where God gives people over to their own self-destructive desires. We see that type of punishment elsewhere in Scripture, like Ezekiel 23.9, Psalm 81.12, and, most famously, Romans 1.24.

The late theologian J.I. Packer put it this way:

> Scripture sees hell as self-chosen; those in hell will realize that they sentenced themselves to it by loving darkness rather than light, choosing not to have their Creator as their Lord, preferring self-indulgent sin to self-denying righteousness, and (if they encountered the gospel) rejecting Jesus rather than coming to him (John 3.18–21; Rom 1.18, 24, 26, 28, 32; 2.8; 2 Thess 2.9–11). … from this standpoint hell appears as God's gesture of respect for human choice. All receive what they actually chose, either to be with God forever, worshiping him, or without God forever, worshiping themselves.[5]

Leave it to the theologians to give such a mouthful of a statement! You might prefer a short and sweet version of the same idea by C.S. Lewis. He says, "There are only two kinds of people in the end: those who say to God, 'Thy will be done,' and those to whom God says, in the end, 'Thy will be done.'"[6]

If this is the view of hell we take, how do we understand the fire? Many people struggle with the fire of hell because fire seems to be used as a method of torture. But here's the thing: fire is not the only description we have of this place. Hell is also described as a place of darkness (Mt 8.12), where "the worm does not die" (Mk 9.48). Revelation calls it a lake (Rev 19.20) and the "second death" (Rev 20.14). Jesus speaks of hell as a

---
[5] Packer, *Concise Theology*, 262–263.
[6] Lewis, *The Great Divorce*, 506.

furnace (Mt 14.32). Paul speaks of it as destruction (2 Thess 1.9). Given the wide array of descriptive terms for hell in the Bible, it appears that hell is presented to us figuratively rather than literally. At the very least, we can't take *everything* literally. Literal fire would give off light, but hell is also a place of darkness.

Likewise, I find the lake of fire in Revelation is to be understood figuratively. It almost *has* to be. After all, death is thrown into the lake (Rev 20.14). You can't literally pick up death, as if death has size and weight to it, and throw it somewhere. So, it's clear that the lake is part of a metaphorical picture being told in Revelation (a book whose apocalyptic genre is known for communicating through figurative language).

To be clear, I am not trying to soften the intensity of hell by arguing for a figurative understanding of fire. The agony of hell is separation from God, and fire is an appropriate illustration of its intensity. That's why the Bible uses fire. The reason for seeing hellfire as figurative is because it helps us understand that hell is not intended for *torture*. We might even say that the fire of hell was lit by human hands.

We may think, "Ah, but if only someone could experience a moment of hell, they would immediately change their ways and want out! How could God keep them in there if their minds are changed?" I'm not so sure people change their minds in hell and become repentant. Look at the story of the rich man and Lazarus in Luke 16. Both men die. The rich man goes to the place of fire. Lazarus goes to heaven. The rich man sees God's servant Abraham in the distance, but he doesn't say to Abraham, "Get me out of this place!" He says, "*Send Lazarus over here* to dip the tip of his finger in water and cool my tongue" (Lk 16.24, NLT, my emphasis). That's telling! Even in that horrible place, the rich man would rather be served like in his prior life than to be brought up into the place of God's presence. The doctrine of hell does not give us an evil god torturing people who never chose to worship him. This is a righteous and merciful God respecting the decisions of those who never wanted to.

As hard as it is to imagine people going through so much agony, I suspect, similar to C.S. Lewis, that if they had the chance to visit heaven, they would want to go back to hell.[7] Their hearts are just not in a place to enjoy God's presence. Also, let's not forget what we learned about the judgment of God. If we died and saw God in his perfect, holy light and splendor, and if, at the same time, we saw the deep, dark depravity of our own sin committed against this holy God, we would be like Isaiah when he cried out, "Woe is me! For I am lost!" If this happened, I don't think God would send us to hell. I think we would escort ourselves.

Once again, Packer offers helpful insight: "Those who are in hell will know not only that for their doings they deserve it but also that in their hearts they chose it."[8] Yes, hell is a hard doctrine and always will be. But hopefully, you can start to see that even when we really dig into the doctrine of hell, the goodness of God is not far to be found.

Three Things to Remember

We have covered a lot in this chapter. We talked about laws. We talked about judgment. We talked about hell. In all this, I tried to demonstrate that these challenging parts of the Bible do not diminish the goodness of God. They proclaim it. If space permitted, we could continue on to many other difficult topics. There are answers for all of them. Even still, at the end of the day, some things will just be very difficult to understand. So, let's land the plane with three important principles to remember when we encounter *any* part of Scripture that challenges our understanding of God's goodness.

First, the Bible tells us explicitly, many times over, that God is good (1 Chr 16.34, Ezek 3.11, Ps 86.5, Nah 1.7, etc.). There is absolutely no ambiguity from Scripture about this, and there are no passages whatsoever that explicitly teach God is not good. So, if the Bible is true, God is good. Period. We may still struggle with laws, judgment, hell, or many other challenging passages or doctrines. But why do we struggle? Because we take them to be true. So, if the Bible is true, and the Bible teaches that God is good, then the only logical way to think about those challenging

---

[7] This is a recurring theme in Lewis's imaginative story *The Great Divorce* where people in hell get to visit heaven.

[8] Packer, *Concise Theology*, 263.

parts is to know there are answers to them that fit into the goodness of God. Even for skeptics—to say that the Bible teaches God is *not good* is utterly impossible without cherry-picking around the clearest affirmations of God's good character. But for Christians, if we seek to understand how God is still good despite difficult passages—even if things feel a little forced at times—we are doing exactly what the Bible encourages us to do. We are reading the Bible rightly.

Second, it makes sense that we wouldn't understand it all. Higher creatures have a higher perspective of reality. A spider doesn't understand the deep things of a dog, a dog doesn't understand the deep things of a human, and a human doesn't understand the deep things of God. God says in Isaiah 55.9, "For just as the heavens are higher than the earth, so my ways are higher than your ways and my thoughts higher than your thoughts" (NLT). So, it makes sense that not everything makes sense! I'm not saying the challenging parts of the Bible must be surrendered to the cheap, dismissive statement that "God works in mysterious ways," but reason only takes us so far. Still, there are enough parts we can understand to reasonably give God the benefit of the doubt for the parts we don't understand.

Lastly, as we have seen, a good God has good reasons for the challenging stories and doctrines in the Bible. But something has gone wrong. The laws of God in the Old Testament were meant to bring life, but instead, they became burdensome. The holiness of God was meant to be beautiful to behold. Instead, we have invoked judgment. Hell was made for Satan and his demons (Mt 25.41); God never wanted to send people there! What happened?

Sin happened. Sin is the poison that dissolves the human heart, corrupts our world, and alienates humanity from God and from each other. But God so loved the world, that he gave his one and only son. His name is Jesus. He came down. He lived and suffered among us. He looked upon all the burdens of the law. He looked upon judgment. He looked upon hell. Ultimately, Jesus looked upon sin. He saw what all of this was doing to us, and he stretched out his hands to be nailed across that wooden beam as if to say, "Over my dead body."

Jesus did this because God is good. Always good. No exception. There is nothing in the Bible we need to be ashamed of. So, we can tell our family and friends that God is truly good. We can show them that, properly read, the Bible is the most potent force for the Gospel ever conceived!

Bibliography

Asimov, Janet. *Notes for a Memoir on Isaac Asimov, Life, and Writing.* New York: Prometheus, 2006.

Butler, Joshua Ryan. *The Skeletons in God's Closet: The Mercy of Hell, the Surprise of Judgment, the Hope of Holy War.* Nashville: Thomas Nelson, 2012.

Copan, Paul. *Is God a Moral Monster? Making Sense of the Old Testament God.* Grand Rapids, MI: Baker, 2011.

Elwell, Walter A., and Barry J. Beitzel. "Gehenna." *Baker Encyclopedia of the Bible.* Grand Rapids, MI: Baker, 1988.

Goldingay, John. *Old Testament Ethics: A Guided Tour.* Downers Grove, IL: IVP, 2019.

Kaiser, Walter C. *Toward Old Testament Ethics.* Grand Rapids, MI: Zondervan, 1995.

Lamb, David T. *God Behaving Badly: Is the God of the Old Testament Angry, Sexist and Racist?* Downers Grove, IL: IVP, 2022.

Lewis, C.S. *The Complete C. S. Lewis Signature Classics.* New York: Harper Collins, 2007.

Morales, L. Michael. *Who Shall Ascend the Mountain of the Lord? A Biblical Theology of the Book of Leviticus.* New Studies in Biblical Theology 37. Downers Grove, IL: IVP, 2015.

Packer, J. I. *Concise Theology: A Guide to Historic Christian Beliefs.* 1st ed. Carol Stream, IL: Tyndale House, 2011.

Tingblad, Matthew, and Josh McDowell. *Why Did God Do That?* Eugene, OR: Harvest House, 2023.

12

Cleverly Devised Myths?
The Historical Reliability of the Gospels and Acts

Nathan Ward

> *For we did not follow cleverly devised myths when we made known to you the power and coming of our Lord Jesus Christ, but we were eyewitnesses of his majesty.* (2 Pet 1.16, ESV)

One of the best known starting points in arguments for the deity of Christ is the trilemma C.S. Lewis made famous in *Mere Christianity*. Lewis urges,

> I am trying here to prevent anyone saying the really foolish thing that people often say about Him: I'm ready to accept Jesus as a great moral teacher, but I don't accept his claim to be God. That is the one thing we must not say. A man who was merely a man and said the sort of things Jesus said would not be a great moral teacher. He would either be a lunatic—on the level with the man who says he is a poached egg—or else he would be the Devil of Hell. You must make your choice. Either this man was, and is, the Son of God, or else a madman or something worse. You can shut him up for a fool, you can spit at him and kill him as a demon or you can fall at his feet and call him Lord and God, but let us not come with any patronizing nonsense about his being a great human teacher. He has not left that open to us. He did not intend to.[1]

The simple logic behind this argument—Jesus is either right or wrong; if right He is Lord; if wrong, He either knew it and lied or did not know it

---

[1] Lewis, *Mere Christianity*, 52. Cf. Haygood, *The Man of Galilee*, 93–97.

and was a lunatic—is powerful and compelling. To that trilemma, however, skeptics have added a fourth L, suggesting that Lewis had not exhausted the possibilities. Jesus, they suggest, may be legend. What if Jesus never existed at all—or if the Jesus who did exist is nothing like the Jesus we read about in the Bible? How can we have confidence in the documents that purport to tell His story? If it can be maintained that Jesus was legend, Lewis' trilemma breaks down.

To the classic trilemma about Christ, Tim McGrew adds a new trilemma concerning the nature of the authors who tell Jesus' story. McGrew argues that they are deceivers, dupes, or direct witnesses.[2] They have either chosen to deceive us, they were fooled into believing something that untrue, or their writings are an accurate representation of eyewitness testimony.

But how might one judge such a thing? There are a variety of criteria proposed to measure historicity. Boyd and Eddy list ten[3] and Evans has seen as many as twenty-five (though he only reviews the six he thinks are best).[4] Although this chapter does not allow for the inclusion of all such tests, it will seek to establish that the Gospels and Acts are highly credible historical documents, based on eyewitness testimony, and that, "When evaluated by the same criteria critical historians typically use to evaluate ancient documents, the Gospels give us many reasons to conclude that the image of Jesus they present is historically reliable."[5] If this can be shown, then the fourth L suggested by critics is not viable and the classic trilemma concerning the deity of Christ stands.

---

[2] T. McGrew, "The Gospels and Acts as History." YouTube. December 7, 2011. Accessed April 11, 2025. http://youtu.be/JAPG3eECaxw.

Tim McGrew's work in historical apologetics has been formative in my thinking on the matter. This chapter was originally to be written by Tim, and I am humbled to step into his place and provide what is certainly an inferior replacement. In the years since I first got to know him and hear him speak on Gospel historicity, his wife Lydia has taken the baton and written extensively on the matter, including four books my own company has published. I am honored to have published her books and blessed to count Tim and Lydia among my friends. My hope is that this essay approaches doing justice to the topic.

[3] Boyd and Eddy, *Lord or Legend*, 77–79. For a far more robust version of their argument, see Eddy and Boyd, *The Jesus Legend*.

[4] Evans, *Fabricating Jesus*, 48–51.

[5] Boyd and Eddy, *Lord or Legend*, 77.

The Historicity of the Gospels and Acts

The Internal Claims. A question preliminary to measuring the accuracy of the documents concerns their nature: are they historical documents? One test of this is self-evident: do they claim to be historical? Luke's purpose statement (1.1–4) is clearly historical. Matthew and Mark do not contain purpose statements, but they are undeniably of the same genre as Luke; if Luke is historical, all the Synoptics are. John's purpose statement (20.30–31), while more theological than historical, is rooted in the historical foundation of the narrative itself: John wants his readers to believe, but their belief is to be based on the accounts he has relayed.[6] All four Gospels, then, intend to convey an accurate history. While the claim itself is not sufficient to prove historicity, it is essential.

Undesigned Coincidences. A stronger argument for the historicity of the Gospels can be found in the undesigned coincidences in the narrative. The Gospels often tell the same stories, but never do so identically. Sometimes they interlock, incidentally touching on overlapping details. An undesigned coincidence is "a notable connection between two or more accounts or texts that doesn't seem to have been planned by the person or people giving the accounts. Despite their apparent independence, the items fit together like pieces of a puzzle."[7] This is unlikely if they were merely copying from one another, improbable if they were working in collusion, and next to impossible if they were independent fabrications.[8] Blunt argues that this establishes that the authors are independent witnesses of the events they record, although they do not require the Gospels to be *completely* independent.[9]

For example, in Matthew 8.14–16, the people of town wait until the evening to bring their sick to Jesus to be healed, an odd move if they

---

[6] Although it is not as frequently noted, Luke's purpose statement is also theological, as he wants Theophilus to be certain of what he was taught (Luke 1.4). Both Luke and John are explicitly theology rooted in history, or history with a theological application.

[7] L. McGrew, *Hidden in Plain View*, 12.

[8] Blunt, *Undesigned Coincidences in the Writings of the Old and New Testament*, 8. Blunt provides the earliest near-exhaustive look into undesigned coincidences. The origin of the argument is Paley, *Horae Paulinae*. Other contemporary authors who argue from undesigned coincidences include Williams, *Can We Trust the Gospels*, 87–96 and Wallace, *Cold-Case Christianity*. Wallace's appeal to undesigned coincidences appears in a variety of places through the argument.

[9] L. McGrew, *Testimonies to the Truth*, 58.

knew Jesus was there and they believed he could heal the sick. Why wait? Mark's account (1.21–32) informs us that it was the Sabbath and they waited until sundown, explaining the detail that Matthew had omitted.

At the Transfiguration of Jesus, the appearance of his face is altered and his clothes become dazzling white. Moses and Elijah appear in glory and speak with Jesus about his departure. A voice booms from heaven, "This is my beloved Son…." After this, according to Luke, the disciples tell no one (Luke 9.28–35). This is, beyond all doubt, the most amazing thing these disciples have ever experienced in their lives and *they tell no one*. The answer to this puzzle is given in Mark's account, where we learn that Jesus told them to keep silent about it until after the resurrection (9.9) and, for once, this command of Jesus was obeyed.

Perhaps even more surprising than the disciples keeping silent about the Transfiguration is Philip taking a lead role in a miracle story, since he is usually far in the background. But when Jesus inquires of his disciples as to where they can purchase food for the crowd following him, he asks Philip (John 6.5). John does not comment on why Philip takes center stage here, but Luke (who does not mention Philip), gives us the setting: Bethsaida (Luke 9.10–11). In other, unrelated texts in John, we learn that Bethsaida was Philip's hometown (1.44; 12.21). Again, the pieces fit together like a puzzle. Luke does not mention Philip; John does not mention Bethsaida. Only by putting them together can we understand why Jesus addresses Philip.

Finally, in John 21.15, Jesus asks Peter if he loves Jesus more than the other disciples do, a shocking question for the one who was constantly at pains to teach his disciples not to make such comparisons. But this question is not to give Peter the opportunity to boast in his great love, but to reinforce that very lesson. Even as the three affirmations of love are parallel to Peter's three denials, Jesus here reminds Peter that he had once made that very boast. John, however, does not record it. In Mark 14.19, Peter proudly declares that he is the most faithful.

One example of an undesigned coincidence might be an accident. If one Gospel were always explaining the others, it would not be nearly so significant. This, however, is not the case. Each Gospel explains the others—multiple times over, if we were to continue this exercise. Beyond the Gospels, there are undesigned coincidences between Acts and Paul's epistles.[10]

Fiction does not work like this. Mythical accounts do not intersect each other in these ways. This will not happen with legends or planned lies. *Mere* copying will not produce these intersections. The cumulative force of the undesigned coincidences in the narrative is overwhelming. As Blunt says, "Truths known independently to each of them, must be at the bottom of documents having such discrepancies and such agreements as these in question."[11] In addition to whatever else may be going on in the composition of the Gospels, there must be an independent historical reality that stands behind the accounts.

The Accuracy of the Authors. With the documents' historical nature firmly in place, the next question is whether they are accurate in their record. Are they accurate in the incidental details? If they repeatedly show that they were not faithful in small things, we should not trust their record of the larger New Testament story either.

The Book of Acts is especially well known for its accuracy. Sir William Ramsay was an archaeologist who was among the foremost authorities on Asia Minor. On his first trip to Asia Minor, Ramsay was skeptical of the accuracy of Luke's narrative. He presumed that it was a second century composition and would not be reliable as a witness to first century conditions. His study in Asia Minor, however, led him to say, "More recently I found myself brought into contact with the Book of Acts as an authority for the topography, antiquities and society of Asia Minor," and, "I gradually came to find it a useful ally in some obscure and difficult investigations."[12] Ramsay concludes that Luke's history is "unsurpassed in respect to its trust-

---

[10] L. McGrew, *Hidden in Plain View*, 131–219. McGrew also points to a variety of other internal clues to authenticity in *Testimonies to the Truth:* unnecessary details (83–113), unexplained allusions (114–133), unexpected harmonies (134–162), unified personalities (163–183), and the unique ("unmistakable") character of Jesus himself (184–219). Her more academic and exhaustive works on the reliability of the Gospels are *The Mirror or the Mask* and *The Eye of the Beholder*. Regarding the apologetic value of Jesus' character, see Gilson, *Too Good to be False* and Haygood, *The Man of Galilee*.

[11] Blunt, *Undesigned Coincidences*, 8.

[12] Ramsay, *St. Paul the Traveller and the Roman Citizen*, second ed., 36.

worthiness"[13] and that "Luke is a historian of the first rank; ... this author should be placed along with the very greatest of historians."[14] Ramsay's testimony to the accuracy of Luke's narrative is especially compelling, since he began his study from a skeptical point of view. Far from his starting point, Ramsay ultimately lauded it as accurate and called it an authority upon which he leaned for help in understanding difficult matters.

Ramsay's work in surveying the accuracy of Acts is continued in the work of the late Colin Hemer, aiming to be a "fresh and rigorous reexamination" of Ramsay's work.[15] Among other things, Hemer lists 84 specific facts from the final 16 chapters of Acts that have been confirmed by historical and archaeological research (e.g., other authors, inscriptional evidence, etc.). Hemer's list includes things like ports, boundaries, landmarks, slang terminology, local languages, local deities, local industries, and proper titles for numerous regional and local officials. If Acts were not written by the historical Luke, but a second-century fraud, it would be difficult if not impossible to accurately relay these types of matters.[16]

For example, in the non-homogenous Asia minor, the governor of Cyprus, the magistrates of Philippi, the official in Thessalonica, the chief executive magistrate in Ephesus, and the ruler of Malta each had different titles. Correctly identifying each of these people with the proper title would be difficult in the information age with access to highly sophisticated search engines and databases filled with encyclopedic information; a second-century imposter could not possibly correctly identify all of them. In fact, skeptics formerly alleged this very argument against Luke, as we will see below—and Luke's supposed misuse of the titles of local and regional leaders was part of their argument.[17]

---

[13] Ibid. 81.
[14] Ramsay, *The Bearing of Recent Discovery on the Trustworthiness of the New Testament*, 222.
[15] Hemer, *The Book of Acts in the Setting of Hellenistic History*, vii.
[16] Williams ("New Evidences the Gospels Were Based On Eyewitness Accounts." YouTube. April 2, 2011. Accessed August 11, 2025. http://youtu.be/r5Ylt1pBMm8) likens the difficulty of such detailed accuracy to a modern English speaker trying to pass off a story written about France 100 years ago as authentically written then and there. In addition to the name accuracy which Williams discusses, the items Hemer enumerates would also be nearly impossible to consistently get right. In his book Williams adds several other items it would be difficult for a forger in another place and time to get correct (*Can We Trust the Gospels*, 51–86). See also L. McGrew, *Testimonies to the Truth*, 22–49.
[17] For an illustration of this in Thessalonica, see McRay, *Archaeology and the New Testament*, 292–295.

Another example from Hemer's list that would be incredibly difficult to use correctly decades later is slang terminology. For a modern comparison, consider how many slang terms over the last 50 years have been used to convey the idea of "something that is really good." Such a thing could be swell, hip, groovy, radical, gnarly, bad, cool, awesome, wicked, tight, sick, dank, or dope, just to name a few. What's more, any adult who tries to use the current slang but misses by a year or two is immediately outed as a poser.[18] While the turnover time for slang in the ancient world might not be quite as quick as it is now, it is highly unlikely that a second-century imposter writing in a different cultural context could correctly use the slang of first century Athens.

The argument against the historicity of Acts is a classic argument from silence: if the matter under discussion is not in any history outside the Bible or has not yet been excavated by archaeologists, it must be wrong. The problem with this argument, other than the inherent logical fallacy, is the presuppositions that it demands. First, it begs the question, presuming at the outset that the Bible is not trustworthy, an overly-cynical stance that is not typically taken when approaching a written historical work. Second, it presumes that we have enough information about the ancient past to make a fair judgment based on a matter not being discussed in other historical documents, though we have lost at least 85% of Christian writings from the second century.[19] Such an allegation lends itself to making the arguer look foolish when new evidence turns up filling in that gap of silence.

Such has been the case many times, as John McRay outlines in his discussion with Lee Strobel.[20] He speaks specifically of Lysanias the tetrarch of Abilene (Luke 3.1), the "politarchs" of Thessalonica (Acts 17.6), and the Pool of Bethesda (John 5), each of which was not known outside the Bible and thus considered a biblical error and proof that the authors wrote well after the alleged date. Ultimately, however, archaeology confirmed

---

[18] Or whatever is the right word for that these days.

[19] Hengel, *The Four Gospels and the One Gospel of Jesus Christ*, 55. Hengel here refers to those documents known to us by title (becuase they are mentioned in other writings). Adding unknown documents would only increase the percentage. It is reasonble to presume that non-Christian writings were preserved at a roughly comparable rate.

[20] Strobel, *The Case for Christ*, 97–99. For more detail, see McRay's *Archaeology and the New Testament*.

the accuracy of the Gospel authors in each case. Tim McGrew adds the example of Frank Zindler questioning the existence of Nazareth, saying that it was "as mythical as the Mary, Joseph, and Jesus family that was supposed to have lived there."[21] Unfortunately for Zindler's allegations, excavations as recently as 2009 by the Jewish antiquities authority—a group with no vested interest in proving the accuracy of the Gospels' record of Jesus' childhood home—have clearly identified the Nazareth of the first century. More shocking, perhaps, is Price's allegation about synagogues in the Gospels: "A major collision between the Gospel tradition and archaeology concerns the existence of synagogues and Pharisees in pre-70 CE Galilee. Historical logic implies that there would not have been any since Pharisees fled to Galilee only after the fall of Jerusalem."[22] There is indeed a certain historical logic to what Price says. The problem is that the excavation of the Capernaum synagogue, portions of which dated to the first century (an "inescapable" conclusion, according to the authors), was published some twenty years *before* Price made this allegation.[23]

The skeptical position amounts to what McGrew calls a "fraud of the gaps" argument:[24] the Bible is wrong in those places, and *only* in those places, where it has not yet been corroborated by extra-Biblical history or archaeology. Or, it seems, in cases where the skeptics choose to willfully ignore the evidence. By contrast, the interactions that the Gospels have with extra-Biblical history and archaeology "have tended to confirm the reliability of the Gospels and disprove novel theories."[25]

The Eyewitness Nature of the Testimony

The nature of the undesigned coincidences in the Gospel narratives and the historical accuracy of the accounts, especially of Luke-Acts, is enough for many to have full confidence in the narratives. For those who seek more, recent study into onomastics (the study of names) has provided

---

[21] T. McGrew, "The Gospels and Acts as History." Incidentally, I would agree with Zindler in principle: it is *exactly* as mythical as they are!
[22] Price, *The Incredible Shrinking Son of Man*, 14.
[23] Strange and Shanks, "Synagogue Where Jesus Preached Found at Capernaum."
[24] T. McGrew, "The Gospels and Acts as History."
[25] Evans, *Fabricating Jesus*, 235.

compelling evidence that these documents are not only historically accurate, but are from eyewitness accounts.[26]

Name popularity changes frequently and is not the same in various places. Conservatives and skeptics alike agree that the Gospel accounts were written somewhere other than Palestine, though skeptics tend to argue for a much later date. Given the frequency with which names change and the distance from the setting of the Gospels, it would be difficult to guess the correct names in the correct proportions and give them the correct features if the authors were not intimately familiar with the setting in question.

A study of 3,000 first century Jewish names yielded much important data about names in Palestine and abroad. First, the names of Palestinian Jews were not at all the same as the Jews of the Diaspora,[27] which would make it incredibly difficult for non-native fraudulent authors to correctly name the characters of the story. What we find in the Gospel accounts, however, is extreme accuracy. For example, the top nine men's names in Palestine accounted for 41.5% of all males; those same nine names account for 40.3% of all the male characters in the Gospels and Acts.[28]

Not only do the authors use the right names in the right proportions, but they have the right features of names. Specifically, some names clarify and some do not. For example, the most common Jewish male name in first century Palestine was Simon. In the New Testament, every Simon is distinguished: Simon Peter, Simon the Zealot, Simon the Tanner, Simon of Cyrene, etc. On the other hand, Philip is simply Philip and Nathanael is simply Nathanael. The names which include this distinguishing feature are all high-ranked names on the frequency charts; those which do not disambiguate are low on the charts.[29] The one exception to this is Jesus, who never has a clarifier attached in narrative even

---

[26] Bauckham, *Jesus and the Eyewitnesses*, 84. For a more recent discussion, see Luuk Vandeweghe, *The Historical Tell*.

[27] Ibid., 83.

[28] Ibid., 71–72. See Bauckham for more detailed charts and data. Women's names do not match quite as closely, as the statistical base is significantly smaller, both in the New Testament and sources in general.

[29] Williams, *Can We Trust the Gospels?* 67–68. See Bauckham, *Jesus and the Eyewitnesses*, 85–89 for a full list.

though his name is the sixth most frequent. This, however, is due to his singular nature as the chief character of the narrative.

In a lecture on this topic, Williams suggests that names are often the most difficult thing to remember, and offers as anecdotal evidence the fact that most people have a hard time remembering names. It is easy, by contrast, to remember stories about people, their children, their physical characteristics, and the like, but there is no logical connection between a person and what he or she is called. Williams concludes, "If the Gospels have correctly got the detail that's the hardest sort of thing to remember, isn't there every reason to think they can get the other things right?"[30]

By contrast, the apocryphal Gospels do not fare so well in regard to the accuracy of the names. For example, The Gospel of Thomas' lead character is Didymos Judas Thomas, which means Twin Judas Twin, an unlikely name in that day. The Gospel of Judas has only two characters with Palestinian names, Jesus and Judas. Further, these apocryphal Gospels fail to differentiate high-frequency names like Mary.[31]

In addition to personal names, the Gospels also excel in place names. The narratives contain not only major cities (like Jerusalem, Tyre and Sidon, and Caesarea Philippi) and towns key to the narrative (like Bethlehem and Nazareth), but they also contain other little-known villages such as Bethphage, Cana, and Nain. In sum, the Gospels speak of 23 cities and villages. More than merely naming them, they know things about them such as geography, climate, travel time, botany, and the like. They know which cities you go up into and which you go down into. They know what time of year the grass is green in Bethsaida. They correctly put Zacchaeus in a sycamore tree in Jericho.[32] By contrast the apocryphal Gospels, as a corpus, list only two cities, Jerusalem and Nazareth.[33] The former is the capital of the region and the latter was famous because of its association with Jesus. Knowledge of these two places is not especially impressive.

---

[30] Williams, "New Evidence."
[31] Williams, *Can We Trust the Gospels?* 69.
[32] Ibid., 52–62.
[33] Ibid., 63.

Skeptics and conspiracy theorists suppose that the apocryphal Gospels are evidence against the canonical Gospels. It is suggested that they were suppressed by the church because they hide the real story of Jesus, telling it in all-too-human terms, as *The Da Vinci Code*, for example, alleges.[34] In reality, however, these documents provide outstanding evidence *for* the canonical Gospels; they give a clear picture of what happens when people make up stories a hundred years later in a different place.

Authorial Bias

Despite their detailed accuracy, it can be alleged that the gospel authors' reporting is not reliable, even if they were eyewitnesses. Critics contend that they are prejudiced regarding what they wrote, which is, after all, merely "propaganda meant to convert people to faith."[35] Given their bias, can we have confidence in their accounts?

An Inconsistent Standard. Perhaps the biggest problem with the insinuation that bias inherently means unreliability is what happens when the rule is followed to its logical conclusion. If this is the case, then all reports by people who believed in their cause must be dismissed. But there is no one who puts pen to paper unless they believe in what they are writing. Objectivity may well be a hypothetical possibility, but in reality, there is no such thing as an unbiased author; true objectivity is an impossibility. Indeed, the skeptics who challenge the bias of the Gospel authors have their own bias, and yet they expect their readers to trust their arguments. But the rule cuts both ways: "If the particular biases of these contempo-

---

[34] Brown, *The Da Vinci Code*, 231, 234–235, e.g., "The Dead Sea Scrolls were found in the 1950s hidden in a cave near Qumran in the Judean desert. And, of course, the Coptic Scrolls in 1945 at Nag Hammadi. In addition to telling the true Grail story, these documents speak of Christ's ministry in very human terms. Of course, the Vatican, in keeping with their tradition of misinformation, tried very hard to suppress the release of these scrolls. And why wouldn't they? The scrolls highlight glaring historical discrepancies and fabrications, clearly confirming that the modern Bible was compiled and edited by men, who possessed a political agenda—to promote the divinity of the man Jesus Christ and use His influence to solidify their own power base" (234). Although *The Davinci Code* is well dated at this point (the novel in 2003 and movie in 2006), it has had a lasting cultural impact. This is to be expected with a book that sold 80 million copies in 44 languages and a movie that grossed $760 million in ticket sales. In spite of the excellent work that was done in debunking it by a variety of scholars (e.g., Bock, *Breaking the Da Vinci Code*), popular-level skeptical arguments still echo its baseless allegations.

[35] Ehrman, *Jesus Interrupted*, 146–147.

rary scholars do not prevent *them* from doing (what they want others to accept as) reliable history, why should we think that the bias of the Gospel authors prevents them from communicating generally reliable history?"[36]

If it is a rule that authorial bias necessitates extreme skepticism on the part of the reader, then all documents must be judged by the rule. Everybody experiences, thinks about, and communicates about the world from their own unique, biased perspective. Either we must admit that humankind can never reliably report events, or acknowledge that while bias can color the truth, it does not *necessarily* undermine it. The Gospel authors, in fact, give us good reasons to believe that they are more interested in reporting an accurate the history of Jesus than creating a biased propaganda meant to further their own agenda.

An Incompetent Propaganda. If the Gospels are propaganda, they are propaganda unlike any other ever written. Far from furthering an agenda by manipulating people into believing sugar-coated half-truths and lies, they give their audience reason to reject Jesus and themselves, and miss multiple opportunities to press the agenda of their own day.

Embarrassing Details. The presence of details that would be embarrassing or otherwise detrimental to the author's purpose adds credibility to an account's historicity. Why, after all, would an author invent something that runs counter to his intent? The Gospel authors consistently include details that are damaging to themselves, their cause, and their chief protagonist.

At the outset of the gospels, Jesus was baptized (Mark 1.4–11) which is still a matter that causes people to ask questions.[37] That his herald, who baptized him, later had doubts (Matt 11.2–6) only exacerbates the issue.

---

[36] Eddy and Boyd, *The Jesus Legend*, 398, italics in original. They add, "[I]t is virtually impossible to imagine certain events being reported by anyone, ancient or modern, in an emotionally detached manner. Consider, for example, Holocaust survivors reporting what transpired in Nazi concentration camps. While historians always must take their limitations and biases into consideration, can anyone imagine dismissing the basic reliability of the survivors' various reports on the grounds that they were 'emotionally involved' and believed 'fervently in the story they [were] telling'? If what they are reporting is remotely close to what actually happened, would it not be positively bizarre if they were *not* 'emotionally involved' and believed 'fervently in the story they [were] telling?'" (398, italics and brackets in original, quotations in the quote are of Funk, "On Distinguishing Historical from Fictive Narrative," 191). See Eddy and Boyd, *The Jesus Legend*, 397–399 for more on the issue of bias.

[37] In addition to how skeptics may raise the issue, I can attest to this question coming up somewhat regularly from sincere undergraduates.

Further, Jesus associated with people of ill-repute and gained a reputation of being a glutton and drunkard (Mark 2.15–16; cf. Matt 11.19) and in collusion with the devil (Mark 3.22, 30), while he disregarded Jewish laws, customs, and cleanliness (Mark 2.23–24).

In regard to miracles, consider that Jesus' family, who did not believe in him (John 7.5), sought to restrain him due to negative reactions to his miracles, thinking him to be mentally unstable (Mark 3.20–35). He was incapable of performing miracles in his own hometown due to the people's lack of faith (Mark 6.5). A Gentile woman, who he first called a dog, out-argues him, convincing him to perform a miracle he didn't really want to (Mark 7.24–30), and, on one occasion, it takes Jesus two tries to get a miracle right (Mark 8.22–26).[38] Further, it is highly unlikely that, when Jesus is already being called a drunkard by his enemies (Matt 11.19), one of his biographers would invent a story about him mass producing the best wine anyone had ever tasted (John 2.1–11)![39]

As to the disciples, they constantly failed to understand what Jesus was teaching and doing. All three times Jesus predicts his death and resurrection, the apostles immediately do something stupid (Mark 8.31–33; 9.30–34; 10.32–37). The betrayer came from among the twelve (Mark 14.10–11), and although all of them boast of their greatness and bravery (Mark 14.31), they sleep when he is in distress (Mark 14.37–41) and flee when he is arrested (Mark 14.50). When told of the resurrection, they do not at first believe (Luke 24.10–11)[40] and are hiding behind locked doors out of fear (John 20.19). Meanwhile, it is women, not considered reliable witnesses in first century Jewish culture,[41] who are the first to give testimony to the resurrection.

Most significantly, Jesus is crucified by the Romans: "It is hard to imagine a more effective way to convince people in a first-century Jewish

---

[38] Evans, *Fabricating Jesus*, 140–41.

[39] Habermas, "Did Jesus Perform Miracles?" in Wilkins and Moreland, *Jesus Under Fire*, 131.

[40] Poor Thomas is unfairly maligned with the epithet nickname of "Doubting Thomas." *All* the eleven doubted, as did the women who went to the tomb and were perplexed at the absence of his body (Luke 24.1–4), asking to where his corpse had been relocated (John 20.13–15). *None* of Jesus' followers responded to the empty tomb with praise that Jesus' predictions of the resurrection had come to pass; *all* had to see him in order to believe—and all, including Thomas, believed the *first* time they saw him.

[41] Josephus, *Antiquities of the Jews*, 4.8.15.

context that someone is *not* the Messiah than by telling them that the would-be savior was executed by Israel's military oppressors! To go further and tell them that this would-be savior died a cursed death on a tree would make the sales pitch all the worse (cf. Deut 21.22–23)."[42]

Of course, the reader might chafe at the negative way I have presented these accounts and suggest an alternate interpretation for some that removes the embarrassment. But that is precisely the point: a forger—and especially a propagandist—would leave no room for the slightest possibility of embarrassment.

Omission of relevant details. The fact that the Gospel authors wrote several decades after the time of Jesus gives us another test of historical accuracy to consider: are they more interested in what Jesus said and did or how his words might solve the issues of their own day? Issues such as the inclusion of Gentiles in the church, the function of spiritual gifts in worship, the role of women in the assembly, and the structure of church leadership *never* come up in the teaching of Jesus. If the Gospel authors had

> generally been inclined to invent Jesus material relevant to their particular concerns, rather than hold as sacred what in fact he did say, *these are precisely the sorts of issues we would have expected the Jesus of the Gospel to address.* That the Gospel tradition retains an amazing amount of embarrassing material on the one hand, and so often fails to insert material that clearly would have been of benefit on the other, testifies to their generally strong interest in, and commitment to, preserving early Christian memory of the earthly Jesus.[43]

Miracles

Although "trust the author until he gives you a reason to doubt" is a reasonable starting point and, as seen above, the authors show themselves to be knowledgeable eyewitnesses in many way, it is also reasonable to question whether a man can, say, walk on top of a lake.[44] Although a full

---

[42] Eddy and Boyd, *The Jesus Legend*, 411, italics in original.
[43] Ibid., 412, italics in original. Here, Eddy and Boyd cite Ben Witherington, *The Christology of Jesus* (Minneapolis: Fortress, 1990), 4 and Craig Blomberg, "Form Criticism," in *Dictionary of Jesus and the Gospels*, ed. J.B. Green, et al. (Downers Grove: InterVarsity, 1992), 246.
[44] Much of the following is modified from Nathan Ward, "This Man Performs Many Signs: The Miracles as History," *The Works No One Else Did*, 15–35.

discussion of miracles cannot be undertaken in a subsection of a single essay, a few things need to be said about the topic.[45]

Historical Criteria. For the sake of space, this essay will not include a thorough discussion of historical criteria in relation to miracles. Many of the standard historical criteria (e.g., multiple attestation, criterion of embarrassment, dissimilarity, etc.) apply to the miracle narratives. Additionally, miracle stories involve undesigned coincidences and other marks of historical authenticity discussed by McGrew and Williams.

The Impossibility of "Demythologizing" Jesus. One particular method of trying to eradicate the miracles from the Gospels is the demythologization of the Gospels.[46] Although there is more to the practice, a hallmark is to strip the miracles from the Gospels. Unfortunately, to demythologize Jesus in this fashion cannot be done—because Jesus was never mythologized to begin with.

Manuscript Evidence. Although no autograph copies of the Gospels exist, fragments of manuscripts go back to within a few decades[47] and an almost-complete copy of Luke and John date to just over a century later.[48] The miracles of Jesus are present in all of these earliest manuscripts. As Bruce says, "Not even in the earliest Gospel strata can we find a non-supernatural Jesus."[49] Not only is there no evidence of mythological development in the manuscripts, the manuscripts are so close to the date of the events in question that there is not enough time for a mythology to develop.

Coherence of the Story. Perhaps even more significant, the Gospels only make sense with the miracles in place.[50] The miracles are not stories made

---

[45] Due to space constrictions, this will only include evidence for the miracles. Replying to the philosophical, naturalistic, historical, and religious objections to miracles is also an important piece of this larger discussion. For further study, see Brown, *Miracles and the Critical Mind*; Collins, *The God of Miracles*; Earman, *Hume's Abject Failure*; Geisler, *Miracles and Modern Thought*; Geivett and Habermas, eds., *In Defense of Miracles*; Keener, *Miracles*; Lewis, *Miracles*; Strobel, *The Case for Miracles*; Swinburne, *The Concept of Miracle*; Twelftree, *Jesus the Miracle Worker*. Many apologetic and historical Jesus works include helpful segments on the topic. Of special note is Eddy and Boyd, *The Jesus Legend*, 39–90.

[46] German theologian Rudolf Bultmann (1884–1976) is among the best known to practice this method.

[47] The oldest currently known fragment is P52, a few verses of John, which dates to as early as AD 125.

[48] P75, containing most of Luke and John, dates to the early third century.

[49] Bruce, *The New Testament Documents*, 62.

[50] Much of this is drawn from Evans, *Fabricating Jesus*, 139–57.

up later and shoehorned into the narrative; they belong there. His healings and exorcisms are an intrinsic part of his proclamation of the kingdom of God (Matt 10.1, 5–8; Mark 3.23–27; Luke 11.20). His miracles were viewed by himself and others as fulfillment of prophetic Scripture (Matt 11.2–6; *cf.* Isa 26.19; 35.5f; 61.1). He understood his entire mission in the context of his miracles, and expected others to as well (Luke 4.16–19). In fact, the Gospel authors saw his miracles as a revelation of his own identity: his authority being equal with that of the Son of Man (Mark 2.3–12 and Dan 7.13–14); people falling down in shame of sinfulness before him like Isaiah did before God (Luke 5.3–10 and Isa 6.5–7); seeing Jesus in action is like seeing God in action (Mark 4.37–41 and Ps 107.23–29). To strip the miracles out of the story is not to demythologize Jesus and figure out who he really was, but to eviscerate the story, leaving nothing at all behind.

The Connection of Jesus to Miracles after the Gospels. The connection of Jesus with miracles does not end with the New Testament. The *Greek Magical Papyrus* (lines 3007–3041)[51] indicates that pagans invoked Jesus' name to perform miracles. The Jewish Talmud discussed the legitimacy of being healed in the name of Jesus, indicating that some rabbis believed that it was better to die than to be healed in his name.[52] Where might this broad testimony of unbelievers, Jew and Gentile alike, connecting the power of Jesus' name and miracles have come from, if not an early source that Jesus himself actually performed miracles?

Summary. Even if we had the space to answer every objection and had provided detailed positive evidence throughout, miracles will not be *proven*. Showing the weakness of the objections and presenting a positive case for the reliability of the historical record are important steps—and there *are* good reasons to believe in the miracles of Jesus—but this is ultimately another aspect of the Christian life that is a matter of faith. The goal throughout this chapter has been to show that it is a reasonable faith, for the Bible never commends blind faith, but the decision to believe or disbelieve the evidence remains in the hands of the reader.

---

[51] See Ibid. 156–57 for the text.
[52] Ibid. 157.

Conclusion

As a whole, the Gospels and Acts show great evidence not only of being historically accurate, but being based on eyewitness testimony. They are accurate in minute details that are peripheral to the story: titles of various people, geographic locations, people's names, and more are all correct. Everywhere we can check it—against history and archaeology—the authors of the Gospels and Acts get it right. The hyper-skeptical position that it is wrong in the places—and *only* in the places—where it cannot be or has not been verified is untenable and illogical.

The miracles, although difficult for some, are a question of metaphysics and worldview, not history. As Poythress says, the God of the Bible is "a personal God, not a mechanical system. So he can bring about exceptions to the regularities when he wishes. Miracles are not only possible but understandable and natural, given the fact that at times God may have special purposes that lead to special actions."[53] Or, to be more succinct, "If there is a God who can act, there can be acts of God."[54]

To conclude where we began, consider again C.S. Lewis. He argues against the legend hypothesis from a literary standpoint saying, "As a literary historian, I am perfectly convinced that whatever else the Gospels are they are not legends. I have read a great deal of legend, and I am quite clear that they are not the same sort of things."[55] To that we would add a great deal of historical and archaeological evidence that suggests the same thing: whatever else the Gospels may be, they are not legend. They do, however, bear the hallmarks of eyewitness history.

Bibliography

Bauckham, Richard. *Jesus and the Eyewitnesses: The Gospels as Eyewitness Testimony*. Grand Rapids: Eerdmans, 2008.

Blomberg, Craig L. *The Historical Reliability of John's Gospel: Issues and Commentary*. Downers Grove: Intervarsity Press, 2001.

⸻. *The Historical Reliability of the Gospels*. Downers Grove: Intervarsity Press, 1987.

---

[53] Poythress, *The Miracles of Jesus*, 20.
[54] Geisler and Turek, *I Don't Have Enough Faith to be an Atheist*, 209.
[55] Lewis, "God in the Dock," 406. Cf. Haygood, *The Man of Galilee*, 31–36.

_____. *The Historical Reliability of the New Testament: Countering the Challenges to Evangelical Christian Beliefs*. Nashville: B&H Academic, 2016.

Blunt, J.J. *Undesigned Coincidences in the Writings of the Old and New Testament: An Argument of Their Veracity*. London: John Murray, 1869.

Bock, Darrell L. *Breaking the Da Vinci Code: Answers to the Questions Everyone's Asking*. Nashville: Nelson Books, 2004.

Boyd, Gregory A. and Paul Rhodes Eddy. *Lord or Legend? Wrestling with the Jesus Dilemma*. Grand Rapids: Baker Books, 2007.

Brown, Colin. *Miracles and the Critical Mind*. Grand Rapids: Eerdmans, 1984.

Brown, Dan. *The Da Vinci Code*. New York: Doubleday, 2003.

Bruce, F.F. *The New Testament Documents: Are They Reliable?* Grand Rapids: Eerdmans, 1965.

Collins, C. John. *The God of Miracles*. Wheaton: Crossway, 2000.

Earman, John. *Hume's Abject Failure: The Argument Against Miracles*. New York: Oxford University Press, 2000.

Eddy, Paul Rhodes and Gregory A. Boyd. *The Jesus Legend: A Case for the Historical Reliability of the Synoptic Jesus Tradition*. Grand Rapids: Baker Academic, 2007.

Ehrman, Bart. *Jesus Interrupted: Revealing the Hidden Contradictions in the Bible (And Why We Don't Know About Them)*. New York: HarperOne, 2010.

Evans, Craig A. *Fabricating Jesus: How Modern Scholars Distort the Gospels*. Downers Grove: IVP Books, 2008.

Funk, Robert, "On Distinguishing Historical from Fictive Narrative." *Forum* 9 (1993): 179–216.

Geisler, Norman. *Miracles and Modern Thought*. Grand Rapids: Zondervan, 1982.

_____ and Frank Turek. *I Don't Have Enough Faith to be an Atheist*. Wheaton: Crossway, 2004.

Geivett, R. Douglas and Gary R. Habermas. *In Defense of Miracles: A Comprehensive Case for God's Action in History*. Downers Grove: Intervarsity Press, 1997.

Gilson, Tom. *Too Good to be False: How Jesus' Incomparable Character Reveals His Reality*. Tampa: DeWard Publishing, 2020.

Habermas, Gary. "Did Jesus Perform Miracles?" *Jesus Under Fire: Modern Scholarship Reinvents the Historical Jesus*. Edited by M. Wilkins and J. P. Moreland. Grand Rapids: Zondervan 1995, 117–140.

Haygood, Atticus G. *The Man of Galilee*. 1889; repr., Chillicothe: DeWard Publishing, 2012.

Hemer, Colin J. *The Book of Acts in the Setting of Hellenistic History*. Edited by Conrad H. Gempf. Winona Lake: Eisenbrauns, 1990.

Hengel, Martin. *The Four Gospels And The One Gospel Of Jesus Christ*. Harrisburg, Pennsylvania: Trinity Press International, 2000

Keener, Craig. *Miracles: The Credibility of the New Testament Accounts*, 2 vols. Grand Rapids: Baker Academic, 2011.

Lewis, C.S. "God in the Dock." *The Collected Works of C. S. Lewis*. New York: Inspirational Press, 1996, 297–537.

———. *Mere Christianity*. 1st HarperCollins ed. San Francisco: Harper San Francisco, 2001.

———. *Miracles: A Preliminary Study*. New York: MacMillan, 1947.

McGrew, Lydia. *Hidden in Plain View: Undesigned Coincidences in the Gospels and Acts*. Chillicothe: DeWard Publishing, 2017.

———. *Testimonies to the Truth: Why You Can Trust the Gospels*. Tampa: DeWard Publishing, 2023.

———. *The Eye of the Beholder: The Gospel of John as Historical Reportage*. Tampa: DeWard Publishing, 2021.

———. *The Mirror or the Mask: Liberating the Gospels from Literary Devices*. Tampa: DeWard Publishing, 2019 .

McGrew, Timothy. "Internal Evidence for the Truth of the Gospels and Acts." YouTube. March 21, 2012. Accessed April 25, 2025. http://youtu.be/9wUcrwYocgM.

———. "The Gospels and Acts as History." YouTube. December 7, 2011. Accessed April 25, 2025. http://youtu.be/JAPG3eECaxw.

McRay, John. *Archaeology and the New Testament*. Grand Rapids: Baker Book House, 1991.

Paley, William. *Horae Paulinae*. London: Society for Promoting Christian Knowledge, 1877.

Poythress, Vern. *The Miracles of Jesus: How the Savior's Mighty Acts Serve as Signs of Redemption*. Wheaton: Crossway, 2016.

Price, Robert M. *The Incredible Shrinking Son of Man: How Reliable is the Gospel Tradition.* Amherst: Prometheus, 2003.

Ramsay, William. *St. Paul the Traveller and the Roman Citizen.* Second ed. Grand Rapids: Baker Book House, 1962.

_____. *The Bearing of Recent Discovery on the Trustworthiness of the New Testament.* New York: Hodder and Stoughton, 1915.

Strange, James and Hershel Shanks. "Synagogue Where Jesus Preached Found at Capernaum." *Biblical Archaeology Review* 9 (1983): 24–31.

Strobel, Lee. *The Case for Christ: A Journalist's Personal Investigation of the Evidence for Jesus.* Grand Rapids: Zondervan, 1998.

_____. *The Case for Miracles: A Journalist Investigates Evidence for the Supernatural.* Grand Rapids: Zondervan, 2018.

Swinburne, Richard. *The Concept of Miracle.* New Studies in the Philosophy of Religion. New York: MacMillan, 1970.

Twelftree, Graham H. *Jesus the Miracle Worker: A Historical and Theological Study.* Downers Grove: IVP Academic, 1999.

Vandeweghe, Luuk. *The Historical Tell: Patterns of Eyewitness Testimony in the Gospel of Luke and Acts.* Tampa: DeWard Publishing, 2023.

Wallace, J. Warner. *Cold-Case Christianity: A Cold Case Detective Investigates the Claims of the Gospels.* Colorado Springs: David Cook, 2013.

Ward, Nathan. "This Man Performs Many Signs: The Miracles as History." *The Works No One Else Did: The Miracles of Jesus.* Florida College Annual Lectures. Temple Terrace: Florida College Press, 2019, 15–35.

Wilkins, Michael J. and J.P. Moreland. *Jesus Under Fire: Modern Scholarship Reinvents the Historical Jesus.* Grand Rapids: Zondervan, 1995.

Williams, Peter J. *Can We Trust the Gospels?* Wheaton: Crossway, 2018.

_____. "New Evidences the Gospels Were Based On Eyewitness Accounts." YouTube. April 25, 2025. Accessed August 3, 2013. http://youtu.be/r5Ylt1pBMm8.

13

The Truth of the Deity of Christ

Robert M. Bowman Jr.

The deity of Christ is such a huge, involved, and profound subject that the reader would properly wish to know what to expect to learn about it in a short presentation. This chapter has relatively modest aims. (1) Surveying the field of alternative views of Christology and contrasting them with the biblical, orthodox Christian position. (2) Explaining what it means—and what it does not mean—to affirm the "deity" of Christ, or to call Jesus "God." (3) Answering some common misunderstandings and objections to the deity of Christ. (4) Identifying the most important passages in the New Testament of relevance to the doctrine. (5) Introducing the broad range of ways in which the New Testament reveals the deity of Christ and showing that this belief is securely based on factual evidence from the life of Jesus.

Many Christologies, One Christ

The apostle Paul affirmed that there is "one Lord, Jesus Christ" (1 Cor 8.6; cf. 12.5; Eph 4.5).[1] Unfortunately, today there are many *Christologies*, or doctrines about Christ, that interpret who and what Jesus Christ is in bewilderingly different ways.[2]

According to ***Islam***, Jesus was a Muslim, a prophet like Muhammad in some ways and unlike him in others. The Islamic view of Jesus is set forth in the Qur'an, Islam's scripture dictated by Muhammad, especially

---

[1] Biblical quotations are taken from the ESV unless noted otherwise.

[2] For detailed introductions to these Christologies see Bowman and Komoszewski, *Incarnate Christ and His Critics*, 43–60. Much of the material presented in this chapter is discussed in more detail in that book.

in suras (chapters) 3–5 and 19. Christians may be surprised to hear that Muslims believe that Jesus was born of a virgin and (perhaps) lived a sinless life—things they do not attribute to Muhammad. We can't even get some Episcopalians to agree on that! On the other hand, they maintain that Jesus, like Muhammad, was nothing more than a human being. They deny that Jesus died on the cross and rose from the dead. Islam teaches that viewing Jesus as God's "Son" is blasphemous false doctrine.

Progressive Christianity views Jesus as a mystic. The term **progressive Christianity** is liable to some misunderstandings. In this context, it refers not to the movement's political perspective (though many progressive Christians are politically "progressive" as well) but to its theological claim that Christianity needs to progress beyond traditional Christian beliefs. Marcus J. Borg (1942–2015) and John Shelby Spong (1931–2021) were highly influential biblical scholars advocating a progressive Christian Christology. Spong was one of those Episcopalian leaders who denied the virgin birth and sinless life of Jesus. According to Borg and Spong, God is not a personal being but is rather the spiritual power or presence in all things. Jesus was an enlightened teacher who showed the way to spiritual union with the divine. Ironically, their view of Jesus is more like the Buddha than the New Testament Christ.[3]

Classically, the term **Unitarianism** refers to the theological tradition that views God as a single person (hence, no Trinity) and Jesus Christ as an exalted man. Unitarians agree with historic Christianity that Jesus was born of a virgin, lived a sinless life, died on the cross for our sins, rose from the dead, and ascended into heaven. However, it denies that Christ existed in heaven before his human life. Only when Jesus ascended into heaven, according to Unitarians, did he become divine, and even then in a subordinate role to the Father, who alone is the real God. Anthony Buzzard and Dale Tuggy are noted contemporary advocates.[4]

The Church of Jesus Christ of Latter-day Saints, popularly known as **Mormonism**, views Jesus in the context of its complicated and highly

---

[3] See especially Spong, *Jesus for thew Non-Religious*; Borg, *Days of Awe and Wonder*; Borg and Riegert, eds., *Jesus and Buddha*.
[4] See Buzzard, *Jesus Was Not a Trinitarian*; Tuggy and Date, *Is Jesus Human and Not Divine*.

unbiblical worldview. According to its founder, Joseph Smith, God was a man of flesh and bones that had not always been God but rather went through a process of exaltation to become a God.[5] Later LDS prophets have taught that Heavenly Father has a wife, known as the heavenly mother, and all human beings were their sons and daughters with "spirit bodies" before coming to the earth in physical bodies. Jesus was their firstborn spirit child and was a God in heaven before receiving a physical body (which is not the usual process in LDS theology). He then came to earth as the "only begotten Son of God in the in the flesh," by which Mormons mean that God and Mary somehow were the literal parents of Jesus in his mortal body.[6]

Jehovah's Witnesses teach that Jesus was God's first and only direct creation. Jehovah God, the Father, created a spirit son for himself known at the time as Michael the Archangel. Michael's "life force" was transferred into the womb of Mary to create a man, Jesus of Nazareth. After his resurrection, Jesus did not rise from the dead in his human body but was instead recreated as an angel again. As the first and greatest creature, Christ is "a god," but he is not equal to Jehovah God in nature or status.[7]

Oneness Pentecostals rejected the doctrine of the Trinity and broke away from the larger Pentecostal movement. According to the Oneness doctrine, Jesus Christ is God, but when we read the "fine print" we learn that this does not mean quite what orthodox Christians mean. In Oneness Christology, the Son did not exist before Jesus was born. Rather, the Son is the human manifestation of the Father. The Logos (Jn 1.1) was not a preexistent divine person but rather God's plan to manifest himself in Jesus. David Bernard, the general superintendent of the United Pentecostal Church International, is also the movement's main biblical scholar and theologian.[8]

All these views are obviously unorthodox from a classic Christian perspective, yet except for Islam they claim to be Christian. In the rest

---

[5] Smith, *History of the Church*, 6.305–6.
[6] See further Bowman and Komoszewski, *Incarnate Christ and His Critics*, 177–80, 341–46.
[7] See Watchtower, *Reasoning from the Scriptures*, 212–20, 334–35, 408–26.
[8] Bernard, *Oneness of God*.

of this chapter, we will explain why these views are erroneous and why we should affirm, as the clear New Testament teaching, that Jesus Christ is God incarnate.

One Monotheistic God

We begin with the foundational truth of biblical Christology: There is one God. This idea is rather basic biblical doctrine and is commonly expressed in Christian theology as the Creator-creation distinction: There is one Creator, called God, and then there's everything else, called the creation. You're either the Creator or you're part of the creation. There's nothing between these two possibilities; there's no semi-creator or anything like that.

Monotheism, the doctrine that there is one creator God, is consistently taught from Genesis to Revelation. Hundreds of texts clearly identify Jehovah or Yahweh (*YHWH*, frequently rendered "the Lord" in English Bibles) as this one God. The generic Hebrew word for God is *Elohim*, a term employed over two thousand times in the Old Testament. It is emphasized almost incessantly throughout the Old Testament that Yahweh is the only God (e.g., Dt 4.35, 39; 6.4; 32.39; 2 Sa 7.22; 1 Ki 8.60; 2 Ki 5.15; 1 Chr 17.20; Isa 44.6, 45.5, 14; Mal 2.10).[9]

One implication of biblical monotheism is that God's nature transcends (or is beyond the limitations of) our universe of space, time, energy, and matter. He's not locked out of the universe, but he's not part of it either. He is eternal (Pss 90.2; 102.25–27) and is infinite spirit (Isa 66.1–2; Jn 4.20–24). He is omnipresent (Gen 28.15; 1 Ki 8.27; Ps 139.7–10), omnipotent (Gen 18.14; Job 42.2; Isa 55.11; Mk 10.27; Lk 1.37; Eph 1.11), and omniscient (1 Ki 8.39; Ps 139.2–6; Isa 41.22–23; Mt 10.30; 1 Jn 3.20). These "omni" attributes belong to God alone. He is therefore unique in essential being, qualitatively different from us in almost unimaginable ways.[10] The Lord God is the only God of all creation. No one and nothing else is, can be, or ever will be a God or be like God in these senses.

---

[9] For a critique of arguments in support of a plurality of gods in the Old Testament, see Bowman and Komoszewski, *Incarnate Christ and His Critics*, 389–410.

[10] On the divine attributes, see Barrett, *None Greater*; Feinberg, *No One Like Him*.

Another implication of monotheism is that whatever other supernatural or spiritual beings exist, they are not to be worshiped or served (Ex 20.3–5; Dt 6.13–15; Rom 1.23–25). This is again Bible 101. You'd be surprised, though, how many different religious groups try to find ways around these biblical teachings when they're confronted with the New Testament's teachings about Christ.

Biblical monotheism rules out Mormonism, according to which Jesus is one of many Gods, and Jehovah's Witnesses, who teach that Jesus is a lesser created god under Almighty God. Their doctrine that God commissioned Jesus (i.e., Michael the Archangel) to make everything else with God's blueprints is ruled out by the simple fact that Scripture teaches consistently that God alone created the universe (Gen 1.1; Isa 44.24).

Our first point is nicely summed up by New Testament scholar Richard Bauckham: "However diverse Judaism may have been in many other respects, this was common: only the God of Israel is worthy of worship because he is sole Creator of all things and sole Ruler of all things."[11]

Two Natures of Jesus Christ

Our second point is that there are two natures of Christ: deity and humanity. This doctrine is known as the *incarnation*, which means that Christ was a divine person who came "in the flesh" (1 Jn 4.2; Latin, *in carne*). Jesus was not a man who became exalted to godhood, as in Unitarianism, but rather *was* God by nature in heaven and humbled himself to become a man. At his ascension, Jesus became exalted as the God-man to his rightful place. Thus, there *is* an exaltation, but it's not a promotion of a nondivine person to a divine status. Jesus goes back to the Father's side as the resurrected, immortal, exalted God-Man. These ideas are laid out for us in a rather complete fashion in Philippians 2.6–11.

Scripture presents several difficult paradoxes about who Jesus is. A *paradox* is an affirmation of two claims that may seem contradictory yet are both true. A paradox is not illogical, but it may be beyond our ability to parse out logically. Here's the basic paradox that establishes the pattern:

---

[11] Bauckham, *Jesus and the God of Israel*, 9.

We find in Scripture that God is not a man (Num 23.19) and that Christ is a man (1 Tim 2.5). Unitarians and others will say, "That's it, we're done here. Jesus is a man. God is not a man. Therefore, Jesus is not God." The problem is that the New Testament also says that Jesus is God (Jn 1.1, etc.). It tells us that he has God's nature and yet became a man. When Paul speaks of Christ "becoming in the likeness of men and being found in appearance as a man" (Phil 2.6–7, lit. trans.), that means he wasn't always one: He was something else first, and then *he became human*. Other New Testament authors tell us the same thing. The Word, or Logos, "was God" and "became flesh" (Jn 1.1, 14). The Son was God and "partook" of flesh and blood for our salvation (Heb 1.8; 2.14).

Other apparent contradictions are more specific instances of this fundamental paradox that Christ was divine and became human. Scripture says God is eternal (Ps 90.2), but Jesus was born (Mt 1.18). Yet he existed before creation (Jn 1.1–2; 17.5; Col 1.17), long before his birth. God is immutable (Ps 102.26–27), but Jesus grew (Lk 2.40, 52). Yet Hebrews applies the text in Psalms about God's immutability to the Son (Heb 1.11–12). God is omnipresent (Ps 139.7–10), but Jesus was in one place at a time, so that if he wanted to go somewhere, he walked (Mt 4.18). Yet Jesus could heal someone at a distance, as though he were there (Mt 8.5–13). Jesus could even tell his disciples that he would be with any two or three of them gathered in his name (Mt 18.20) and that he would be with all his disciples until the end of the age (Mt 28.20). That's quite a trick if you're simply a prophet, or even an archangel. God knows all things (Isa 41.22–23), but Jesus did not know the day or the hour (Mk 13.32). Yet the New Testament also teaches that Christ knows all things, even what is in people's hearts (Jn 16.30; Rev 2.23). God is immortal—he cannot die (1 Tim 1.17), but Jesus died (Jn 19.33). Yet Jesus could not have his life taken from him but had to lay it down voluntarily (Jn 10.17–18).

At some point you should notice a pattern here as you see these paradoxes, one after another after another. The key to understanding the paradoxes is the New Testament teaching that Christ was the preexistent Son, God by nature, who became human (Jn 1.1, 14; Phil 2.5–7;

Heb 1.8; 2.14). Indeed, if Christ was deity incarnate, we would *expect* such paradoxes.

Perhaps the most difficult of these paradoxes has to do with Christ experiencing temptation. The argument takes the familiar form: God cannot be tempted (Ja 1.13), but Jesus was tempted (Heb 4.15). Yes, but Hebrews 4.15 says that Jesus "in every respect has been tempted as we are, *yet without sin.*" That last part ought to make people think twice. Everybody who gets tempted eventually succumbs to temptation. "All have sinned" (Rom 3.23). In all of human history, only one person has experienced the full range of temptations to sin and yet never sinned—Jesus. In fact, Jesus claimed that as "the Son," he "can do nothing of his own accord, but only what he sees the Father doing" (Jn 5.19). That statement entails not just that Christ was sinless but also that, like God, he *couldn't* sin. Of course, physically speaking, Jesus could have stolen a piece of bread or done other sinful things. But in terms of his own moral, spiritual, mental constitution, Jesus never gave into sin, never gave into temptation, *because of who he was*—the Son of God.

Everything in creation belongs to God, and no one gave it to him (Job 41.11). But Jesus told his disciples, "All authority in heaven and earth has been given to me" (Mt 28.18). How can God be given authority? The answer is that Jesus is God the Son who humbled himself as the Servant for our sake, putting himself in a position of dependence on the Father to exalt him. Jesus is "the Son of Man" who "came . . . to give his life as a ransom for many" (Mt 20.28). He did so by humbling himself to become a human being, suffer, and die. Having humbled himself to do all that, he has been raised from the dead and given all authority in heaven and earth. The One to whom this universal authority has been given is not simply God the Son, but is the divine Son incarnate.

By the way, if Christ has all authority in heaven and earth, that makes him, at least functionally, God. The One in charge of everyone and everything, who decides where we will spend eternity (Mt 25.31–46), is God.

You have basically three choices as to how you will understand this pattern of apparent contradictions. (1) You can conclude that these presentations of Jesus are actually contradictory and that the New Testament is hopelessly incoherent. The problem with that explanation is that the paradoxes are a pattern throughout the New Testament and are often found in the same book. For example, as we showed earlier, Matthew presents Jesus as both located in one place at a time and as able to heal someone at a distance.

(2) You can agree with one side of these statements, but not the other, by insisting that all those places in the New Testament that seem to teach that Jesus was God can't really mean it. This option requires a lot of fudging and fixing of the New Testament either in retranslating or reinterpreting all those texts to fit your assumption that God could not have become incarnate.

(3) You can embrace the apparent contradictions as paradoxes arising from the fact that the divine Son humbled himself to share in our finite humanity. This has been the orthodox choice from very early on in Christian theology after the New Testament was written. Irenaeus, writing before the end of the second century, said, "Thus he took up man into himself, the invisible becoming visible, the incomprehensible being made comprehensible, the impassable [which means unable to suffer] becoming capable of suffering, and the Word being made man, thus summing up all things in himself."[12]

The doctrine of the incarnation rules out Unitarianism, according to which Jesus was just a man elevated to divine status. It also rules out Islam, in which Jesus was a great prophet but nothing more. The alternative Christologies are falling to the wayside, and we've only gone through two points: There is *one* Creator God, and there are *two* natures in Christ.

Three Divine Persons

Our third point is that there are three divine persons. Although the word Trinity isn't in the Bible, the triunity of the Deity is all over the New Testament. Depending on how we count them, the New Testament has anywhere between about 85 and 115 "triadic" texts in which the Father, Son,

---

[12] Irenaeus, *Against Heresies* 3.16.6, in *The Ante-Nicene Fathers*, 1.443.

and Holy Spirit are presented in a coordinated way.[13] The most famous such text is Matthew 28.19, "Go therefore and make disciples of all nations, baptizing them in the name of the Father and of the Son and of the Holy Spirit." Critics offer some creative and desperate responses, saying things like, "Well, it doesn't say the three are one God." But that is an argument from silence. We already know from other Scriptures that there is only one God. What *does* this text say? It says that disciples are to be baptized "in the name of"—and then three persons are named. We know the Father and the Son are persons, and since the term *spirit* commonly refers to a person and the word *name* is used of all three, the statement implies that the Holy Spirit is also a person. Moreover, baptizing is a religious rite of initiation into the people of God, in which you are confessing the object of your faith. According to Matthew 28.19, the object of faith is the Father, the Son, and the Holy Spirit. The text doesn't use the later technical terminology of the Trinity, but it does reveal three divine persons as the joint object of Christian faith confessed by name in the initiatory rite of baptism. This one statement, then, brings us a long way toward the doctrine of the Trinity.

Another famous Trinitarian text is 2 Corinthians 13.14, "The grace of the Lord Jesus Christ and the love of God and the fellowship of the Holy Spirit be with you all." Notice a couple things with me. First, if Christ is inferior to the Father, then Paul put the three persons in the 'wrong' order. Paul can list the three persons in basically every order that there is, because he is not worried about detracting from the honor of the Father by doing so (e.g., Rom 15.16, 30; 1 Cor 12.4–6; Eph 4.4–6). Notice also that grace is attributed to Christ and love to God. But elsewhere in Paul's epistles—even in the same epistle—sometimes it's the grace of God (2 Cor 9.14) and the love of Jesus Christ (2 Cor 5.14). There are no hard and fast lines being drawn here. It's not that grace is Christ's job and love is the Father's job. No. All three persons are involved in all these blessings. It's just put that way in this case.

Many other texts speak of the Father, Son, and Holy Spirit together in the context of related divine functions. Here again, we find a pattern

---

[13] On these texts, see Robert M. Bowman Jr., "Triadic New Testament Passages and the Doctrine of the Trinity," *Journal of Trinitarian Studies and Apologetics* 1 (Jan. 2013): 7–54.

throughout the New Testament. It's in the Gospels (e.g., Mt 3.16–17; Jn 14.16, 26), Acts (2.33; 7.55–60), the epistles (1 Cor 12.4–6; Eph 4.4–6; 1 Pt 1.2), and Revelation (1.4–5). This pattern consistently reveals Christ to be a divine person alongside the Father and the Holy Spirit.

Scott Harrell of Dallas Seminary says, "The threefold experience of the personal God is densely woven throughout the New Testament."[14] The deity of Christ and the doctrine of the Trinity do not rest on isolated proof texts. There are lots of proof texts, but the doctrines don't rest on this or that verse. It's part of the fabric of the whole New Testament.

The Trinity rules out Oneness Pentecostalism, which teaches that Jesus was the Father manifested in the flesh, and it rules out all the other heretical views that I have mentioned. The one thing they all have in common is a rejection of the doctrine of the Trinity.

Four Main Christological Passages

I have just stated that the deity of Christ is part of the fabric of the New Testament. That having been said, it is laid out more directly and fully in some places than in others. There are four main Christological passages: John 1.1–18, Philippians 2.5–11, Colossians 1.12–20, and Hebrews 1.1–13. Now you may be thinking: "Rob, where do you get off saying these are the main ones? It's just because you like these passages more." I do like these passages a lot, but that's not why. These are the main passages in which Christ's divine nature is laid out in a detailed, extensive manner. Notice that they are all sizable passages, not short, one-verse proof texts. True, some of our favorite proof texts are embedded in these passages, such as John 1.1. But it's not just John 1.1 that is significant on the subject; it's John 1.1–18. We ought to build our Christology on these main passages because they are the longest and most detailed, extensive expositions of who Jesus is.

So, we should start with these passages. That doesn't mean we ignore isolated verses that may sound like they're saying something else, but we don't make such texts primary. That's what the heretical religions do. They

---

[14] Horrell, "The Eternal Son of God in the Social Trinity," in *Jesus in Trinitarian Perspective*, ed. Sanders and Issler, 45.

start with an isolated proof text and announce, "We're done. We've proved that Jesus can't be God, just from this one verse all by itself. You don't even have to read the verse before or the verse after. This verse alone proves it."

Not only are those four passages the most substantial expositions of Christology in the New Testament, but they exhibit the same pattern of divine Christology. They don't rigidly say the same thing in the same words, but they exhibit the same pattern, and they often use the same or parallel terminology. Two of these passages call Jesus "God" (Jn 1.1; Heb 1.8); one calls him "Lord" in a context that has to mean Yahweh (Phil 2.9–11); and one says that the fullness of deity dwelled in him (Col 1.19, cf. 2.9). Those statements are very similar in meaning, even though they use different words.

Three of these passages say that all things came into being through the Son or the Word (Jn 1.3; Col 1.16; Heb 1.2). Three of them express Christ's divine Sonship in different terms, calling him the "unique Son" or "only-begotten" (Jn 1.14), the Father's "beloved Son" and "the firstborn" (Col 1.13, 15), and "the heir of all things" and "the firstborn" (Heb 1.2, 6). These are surprisingly similar terms used by writers that probably didn't even read each other's works. John states that the Son "is at the Father's side" (Jn 1.18, lit., "in the bosom of the Father"). Paul says that God "highly exalted" Jesus above all creation (Phil 2.9–10) and that God's purpose for his Son is "that in everything he might be preeminent" (Col 1.18). Hebrews says that the Son "sat down at the right hand of the Majesty on high" (Heb 1.3).

On the one hand, these passages all distinguish between Christ and the Father. Jesus isn't God the Father. When Paul says that "God has highly exalted him" (Phil 2.9), the title *God* there refers to the Father. On the other hand, these passages all understand Jesus to have the same divine status and power as the Father. Sitting at the right hand of the Father doesn't mean that Christ is second in place, but that he shares with the Father that highest position of ruling over all creation. This is the consistent teaching not only of these four main Christological passages but of texts found throughout the New Testament.

Five Reasons We Know that Jesus Is God

Finally, the New Testament gives us five different kinds of reasons for believing that Jesus is God, which Ed Komoszewski and I present in our two books through the acronym ***HANDS***[15]: Jesus receives the *H*onors due to God, possesses the *A*ttributes of God, bears the *N*ames of God, performs the *D*eeds that God does, and sits in the *S*eat of God's throne. We believe that Jesus is God incarnate not just because he gets called God a few times but because of everything that the New Testament says about Jesus.

First, Jesus receives the *honors* due to God. For example, he receives worship (Mt 28.17; Lk 24.51–52; Heb 1.6; Rev 5.14). He is the object of faith (Jn 3.15–16; 20.31; Ac 16.31; Rom 10.11; 1 Jn 5.13). He receives prayer (Jn 14.14; Ac 7.59–60; Rom 10.12–13; 2 Cor 12.8–9).

Second, Jesus possesses the *attributes* of God. He existed before creation and is thus uncreated (Jn 1.1–3; 17.5; Col 1.16–17; Heb 1.2). He is omnipotent (Eph 1.19–21; 1 Pt 3.22), omniscient (Jn 16.30–31; 21.17; 1 Cor 4.5; Rev 2.23), and omnipresent (Mt 18.20; 28.20; Eph 4.10–11).

Third, Jesus bears the *names* of God. He is called "God" about eight times (Jn 1.1, 18; 20.28; Rom 9.5; Titus 2.13; Heb 1.8; 2 Pt 1.1; 1 Jn 5.20). Jesus is also called "Lord" (Greek, *kyrios*) hundreds of times in the New Testament, many of which clearly use the title to represent the divine name Yahweh, usually translated with *kyrios* in the Greek Old Testament (e.g., Mk 1.2, cf. Isa 40.3; Rom 10.9–13, cf. Joel 2.32; 1 Cor 8.6, cf. Dt 6.4; Phil 2.9–11, cf. Isa 45.23). Jesus is called "Savior," sometimes coupled with other divine titles as in Titus 2.13, "our great God and Savior, Jesus Christ" (similarly, 2 Pt 1.1). Faced with all the texts calling Jesus God, Lord, Savior, the First and the Last, the Beginning and the End, etc., critics try to argue that Jesus isn't really any of those things; he's just *called* those things because he acts on God's behalf. At some point you have to ask, is that really the best explanation of these texts? No, it isn't: Jesus bears these names of God because he *is* God.

Fourth, Jesus performs the *deeds* of God. John 5.19 is a rather startling statement: "The Son can do nothing of his own accord, but only what he

---

[15] Bowman and Komoszewski, *Putting Jesus in His Place; Incarnate Christ and His Critics*.

sees the Father doing. For whatever the Father does, that the Son does likewise." So, Jesus does *only* what God would do, and he does *everything* that God does. Doesn't that make him God?

Let's consider some specific examples of the divine deeds performed by Jesus. First, Christ made the universe. The book of Hebrews applies the words of Psalm 102.25 to the Son: "You, Lord, laid the foundation of the earth in the beginning, and the heavens are the works of your hands" (Heb 1.10). The same epistle, along with John and Paul, make it clear that Christ did not do this apart from God the Father, saying that the world was created or made through the Son (Jn 1.3, 10; Col 1.16; Heb 1.2).

Now wait a minute, skeptics may be thinking. How do we know that Jesus did the work of creation? No human was able to witness him doing that. Well, Jesus did many things that people did witness that revealed his divine power and authority. For example, Jesus forgave people's sins. I'm not talking here about Jesus forgiving someone who stepped on his toe or took something that belonged to him. When some men brought a paralyzed man to Jesus for healing, Jesus immediately forgave all the sins that the paralytic had ever committed in his life. No wonder the scribes said, "Why does this man speak like that? Who can forgive sins but God alone?" (Mk 2.5–7). Jesus then demonstrated his authority to heal the man spiritually by healing him physically, telling him to stand and go home (Mk 2.8–12).

Now, of course, other people did miracles, such as Moses, Elijah, and Elisha. However, Jesus did miracles with simple commands. He never prayed that the Father would do the miracles; Jesus just did them. For example, Jesus was in a fishing boat on the Sea of Galilee with some of the disciples, and he fell asleep—a very human thing to do, of course. The disciples rouse Jesus. "There's a big storm. Don't you care? We're dying here." Jesus looked out at the storm, and said, "Shut up." And it did! That's a pretty accurate paraphrase that better reflects the tone of what Jesus said than "be still." There was no long ritual prayer, no working himself up into an altered state of consciousness—none of that stuff. He just said, "Shut up" (*pephimoso*, Mk 4.39). That sort of demonstration of power over creation supported the earliest Christians in their belief that Jesus Christ was the preexistent Son through whom God made all things.

Finally, Jesus sits on the *seat* of God's throne. Jesus himself claimed that he would sit at God's right hand in heaven (Mk 14.62), and this idea is affirmed throughout the New Testament (Ac 2.33–34; Rom 8.34; Heb 1.3–6; 1 Pt 3.22; Rev 22.1–3). The imagery here is not that of a king's child who gets to sit on his daddy's lap while daddy runs the kingdom. Rather, Jesus rules over all existence from God's throne, and he does so forever (Mt 28.18; Lk 1.33; Phil 2.10; Heb 1.8). This is not an honorary or token position. Jesus is ruling and will rule forever and ever from the throne of God.

Summing Up

You may have noticed that I have organized the argument for the deity of Christ using the numbers 1 through 5, with the hope that this outline will make it easy for you to remember the main points. To review: there's *one* God (the Creator), *two* natures of Christ (deity and humanity), *three* divine persons (Father, Son, and Holy Spirit), *four* main Christological passages (Jn 1.1–18; Phil 2.5–11; Col 1.12–20; Heb 1.1–13), and *five* reasons for believing that Jesus is God (*HANDS*—*h*onors, *a*ttributes, *n*ames, *d*eeds, and *s*eat). With these points in mind, you're ready to defend the truth of the deity of Christ.

Bibliography

Barrett, Matthew. *None Greater: The Undomesticated Attributes of God.* Foreword by Fred Sanders. Grand Rapids: Baker, 2019.

Bauckham, Richard. *Jesus and the God of Israel:* God Crucified *and Other Studies on the New Testament's Christology of Divine Identity.* Grand Rapids: Eerdmans, 2009.

Bernard, David K. *The Oneness of God.* Pentecostal Theology, Volume 1. Rev. ed. Hazelwood, MO: Word Aflame Press, 2001.

Bird, Michael F. *Jesus among the gods: Early Christology in the Greco-Roman World.* Waco, TX: Baylor University Press, 2022.

Borg, Marcus J. *Days of Awe and Wonder: How to Be a Christian in the Twenty-first Century*. New York: HarperOne, 2017.

Borg, Marcus J., and Ray Riegert, eds. *Jesus and Buddha: The Parallel Sayings*. Berkeley: Ulysses Press, 1997.

Bowman, Robert M., Jr. "Triadic New Testament Passages and the Doctrine of the Trinity." *Journal of Trinitarian Studies and Apologetics* 1 (Jan. 2013): 7–54.

Bowman, Robert M., Jr., and J. Ed Komoszewski. *The Incarnate Christ and His Critics: A Biblical Defense*. Grand Rapids: Kregel, 2024.

—————. *Putting Jesus in His Place: The Case for the Deity of Christ*. Grand Rapids: Kregel, 2007.

Buzzard, Anthony F. *Jesus Was Not a Trinitarian: A Call to Return to the Creed of Jesus*. Morrow, GA: Restoration Fellowship, 2007.

Feinberg, John S. *No One Like Him: The Doctrine of God*. Foundations of Evangelical Theology. Wheaton, IL: Crossway, 2001.

Loke, Andrew Ter Ern. *The Origin of Divine Christology*. SNTSMS 169. Cambridge: Cambridge University Press, 2017.

Pitre, Brant. *Jesus and Divine Christology*. Grand Rapids: Eerdmans, 2024.

Roberts, Alexander, and James Donaldson, eds. *The Ante-Nicene Fathers: Translations of the Writings of the Fathers Down to A.D. 325*. Revised by A. Cleveland Coxe. New York: Charles Scribner's Sons, 1903 (orig. 1885).

Sanders, Fred, and Klaus Issler, eds. *Jesus in Trinitarian Perspective: An Intermediate Christology*. Foreword by Gerald Bray. Nashville: B&H Academic, 2007.

Smith, Joseph. *History of the Church of Jesus Christ of Latter-day Saints: Period I, History of Joseph Smith, by Himself*. Introduction and notes by B. H. Roberts. 7 vols. Salt Lake City: Deseret, 1902.

Spong, John Shelby. *Jesus for the Non-Religious: Recovering the Divine at the Heart of the Human*. New York: HarperOne, 2007.

Tuggy, Dale, and Christopher M. Date. *Is Jesus Human and Not Divine? A Debate*. Apollo, PA: Areopagus Books, 2020.

Watchtower Bible and Tract Society. *Reasoning from the Scriptures*. Wallkill, NY: Watchtower, 1995.

14

This World is Messed Up But God Raised Jesus from the Dead
Addressing the Pastoral Problem of Evil

Robert B. Stewart

Deep down inside, all of us—Christians or non-Christians, theists or nontheists—have this sense that there's something wrong with this world. In fact, every worldview has to try to answer these questions: "What's wrong in this world?" and "What's the solution to what's wrong?"

Let me share with you two true stories.

Story #1: One of the people who died in the terrorist attack in New Orleans on New Year's Day 2025 was a young man that I baptized approximately five years ago. His name was Brandon. Brandon started coming to our church because he recognized that something was missing in his life. Over two decades earlier, he had come to the church as a child for Vacation Bible School. He said that he knew he would be safe and welcome. (That shows how small things can bear fruit many years later that we rarely recognize.) Brandon was painfully shy; he always arrived in time for Sunday School but would just sit in the fellowship hall and read his Bible. Then he would come to church. I preached Brandon's funeral yesterday. There were a lot of tears. He was engaged to be married. He had his life in front of him.

Brandon's mother, Mary, had two children, both sons. Brandon's brother died of a heart attack less than two years ago. His mother has lost both her sons in less than two years' time. No parent should have to stand beside the coffin of his or her child, much less two.

Story #2: Kolja was my teaching assistant. Kolja was a young German man from Hamburg. He was very bright and a deeply committed believer. He was a Ph.D. student in philosophy at the University of Rochester in upstate New York. He was writing his dissertation in epistemology under the direction of Richard Feldman, a prominent philosopher. Kolja was also pastoring a small Baptist church in downtown Rochester. He had pastored it for years, but after Covid, he insisted on doing so for no pay. He was 37, in the prime of life, and didn't have an ounce of fat on his body. Kolja had a wife and three young daughters.

Late in march of 2023, I was team-teaching a Ph.D. seminar in philosophical hermeneutics and received a text from my son, Ray, who was also close to Kolja—they both went to Western Michigan University, where they earned M.A. degrees in philosophy. Ray's text said that Kolja had died the day before. I excused myself from the seminar, went out to my car, and wept like a baby. I preached Kolja's funeral too. Kolja died of a strep infection that turned septic. No little girl should lose her daddy to strep throat. I repeat—something is wrong in this world.

We all suffer in some way, at some time; suffering is a universal experience. Although pain and suffering are universally experienced, they are not equally experienced. The intensity and frequency with which we suffer differs from person to person—but we all suffer.

The problem of pain is a complex problem. When I say it's a complex problem, what I mean is that it is multi-dimensional. The problem of pain and suffering is one of the head and the heart! It's an *intellectual problem*, but it's also an *existential problem*.

We have to address pain and suffering as an apologetics issue. But suffering is also a pastoral issue. Committed Christians who aren't doubting still struggle with pain and suffering. We need to hear their cries for help. If we as Christians don't deal well with the pastoral problem of pain, both in terms of bearing pain, and in responding to the pain that others bear, we will falsify our claims concerning the various intellectual problems of pain.

One of my all-time favorite authors, perhaps my favorite author, is C.S. Lewis. Lewis's life offers us some helpful pointers on how to think about pain and suffering. Lewis wrote two books on suffering. The first book, *The Problem of Pain* was a commissioned book, published in 1940. He wrote the second book, *A Grief Observed*, 20 years later, after his wife, whom he married late in life, died of cancer.

In the preface of *The Problem of Pain* Lewis wrote this:

> I must add, too, that the only purpose of the book is *to solve the intellectual problem raised by suffering*; for the far higher task of teaching fortitude and patience I was never fool enough to suppose myself qualified, nor have I anything to offer my readers except my conviction that when pain is to be borne, a little courage helps more than much knowledge, a little human sympathy more than much courage, and the least tincture of the love of God more than all.[1]

The two books are very different. *The Problem of Pain* is analytical and theoretical, while *A Grief Observed* is a journal of Lewis's grief, a type of lament. *A Grief Observed* is raw and honest. It's Lewis working through his own personal pastoral problem of pain. Lewis wrote *A Grief Observed* under a pseudonym: "N. W. Klerk." In Old English that means "an unknown scholar." It was never published under Lewis's real name in his lifetime. From time to time people who knew that he had lost his wife mailed him his own book thinking it might help him!

When we suffer, we are sometimes tempted to doubt either God's goodness or his greatness. I say that we are sometimes tempted—I don't think that there is a necessary connection between suffering and doubt. But there is frequently the temptation to doubt.

In *A Grief Observed* Lewis clearly is not doubting that God exists but rather he doubts God's goodness. Early in the book he wrote this:

> Not that I am (I think) in much danger of ceasing to believe in God. The real danger is of coming to believe such dreadful things about him. The conclusion I dread is not "so there's no God after all," but "so this is what God's really like. Deceive yourself no longer."[2]

---

[1] Lewis, *The Problem of Pain*, vii-viii.
[2] Lewis, *A Grief Observed*, 6–7.

Some have thought that Lewis lost his faith after his wife's death. Not so. Those who read all the way to the end of *A Grief Observed* will see that he retained his faith. Near the end of the book, he wrote:

> When I lay these questions before God I get no answer. But a rather special sort of "no answer." It is not the locked door. It is more like a silent, certainly not uncompassionate, gaze. As though he shook his head not in refusal but waiving the question. Like, "peace, child; you don't understand." Can a mortal ask questions which God finds unanswerable? Quite easily, I should think. All nonsense questions are unanswerable. How many hours are there in a mile? Is yellow square or round? Probably half the questions we ask—half our great theological and metaphysical problems—are like that. And now that I come to think of it, there's no practical problem before me at all. I know the two great commandments, and I'd better get on with them.[3]

Lewis came to see something that Karl Marx and Friedrich Engels also saw and stated succinctly in their *Theses on Feuerbach*: "The philosophers have only interpreted the world, in various ways; the important thing is to transform it."[4] Marx and Engels were wrong on a number of points, but they were correct on this point: no philosophy is worth a hoot if it can't be lived. Christianity can be lived, but not easily. Nevertheless, it can be lived.

Lewis admittedly didn't have all the answers to the problem of pain. It's okay not to know everything. I teach a class on the problem of evil. I can't answer every question about evil and suffering.

Sometimes, given the evidence we have, we have to be satisfied knowing that two things are true that we can't fully reconcile to each other. For instance, physicists tell us that both *relativity* and *quantum mechanics* are extremely well-tested theories. They also tell us that they can't perfectly reconcile them. But they don't conclude that one or the other is false. Why? Because both scientific theories have evidentially been confirmed over and over. Physicists hope—eventually—to understand how they work together. But in the meantime, there is a tension.

---

[3] Lewis, *A Grief Observed*, 69–70.

[4] Marx and Engels, *Thesen* über *Feuerbach*, 3rd Revised Edition (Bonn: 2022), 30. The original German reads, "Die Philosophen haben die Welt nur verschieden interpretiert, es kömmt drauf an, sie zu verändern."

The existence of evil and suffering is evident; we have only to look around. What evidence do we have that God loves us? The answer to that question is simple—but it's not easy. The answer is the cross.

Sometimes the best response—and the best answer—we can have is "just trust God." That's right! You read me correctly! So often I have heard apologists belittle that answer—just trust God—and with good reason. "Just trust God" is a horrible answer to the question, "Does God exist?" It's an awful answer to the question, "Why should I believe that the Bible is true?" or "Why should I believe in miracles or that Jesus was raised from the dead?" But sometimes when we are hurting, and crying out to God for an explanation—or a way to endure our pain—the best answer is, "Trust the one who loves you enough to put his Son on the cross." Have we never told our children, or friends, "I can't explain it to you right now—you just have to trust me that I have your best interest at heart"?

My observation has been that—in general—there are good theoretical answers to the various problems of evil; the deductive problem; probabalistic problem; existential problem—writ large—as classes of problems. Most of the time, it seems like I can make sense of evil at the macro-level. But at the same time—at the micro-level—the individual instance of evil—there are many, many instances of evil that neither I nor anybody else can make sense of.

Sometimes a believer suffers and there is an immediate, obvious good that comes from that suffering even if not everyone calculates that that good is a greater good or an equal good to the evil of that particular instance of suffering.

Often, we're not in position to calculate these sorts of things. The story of Joseph in Genesis is a well-known example of greater good coming from suffering. In the final chapter of Genesis, after their father has died, Joseph tells his brothers that he will not seek vengeance upon them, when he says:

> "Don't be afraid. Am I in the place of God? You intended to harm me, but God intended it for good to accomplish what is now being done, the saving of many lives. So then, don't be afraid. I will provide for you and your children." And he reassured them and spoke kindly to them. (Genesis 50.19–21, NIV)

"You intended to harm me, but God intended it for good." But when Joseph was sitting in an Egyptian prison for refusing to sin against his God and his earthly master, he didn't say, "This is going to result in the salvation of my entire people group." He learned this many years later, after much suffering and many years of trusting God—and God proving to Joseph that he was worthy of his trust.

As a philosopher I think we get many helpful insights from philosophy that help us in understanding evil and also in responding to the problem of evil, but typically philosophers are concerned to arrive at philosophical defenses rather than practical advice for how to live in a world filled with pain and suffering. Philosophers also tend to work as "natural theologians." Natural theologians work with nature and human reason, but exclude the data of special revelation, i.e., Scripture, from their thinking. They may be Christians but for the sake of their work as philosophers they choose intentionally to bracket Scripture as an authoritative source in their work. (Note well: They may use Scripture as a source of information as to what Christians believe about God, but they do not use Scripture as a source of authority, i.e., a statement of truth about God.) This is often useful, but it also results in a pretty minimal picture of God, humans, the meaning of life, etc.

In a moment, I want to try a different sort of experiment. I want to start with the Bible and see if it offers us a thesis, and if we can test that thesis against what we know from reason and experience. This is, in fact, what scientists, historians, detectives, and jurists do—test a theory against the facts (evidence) that they have. What I'm not going to attempt to do is give you a neat, one-size-fits-all answer to the problem of pain and suffering. There is no silver bullet that will deal with all pain and suffering.

I hope that I've learned some things about how suffering has worked in my life—and from thinking about it as a philosopher and theologian—that help me understand God, life, and suffering at points. But mostly I am a fellow traveler through life. I know many have suffered far more than I. I am not an expert! So, I don't have a pithy phrase, or philosophical argument, that will deal with the experience of pain and suffering once and for all, for everyone in every place.

Just as the intensity of pain and suffering differs from person to person, the response to pain and suffering does too. Some people pull away from God as a result of suffering, while others draw closer to him. Allow me to tell you about a lady who was part of the first church that I served fulltime as a minister. Her name was Ann. Ann was a wonderful lady who had a life filled with trauma and loss. She was mother to two mentally-challenged sons, and one daughter, who helped her raise her two sons—until her daughter was diagnosed with inoperable, terminal brain cancer. Ann had been married three times, and each of her husbands died. One of her husbands was actually murdered, and the police never discovered who had killed him or why. Yet Ann was the most positive, encouraging person you would ever want to meet. She was not well off financially but she regularly brought little gifts, like home-baked desserts or canned goods she'd grown in her garden to the church staff, and served in other ways. Nobody, upon first meeting her, would know the challenges and loss that Ann had experienced.

Let me share with you about another person. I'm going to call him John, although that is not his name. John is a graduate of New Orleans Baptist Theological Seminary with a masters degree in Christian Apologetics. He went on to become a Ph.D. student at the seminary. Soon after he entered the Ph.D. program, he learned that his wife had had an affair. To make matters worse her affair had been with one of his groomsmen. Talk about double betrayal! John wanted to work it out with her but she refused. In short order, he failed out of the Ph.D. program, his wife divorced him, and he found himself out of the ministry.

Soon after all these things, John came to my office, and we had a conversation that went approximately thus:

John: "Doc, I'm doubting this whole Christianity thing."
Me: "Do you have any reason—any reason at all—other than your feelings—to doubt that God raised Jesus from the dead?"
Long Pause
John: "No."
Me: "So, you have no rational reason to doubt?"

Second Long Pause

John: "Thanks, Doc! I really needed that!"

John's doubting was rooted in his emotions, not in his intellect. It was rooted in what he was experiencing, not what he knew. We can't trust our emotions because our emotions fluctuate, they come and go.

Please understand this—I am not for one minute trying to say that our emotions don't matter. God made us with emotions, just like he made us with minds. He wants us to train both and to use them for his glory. Furthermore, sometimes our emotions tell us that something is off before our minds do.

To make my point, allow me share with you about another person, before returning to John. In the last church that I served as senior pastor before joining the seminary faculty, we had a wonderfully gifted youth minister named Chuck (not his real name). The church was a relatively large church whose members were financially well off, but certainly not a mega-church. Chuck came to us from one of the larger churches in Tennessee and was about to enter the Ph.D. program in counseling at Southwestern Baptist Theological Seminary. He was a gifted communicator, singer, and athlete. Our youth group thrived under his leadership. He and I were close to and frequently spent time together beyond our roles at the church. At some point, however, I began to sense that something was wrong with Chuck but couldn't tell what. Still, I knew that I was bothered. I recall very clearly driving home alone one night after church and praying, "God, if it's me, show me what's wrong. But if it's Chuck, please show me what's wrong in his life." The very next morning, we had our weekly staff meeting. My secretary told me that Chuck had called and said that he couldn't make it in that morning because he had to help a friend with a serious personal problem. He didn't make it in that afternoon, either. The following day, when I arrived at the office, my secretary told me that I needed to call the chairman of our personnel committee. When I did, he asked me if I had talked to Chuck. I said no. He said, "You need to, he has left his wife." (The daughter of our personnel committee chairman's adult daughter was very close to Chuck's wife.) I immediately called Chuck, and he said that we needed to talk, which was an understatement. When he arrived at the church, I asked him if it was true. He said it was. I then asked him, "Have you slept with this woman?" He said, "Not yet." I then asked, "Don't you realize how serious a sin this is?" His reply was, "God will forgive us." In other words, he was presuming God's forgiveness.

I share that story for two reasons. One is to warn all of us, myself included, that nobody is immune to temptation and that all of us are capable of far greater sins than we think we are. We must guard our hearts and walk humbly before God. But the primary reason I share that story is to demonstrate the value of our emotions. I knew something was wrong in his life in my spirit and my emotions before I knew what was wrong. Our emotions matter.

Emotions are especially important when dealing with the problem of pain. Sometimes people just need to share their pain with someone. They need to grieve and to know that others are grieving with them. But what John needed from me that day was to be reminded of what he knew to be true. He didn't need me simply to hold his hand and tell him it would be okay—he needed me to remind him that God raised Jesus from the dead. He needed to be reminded that Christianity is based on historical facts, not simply our feelings.

John's case was unique. *Everyone's case is unique.* None of us is the norm. When we deal with the problem of evil, we need to be sharp-minded but also gentle-hearted. We need to approach the issue both intellectually but also pastorally.

In general—I repeat, in general—those dealing with suffering as an intellectual question need *information* to *understand* the issue. They want to know how pain and suffering make sense in the biblical worldview. In general—again, I repeat, in general—those dealing with suffering as an existential problem need encouragement, instruction, and support to cope with the experience of suffering. But the two cannot be entirely separated, because if the pastoral instruction isn't grounded in truth, then no matter how effective it is for the moment, it isn't ultimately useful because if it's not true, it's only accidentally helpful.

Please allow me to be very transparent with you for a moment. I want to share with you one of the greatest failures of my pastoral career. I was pastoring the First Baptist Church in a small town in Texas. This town had a population of less than a thousand people. Many of the people in my congregation were related to one another either biologically or by marriage. We had many extended families that had members in both our congregation and the town's Church of Christ, the other significant congregation in town due to marriage. Everybody knew everybody.

One afternoon, tragedy struck. The eleven-year-old grandson of one of our deacons was killed after being struck by a car driven by a teenager. The situation was this: It was his mother's birthday. She had taken her children to the store to buy sweets and decorations for her birthday party, which was to be that evening. They lived in the country, and when they arrived home, he asked if he could get the birthday cards out of the mailbox. She said yes. Unfortunately, their mailbox was on the other side of the country road from their house, and he was so excited that he dashed out into the road without looking, and was struck by a car that had just crested a slight hill. His life was snuffed out in an instant.

Our community was traumatized. The large extended family of the young boy was obviously in shock. But the young lady who was driving the car was also a victim. She too needed pastoral care.

My wife and I went to see and pray with both families. And I changed my prepared sermon to address the situation. I was pleasantly surprised to see the family of the driver in church that Sunday. The grandfather and grandmother of the young boy were also present. I preached from the book of Job on God's sovereignty. There are many lessons in Job about suffering and sovereignty. Unfortunately, what I focused upon in Job wasn't helpful, largely because at that time I didn't understand the overall message of the book. What I said that morning was true, so far as it went, but it was also distorted, insensitive, and brutal. Nobody ever told me so, but as I've reflected on it over the years, I can see that I badly mismanaged an opportunity. The young lady and her family never darkened the doors of our church again.

Sometimes what people need is not information. Sometimes they need consolation. Apologetically, consoling the grieving is often the greatest single thing we believers can do. It's our job to know when to speak the truth in love and when to love and shut up.

We must understand that the world is watching how we Christians live, and if we don't deal well with the pastoral problem of pain, often they see no reason to listen to our thoughts about the intellectual problem of pain. If we Christians don't suffer well, then we will falsify our rational explanations for evil and suffering. Note Well: Suffering well doesn't mean not grieving, but rather grieving with hope (1 Thess 4.13).

Nowhere in the Bible do we read something that we frequently hear from liberal theologians and pastors: "It doesn't matter if it's true, what matters is this: 'does it help you.'" Rudolf Bultmann wrote this: "Does he help me because he is God's Son, or is he the Son of God because he helps me?"[5] My question for Bultmann would be this: How can he help me if he is not the Son of God?

We can't divorce the intellectual from the pastoral even though they are distinct. We can *distinguish* between them but we cannot *divide* them. Pastorally we are looking for something that helps with feelings of despair—but to truly be helpful, our assistance has to be based on facts. It can't be all sweetness and sunshine. People who are satisfied with something that just makes them feel better are like fools who turn up their car radios so that they won't hear the actual problem in the engine. Truth and love go together; they are like two wings of an airplane. We have to be loving when we address the apologetic dimension and truthful when we deal with the pastoral dimension. The apostle Paul makes it very clear in Ephesians 4.15, "Instead, speaking the truth in love, we will grow to become in every respect the mature body of him who is the head, that is, Christ" (NIV).

To some degree, how we think about pain and suffering is culturally contextual. Michael is a British friend of mine who grew up in Saudi Arabia. There was far more death and suffering in the region where he

---

[5] Bultmann, *Essays: Philosophical and Theological*, 280.

grew up than there typically is in North America or Europe *but Michael never heard the problem of pain raised as an objection against Christian faith or belief in God.* The intellectual problem of evil simply wasn't an apologetics issue where he grew up—like it was in Europe, especially in Oxford, where he was teaching at the time. Let me be very clear on this point: Michael did *not* say that suffering was *not a problem* in Saudi Arabia. But it was not an *apologetic* problem there.

This shows us that *sometimes* suffering is an *intellectual* problem—but it is *always* a *pastoral* and *emotional* problem because pain always hurts. Furthermore, we don't live in the Middle East. We live in America—and people in America don't expect to suffer; they expect life to be comfortable. Sometimes we even appear to think that we deserve to be happy and that God has no right to allow us ever to suffer. This tells us that something is wrong with American Christianity. I think that we've bought into a lie that says that "if you know God, then your life will be all puppies and lollipops. Name it and claim it and you'll be healthy and wealthy. Jesus removes all of your problems." That is most definitely not the message that we find in the Bible.

Questioning God about suffering—particularly our personal suffering—is all over the Bible. Job, Jeremiah, and Jesus are biblical examples that come to mind. The Bible is filled with laments. Lament is crying out to God from an experience of pain. Frequently, lament is *complaining to God* about seeming injustice.

Job 3.11 says: "Why did I not perish at birth, come forth from the womb and expire?" (NASB)

In Jeremiah 15.18a we read: "Why is my pain unending and my wound grievous and incurable?" (NIV)

On the cross, Jesus quoted Psalm 22 in his cry of desolation: "My God, My God, why have you forsaken me…?" (Matthew 27.46 NASB 1995)

Roughly one-third of the psalms are psalms of lament. There's even an entire book of the Bible named Lamentations!

Understand this: Experiencing pain is not necessarily a bad thing. We tend to misunderstand physical pain. Physical pain is not an illness; it's an indicator. A fever is not an illness—it's a response to an illness. It tells us something is wrong. It's a symptom, not the problem.

Pain and suffering are symptoms of a deeper problem. What is that problem, biblically speaking? In a word it is "sin." To understand the problem, we need to see the biblical story in context. The biblical story begins with God (rather than with an argument for God's existence): "In the beginning God…" Just four words (in English—only three in Hebrew). The biblical God is great. He is almighty. He is sovereign over history. Lamentations 3.37–38 captures it well:

> Who is there who speaks and it comes to pass,
> > Unless the Lord has commanded *it*?
> *Is it* not from the mouth of the Most High
> > That both good and ill go forth? (NASB 1995)

This sort of sovereignty bothers a lot of people. Not me. It tells me that God has a reason for all my suffering—even if I don't know what that reason is.

The biblical God is also loving. Everything he made was good. But the Bible also tells a story about a spiritual enemy who wreaks havoc in this world. And he comes on the scene in Genesis 3. He sows seeds of doubt "has God said…?" He lies, "You won't die." And our first parents bought what he was selling. Simply put, *we are fallen people living in a fallen world.*

Okay, I'm ready now to run my experiment. To do so, we need to look at the biblical story. I want us to ask this question of the biblical story. "Does the biblical story lead us to be surprised that we find ourselves in a world with suffering, or does it lead us to expect that to be the case?"

I am aware that a skeptic might object to my using the Bible. Frequently, skeptics will say something like, "You can't use the Bible to make your case."[6] I admit that it would be wrong for me to use the Bible if I

---

[6] Often skeptics want to challenge Christians to give an answer to their questions without using the Bible in any way. In other words, they demand an answer from the Christian worldview on one hand, but on the other hand they wish to deny us access to the Christian worldview. I grant that it is viciously circular to appeal to the truthfulness of the Bible by pointing out that the Bible says that it is truthful, but there is nothing circular about appealing to the worldview narrative that unfolds in the Christian Scriptures.

were to use the Bible as a source of *authority*. But I'm not going to use the Bible as a source of authority but rather as a source of *information*.

What sort of information am I seeking? Not historical information but rather theological information. I am not insisting that the Bible is true (although I believe that it is), but rather I am pointing to what the Bible teaches that Christians believe. I am definitely not reasoning in a circular manner or begging the question.

In the biblical story, there are five acts.

Act 1: The world before the fall.

Act 2: The world after the fall but before Jesus Christ.

Act 3: The ministry of Jesus—including his death, resurrection, ascension, and Pentecost.

Act 4: The world with the Gospel and the Spirit—after the cross, resurrection, and coming of the Spirit—set right in an already but not yet fully-realized sense.

Act 5: The world to come, new heavens and new earth.

Presently, we're in Act 4! Let's see what Romans 8.19–23 has to say about Act 4:

> For the creation waits in eager expectation for the children of God to be revealed. For the creation was subjected to frustration, not by its own choice, but by the will of the one who subjected it, in hope that the creation itself will be liberated from its bondage to decay and brought into the freedom and glory of the children of God. We know that the whole creation has been groaning as in the pains of childbirth right up to the present time. Not only so, but we ourselves, who have the firstfruits of the Spirit, groan inwardly as we wait eagerly for our adoption to sonship, the redemption of our bodies. (NIV)

The entire universe is groaning and hoping for redemption—like we are. Biblical hope is certain but what is hoped for is out in the future. Why doesn't it say "wishing for redemption?" Because of Jesus.

Let's see what my experiment has yielded. Given where we are right now—Act 4—it's not surprising that we find lots of good and evil, success and failure, and horrendous sorts of evil in this world. In fact, this is exactly what the Bible leads us to expect. *But if evil and suffering are not surprising, how exactly do they work against the Christian worldview?* The answer seems obvious: They don't!

Note Well: We can know *that* evil and suffering have a purpose. Romans 8.28 tells us that "all things work together for good for those who are called according to his purpose." It does *not* tell us that all things are good. Nor does it say that we will know *how* all things work for good.

Did you catch verse 23 of Romans 8? It reads, "Not only so, but we ourselves, who have the firstfruits of the Spirit, groan inwardly as we wait eagerly for our adoption to sonship, the redemption of our bodies." Paul is talking about Resurrection. Resurrection is the Christian answer to what's wrong with the world! Resurrection is part of God's ultimate plan for creation. God created a perfect world—and we messed it up royally. Resurrection is God's answer to the sorry state of the world we live in.

Resurrection was a Jewish belief before it was a Christian belief. Most Jews believed in resurrection before Jesus was born.[7] The main reason that most Jews came to believe in resurrection before the birth of Christianity was that their Scriptures told them that because their God was faithful to his people, he was going to reverse the curse—he was going to clean up the mess they made—he was going to set creation right. But if death were not defeated, then creation would not be set right.

One sometimes hears at funerals that death is a friend. The Bible doesn't teach such a thing. The Bible calls death an enemy. Physical death separates us from our loved ones. Spiritual death separates us from God. And spiritual death coupled with physical death separates us from God forever. Death is the opposite of what Jesus is. Jesus is the bread of *life* (John 6.35), he is the way, the truth, and the *life* (John 14.6), and he is the *resurrection* and the *life* (John 11.25). Death is not anybody's friend.

Death is so bad that if Jesus was not raised from the dead, nothing matters. But if Jesus was raised from the dead nothing matters more. Death—and sin—are so bad that God the Father put his Son on the

---

[7] Not all Jews believed in it. The Pharisees believed in resurrection, as did the Qumran community, but the Sadducees and the Essenes did not. The Sadducees did not reject the idea of resurrection because they were liberal. They denied the resurrection because they were biblical literalists and gave priority to the Torah over the oral law.

cross to deal with it! But God is so good that he put his Son on the cross to deal with sin. And because God raised Jesus from the dead, death is a defeated enemy. When Jesus comes back he will call us all from the dead. And death will be no more. Jesus' resurrection is a testimony to the faithfulness of God. *Our God does not abandon his people.*

Resurrection means that death is really, really bad, but resurrection also means that God is greater than the evil of death, and that death is defeated. Resurrection is not simply a new, positive way to think about death, it's not a reconstrual of death, it's not a new understanding of death. It's not a way to say death isn't so bad after all. Resurrection is the defeat of death. It's the death of death!

Jesus' resurrection means that all that tyrants can do is kill you. And Jesus has already defeated death. Jesus' resurrection is why middle-eastern Christians can die singing as ISIS executes them. Because they know that their redeemer lives and on this earth again shall stand!

Resurrection means that there will be final justice. Resurrection means that Hitler didn't get away with it. Stalin didn't get away with it. ISIS won't get away with it. No tyrant ever will.

Resurrection also means that we won't get away with our sins. Resurrection is a reminder to put your faith in Jesus in this life because each of us will have to answer to God in the next.

Resurrection means that your deepest pain—no matter how painful—is going to be dealt with. Resurrection means that a day is coming when God will remake our present world, and Jesus Christ will wipe every tear from every eye and there will be no death, no disease, no injustice, and no mourning. That's what resurrection tells us!

Bibliography

Bultmann, Rudolf. *Essays: Philosophical and Theological*, trans. James C. G. Greig. London: SCM, 1955.

Lewis, C.S. *The Problem of Pain.* New York: Macmillan, 1947.

Lewis, C.S. *A Grief Observed.* San Francisco: HarperSanFrancisco, 1996.

Marx, Karl and Friedrich Engels. *Die Deutsche Ideologie.* Kindle Edition, 733.

15

Witnessing to Mormons with the *Book of Mormon*

James K. Walker

Introductory Remarks

Just imagine two eager Latter-day Saint missionaries show up at your front door and *you* are equipped to use their very own Book of Mormon (BoM) as a witnessing tool for the truth of Christianity! If you cannot even begin to imagine how this would be possible, this chapter is for you. Here we will examine some of teachings of the Church of Jesus Christ of Latter-day Saints (LDS), right from the Book of Mormon so you can be better prepared to answer the missionaries' knock at your door.

Growing up as a fourth-generation LDS, I had some Christian friends in school who knowledgeably and compassionately asked me questions about LDS doctrine. They started me on a journey from being a believing Mormon who knew it was true without a shadow of a doubt, to having a few concerning questions. Those questions grew into doubts. And those doubts eventually became a full-blown crisis.[1] I finally came to realize that the BoM and the LDS gospel were not true. But this also left me with some doubts and skepticism about the veracity of the Bible. Over time I was able to resolve those concerns; I now see the Bible as a useful tool for testing some of the truth claims of the BoM and for

---

[1] For more on my background and ministry, see http://www.watchman.org/staff/JamesWalker-Bio5.pdf

better understanding and contrasting the beliefs of LDS with those of traditional Christian denominations and churches.

I. The Right Attitude

First let us begin with the Bible. Scripture exhorts us to have a gentle and respectful approach when we attempt to share the gospel with people of other faiths, including Mormons. Consider Ephesians 4.14–15. The Apostle Paul writes that we must henceforth be "no more children"— we must no longer be spiritually immature, for we are vulnerable in a state of spiritual immaturity, and we will be "tossed to and fro, and carried about with every wind of doctrine by the sleight of men and the cunning craftiness whereby they lie in wait to deceive." The spiritually immature are vulnerable to false teaching, to spiritual abuse, and to a myriad of other problems. By the grace of God, we must examine ourselves before diving headlong into spiritual conversations with passionate believers from other faith traditions and be able and empowered by the Holy Spirit to speak the truth in love (Eph 4.15). This is especially true for engaging zealous and dedicated Latter-day Saints.

There is always the ever-present danger of trying to win an argument with a non-Christian but losing the person. Apologetic arguments can easily become a clanging cymbal in the ears of non-believers (1 Cor 13.1). Instead, we want to be "Ephesians Four" type of Christians. When we share the gospel, we want to speak both truth *and* love. And if we were honest with ourselves, we can all probably remember a time or two when our words were more like clanging brass than love.

As a former fourth-generation Latter-day Saint, I had some Christian friends in school that were kind and loving. They asked good questions and made me think. But I also had a few Christian friends who were not so nice. They wanted to belittle, criticize, and make fun of me. Even if everything they told me about LDS and the Bible was true, I wasn't going to pay any attention to them because they didn't show me much in the way of love.

There is also the opposite danger of being "all love" and no truth. Sometimes we value the relationship we have with someone so much that we don't want to do anything that we think might potentially harm the relationship. We end up never getting around to telling them that they need the Gospel of Jesus Christ, that Jesus is the only way of salvation, and that their present path, though it may seem right to them, leads to death.

Where to Begin with Latter-day Saint Missionaries

ComeuntoChrist.org is one of the official websites of The Church of Jesus Christ of Latter-day Saints (LDS). When you visit the site, scroll down close to the bottom of the page. There you will see a link to request a free copy of the BoM. If you click that and put in your name and address, your new BoM will likely arrive faster than if you ordered it from Amazon Prime! And your new BoM will be hand-delivered by two bright-eyed, passionate Mormon missionaries who will be quite eager to discuss it with you. We have prepared a free documentation guide containing full-page scans of key LDS source materials to help with your discussions.[2]

So, let's jump right in. This chapter will provide you with a few approaches you can intelligently and compassionately employ with LDS friends, using the BoM.

II. Using the *Book of Mormon* with Mormons

When LDS missionaries deliver a BoM to you, they will oftentimes underline a few key passages from it. They will likely ask: "After you've had a few days to read over and pray and think about it, may we come back and see if you have any questions?" After reading this chapter, you should be confidently able to say to them, "Absolutely!"

One of the late Mormon apostles, Bruce R McConkie (d. 1985) wrote the long-standing introduction to the contemporary *Book of Mormon*. In the introduction, McConkie claims that the BoM is "a volume of holy scripture comparable to the Bible." But is the Book of Mormon really on the same level as the Word of God, the Bible? Mormons have several sources of Scripture. They use the King James Version of the Bible and the BoM. A third scripture is the *Doctrine and Covenants*, which is

---

[2] Download the documentation guide, *Witnessing to Mormons with the Book of Mormon*, containing the primary LDS sources and training video here: http://uhop.me/classpass52.

largely a collection of prophecies received by the Mormon prophet Joseph Smith. There is also a fourth source of sacred scripture for LDS called the *Pearl of Great Price*, which includes The Book of Abraham. Joseph Smith claimed that this text was written by the biblical patriarch Abraham, and was among a collection of Egyptian papyri which he acquired in Kirtland, Ohio in 1835, and later translated.

It is essential to understand how LDS claim to know the BoM is true. In one sense, it is similar to how we as Christians know Jesus is the way, the truth, and the life. But in another sense, it is radically different. How we know what we claim to know is a question of epistemology—the philosophy of knowledge. Following the Latter-day Saint hermeneutic, the chief means by which a Mormon arrives at the truth is via personal revelation. Christians also believe that God reveals Himself to us personally, but with LDS, there is a significant difference. Their "personal" revelation trumps everything else. It is more or less a feeling, a "burning in the bosom," as many LDS describe it. Your missionary interlocutors will likely take you to one of the most often-quoted verses in the BoM in support of this foundational epistemic conviction of LDS theology. It comes from the book of Moroni: "And when ye shall receive these things, I would exhort you that ye would ask God, the Eternal Father, in the name of Christ, if these things are not true; and if ye shall ask with a sincere heart, with real intent, having faith in Christ, he will manifest the truth of it unto you, by the power of the Holy Ghost" (Moroni 10.4).

In short, when you get a *Book of Mormon*, the missionaries will encourage you to pray about it, ponder it, and ask "Heavenly Father" if the BoM is true or not. By following these steps, the missionaries will tell you that God will reveal to you that the BoM *is true*. Mormons will frequently cite this spiritual testimony, often even in the face of contradictory evidence emanating directly from the BoM itself. If you end up having a follow-up visit with the missionaries, you will likely be peppered with questions like, "Did you pray the prayer? Did you ask Heavenly Father if the book is true? When you prayed that prayer, did you sense that burning in the bosom that told you these things were true?"

Maybe at this point you might be thinking you have arrived at an epistemological impasse. Maybe you even have some questions yourself. If we as Christians can pray and receive an answer to our prayers, why can't Latter-day Saints do the same? What's the difference between us? Ok, while I don't believe Mormonism is true, how can my personal experience as a Christian prove to be any different than those experiences of Latter-day Saints? How is it possible to decide whose "personal revelation" is correct?

Now, I certainly believe God answers our prayers. But *prayer alone* does not appear to be the biblical way that we arrive at truth, for several reasons. First, most every religion in the world today teaches the necessity of prayer or meditation. And most every fervent adherent of a praying faith tradition also has a testimony of some kind, a spiritual experience which seems to confirm for them that what they believe is true. Consider Islam. Muslims must pray five times a day. They too have a spiritual testimony about a prophet and a book—their prophet Muhammad and their book the Qur'an.

It is virtually an identical situation in Mormonism. Their prophet is Joseph Smith, and their book is the Book of Mormon. The problem of course is that personal prayer and personal experience are quite subjective. The Bible also explicitly warns us about false religious experiences. Many will find out too late that their spiritual experiences in doing "many wonderful works" allegedly in Jesus' name were merely works of iniquity. How then do we break this subjective impasse? How can we demonstrate whose personal experience is the correct personal experience?

One way we can uncover what informs someone's personal experience is by *testing* the spirits. As 1 John 4.1 states, "Beloved, believe not every spirit, but try [or test, δοκιμάζω] the spirits whether they are of God: because many false prophets are gone out into the world."[3]

Does the Holy Spirit affirm the truthfulness of the BoM? If the Holy Spirit is also the Author of the Bible, then the message of the Holy Spirit should agree doctrinally with the content of the Bible.

---

[3] King James Version (KJV). In most cases it is best to use the KJV in conversations with LDS as this is the Bible translation they have officially endorsed and that they most trust.

Keep in mind that as a former fourth-generation Latter-day Saint, I gave my life to Mormonism and was fully prepared to go on a two-year mission to tell people that I knew beyond a shadow of a doubt that the BoM was the Word of God. I had received the Aaronic Priesthood. I had done baptism work for the dead in the Salt Lake City Temple in Utah.

So how could I have been so wrong about the BoM? I had prayed the prayer. I had received the burning in the bosom. I had what I believed was indeed a veridical spiritual testimony. The question, though, is how did I know it was the Holy Spirit? Could it actually be a different spirit besides the Holy Spirit? The Bible says that indeed it could have been another spirit (1 John 4.1; Eph 6). Even Satan himself can transform into an angel of light (2 Cor 11.4). What is perceived to be God's voice through the Holy Spirit could be conflated with emotions, psychology, or compromised by confirmation bias. The Bible also warns that in some cases spiritual experiences can be real while not being true. In 1 Timothy 4.1, Paul writes: "Now the spirit [the Holy Spirit] speaketh expressly, that in the latter times some shall depart from the faith, giving heed to seducing spirits, and doctrines of devils." So, whether we get a "message" from an imam in Istanbul, a prophet in Provo, or a Baptist on Bourbon Street, our command is the same. Beloved, *test* the spirits. And with the Book of Mormon, we have ample means to perform several tests, right from its very own pages.

III. How the *Book of Mormon* Came to Be

High atop most of the 200 or so Mormon temples throughout the world, there stands a gold-covered angel named Moroni.

Long before Moroni was an angel, however, according to the story in the BoM, he was a man, a human being, a 5th century AD prophet who allegedly lived in the ancient Americas. The main story of the BoM, however, begins much earlier. It opens with the account of a Jewish man, Lehi, who lived in Jerusalem shortly before the Babylonian destruction of Judah when the Southern Kingdom fell. Lehi was warned by God to flee because of the coming destruction of Jerusalem and Judea. Lehi and his family built a boat and allegedly undertook an improbable trans-Atlantic journey to the New World, arriving around 600 BC on what the BoM describes as a "narrow neck of land," which most Latter-day Saints interpret to be somewhere in Central America.

Upon landing, Lehi and his family find the land uninhabited. The BoM then describes in the centuries that followed how this one Jewish family multiplied and became a great nation of people, eventually two great nations, made up primarily of the descendants of Lehi, his sons Laman and Nephi.

Laman became the father of a tribe of people known as the Lamanites. His brother Nephi became the Nephite's progenitor. In the subsequent centuries, a number of wars and great battles took place between the Nephites and the Lamanites. For the most part, the Nephites were godly, while the Lamanites had become unrighteous. For nearly a thousand-year period, from 600 BC to 421 AD, warfare continued between the Lamanites and the Nephites, who perpetually attempted to annihilate one another. Their battles were bloody and involved millions of people who lived in enormous, fortified cities. Eventually, the Lamanites prevailed, leaving the prophet Moroni as the last surviving Nephite at the close of the BoM.

Shortly before Moroni died in 421 AD, however, he allegedly buried sacred gold plates or gold tablets in a hill called Cumorah. These gold plates contained engravings in a language that Joseph Smith called Reformed Egyptian Hieroglyphics and which, according to Smith, contained a record or scripture of the Nephites and Lamanites living in ancient America.

What Latter-day Saints claim is that these gold plates allegedly contain "another testament of Jesus Christ" which eventually became the Book of Mormon. The Hill Cumorah is located in upstate New York, fortunately within walking distance of Joseph Smith's home in Palmyra. LDS church history tells us that the angel Moroni appeared to Smith in September of 1823 and told him where, how, and when to dig up the plates.

What we learn at this point is the answer to a significant historical question many people of Smith's day were asking: "From where did the Native Americans come?" The answer, according to the BoM, is that they all are of Jewish descent. According to the introduction of the BoM, the Lamanites are the "principal ancestors of the American Indians."[4]

Joseph Smith allegedly made this discovery upon "translating" the gold plates into English. In 1830, Smith's translation of the gold plates became the first edition of the BoM. The belief that Joseph Smith was able to translate the plates by "the gift and power of God" remains to this day a foundational belief for LDS. Smith, however, had no formal schooling, nor did he take a course in translating reformed Egyptian hieroglyphics. In fact, there is no historical or archaeological evidence of Reformed Egyptian. No Egyptologist in the field before or since Smith's time has ever been able to verify it as a legitimate language. No one, not even Latter-day Saints, know what it looks like.

Nonetheless, Smith supposedly translated this enigmatic language by the gift and power of God. Smith even went on to claim that his translation was the most correct of any book ever written, *even the Bible*! As Smith himself said, "I told the brethren that the Book of Mormon was the most correct of any book on earth, and a man would get nearer to God by abiding by its precepts than by any other book."[5]

As a Mormon, I was taught that there are four scriptures: the Bible, BoM, *Doctrine and Covenants*, and the *Pearl of Great Price*. Of the four, I was also taught that only *one* of them, the Bible, contains errors. It was not translated correctly. So, where are these translation errors? The Mormon church actually does not publish any official list of errors. It is also important to keep in mind that when LDS say "translated correctly," they really mean *transmitted* correctly. There are LDS scholars at Brigham Young University who are experts in Greek and Hebrew, so it is finally not an issue of translation. They believe that over the centuries the text of the Bible had become corrupted, similar to what agnostic-atheist and New Testament scholar Dr. Bart Ehrman popularly argues.[6]

---

[4] After critics cited DNA studies disputing the genetic connection between Jews and Native Americans, the LDS church has now reworded the 1981 introduction from "The Lamanites, and they were the *principal* ancestors of the American Indians" to "The Lamanites, and they are *among* the ancestors of the American Indians." (italics added).
[5] Joseph Smith, *History of the Church of Jesus Christ of Latter-day Saints*, 4.461.
[6] Ehrman, *Misquoting Jesus*.

LDS do affirm that the Bible is sacred Scripture. But there was this subtle feeling I had as a Mormon that anytime something in the Bible seemed to go against what I read in the BoM or heard from the church, the BoM, *Doctrine and Covenants*, and *The Pearl of Great Price* held authoritative sway.

IV. Testing the Claims of the *Book of Mormon*

The claim that the BoM is the most correct book is finally a testable claim. Take for example that the BoM talks about a populous civilization in the New World, allegedly with millions of people. In one battle alone which is said to have taken place on Hill Cumorah, almost a quarter of a million Nephites died, a number which represents only the Nephite casualties.[7] *A quarter of a million people.*

The BoM also describes fortified cities such as the city of Bountiful and the city of Zarahemla. The problem is that to date, archaeologists have not uncovered any ruins that can be identified as of any of the cities mentioned in the BoM. No mass graves. No human remains. No weapons. Nothing. Mormons will sometimes cite cities like Chichén Itzá on the Yucatan Peninsula and suggest such places could be evidence of a Nephite or Lamanite city. But the history and archaeology of such cities turn out to be not only chronologically out of sync with the BoM but out of sync in many other details as well: in language, customs, dress, etc.

In contrast, most Bibles contain an index of maps of Israel and the ancient Near East. There is a Bethlehem, there is a Jerusalem, there is a Capernaum. All these locations have been archaeologically verified. Contemporary archaeology and geography thus confirm the existence of places mentioned in the Bible, but there is to date no geography or archaeology which coincides with the BoM.

Consider certain coins mentioned in the BoM. There existed a monetary system in the BoM, comprised of gold and silver. Earlier editions of the BoM even identified them as "Nephite coinage."[8] Gold and silver

---

[7] BoM, Moroni 6, about 385 AD.
[8] Some LDS apologists argue that the gold and silver comprised a "monetary system" of weights and measures and not "coins" per se. In 2013, the LDS church edited the "chapter headings originally

coins, including senine, senum, and shiblum are mentioned in the BoM, along with a denominational structure to the coinage (Alma 11.3–4). Yet to date, archaeologists have found no trace of any coins pertaining to the BoM. Not one.

Contrast this with coins mentioned in the Bible: shekels and the widow's mite, for example. These coins have been found *in abundance.* There are so common you can find biblical coins for sale all over the Internet. If you want a 2000-year-old coin, the likes of which Jesus handles or mentions, you don't need to be a professional archaeologist to find one or even own one. This is not true of "Nephite coinage."

Another archaeological problem with the BoM involves anachronisms, when a phrase or word does not properly fit the time frame of when events in the BoM take place. The BoM describes domesticated horses pulling chariots in the New World (Alma 18.9–10; 3 Nephi 6.1). Horses, however, were not introduced to the New World until 1492 when Columbus landed in what is now San Salvador Island in the Bahamas. The conquistadors who followed in Columbus' footsteps brought further European contact with the New World and are primarily responsible for introducing the horse to the New World. By the turn of the 19th century, in Joseph Smith's day, there were millions of horses in America, many of which were wild. Native Americans are credited with domesticating the horse.

Simply put, during the primary BoM timeline of 600 BC through 421 AD, there were *no horses* in America, and the wheel had no practical use among Native Americans until contact with Europeans. In short, there were no wheeled vehicles of any kind, no wagons and no chariots, in the Americas before 1492, over a thousand years after the events described in the BoM.

If you bring this question up with a Latter-day Saint, they may respond by telling you that the word "horse" may not be the best translation

---

written by Apostle Talmage and published in the 1920 edition of the Book of Mormon. Gone are the references to 'Nephite coins' in the [chapter] heading of Alma 11. New editions [2013] now say, "The Nephite monetary system is set forth." Bill McKeever and Eric Johnson, "Are Ancient Coins Mentioned in the Book of Mormon?" Mormonism Research Ministry, http://mrm.org/coins.

and that perhaps "tapir" is meant. A tapir is a South or Central America pig-like animal, which theoretically speaking, *might* be able to pull a chariot. Or some Mormons may say that the word "horse" in the BoM is a reference to a very large deer.

Regarding chariots, Mormons will sometimes explain that these chariots didn't necessarily have wheels, they could have been something more like a sled. Instead of horses and chariots, then, LDS are left with coming up with the idea that the Nephites and Lamanites used pigs, tapir, or deer to pull sleds. At this point, you might be tempted to mock, as some of my Christian friends did when I was still a Mormon. But remember the exhortation to speak the truth in love and consider that for some LDS, especially younger missionaries, bringing this up may be the first time they have ever heard this objection. And also keep in mind how devastating such an objection might be to a missionary who is totally devoted to his LDS faith. How would you want someone to tell *you* bad news?

A third significant problem with the BoM is DNA. Recall that the BoM claims that Native Americans are descendants of the original Israelites (Lehi and his family) who supposedly came over to the New World in 600 BC. But this too can be and has been thoroughly tested. Scientists have since extracted DNA from virtually every Native American group such as Cheyenne, Apache, Seminole, and Eskimo, in addition to the ancient indigenous peoples such as Aztec, Maya, Inca, and Toltec. None of the Native American DNA matches DNA from Israeli descent. The primary marker in Native American genes comes from Northeast Asia, not Israel. The current consensus is that Native Americans came from Siberia, Mongolia, and Northeast Asia, not Israel or the Middle East.[9]

V. Doctrinal and Historical Issues in the *Book of Mormon*

We as Christians take it for granted that Jesus was born in Bethlehem. Yet in the book of Alma, one of the books of the BoM, there exists a prophecy about where Jesus would be born. "And behold, he [Jesus] shall be born of

---

[9] An LDS geneticist, Dr. Simon G. Southerton, left the LDS Church largely over the issue of DNA and the Book of Mormon. See, Southerton, *Losing a Lost Tribe: Native Americans, DNA, and the Mormon Church.*

Mary at Jerusalem, which is the land of our forefathers. She being a virgin, a precious and chosen vessel..." (Alma 7.10).

But the Bible is emphatically clear about the location of Jesus' birthplace being *Bethlehem* (Micah 5.2; Matt. 2.1; Luke 2.4), not Jerusalem. Many Mormons with whom I have spoken over the years are already familiar with this objection and have what they consider to be a simple solution. Interestingly enough, the Latter-day Saints sing "O little town of Bethlehem," just like we do. Many LDS will attempt to explain that Bethlehem and Jerusalem are very close to each other, as if Bethlehem were something like a suburb of Jerusalem. Bethlehem is only about six miles from Jerusalem, no big deal, right?

Not quite. In a short video clip from the documentary, *The Bible vs. Joseph Smith*, Joel Kramer, a Christian apologist living in Jordan, talks to Greg Gifford, who is a Latter-day Saint elder. They are not actors. This is a real Christian apologist and a real Latter-day Saint in conversation in Israel. Greg Gifford was willing to go to Israel with Joel and actually go to these sites, go to Bethlehem, go to Jerusalem, go to these places to see and discuss the evidence firsthand. By the end their short exchange about the Bethlehem-Jerusalem controversy, Gifford was incredulous and seemed almost desperate when he confesses to Kramer "I think that it's just a mistake. I don't know what else to say about it."[10]

I hope you see and understand the need to be gracious and compassionate when bringing up these problems with LDS. These issues can be and often are devastating for them once they realize, maybe for the first time, that there might indeed be significant problems with what they've believed for most of their lives.

In my own journey from Mormonism to Christianity, I was more troubled by some of the more significant theological difficulties. As a Latter-day Saint, I was routinely taught that our Heavenly Father, Elohim, was once a man on another world, and he was married to our Heavenly Mother. In Mormonism there exists both Heavenly Father *and* Heavenly Mother, and when Heavenly Father was a mere man with his wife on this

---

[10] You can watch this 6-minute excerpt from the video documentary, *The Bible Vs Joseph Smith*, here: www.watchman.org/BibleVsJoseph.

other world, he had a god over him whom he worshipped. Interestingly, the god Heavenly Father worshiped had also once been a man on a different world and worshipped a god who had once been a man, and that god had a god over him who had once been a man, and so on.[11]

I was taught that if I was obedient to celestial principles, if I went through the secret Mormon temple ritual, and if I obeyed all the laws and ordinances of the gospel, I had the same potential to become a god myself one day. Now, *that* is a striking theological problem, especially when compared to what the Bible says about other gods,[12] but it is even a problem when you compare it to the BoM itself.

In the Book of Alma (11.22–31), for example, it clearly teaches *there is only one true God*. "And Zeezrom said unto him, thou sayest, there is a true and living God. And Amulek said, 'Yea, there is a true and living God. And now Zeezrom said, 'Is there more than one God? And he answered, no.'"

So, according to the BoM, how many true gods are there? Just one. At first glance, the Book of Mormon appears to consistently affirm monotheism. Yet elsewhere in the Mormon scriptures it seems that there is indeed more than one God. In the Book of Abraham found in *The Pearl of Great Price*, for example, it reads "And then the Lord said, Let us go down. And they went down at the beginning. And they, that is, the Gods organized and formed the heavens and the earth. And they the Gods said, 'Let there be light,' and there was light and the Gods called the light day, and the darkness they called night." If you go through the whole of chapter four where these lines appear, a dozen times it uses a capital 'G' for "Gods."

At this point it would be appropriate to ask your LDS interlocutor: "Does the Book of Mormon teach that there is only one God or many Gods? Alma seems to say there is only one God, but the Book of Abra-

---

[11] This concept, sometimes called "The Law of Eternal Progression," seems to imply an almost infinite chain of contingent Gods and raises the problem of an infinite regress. For a discussion of this issue see the chapter Paul Copan and William Lane Craig's chapter "Craftsman or Creator?" in Beckwith, Francis J., Carl Mosser and Paul Owen, gen. eds. *New Mormon Challenge*.

[12] God says, "… I am he: before me there was no God formed, neither shall there be after me." (Isaiah 43.10). "Is there a God beside me? yea, there is no God; I know not any." (Isaiah 44.8). Paul acknowledges that there are deities that are *called* gods (1 Cor 8.5) but in the context of verse 1 he is clearly speaking of idols or false gods.

ham clearly teaches that there are many Gods. Which do you think it is?" Mormonism today is *clearly* polytheistic, but at the same time, the BoM disagrees with the Book of Abraham. This is a significant problem for LDS today.

And this brings us to a problem with which the Latter-day Saint faith has been plagued nearly since its beginning.

Polygamy.

As with God/Gods, the LDS Scriptures seem to contradict themselves about men having multiple wives. In one instance the BoM teaches that polygamy is wrong and cites as a prime example King David and his son Solomon who "had many wives and concubines" (BoM, Jacob 2.24). The BoM says polygamy is an abomination to God, but by the 1840s the *Doctrine and Covenants* (D&C) section 132 verse 39 clearly states that God authorizes polygamy and that God gave all the wives and concubines to King David. It was *God's idea*, not David's. The exception was one flawed case, with Bathsheba and Uriah. *That* was a sin, but with all the other wives and concubines which God gave to David, David did not sin. These women were a gift from God to David, and God not only authorized, but actually *commanded* polygamy.[13]

In addition to these and other historical and doctrinal challenges in the BoM, I was personally more troubled by some of the changes in the text of the BoM. I had been taught that there had been no alterations to the text of the BoM except for a few grammatical edits.

In reality, there have been over 4,000 word changes since the 1830 first edition of the BoM. Now, most of these changes are grammatical in nature, but even the grammatical changes create a serious problem and actually are substantial evidence for plagiarism in the BoM.[14]

---

[13] On their official website, the LDS Church has recently acknowledged that Joseph Smith married as many as 40 wives including women already married to other Mormon men and at least one girl who was only 14. The church explained that God repeatedly commanded Joseph to marry these women but he refused until God threatened him by sending an angel with a drawn sword to kill him if he failed to comply. "Plural Marriage in Kirtland and Nauvoo," Gospel Topic Essays: https://www.churchofjesuschrist.org/study/manual/gospel-topics-essays/plural-marriage-in-kirtland-and-nauvoo.

[14] The poor grammar of the original 1830 BoM has been cleaned up in later editions. A careful comparison however shows that portions of the 1830 BoM that are also found in the Bible (content from Genesis, Isaiah, the Sermon on the Mount, etc.) are grammatically superior. In fact, for

One significant change begins with the original 1830 BoM. It says in the Book of Mosiah, chapter 21, verse 28: "And now Limhi was again filled with joy on learning from the mouth of Ammon that King Benjamin had a gift from God whereby he could interpret such engravings. Yea! And Ammon also did rejoice."[15]

Note that everyone is excited and happy because *King Benjamin* is able to interpret these important engravings. You would never notice a problem, however, unless you had a little more context and familiarity with the Book of Mosiah.

Let us go back a few chapters to Mosiah chapter six and look at verses three through five. It says this: "King Benjamin had made an end of all these things and consecrated his son Mosiah to be a ruler and king." Verse five: "And King Benjamin lived three years, and he died." *What happened* to King Benjamin in chapter six? He died! What happens to him in chapter 21? He is alive and well, interpreting engravings and making everyone happy, no less.

Let us now look at the Mosiah 6.3–5 from 1981 edition of the BoM. "And now Limhi was again filled with joy on learning that *King Mosiah* had a gift from God whereby he could interpret such engravings." King Mosiah has replaced King Benjamin. If you mention this issue, again, remember to maintain gentleness and respect, as this can be rather devastating to LDS who discover it for the first time. You may also hear LDS respond by asking you "Aren't there different translations of the Bible?"

The simple answer is that in contemporary English translations of the Bible, no translator has ever replaced the name of a dead king with someone else's name. Benjamin/Mosiah is not a simple grammatical adjustment, or a matter of a word spelled a little differently. As a Latter-day Saint, this problem deeply troubled me.

---

the most part they are reproduced virtually verbatim from the 1769 revision of the King James translation of 1611.

[15] For access to complete copies of the original 1830 BoM, see Tanner, *3,913 Changes in the Book of Mormon* and Wood, *Joseph Smith Begins His Work, (Vol. 1).*

VI. Conclusion

Whenever I find myself in a conversation with a Latter-day Saint and mention any one of these issues, instead of approaching with the attitude of "You're wrong and I can prove it," I will often flip it around. I say, "I have a problem. Maybe you can help me. I've lost my confidence, my testimony, and my faith in the BoM. I have learned over the years, however, that there are two sides to every story. If I'm misunderstanding something, what I need is a Latter-day Saint who will love me enough to be patient with me and help me work through my problems. Can I show you some of the challenges I have been dealing with for a number of years?" I want to present the information as a partner, not as an adversary. "Let's see if we can resolve this together. Can you make some phone calls? Do you have any friends that may know the answer to this?" I have discovered that in many cases, my questions can be very contagious. But I'm not trying to win the argument, I'm trying to get them to engage what the text actually says and hopefully get them on the path to the way, the truth, and the life.

With this in mind, it is helpful to also have a basic understanding of the historical reliability of the Bible in comparison. One should be prepared to discuss basic questions about canonicity, textual transmission, and the history of English translations of the Bible. Whenever someone begins to doubt their core beliefs in the BoM, it is natural to for them to wonder if they can have confidence in the Bible or any scripture.

Bibliography

Beckwith, Francis J., Carl Mosser and Paul Owen, gen. eds. *The New Mormon Challenge: Responding to the Latest Defenses of a Fast-Growing Movement.* Grand Rapids, Zondervan, 2002.

Bowman, Robert M., Jr. *Jesus' Resurrection and Joseph's Visions: Examining the Foundations of Christianity and Mormonism.* Tampa, FL: Deward Publishing, 2020.

Ehrman, Bart D. *Misquoting Jesus: The Story Behind Who Changed the Bible and Why.* New York: HarperOne, 2005.

Southerton, Simon *Losing a Lost Tribe: Native Americans, DNA, and the Mormon Church.* Salt Lake City: Signature Books, 2004.

Smith, Joseph, Jr. *History of the Church of Jesus Christ of Latter-day Saints* (7 Volumes). Salt Lake City: Deseret Book Co.; ed. B. H. Roberts, 2nd ed. rev. 1957.

Tanner, Jerald and Sandra. *3,913 Changes in the Book of Mormon.* Salt Lake City: Utah Lighthouse Ministry, 1987, 1996. A photo reprint of the original 1830 edition of the Book of Mormon with all the changes marked (compared to the 1964 edition).

Wood, Wilford C. *Joseph Smith Begins His Work, Vol. 1.* Wilford C. Wood, 1958. A photomechanical reprint of the original 1830 edition of the Book of Mormon. This reprint was produced by a faithful Latter-day Saint which mitigates the charge of "anti-Mormon literature."

PART FOUR

Anthropological Truth

Human Nature and Communication

16

I Think, Therefore I'm Trans
A Closer Look at Transgenderism

Alycia Wood

I. Introduction

I've been an Apologist for over a decade, but there's no Apologist training that teaches you how to help others know if they are a boy or girl. But we live in an era in which our culture is confused on gender issues and consequently, as an Apologist, this has become a topic that I've had to do a lot of research on. What I want to do in this chapter is provide a practical overview of the gender issue. We're first going to look at a little bit of background and history to see what is pushing our modern gender trends. Then we're going to start looking at what actually happens during gender transitioning. Finally, we will explore where we can go for help.

People are always asking me, what good resources are there that address this? I really encourage you to read Abigail Shrier's book, *Irreversible Damage*.[1] It's the book that exposed what was happening in young girls. There's also a fantastic interview by Jordan Peterson of detransitioner Chloe Cole[2] and an article by The Free Press titled "Gender Affirming Care is Dangerous: I know because I helped pioneer it"[3] by Finnish doctor Riittakerttu Kaltiala. Her 2023 article helps give an overview of how we developed the treatment protocol for Gender Dysphoria (GD).

---
[1] Shrier, *Irreversible Damage*.
[2] Peterson, "The Wounds That Won't Heal."
[3] Kaltiala, "Gender-Affirming Care is dangerous."

If you look at the culture and media, they are painting this topic as a war between Christians, Conservatives, or Republicans vs. the LGBTQ community, Democrats, or the left. I assure you, this narrative is not true. In fact, Christians are the quietest on this topic because a lot of Christians don't even know how to address it. To demonstrate this point, I'm not going to use a single Christian resource throughout this entire chapter until I get to the end that says, God help! I will use medical journals, news sources, individual personal stories etc. so as to present the issue as fairly as possible—meaning without any Christian bias. I'm doing this because the loudest voices against Gender Affirming Care are the secular culture. The well-known atheist Richard Dawkins himself has commented on how ridiculous this movement is because as a scientist, male and female is basic biology.[4]

II. Background & History of Transgenderism

It's important to define some of the terms that you'll hear in the transgender discussion.

Non-binary: refers to someone whose gender is fluid (meaning it changes), someone who identifies as gender neutral, or someone who doesn't identify as any particular gender at all.

Trans man and trans woman: These terms mess people up, so let me use myself as an example. If you were to say, "What is Alycia?" you'd say she's a woman. Therefore, a trans woman is something different than a woman. A trans woman is someone who is born biologically male but transitioned to a woman. Similarly, a trans man is not the same as a man. It describes someone who is a biological woman who transitioned to a man. With that understanding, let's get a lay of the land.

According to the Pew Research Center in June of 2022, 1.6% of all American adults 18+ identify as transgender. That doesn't seem like a very big number, right? Let me break this down by different age groups. Between the ages of 18–29, 5.1% of people identify as transgender. Between the ages of 30 to 49, the percentage drops to 1.6% and for 50 and over 0.3%.[5] While these are relatively small numbers in comparison to the

---

[4] Dawkins, "Trans: When Ideology meets reality," 2.49–3.41.
[5] Brown, "About 5% of young adults."

population, we all know there's been a massive rise in the numbers of people that have identified as transgender in recent years. What is going on?

Historically, GD was male to female. Little boys between the ages of 2–4 felt like they were girls. Maybe they liked dressing up like mom with skirts and high heels, or maybe they wanted to wear mom's makeup. Regardless, they felt like they were a girl from a very young age. They'd then grow up, become adults, and then maybe they would start taking estrogen, cross-dressing, and for some doing surgery to live as females.

However, a 2011 study, and a follow-up done in 2014, called the Dutch Protocol laid out an evidence-based framework for the modern-day Gender Affirming Care (GAC) practices based off of their results of 70 patients between 2000–2008. While the Dutch protocol ideas had been around for years prior, even being adapted globally, it was then that its influence grew. It shifted GAC from men to adolescents, claiming that medically transitioning young people using puberty blockers was beneficial to their emotional and behavioral health.[6] This was seen as an effective method to treat GD, because "after gender reassignment… the GD was alleviated and psychological functioning had steadily improved."[7] Also, the benefit of starting transitioning younger is that it makes it easier for people to pass better as opposite sex adults. Why? Because if you started treatment early and blocked puberty, the male facial hair that develops during puberty, for example, would not be visible if they transitioned to female later. So, puberty blockers at 12, cross-sex hormones at 16, and surgery at 18 became the suggested model. The news spread. Unsurprisingly, the number of young people with GD increased significantly. But now we were transitioning adolescents, 12–14 years old, both male *and* female.[8]

But the subjects in the study were different than what we are seeing today. They were mostly males who had struggled with GD since they were very young, were mentally well, and were very high functioning. Regardless, the influence of the Protocol for Gender Affirming Care spread around the world faster than before. The World Professional Association

---

[6] Vries, "Puberty suppression."
[7] Vries. "Young adult psychological outcome."
[8] Kaltiala, "Gender-Affirming Care is dangerous."

for Transgender Health (WPATH) even used the Dutch protocol in their Standards of Care version 7.

In the US, between 2016 to 2017, gender surgeries for female to male became the fastest rising population group. Female to male gender surgeries increased fourfold and comprised 70% of gender surgeries. In 2018, the UK reported a staggering rise in female to male gender treatments of 4,400% in comparison to the previous decade.[9] Likewise, Sweden's Board of Health and Welfare confirmed a 1,500% rise between "2008 and 2018 in gender dysphoria diagnoses for 13- to 17-year-olds born as girls."[10] With these massive rises of young girls suddenly starting to transition, you need to know that before 2012, "there was no scientific literature on girls ages 11 to 21 ever having developed gender dysphoria at all."[11]

In looking at some of the demographics of these young girls, many are upper middle class, do great in school, are well behaved, never smoke a cigarette, don't drink, are not sexually active, and many have never had a kiss, either with a boy or a girl. But they are in lots of pain.[12] In Sweden, they found that of their 13–17 year olds, 32.4% of these young girls had diagnoses for anxiety, 28.9% for depression, 19.4% for ADHD, and 15.2% for autism.[13] These, what I call the Golden 4, we find in almost every single case of GD in young girls and boys as preexisting *before* any feelings of GD began. They are already depressed, anxious, ADHD or autistic, and then all of a sudden they think they are Trans. For many of these young girls, it's not so much that they have a strong desire to be a boy. The strong desire is that they don't want to be a girl. Which explains why after transitioning, many of these girls don't adopt the stereotypical boy habits. They're not like, "I'm a boy! Let's go to the gym or watch football!"[14] It's more that they just don't want to be themselves. Why is that? Well, there are plenty of reasons.

---

[9] Shrier, *Irreversible Damage*, 26.
[10] Orange, "Teenage Transgender Row Splits."
[11] Shrier, *Irreversible Damage*, xxvii.
[12] Shrier, *Irreversible Damage*, 6.
[13] Orange, "Teenage Transgender Row Splits."
[14] Shrier, *Irreversible Damage*, 7–8.

III. Why Transition?

Number one: they are uncomfortable with themselves. Puberty is tough! The changes that happen are not always easy. Some girls may not be as tall as they wanted to be, maybe they have acne or aren't as pretty as they wish. Additionally, many children and adolescents don't conform to societal gender stereotypes. Maybe she's a girl who hates pink and dolls but loves sports! In other words, she's a Tomboy and feels pressure to fit stereotypes of a more feminine nature than she wants.

Number two: some have experienced abuse. For some, in the form of sexual, for others in the form of bullying because they are masculine women or don't fit girl stereotypes. They think that if they can transition to being a boy, they won't be abused anymore because if they're a boy, they'll be safe. They can protect themselves. Or they think that people just sexually abuse girls, which isn't true. Either way, the desire to protect herself from further abuse can be a motivator for transitioning.

Number three: many people with GD are actually gay, so a young girl will think that since she is attracted to girls, she must really be a boy. This leads her to think that instead of being a girl who's attracted to girls and is therefore a lesbian, if she transitions to being a boy, then she's a boy attracted to girls and is heterosexual. This is one of the reasons why the LGB has a lot of problems with the T because the LGB community feels like parents are transitioning kids who would grow up gay *out* of their community; let alone the deception the LGB community feels going into gay bars and meeting someone, only to find out they're actually biologically the other sex.

IV. The Discovery

Lisa Littman, a former Ob/Gyn now working in public health, noticed on Facebook in 2016 that several, mostly adolescents girls, were coming out as trans. But she also noticed that when one young girl came out as Trans, her friends also came out as trans. This happened multiple times. Statistically, this seemed odd. Doctor Littman formed a hypothesis that this was peer contagion, or the phrase she coined, "Rapid Onset Gender Dysphoria" ("ROGD"). She developed a survey and gave it to 256 parents whose daughters were identifying as boys, and one thing that became very obvious was that for 65% of the girls, the GD came after a long time of being heavily immersed in social media.[15]

Her results were interesting. Over 80% were natal females, meaning born biological females, with a mean age of 16.4. Most were living at home with parents when they came out as trans and the vast majority had zero history of GD as children.[16] Now that's important. Remember that historically GD involved little boys 2–4 years old, but these girls had no history of that. One minute everything is fine with their gender, then all of a sudden, "I'm a boy." And this can happen in adolescence or even in their 20s. You can imagine the parents are caught off guard: Where did that come from?

A look at the demographics can help us find that answer: As previously stated, a majority of transitioners had one or more psychiatric diagnoses, and almost half were engaging in self-harm prior to the onset of GD. Nearly 70% belonged to a peer group where someone had come out as trans, and over 90% were white. Over 85% of the parents supported gay marriage. And an even higher amount, 88% of the parents overwhelmingly are in support of trans rights. But in spite of this, they're saying, "not my child." Something is wrong here. To make it worse, less than 13% believed that their child's mental health improved after identifying as trans. In fact, 47% said it got worse.[17] This is where the Dutch protocol failed us all.

According to the Journal of Sex and Marital Therapy in 2023, the Dutch protocol was heavily biased in that it only included the most successful cases for each stage of treatment. Furthermore, the Dutch protocol didn't discuss the health risks of being on puberty blockers and cross-sex hormones, nor address post-puberty GD of girls coupled with mental illness because the people in the original Dutch protocol study were mentally well.[18]

---

[15] Shrier, *Irreversible Damage*, 25–27.
[16] Shrier, *Irreversible Damage*, 37–38.
[17] Shrier, *Irreversible Damage*. 37–38.
[18] Abbruzzese, "The Myth of Reliable Research."

Doctor Kaltiala adds that the Dutch protocol failed to account for the large number of detransitioners (someone who transitions only to later transition back to their original gender) that would ensue. So, in their follow up, they didn't include them. They also failed to mention that one of the participants actually died during the study due to complications from surgery.[19]

Oftentimes people say to me, okay, we can understand why a 12-year-old might say, "I think I'm a boy," but what is wrong with the parents? Why would the parents allow their child to transition? You need to understand that parents are unsure of how to deal with their child's GD, so they go to the people that are the most knowledgeable and can give the best advice—therapists and doctors. Problem is, they are told they need to transition their daughter because if they don't, she's going to commit suicide, "And would you rather have a dead daughter or an alive son?" they say. This statement given over and over terrifies parents, and so they suspend their judgement and follow the advice of the "experts."

Here's the sad truth: That was a bold-faced lie. There's not one single study that supported the threat that if parents did not transition their children they would take their own lives. The closest study we can gather some information from is the clinic that served England, Wales and Northern Ireland, the Tavistock Clinic. In an approximate ten-year period, Tavistock tracked 15,032 patients. Of the 15,032 patients, four committed suicide. Two were actually getting treatment and the other two were still on the waiting list to be seen.[20] While every death matters, that is very different than the guarantee of suicide many parents were presented with. The suicide threat was a lie to scare parents into transition.

So why does ROGD seem to happen in young girls at such high numbers compared to boys? Because of the ways that girls relate and engage with each other. If one friend in a group of girls shares about how depressed she is and how much she doesn't like herself and thinks she is a boy, her girl friends sympathize with her and take on her pain. They say, "Well, you know what? I haven't been happy either. Maybe that's my

---

[19] Kaltiala, "Gender-Affirming Care is dangerous."
[20] Biggs, "Suicide by Clinic-Referred."

problem. I didn't realize it, but it makes sense. I've always liked sports instead of playing with dolls, so I must be a boy too. Don't worry. I'll do it with you. We'll do it together." And so they transition in groups.

Boys don't relate the same way, so we don't find the same group mentality in them. When a boy comes out to their guy friends saying they're a girl, their friends respond very differently. While they're listening, when he finishes the friend might just change the subject. Contrary to how girls respond, boys don't take on each other's pains. They aren't interested in relating on that same level.

At the core, for both females and males, there is a desire to escape the inner pain they are experiencing. We've created a culture where we've told people that it is your right to not experience pain. Anything that brings you pain should be avoided or fought against. If somebody says something that's hurtful, they should be cancelled since it is your right to be happy.

But that's not how all of humanity has worked. All of humanity has suffered pain and loss. We used to say things like "No pain, no gain" when it came to sports. There was this understanding that when you experience pain, it helps develop you and change you. I'm not talking about all pain, of course, but the idea was that we should push through pain and become stronger, tougher people. But now we've created a culture where we told people it's their right to never hurt, and so we as a society don't know how to live in pain, how to thrive when it hurts. And so the response to pain isn't to learn how to push through, but to avoid it or change it no matter the cost. This pain-free expectation plays into both the personal expectation of the person experiencing GD and the societal support behind it.

Reasons behind why adults transition are both similar and different to what we see in adolescents. For men, in addition to GD experienced by young boys 2–4 years old, there are other contributing factors. One is Autogynephilia, a condition where adult men get sexual pleasure dressing up as a woman or by the thought of themselves as a woman. Pornography also plays its part in male GD as it promotes distorted pictures of the other sex.[21] Someone with Narcissistic personality can find transition

---

[21] Much of the Trans movement has been about sexualization of children. There's an actual Twitter page, Gays Against Groomers, of people who belong to the Lesbian-Gay-Bisexual community

attractive because with this condition, they are so completely in love with themselves: since they are the best man that exists, then the best woman that exists would have to be a female version of them. Finally, the complete infatuation with the female body cannot be overlooked. You may have noticed that when somebody transitions to being a female, oftentimes they transition to being this overly sexualized female, fitting the stereotype of what a perfect woman should be—high heels, lots of makeup, tightfitting dresses, large chest, etc. It isn't the personality of a woman they are obsessed with, it is her physical body. This obsession and infatuation becomes so intense that you take it on yourself and transition to it.

In regards to adult females, previously mentioned things apply such as not liking themselves, narcissism, mental health issues, abuse, and bullying. Regardless of if it is an adult male/female, both sexes struggle with pre-existing comorbidities such as complex PTSD, bipolar, and the Golden 4—depression, anxiety, ADHD and autism.

V. Gender Transitioning

Gender transitioning happens in stages. The first stage is a combination of not liking oneself, going through puberty, and struggling with mental health. In this unhappiness, adolescents turn to social media because that's where they go to help figure themselves out. Social media tells them, "The reason why you don't like yourself is because you're a boy. If you transition you'll feel better." They believe this and begin the process—changing their name, clothes, and maybe informing their parents.

As you can imagine, most parents are caught off guard and feel inadequate to help their child. So in the second stage the parents bring the child to "the experts" also known as the therapist. But as soon as the child mentions that they are a boy in a girl's body or vice versa, then after one, maybe two visits, the therapist affirms the *child's* self-diagnosis of GD and sends them for medical help.

Stage three involves an endocrinologist or primary care doctor, who begins to prescribe puberty blockers. Note that no one so far has ad-

---

who, amongst other things, will go and speak at school board meetings, objecting to books being shown to young children of extremely sexual behaviors as they see it as grooming.

dressed any existing autism, depression, or whatever else is going on under the surface, rather it is straight to affirmation and prescriptions. Puberty blockers do what it sounds like they do. They stop puberty where it is. If I'm 14 and I've begun puberty, it will stop. If I haven't started puberty, then it will make sure it doesn't start. Puberty blockers' effects are tremendous, including the delay of sexual development, the disruption of normal brain development, and preventing the start of women's periods. It's going to slow bone growth and impact bone density. Their future could consist of a lack of sexual pleasure, issues with fertility, and sexual dysfunction. We simply don't know what the long-term effects are because we have never given blockers to thousands of children going through normal puberty before.

With effects like this, it is no wonder that countries like Norway, Finland, Sweden, the UK, and Italy have now switched direction by limiting or restricting puberty blockers in minors and have shifted their treatment of GD to mental health counseling.[22] The US is quickly following suit.

After a period of time on puberty blockers, the fourth stage begins: cross-sex hormones—testosterone or estrogen. Testosterone (T) for an adolescent female brings a litany of effects including the deepening of her voice. She will have increased body and facial hair and muscle mass, and possibly thinning hair or premature balding. Her body fat will begin to shift, leading her to look more masculine, including in her face.[23] The changes in hair and voice, once these kick in, become permanent—even if she stops taking T. Additionally, T will cause her blood to thicken, increases moodiness and irritability, muscle aches, sweating, and aggression.[24] There are also some concerns about the long term effects of taking T and the development of Endometrial cancer.[25]

As if this wasn't enough, taking T will do to the female body what it's designed to do to the male body, which means it will cause her genitalia to grow.[26] That is also permanent.

---

[22] "Italy Joins the List of Countries Recommending Restrictions."
[23] Deutsch, "Information on Testosterone."
[24] Shrier, *Irreversible Damage*, 169–170.
[25] To read more: https://doi.org/10.1016/j.gore.2023.101199.
[26] Deutsch, "Information on Testosterone."

The effects of men taking Estrogen are no less serious. Men will see an in increase in breast growth, a loss of muscle definition and body hair, decreased sweating, increased body fat collecting around the hips and thighs (which is where ladies store their fat), and a shifting of body fat in the face, making it look more feminine.[27] Ordinarily, while the risk is small, men can get breast cancer. However, when you're taking estrogen, studies seem to be pointing in the direction that the risk increases.[28] Finally, when a man takes estrogen, it will cause a shrinkage of part of his genitalia.[29] That is permanent.

If after all the changes are made and one still wishes to continue, they can move on to Stage five which is surgery—a double mastectomy for women, breast implants for men and "bottom surgery," or genitalia surgery, for either men or women.

VI. Stories of Gender Transitioners and Detransitioners

When you watch videos posted by detransitioners, they will tell you with tears pouring down their faces, "Nobody told me what was going to happen to my body when I transitioned. I was 12 years old. How was I supposed to understand?" Chances are, either you or somebody you know is struggling with GD, and I don't want anybody who hears me speak to ever say, "Nobody ever told me." So let me introduce you to a few detransitioners.

Tulip Ritchie, as his Twitter name says, was born male, transitioned to female, and has now detransitioned back to male. Tulip transitioned in his late 20s, after going through full male puberty and struggling with mental health. He had been on estrogen for several years when therapists pressured him into getting bottom surgery or face being discharged from therapy. Scared to lose his therapy, he reluctantly got surgery, and now he has completely regretted it. In one Twitter post about his surgery, he says: "I want to tell everybody what they took from us. What irreversible really means and what that reality looks like for us. No one told me any of what I'm going to tell you now." He then goes on to share his story of how bad-

---

[27] Deutsch, "Information on Estrogen."
[28] Villalba, "Breast Cancer in a Transgender Woman."
[29] Unger, "Hormone Therapy."

ly the genitalia surgery went, leaving his genitalia completely numb and him now being incontinent for the rest of his life.

Another detransitioner is Chloe Cole. Remember the Golden 4? Well, Chloe is autistic. She took testosterone and puberty blockers at 13, had a double mastectomy at 15, and detransitioned at 16 years old. She travels and speaks on the harm of gender affirming care, including going before U.S. Congress to advocate against transitioning children.

Finally, consider Sinead Watson. Due to the harm caused by transitioning, which included a double mastectomy, she suffers from extreme depression, alcoholism, and is suicidal. She puts her whole life on Twitter and it can be so hard to read sometimes. She's said that, if she ends up dead, just know it was transitioning that ruined her life. It absolutely breaks my heart to know the regret pain she feels.

VII. God Help

I mentioned early on that I would not use Christian sources until now, but now that we have become more familiar with Gender Affirming Care, it is vital that we look to someone who can bring clarity to our confusion.

Let's start by asking, what does it mean to say, "I feel like a man?" What is that feeling actually? How do I know what it feels like to be something I'm not? I can make good guesses, but as someone born in America, would anyone take me seriously if I said that I felt like a Rwandan? In our culture we act like feelings are truth, but if they're true, that means that if I feel like I'm a boy, I'm a boy! The question then follows, why transition? If you feel it, you are it! Let's say this another way using me as an example. The GD that I am experiencing is that I am in a female body, but I feel like a boy. The question that then follows is, which one is right? The body or the feeling? The pro-Trans movement says the body got it wrong. You are really a boy because that's what you feel like. The body is wrong and irrelevant for truth. So my question is: If the feeling is truth and I say that I'm a boy, that means I am a boy. But the minute I get surgery, or I take testosterone, I'm actually admitting that the body *does* matter and conveys truth. Once I start making physical changes, such as growing a beard and getting a double mastectomy, I'm saying that the human body does have a boy biology. What I don't say is, "I feel like a boy, so I'm going to get cat ears and a tiger tail." Why not? Because those are not male characteristics of humans. The minute you get surgery or cross-sex hormones, you're affirming that the body does play a role in identifying your gender. But on the front end, you said the body was irrelevant in identifying your true gender and went with the feeling. So which is it? If the body is irrelevant and feelings are all that's true, then I should never need any kind of surgery or any kind of medical intervention. The minute I get that, I affirm that there actually is a biological aspect to the truth of being male that carries weight, although I devalued that truth being female on the front end. Do you see that contradiction? You can't have it both ways. If our emotions and feelings convey truth, then you don't need surgery. But yet we get the surgery, thereby acknowledging that the physical body conveys the truth of gender.

Secondly, what's fascinating to me about this whole conversation is how contrary to feminist philosophy it is. Think about it. Feminists have spent years emphasizing that women are more than just cooks and pretty people with dresses and heels. There's more substance, intellect, and skill to us. And then what happens? Somebody says, "I want to be a girl" and what do they do? They grow their hair long, they get long nails, put on makeup, pluck their eyebrows, and shave their legs. They wear heels and tighter form fitting dresses, and then say, "I'm now a woman!" But what does this now mean? Essentially, that all there is to being a woman is makeup, long hair, a cute shape, large chest, and high heels etc. and you've just undone years of feminism that says women are more than just physical or sexual objects!!

The messaging here need not be missed. What are we saying about what is a woman? If you're a woman who doesn't like high heels because they're horrible for your feet, are you less female than somebody else? Or what about a girl who wants shorter hair or doesn't wear makeup? Is she somehow a man? I have yet to hear someone say, "I am a woman" and so begin studying mathematics. Don't women do that too, or is their only job to be sexually appealing?!

Aren't there more differences between men and women than just surface physical appearances? Absolutely! Women have better muscle endurance than men, and their muscles recover faster. However, men have more muscle mass than women, and those muscles are faster and more powerful! Women have bigger memory centers than men (see ladies, it's not their fault, okay?). Women function better during sleep deprivation than men, have 10% more fat, more taste buds, and have a better sense of smell and taste. Men typically have 25% thicker skin, more blood cells than women per microliter, are more likely to be colorblind, and have stronger bones, ligaments, and tendons.[30] Men also have significantly greater sensitivity for fine detail and rapidly moving stimuli in their eyes than women do.[31] Even male/female skulls are different in regards to size, brow shape and chin shape. Fascinating!

Finally, Genesis 1.27, "So God created mankind in his own image, in the image of God he created them; male and female he created them" (NIV). This verse is important to helping us understand what male/female is. When you look at the Hebrew for create, it means to shape, to create, to form, as in a physical description. In other words, Adam and Eve were created, shaped, and formed male and female. These are physical biological descriptions. It wasn't, "He's a male because he can throw a spear. She's female because she's shorter." They are physically shaped, male or female. Our sense of who we are or our feelings are not part of the criteria. From the beginning, God knew that we would struggle with identity, with liking ourselves, and so from the very first chapter of the Bible he gives us this clarity. Our gender doesn't have to do with our feelings or with societal stereotypes, but biology. And that biology goes beyond surface level to our gametes (egg or sperm) which make our male/female division even clearer. No amount of testosterone will cause a biological female to produce sperm. And no amount of estrogen will cause a biological male to produce eggs. A woman simply cannot become a man.

I've heard people say, "I've got a female body and a male brain," but that's biologically impossible because the brain is a sex-typed organ. As Dr.

---

[30] Staff, "25 Fun facts."
[31] Abramov, "Sex and vision."

Debra Soh says, "At about seven weeks, if the embryo is male, the testes will begin to secrete testosterone, masculinizing the brain. If the embryo is female, this process doesn't occur."[32] This process leads to differences in brain and neuron function, including amygdala and hippocampus size and functioning, memory,[33] and even toy preference once born to name a few! Hormones secreted from the brain, while the same, are secreted as pulses in females and nearly constant in males![34]

Paul Brand was a medical doctor who worked in India for many years with leprosy patients. He studied the skeletons of 600 people who had died from leprosy and knows the size/shape of the pelvis tells you whether it's male or female (which is why Archaeologists can dig up a body and, by looking at the bones, identify it as male or female). The female pelvis is shallow and broad, with an inner ring that's smooth and a unique opening for childbirth; a male's pelvis is narrower, heart-shaped, and formed with heavier bones.[35]

From looking at the bones, Doctor Brand can tell a lot. He mentions,

> The female runner still lags behind the male, and blame rests on the pelvis. The projections on the man's pelvis allow for more powerful muscles, but a woman equipped with them could not bear a child. Similarly, a man's hip sockets are closer together, nearer the center of gravity, which enables more efficient movement. If a woman's were similarly designed, there would be no room for the baby's head to extrude. So the odd pelvic bone represents a summation of many different requirements. When a woman wishes she could run faster or sway less or have a narrower base, let her know that the survival of the human race depends upon her being just the shape she is.[36]

We are all beautifully and intentionally designed and made. We are not accidents. Stasi Eldredge said, "It breaks my heart when women look at the sky and think 'Wow! God is amazing!' But look in the mirror and say, 'Ugh!', as if He did not make both."[37]

---

[32] Soh, *The end of Gender*, 18.
[33] Goldman, "Two Minds."
[34] Glezerman, "Yes, there is a female and a male brain."
[35] There is no current evidence that taking testosterone or estrogen will change your skull or pelvis structure.
[36] Brand, *In the likeness of God*, 87.
[37] Stasi Eldridge, Facebook, 6/15/19.

If you or someone you know is struggling with transgenderism, here's some advice. Number one, get off social media and/or change your friend groups. Two, consider changing schools or University. Three, seek mental health therapy, not therapy for GD. And lastly, please, under no circumstances take hormones, puberty blockers, or get surgery. Being a feminine guy doesn't make you a girl. Being a masculine female doesn't make you a boy. Generally, the overwhelming majority of people, by the time they hit around 25, will like themselves! Just give yourself time. You're going to be okay.

Suicide rates are higher in the trans community, not because of GD but because of pre-existing mental health conditions. Our society is struggling to find a reason to live. As believers, we need to do our best to help bring clarity to the confusion that we see around us, and the only way to do that with compassion is to see people through the eyes of God. We as Christians have done a horrible job of loving the sinner in our past. I remember our response to the LGB community in the 80s and 90s, and I remember being embarrassed and horrified by some of the stuff being said from the stage in churches when people were dying of AIDS or were gay. Please don't look down on those who are struggling with gender identity. Recognize that you are who you are because of the way Jesus has transformed your life. While you personally may not struggle with GD, that doesn't mean you're better than them. "Goodness" isn't determined in comparison to others, but in comparison to Jesus, and we all fall short of Him. We all are in need of His transformation. Don't forget that. Remember, the strongest voices against transitioning are the secular culture, and as the trans community continues to get rejected by them, will they find a home with Christians? Will they find a Christian who says, "I still love you and I still think you are valuable and matter." I hope so. We should be willing to embrace the sinner, the way we were embraced by Christ.

Bibliography

Abbruzzese, E., Stephen B. Levine, and Julia W. Mason. "The Myth of 'Reliable Research' in Pediatric Gender Medicine: A Critical Evaluation of the

Dutch Studies—and Research That Has Followed." *Journal of Sex & Marital Therapy* 49, no. 6 (January 2, 2023): 673–99. https://doi.org/10.1080/009262 3x.2022.2150346.

Abramov, Israel, James Gordon, Olga Feldman, and Alla Chavarga. "Sex & Vision I: Spatio-Temporal Resolution." *Biology of Sex Differences* 3, no. 1 (September 4, 2012): 20. https://doi.org/10.1186/2042-6410-3-20.

Biggs, Michael. "Suicide by Clinic-Referred Transgender Adolescents in the United Kingdom." *Archives of Sexual Behavior* 51, no. 2 (January 18, 2022): 685–90. https://doi.org/10.1007/s10508-022-02287-7.

Bramble, Matthew S., Lara Roach, Allen Lipson, Neerja Vashist, Ascia Eskin, Tuck Ngun, Jason E. Gosschalk, et al. "Sex-Specific Effects of Testosterone on the Sexually Dimorphic Transcriptome and Epigenome of Embryonic Neural Stem/Prrogenitor Cells." *Scientific Reports* 6, no. 1 (November 15, 2016). https://doi.org/10.1038/srep36916.

Brand, Paul, and Philip Yancey. *In the likeness of God*. Grand Rapids, MI: Zondervan, 2004.

Brown, Anna. "About 5% of Young Adults in the U.S. Say Their Gender Is Different from Their Sex Assigned at Birth." Pew Research Center, June 7, 2022. https://www.pewresearch.org/short-reads/2022/06/07/about-5-of-young-adults-in-the-u-s-say-their-gender-is-different-from-their-sex-assigned-at-birth/.

Dawkins, Richard. "Trans: When Ideology Meets Reality- My Conversation with Helen Joyce." YouTube, July 29, 2023. https://www.youtube.com/watch?v=hu72Lu5FqE4.

Deutsch, Maddie. "Information on Estrogen Hormone Therapy." UCSF Transgender Care, July 2020. https://transcare.ucsf.edu/article/information-estrogen-hormone-therapy.

Deutsch, Maddie. "Information on Testosterone Hormone Therapy." UCSF Transgender care, July 2020. https://transcare.ucsf.edu/article/information-testosterone-hormone-therapy.

Glezerman, Marek. "Yes, There Is a Female and a Male Brain: Morphology versus Functionality." *Proceedings of the National Academy of Sciences* 113, no. 14 (March 8, 2016). https://doi.org/10.1073/pnas.1524418113.

Goldman, Bruce. "Two Minds." *Stanford Medicine Magazine*, May 22, 2017. https://stanmed.stanford.edu/how-mens-and-womens-brains-are-different/.

"Italy Joins the List of Countries Recommending Restrictions on Puberty Blockers for Gender Dysphroia." *Society for Evidence Based Gender Medicine*, December 19, 2024. https://segm.org/Italy-Puberty-Blockers-Therapy-Bioethics#:~:text=%22The%20use%20of%20tryptorelin%20%5Bpuberty,articulation%20of%20National%20Health%20Systems.%22.

Kaltiala, Riittakerttu. "'Gender-Affirming Care Is Dangerous. I Know Because I Helped Pioneer It.'" *The Free Press*, October 30, 2023. https://www.thefp.com/p/gender-affirming-care-dangerous-finland-doctor.

Orange, Richard. "Teenage Transgender Row Splits Sweden as Dysphoria Diagnoses Soar by 1,500%." *The Guardian*, February 22, 2020. https://www.theguardian.com/society/2020/feb/22/ssweden-teenage-transgender-row-dysphoria-diagnoses-soar.

Peterson, Jordan. "The Wounds That Won't Heal | Detransitioner Chloe Cole | EP 319." YouTube, January 2, 2023. https://www.youtube.com/watch?v=6O3MzPeomqs.

Shrier, Abigail. *Irreversible damage: The transgender craze seducing our daughters*. Washington, DC: Regnery, 2021.

Soh, Debra. *The End of Gender: Debunking the myths about sex and identity in our society*. New York, NY: Treshold Editions, 2020.

Staff. "25 Fun Facts about What Makes Men and Women Different." Ask The Scientists, December 30, 2019. https://askthescientists.com/men-women-different/.

Unger, Cécile A. "Hormone Therapy for Transgender Patients." *Translational Andrology and Urology* 5, no. 6 (December 18, 2016): 877–84. https://doi.org/10.21037/tau.2016.09.04.

Villalba, Michael D., Haley P. Letter, Kristin A. Robinson, and Santo Maimone. "Breast Cancer in a Transgender Woman Undergoing Gender-Affirming Exogenous Hormone Therapy." Radiology Case Reports 18, no. 7 (July 2023): 2511–13. https://doi.org/10.1016/j.radcr.2023.04.032.

Vries, Annelou L.C. de, Jenifer K. McGuire, Thomas D. Steensma, Eva C.F. Wagenaar, Theo A.H. Doreleijers, and Peggy T. Cohen-Kettenis. "Young

Adult Psychological Outcome after Puberty Suppression and Gender Reassignment." *Pediatrics* 134, no. 4 (October 1, 2014): 696–704. https://doi.org/10.1542/peds.2013–2958.

Vries, Annelou L.C. de, Thomas D. Steensma, Theo A.H. Doreleijers, and Peggy T. Cohen-Kettenis. "Puberty Suppression in Adolescents with Gender Identity Disorder: A Prospective Follow-up Study." *The Journal of Sexual Medicine* 8, no. 8 (August 1, 2011): 2276–83. https://doi.org/10.1111/j.1743-6109.2010.01943.x.

17

Sex Matters
Understanding the Differences Between Male and Female and Why It's Good

Erin Kunkle

I. The Question Our Culture is Asking

Let me begin with a simple but pressing question: *Is there a difference between males and females?*

That question, the answer once considered self-evident, now evokes a surprising range of reactions. Recently, I posed it to a room full of *Christian* junior high students, and their wide variety of answers reflect the confusion that's become commonplace in this cultural moment. What used to be basic biology has now become a battleground of ideas.

In 2016, the Family Policy Institute of Washington interviewed students at Seattle University to explore public attitudes about gender identity. The video interviews[1] capture, with disturbing clarity, the prevailing mindset of a younger generation.

The interviewer, Joseph Backholm, begins by asking students whether they're aware of the ongoing discussions around gender identity and gender expression. Most students nod affirmatively and mention things like gender-neutral bathrooms and the freedom to choose restrooms based on one's personal sense of identity. When he presses further, asking whether there's any real difference between men and women, many hesitate. Their

---

[1] "Do College Kids Know the Different Between Men and Women?" You can view the entire video interview here: https://www.youtube.com/watch?v=-4S0gHlKiho.

answers range from tentative "yeses" to outright denials. Some assert gender is fluid or a mere social construct. Others are reluctant even to guess the interviewer's gender (clearly, Joseph Backholm is a man!).

At one point, Backholm asks students whether they think it matters at all that we have categories like "male" and "female." Many respond with a simple "no." Others couch their responses in the language of modern-day expressive individualism: "As long as no one's hurt" or "Everyone should be free to identify how they want." One young man confidently proclaims, "There is no need for the difference to exist scientifically or logically." Let that sink in: the idea that there is no scientific or logical reason for distinguishing male from female. And this from students at a major American university.

Backholm concludes with a thought-provoking observation: "There may be nothing more self-evident in the natural universe than the fact that every animal species is divided into two halves—male and female. Yet the most intelligent of those species seems to be wrestling with whether male and female are even real. Have we discovered something new, or have we become too clever for our own good?"

This video offers more than just viral sound bites. It provides a window into the minds of young adults deeply influenced by modern ideas of gender. And more troublingly, it reveals a profound uncertainty about the most basic aspects of our humanity.

I share this not to mock or criticize those students. I'm not interested in scoring cultural points. I share it because their answers reflect something very real and very serious. Our culture's confusion over sex and gender is no longer confined to academic debates. It's shaping the way young people see themselves, each other, and the world. We're watching in real time as the meaning of manhood and womanhood is being deconstructed—and redefined—before our eyes.

Think about what's at stake here. If we cannot even agree on what it means to be male or female, how can we possibly build a coherent view of family, parenting, sexuality, or even friendship? If our identities are entirely self-determined—if biology is irrelevant, and the body merely incidental—then the God-given foundation for human relationships begins to crumble.

This is why we must talk about these things. This is why I'm passionate about this topic. Because it's not just about culture wars or political battles, it's about truth. It's about the nature of reality. It's about human flourishing.

So, we must ask and answer these questions: *What does it mean to be male or female? Are those differences real? And if they are, are they good?*

Our answers will shape the way we understand ourselves, the way we raise our children, and the way we live faithfully in the world God has made. And while our culture may be stumbling around in the dark, I believe Scripture speaks clearly—and beautifully—into the confusion.

II. Unpacking the Confusion by Defining our Terms

To make sense of the cultural confusion, we need to uncover some of the lies our culture tells—lies that have deeply shaped how we think about sex and gender. And the first lie is this: *You decide your own gender.*

According to this narrative, feeling discomfort with your biological sex means you might actually be the opposite sex. This idea rests on the claim that gender is a *social construct*. A social construct is something that doesn't exist independently in the natural world but is instead created by society. It's an agreed-upon convention, not an observable reality. For example, speed limits are a social construct. Your local city council didn't consult nature to decide that the safe speed on a road should be 35 mph. That number is arbitrary, decided upon by people for practical reasons. Local laws are full of social constructs, some even humorous. Did you know that in Portland, Oregon, it's illegal to walk down the street with your shoelaces untied? In Waterville, Maine, it's illegal to blow your nose in public. In Alabama, wearing a fake mustache in church is forbidden. In Alaska, you can't drive with your dog tethered to your car (which actually sounds wise), and in Los Angeles, where I live, it's illegal to wash your neighbor's car without their permission. These are all examples of things we've simply made up.

So, *is gender like that?* Is gender merely something society has invented? Is it something with no basis in nature, that we can change whenever we want? And if we claim that everything is a social construct, why not say the same about gravity? Is gravity a social construct? Of course not. So, what makes gender different? And if someone says, "Reality is a social construct," we must ask—*is that statement itself a social construct?* You can see how quickly this idea unravels.

To think clearly about this, we need to define several key terms. Let's begin with the most foundational one: *sex*. Biological sex is a physical reality. It refers to the two categories of male and female, into which humans and other living organisms are divided based on their reproductive function. Sex refers to the way the body is organized for the purpose of reproduction. Simply put, males have smaller gametes (sperm) and women have larger gametes (ova or eggs). There are two important things to note about this definition. First, biological sex is unchanging, and second, it's almost always immediately obvious. There is no "spectrum" of sexes. There is no third category.

At this point, someone might bring up the issue of intersex individuals, people born with ambiguous genitalia. It's a common objection, so let's address it. Intersex conditions represent a biological abnormality. They are a deviation from the way things are supposed to be, much like being born with a cleft palate or a congenital heart defect. These do not represent new categories of sex, but are exceptions due to the brokenness of our fallen world. Therefore, we shouldn't treat intersex as a third sex or claim that God created people intersex by design. It reflects the same kind of physical disorder we see in many other areas of life.

Next, let's define *gender*. Gender refers to how we identify and then present ourselves to the world as male or female. It's expressed in how we dress, speak, or act. Historically, gender has always been connected to biological sex. That connection is even built into the word itself. The root word "gen" means "birth" or "origin." That's why we find it in words like *genesis*, *genitals*, and *gender*.

Here's an easy way to remember the current cultural distinction between sex and gender:

sex = biology
gender = psychology

Sex is about the body. Gender is about the mind. For thousands of years, humanity did not separate the two. It's only in recent history that our culture has attempted to pull them apart.

This brings us to another important term: *gender dysphoria*. Gender dysphoria is the condition of experiencing a psychological or emotional disconnect between one's biological sex and one's internal sense of gender. A person with gender dysphoria may feel as though they are, or should have been, the opposite sex. However, not everyone with gender dysphoria goes on to identify as transgender.

Transgenderism is the belief that a person's self-declared gender identity determines their actual gender. According to this view, a boy who identifies as a girl *is* a girl, not simply a boy who feels like one. Thus, trans activists will simply assert that trans women *are* women. Not only does this view insist that a person can be the gender opposite their biological sex, but that everyone else must affirm this as true. But here's the critical question: *Why do we think we can or should disconnect gender identity from our bodies?* On what basis do we believe that our thoughts should override biological reality? Our culture's answer boils down to one thing: feelings. However, this answer should lead us to ask a second question: *Can our thoughts and feelings ever be wrong?* Of course they can. And deep down, we all know this.

Even today, there are areas in our culture where we refuse to accept someone's feelings as the final authority. Take, for example, Rachel Dolezal. A few years ago, she made headlines for leading a chapter of the NAACP in Spokane, Washington, while presenting herself as a black woman who advocated passionately for African American causes. The problem? Rachel is white. She grew up in a white family and is biologically European. Yet she *felt* black. She *identified* as black. Nonetheless, the culture did *not* affirm her feelings. It rejected them. She was accused of lying and forced to resign from the NAACP. Why? Because feelings don't change reality. You don't get to *become* another race simply because you feel like you are.

Or, consider the example of plastic surgery. Suppose I have cosmetic surgery that makes me look 20 years younger. Do people then say, "She's actually 28 year old now?" Of course not. My age hasn't changed. No one believes that modifying my appearance rewrites the biological facts. My cells, my DNA, my entire biology still testify to my real age.

Consider a more tragic example, anorexia. Many girls—and some boys—suffer from this painful condition. Despite being dangerously underweight, they look in the mirror and see someone who is overweight. Their perception doesn't match reality. And how do we help them? Not by affirming their distorted self-image. We don't say, "Well, if you feel overweight, then you must be. Let's put you on a diet immediately." No, we seek to bring their mind back into alignment with the truth. We help them see their body as it truly is and not as they imagine it to be.

So why, in the case of gender, do we suddenly flip the script? Why do we affirm feelings over facts? Why do we deny biology in favor of identity?

These are the contradictions we must face head-on because when it comes to the question of what makes us male and female, truth matters. And when we detach identity from the body, we don't just create confusion, we cause real harm.

III. Ideas That Have Captured Culture

In her book *Irreversible Damage,* Abigail Shrier uncovers a startling statistic: over 70% of transgender surgeries are performed on girls.[2] That figure may surprise you. It certainly surprised me when I first began reading her book. I found myself asking, *Why are girls so disproportionately represented in this movement?*

The answer, as Shrier explains, is that the transgender movement taps into a particular vulnerability that many young women experience—deep discomfort with their changing bodies, especially during puberty. In an oversexualized culture, where girls are bombarded with impossible beauty standards and distorted messages about femininity, it's not unusual for them to feel out of place in their own skin. Their bodies begin

---

[2] Shrier, *Irreversible Damage*, 26.

to change, they feel strange or awkward, and it's easy to conclude, *Something must be wrong with me.*

But what do we do with that discomfort? Do we affirm it as truth? Do we treat the body as the problem to be fixed? Or do we guide these young women toward the truth that there's nothing wrong with them, that these feelings are often a normal part of growing up, and that their bodies are good?

As Christians, we need to understand that ideas are never neutral. Ideas have consequences, and bad ideas have victims. When a culture embraces the idea that identity is self-determined and detached from biological reality, confusion and brokenness inevitably follow.

So, how do we respond? What should the church do in a cultural moment like this?

It's not enough to simply say *no* to the lies of the gender revolution. We must also present an alternative, a true and beautiful vision of what it means to be made male and female in the image of God. In the face of confusion, we need clarity. And we need to offer something true, good, and beautiful.

Let me give you a simple analogy that helps illustrate the goodness of design. Imagine my washing machine at home. It's a wonderful tool for cleaning clothes. It was made for that purpose, and it works well. Now imagine someone sees the washing machine and thinks, *If this thing cleans clothes, maybe it can clean dishes too!* So they load up the plates and bowls and give it a try. We all know how that would end. Using the machine for something it wasn't designed to do would only lead to broken dishes and eventually, a broken washing machine.

Now, if my washing machine starts leaking or making weird noises, I don't simply guess what the problem is. I consult the manual. Why? Because the manual was written by the one who designed the machine. The one who created it knows how it was meant to function.

In the same way, if we want to understand who we are—if we want clarity about our identity, purpose, and how we are to properly function—we need to turn to the One who made us. Only the Creator can define the creature. And this is the heart of our modern confusion: identity. What do we root our identity in? Or better yet, *Who* do we root our identity in? You cannot know who you are until you know whose you are.

But how do we discover that? How do we know who made us and what He made us for?

IV. God's Design for Male and Female

According to the Christian worldview, we have two primary sources of knowledge about God: His Word and His world. First, we look to Scripture. We have good reason to believe that the Bible is the true and trustworthy Word of the God who made us. It reveals who He is and what He has done. Second, we look to the natural world—what God has made—which also speaks about Him. As Romans 1.20 reminds us, God's "eternal power and divine nature have been clearly seen, being understood from what has been made."

Let's begin with God's Word. The opening pages of Scripture take us straight to the foundation in Genesis: "In the beginning, God created the heavens and the earth…" (Genesis 1.1). From the very first chapter, we see that God is the Creator of all things. Then, in verses 26 and 27, we read something truly remarkable: "God said, 'Let us make mankind in our image, in our likeness…' So God created mankind in His own image; in the image of God He created them; male and female He created them."

This is the starting point for understanding human identity. What gives every human being—man or woman—equal worth and value? What do we all share, no matter our sex? *We all bear the image of God.*

This foundational truth is utterly unique to the Christian worldview. No other worldview provides such a solid basis for human equality, dignity, and purpose. And when God looked at His creation, including men and women, He declared it all "very good" (Genesis 1.31). God doesn't just tolerate the differences between men and women, He delights in them.

We've seen what Scripture says, but now let's look at the world God has made. Nature itself bears witness to the reality that humans are made male and female. The differences are not merely external. They go far deeper than reproductive organs. We're talking about DNA, hormones like testosterone and estrogen, brain structures, muscle mass, fat distribution, heart and lung capacity, and more. These differences are real, measurable, and meaningful.

Let me give you a striking example. Compare photos of male and female Olympic swimmers. These are elite athletes, each at the peak of human performance. And yet, the differences between the male and female bodies are plainly visible. You can see it with your own eyes.

Or take Lia Thomas (formerly Will Thomas), a swimmer who competed for three years on the men's team at the University of Pennsylvania before switching to the women's team. In his final year, he won the NCAA women's championship in the 500-yard freestyle, beating out biological females. There he stood on the podium, holding the trophy, flanked by the two women he had just defeated. When you look at the photo of the athletes standing on the winner's podium, is there any real question about whether males and females are different? The evidence is right there in front of us. But our culture has reached the point where even stating the obvious is considered controversial—or dangerous.

Now, maybe you're not struggling with *what* you see, but with *how* to interpret it. You might wonder: *Are these differences good?* And that's a question many young people are sincerely asking.

A few years ago, I gave a similar talk to a group of junior high students at a youth conference in Arkansas. Afterward, a small group of girls approached me, visibly upset. They told me that one of their friends was so offended by my statement that men are generally bigger than women, that she couldn't even come talk to me. I didn't argue the point. I simply asked, "What's wrong with that? Why is it bad that men and women are physically different?"

That's the question we need to wrestle with. If God is good—and He is—why did He make humanity in two distinct categories, male and female? And are these differences merely physical, or do they reflect something deeper, something about who God is and how we bear His image?

V. Lie #1 — Men and Women Are the Same

One of the most pervasive cultural lies today is that men and women are essentially the same. We're not just equal in value, but identical in nature. However, social science, common sense, and our own experience tell a different story.

When researchers examine different times, places, and cultures, they find something remarkably consistent. Men and women are different and not just physically, but behaviorally, emotionally, and psychologically. Of course, when we start talking about male-female differences, people often get defensive. I've heard responses like, "Well, I know a guy who doesn't fit that mold," or "That doesn't describe my daughter at all." And that's fair. So let's be clear that we're talking in generalities. There are always exceptions, but general patterns still matter, and they help us see God's purposeful design.

So, what are some of the consistent differences social scientists have found? First, men tend to be *builders*, and women tend to be *nurturers*. That is, men are often drawn toward constructing, protecting, and physically engaging with the world, while women often lean toward caring for and developing relationships. This distinction is reflected everywhere, even among children. If you doubt this, try volunteering in your church's children's ministry. Watch how the two- and three-year-old boys and girls play. In general, the boys are building things (and often knocking them down!), chasing each other, making loud noises, and wrestling around. The girls, on the other hand, are more likely to be playing cooperatively, setting up pretend picnics or caring for dolls. These behaviors reflect deeper tendencies that often continue into adulthood.

Why is it that 99.9% of construction workers are men? And why are the vast majority of nurses—about 95%—women? That's not a coincidence. It says something about how men and women are wired. That doesn't mean men can't be nurturing or that women can't build. In fact, one of the pastors at our church in California is a full-time nurse, a husband and father of four. He's great at what he does. But the broader pattern remains.

Think about your own childhood. When you were sick, whom did you instinctively go to for comfort, your mom or your dad? Most kids go to mom. Again, that speaks to something deep and good about how women are made.

Here's another common difference: *men tend to take risks*, while *women tend to seek security*. In your own home growing up, or even now in your marriage, who was more likely to suggest a big move across the country or a bold new career change? Often, it's the man who initiates the risk, while the woman voices concerns about security and stability.

Insurance companies know this too. Why do they charge significantly more to insure teenage boys than girls? Unless we think the entire industry is sexist, the answer is clear: boys take more risks. They drive more aggressively, and they get into more accidents. Even in parenting, the difference shows up. Who was the more protective parent in your household? Who said things like, "Drive safe," "Wear your seatbelt," or "Call me when you get there"? Probably your mom. Dads don't usually think of those things, not because they don't care, but because their instincts are wired differently.

Social scientists have noted another pattern: *men tend to compete*, while *women tend to connect*. Think of your last big family gathering. The men were probably outside tossing a football, watching a game, or playing cards—doing something competitive. The women? Most likely gathered around, talking and catching up. I saw this difference play out during COVID.

Early in the lockdowns, when we were all stuck at home, we decided to create a family Settlers of Catan board game tournament. We even kept score on a chalkboard. One night, after a particularly tense and competitive game, I was frustrated. As we got ready for bed, I told my husband Brett, "You guys ruined the game. You argued the whole time. It was supposed to be about family bonding." He looked at me and said, "Wait, you were playing Settlers for the purpose of spending time as a family? I was trying to win!" Brett wasn't thinking about connection. He was focused on the competition. That's not bad, it's just different.

Of course, women can be competitive too. Two of our daughters were fiercely trying to beat their dad in that same tournament. And yes, men can be deeply relational. These are general *tendencies*, not rigid rules.

Let me share another humorous but telling example. We have five kids: three girls and two boys. One evening, before dinner, one of our children offered the following prayer: "Dear Lord, give the superheroes strength in the movies, and for our family to be strong to punch the bad guys and the trolls, and for us to get an axe. Amen." Now, do you think that was one of our daughters or one of our sons? Of course, it was our son Jonah, who was three years old at the time.

Brett's reaction? He was so proud of his boy! He immediately wrote the prayer down, so that we could preserve it and share it with generations to come. My reaction? I was slightly alarmed! "An axe? Is this a red flag?" But to Brett, it was just the brave heart of a little boy. And honestly, he was right. These general patterns resonate with what we see every day.

As Christians, we do need to be careful that generalities don't morph into stereotypes. We must leave room for the wide range of personality and preference within male and female design. For example, what if you're a boy who doesn't like football or wrestling or video games? Maybe you prefer reading, music, or philosophy. That's okay. You're still a boy. You're not less of a man because you enjoy different things. Think about men like Mozart, C.S. Lewis, Shakespeare, da Vinci—men of intellect, creativity, and imagination. You're in good company.

I once gave this message to a youth group, and a junior high boy waited until everyone had left to come speak to me. He said, "Thank you for saying that. I don't like football, and everyone tells me I'm gay, but I'm not." Apparently, I was the first adult who had ever told him that he was just fine the way he was.

And what about the girls? If you're a girl who doesn't like shopping or romantic comedies or Taylor Swift but would rather be outdoors fishing with your dad or playing sports or fixing cars, you're still a girl. There's nothing wrong with you.

That was my story. I was a tomboy growing up. I refused to wear dresses. I played baseball and kickball at recess while my sisters played with dolls. My mom still made me wear a dress to church, but I didn't like it.

The category of "tomboy" has almost disappeared from our cultural vocabulary. Today, girls like I once was are told something far more damaging: *Maybe you're not really a girl at all. Maybe you were supposed to be a boy.* But that's not true. If you're a girl who loves football like I do, you're just a girl who loves football. You're not a boy. And you're certainly not a mistake.

VI. Lie #2 — There Is a Spectrum of Genders

Our culture's second major lie is that gender exists on a spectrum. According to this view, there aren't just two genders, male and female, but dozens and maybe even hundreds of variations. Gender, we're told, is fluid. You can be one gender today and another tomorrow. Or maybe you're a blend of both. Or maybe something entirely new. In fact, Facebook once offered over 50 gender options for users to choose from. But the truth is, this kind of thinking misunderstands something very important: it confuses *gender* with the traits of *masculinity and femininity*—real qualities that do exist on a spectrum *within* each sex.

For example, when it comes to masculinity, not all boys are the same. Some boys are more sensitive, reflective, and gentle. Others are more assertive, rough-and-tumble, and active. And most fall somewhere in between. But no matter where a boy lands on that masculine spectrum, he is still male—and that is good.

The same is true for girls. Some are what we might call "girly girls," who enjoy dresses, dolls, and all the cultural norms of femininity. Others prefer competitive sports or roughing it in the outdoors. And most are somewhere in the middle. But wherever a girl lands on the spectrum of femininity, she is still female—and that, too, is good.

This diversity of expression within male and female shows the richness of God's design. He made two sexes. He made them different. And He called them *good*.

When we begin to appreciate the differences between male and female, not as limitations or social constructs but as part of God's beautiful design, we begin to see the value in honoring both. This kind of clarity shouldn't lead to arrogance or division between men and women. It should lead us to *reverence* and *respect*.

In Matthew 22, Jesus gives us the two greatest commandments: love God and love your neighbor. So how do we love those who are struggling with gender identity? How do we love our LGBTQ neighbors, friends, and family members? We must begin by clarifying what love is.

In our culture, love is often defined as *total affirmation*. If you love someone, you accept, affirm, and support whatever they feel or desire. But that's not the biblical definition. Scripture gives us a different vision of love, one rooted in truth. 1 John 3.18 says, "Let us not love with words or speech but with actions and in truth." And in 1 Corinthians 13, often referred to as the "love chapter" of the Bible, we're told that "love does not rejoice in unrighteousness, but rejoices with the truth."

Take Sidney, a young woman who shared her story online.[3] She writes, "Doctors failed me at every turn." Sidney explains that as she began questioning her identity, everyone from friends to medical professionals to her own parents affirmed her desire to transition—everyone, that is, except her grandfather. Her grandfather pleaded with her to reconsider. At one point, he sat down with tears in his eyes and simply asked her to stop. And something in that moment broke through. She writes, "He was the only person whose opinion I ever really cared about… I just couldn't tell him no." In that moment, her grandpa's love *and* courage to speak the truth may have saved her life.

Scripture binds love and truth together. As C. S. Lewis put it, "Love is not affectionate feeling, but a steady wish for the loved person's ultimate good as far as it can be obtained."[4] If you're a parent, you understand this instinctively. Loving your child doesn't mean affirming their every desire. It means guiding them toward what is objectively good for them, even when it might be refused or rejected.

---

[3] Wright, "I Spent a Year as a Trans Man Where Doctors Failed Me at Every Turn."
[4] Lewis, *God in the Dock*, 49.

VII. Lie #3 — Transitioning Leads to Wholeness

One of the most damaging lies told today is that transitioning your gender leads to wholeness and happiness. The culture says that if someone feels like they are the opposite sex, the loving and supportive thing to do is to help them transition, not merely through social changes but through hormone therapies and surgeries, so they can finally "be who they really are." But we've been running this cultural experiment for over a decade now and the results are heartbreaking.

Maybe the most powerful way to debunk this lie is by telling the thousands of stories of detransitioners like Prisha Mosley. In an online video,[5] she recounts being promised that transitioning would bring her peace. After undergoing hormone treatments and a double mastectomy, she describes feeling not liberated, but *ruined*, as she begins to sob. In another video,[6] Mosley recounts how her medical transition did not relieve a host of mental health issues, rather it exacerbated them and in addition, left her with a host of irreversible physical issues that she will deal with for the rest of her life.

Thankfully, by God's grace, there is hope and healing for those who have journeyed down the road of transition. The only hope for wholeness is found in God. Indeed, Revelation 21.4 promises that one day, God "will wipe away every tear from their eyes… neither shall there be mourning, nor crying, nor pain anymore, for the former things have passed away." Even a body that has been mutilated in this life will eventually be restored.

That's our hope. That's the hope we offer to those who are hurting. The growing community of *detransitioners*, people who went down the path of transition and now deeply regret it, desperately need the love, hope and healing only the Gospel can bring. And we can be conduits of God's love for this community.

---

[5] Mosly, "Opening up/DetransDiary/Entry 1."
[6] Alliance Defending Freedom. "Transition Did Not Fix My Distress," YouTube, November 26, 2024. https://www.youtube.com/watch?v=hFsCmgheHRE.

VIII. Be Prepared for the Social Cost of Speaking the Truth

Speaking the truth about gender in today's culture is not without risk. Those who do often face mockery, rejection, or worse.

Korbin Albert, a professional soccer player, found herself at the center of controversy simply for reposting a video.[7] It featured a young man with an intellectual disability who shared candidly about his struggles with same-sex attraction and gender confusion, and how the church helped him find hope. Korbin reposted the video and liked it. The backlash was immediate. Prominent voices in the LGBTQ community—some of them fellow athletes—condemned her. Under immense pressure, she issued a public apology for sharing what was considered "offensive content." This is often the cost of speaking the truth in love.

But Jesus prepared us for this. In John 15.18–20, He says, "If the world hates you, keep in mind that it hated me first... If you belonged to the world, it would love you as its own. But I have chosen you out of the world. That is why the world hates you... If they persecuted me, they will persecute you also."

We must not be surprised by resistance. And we must not back down in fear.

IX. Hope, Not Despair

In the face of cultural confusion, we do not respond with despair. We respond with hope.

Why? Because Jesus is our Redeemer. He took Saul of Tarsus, a persecutor of Christians, and made him the Apostle Paul. He redeemed Augustine, a young man steeped in sin, who became one of the greatest theologians in church history. He redeemed me, a teen mom at seventeen, and God has redeemed you, as well. There is no one beyond His reach.

Furthermore, God's design for men and women and the complementarity of the sexes, offers our culture a *beautiful* way forward through the confusion and chaos of modern gender ideology. I was reminded of this truth while watching the 2022 Winter Olympics. One of my favorite

---

[7] Associated Press, ""U.S. midfielder Korbin Albert..."

events is couples ice skating. It's graceful, yet powerful, and even terrifying, if you've ever tried skating yourself! But what struck me most as I watched was how the pairs displayed the beauty of difference.

The man and the woman don't move identically. They don't do the same things. Their roles are different and their bodies are different. But together, they create something breathtaking. That's what God's design does. It doesn't erase our differences. It celebrates them. It harmonizes them. And when we live according to that design—when we proclaim it, embody it, and hold it out to a confused world—we offer not just a truth, but a beauty too compelling to ignore.

Bibliography

Alliance Defending Freedom. "Transition Did Not Fix My Distress," YouTube, November 26, 2024, video, https://www.youtube.com/watch?v=hFsCmgheHRE.

Associated Press. "U.S. midfielder Korbin Albert apologizes for sharing 'insensitive and hurtful' social media posts," accessed April 1, 2025, [https://apnews.com/article/korbin-albert-apology-uswnt-tiktok-lgbtq-14b416d-f34354278ad0174bb7fedcad3].

Lewis, C.S. *God in the Dock*. Grand Rapids, MI: Eerdmans Publishing Company, 1970.

Mosley, Prisha. "Opening up/DetransDiary/Entry 1," YouTube, October 2, 2022, video, https://www.youtube.com/watch?v=Utncd9-VxPg.

Shrier, Abigail. *Irreversible Damage: The Transgender Craze Seducing Our Daughters*. Washington, DC: Regnery Publishing, 2021.

Wright, Sydney. "I Spent a Year as a Trans Man Where Doctors Failed Me at Every Turn," accessed March 29, 2025, [https://theohiostar.com/uncategorized/commentary-i-spent-a-year-as-a-trans-man-but-doctors-failed-me-at-every-turn/ohstarstaff/2019/10/09/].

Further Resources

Pearcey, Nancy. *The Toxic War on Masculinity: How Christianity Reconciles the Sexes*. Grand Rapids, MI: Baker Books, 2023.

Stanton, Glenn. *Secure Daughters Confident Sons: How Parents Guide Their Children into Authentic Masculinity and Femininity.* Colorado Springs, CO: PRH Christian Publishing, 2011.

18

"Am I Not a Man and a Brother?"
Scripture and Slavery in Ancient and Modern Contexts

Paul Copan

I. Introductory Remarks

"Am I not a man and a brother?" That famous quotation and accompanying engraving comes from the British abolitionist Josiah Wedgwood. Along with Olaudah Equiano, William Wilberforce, and the Clapham Sect, he defended the humanity of the chattel slaves, who had been kidnapped and transported to Britain and its colonies. And we know the good outcome of this noble struggle. But when it comes to the Old Testament, what was the status of the "slave" or "servant" (*ebed*)? Was he considered *man* and *brother*? Atheist Sam Harris thinks not. He has claimed that slaves were treated as "farm equipment" in the Old Testament.[1]

What I write on this topic in my books *Is God a Moral Monster?*[2] and *Is God a Vindictive Bully*,[3] and more recently in a chapter in my coedited *Christianity Contested*,[4] I can only distill and summarize here. After some general comments on the history of slavery, I will, first, make summary comments on the term "slave" in light of biblical translations. I then compare visions of humanity in the Old Testament to other ancient Near Eastern cultures.

---

[1] Harris, *Letter to a Christian Nation*, 14.
[2] Copan, *Is God a Moral Monster?*
[3] Copan, *Is God a Vindictive Bully?*
[4] Copan, "'Slavery' in the Old Testament," in *Christianity Contested*.

Third, I explore provisions and various accommodations for servants in Scripture. Fourth, I inspect illustrations in three troubling servitude texts.

II. Humanity and the History of Slavery

Slavery has been with us for millennia. In his book *Colonialism: A Moral Reckoning*, Nigel Biggar documents just how widespread and longstanding it has been—from the ancient Mesopotamians, Greeks, Carthaginians, and Romans to the Chinese, Japanese, and Koreans to the Incas, the Aztecs, and the Comanches. The ever-growing Islamic militaristic dominance inspired by Muhammad continued the practice of taking women as sex slaves after war. Vikings provided Arab Spain and Egypt with white slaves from Eastern Europe and the British Isles. Raiders from Tunis, Algiers, and Tripoli alone enslaved between 1 million and 1.25 million *Europeans*, according to one estimate. The Muslim slave trade as a whole, lasting until 1920, transported about 17 million slaves, mostly African, exceeding the estimated 11 million shipped by Europeans across the Atlantic. And for a long while, Africans enslaved other Africans and even offered them up as sacrificial victims in their religious rituals.[5] The slave's conditions differed, and the right to ownership was not always absolute.

Biggar notes that work could be laborious, legally compelled due to unfair contract, and even soul-destroyingly tedious, but without amounting to slavery. Such work

> may have been performed under terms of an unfair indenture or contract, to which the employee has consented only under duress. And yet, an *exploited* employee does not quite make a slave. Even "forced labour" can fall well short of slavery. There is nothing necessarily wrong with requiring members of a community, by law or custom, to spend some of their time and energy on public works or in public service.[6]

What distinguishes and specifies slavery is that

> the slave's time and employment are owned, not voluntarily, under certain conditions, for certain purposes and for a certain length of time, but absolute-

---
[5] Biggar, *Colonialism*, 47–48.
[6] Ibid., 48.

ly. The slave is the slave owner's disposable property to be put to whatever use the owner decides and to be bought and sold—and perhaps even killed—at will. That is the pure form or paradigm of slavery, and it is the treatment of another human being as absolutely disposable property that makes it categorically worse than other forms of unjust employment.[7]

This illustrates what Harriet Beecher Stowe, author of *Uncle Tom's Cabin*, wrote of antebellum Southern slavery that "the legal power of the master amounts to an absolute despotism over body and soul …. there is no protection for the slave's life."[8]

III. Examining Versions: "Slave" and "Slavery" in Translation

Contrary to Sam Harris's accusations, Biggar's definition, and Stowe's description, Old Testament servitude was *very* different from the quintessential evil of slavery. For starters, let's consider our modern Scripture translations. Given the history of modern slavery, the US Civil War, and the abolition of slavery, how strange it is to have the emotion-laden *slave/slavery* language in our modern Old Testament translations! This is all the more startling when compared to less-harsh sounding older translations (*servant/serve*)—not just in English but German, Spanish, and other languages as well. For example, the King James Version (1611) mentions *slave* only used once in the Old Testament. By contrast, modern versions *often* use the strong, misleading language of *slave* and *slavery*. For example, the New International Version (1984) uses the term *slave* (*ebed*) 104 times and *slavery* (*ebedim/abduth*) 17 times. No wonder readers often wrongly infer a resemblance to the antebellum South!

However, a rendering like *servant* or *hired worker* would be a more accurate rendering for the Hebrew term *ebed*. It refers to a worker's dependency relationship, and it is not intrinsically negative. For example, Moses and Joshua are each called "the servant of the LORD"—an honorific title.

This biblical dependency-relationship language, though not identical, is akin to our transactional modern-day sports world. Basketball players are *traded* or *sold*, teams are *owned*, and so forth. Rightly un-

---

[7] Ibid.
[8] Stowe, *A Key to Uncle Tom's Cabin*, I.10, 139.

derstood, this isn't dehumanizing. Likewise, we should see that same non-dehumanizing, legal, contractual, transactional servitude language in the Old Testament as well.

Again, the term *servant* is neutral and not inherently negative. In the book of Exodus, the Israelites are called Pharaoh's *servants*—no surprise there. But the *Egyptians* are also called Pharaoh's servants (Ex 5.21). Yet God commands Moses to tell Pharaoh to let Israel go so that "they may serve [*abad*] me in the wilderness" (Ex 7.16).[9] The Israelites are moving from *oppressive* servitude to *liberating* servitude. The same neutral language used to illustrate dependency can be positive or negative.

IV. Comparing Visions: Humankind, Scripture, and the Ancient Near East

Beyond translations and versions, it's helpful to examine the biblical visions of humanity in contrast to other ancient Near Eastern cultures. In doing so, we should distinguish between specific *laws* and a broader moral *vision*. Jesus referred to legislation permitting divorce (Deut 24.1–4), declaring that this concession was due to human hardheartedness (Mt 19.8); by contrast, God desired marital permanency (Gen 2.24). Certain laws are less-than-ideal and concessionary, and they assume humans will sin; they don't reflect the divine ideal.

In his condescending activity towards humans, God doesn't begin with pristine conditions; he starts where people are—with their fallen structures and mindsets—and gives them specific steps to move in a redemptive direction. Deuteronomy 4.6 assumes that Israel's distinctive laws, contrasted with other nations' laws, are morally and righteously superior: If Israel obeys them, this "will be your wisdom and understanding in the sight of the peoples, who, when they hear all these statutes, will say, 'surely this great nation is a wise and understanding people.'"

One key area of Israel's vision is its *concern for the marginalized*, who can most easily be taken advantage of. This begins in Genesis 1 with the fact that *all* persons bear the image of God in the biblical vision: all hu-

---

[9] Unless otherwise noted, all Scripture citations are from the New American Standard Bible (NASB).

man beings are God's representatives on earth and are created to be co-regents with God (vv. 26–28). By contrast, *kings* alone were the divine image-bearers in the rest of the ancient Near East. Other creation accounts show a more contemptuous attitude toward humans. In the Mesopotamian *Atrahasis* account, humans are created from a lesser deity's blood and the spit of an assembly of deities. And humans are created to dig irrigation ditches—the task the lesser gods despised.

Furthermore, the Old Testament also presents servants, not just employers ("masters"), as fully human. Job 31.13–15 emphasizes master and servant come from the same place—the mother's womb; they are fundamentally equal. And God says he'll pour out his Spirit on male and female servants (Joel 2.29). This biblical vision—rooted in creation—stands in contrast to, say, ancient Greece, which denied such equality and dignity. Aristotle claimed that some people are slaves by nature and that slaves are merely animated tools.[10]

In addition, in the Mosaic Law, persons receive far higher priority over property. By contrast, other ancient Near Eastern law collections prioritize property over persons, with property crimes treated with greater severity than personal crimes.

Also, Israel's laws reflect a more democratized understanding of society. This was different from the strongly hierarchical structures of the surrounding nations; those lower on the social ladder would get punished more severely while those at the top had lighter punishments. In Israel, however, kings and priests were to be held to the same standards as the common person. Consider 2 Samuel 12, where Nathan confronts King David for his murder and his adultery: the king can't simply get away with such wickedness.

Other differences include the fact that God established a loving relationship with Israel, which is much more personalized than other ancient Near Eastern covenants, whose gods were more detached covenant-makers. By contrast, Yahweh showed deep concern for Israel; his personal involvement in Israel's history included bringing them out of

---

[10] Aristotle, *Politics*, I.3–6; *Nicomachean Ethics*, 8.11.

Egypt with signs and wonders and renewing his covenant after Israel has repeatedly broken faith with him.

Israel's neighbors' laws also didn't show much concern for foreigners, the downtrodden, or the poor. They made no provisions for the poor whereas Israel's gleaning laws benefited the poor. Also, other nations had no time limits on servitude, although their kings might haphazardly pronounce amnesty for slaves—but this was not a matter of fixed legislation. And unlike Israel, other nations had no interest-free loans; lenders engaged in loan-sharking with high interest rates that pushed the poor further into poverty. Individuals had rights in Israel, whether they were war captives (Deut 21.10–14), runaway slaves (Deut 23.15–16), or the socially vulnerable (Deut 14.28–29; 26.12–13). They had rights and were to be treated as free agents: they were not considered things or objects. In other parts of the ancient world, no such rights existed. (See David L. Baker's book *Tight Fists and Open Hands*, which contrasts Israelite law with that of the nations surrounding Israel.[11])

In sum, the vision behind Old Testament law tends to benefit those at the margins of society. By contrast, other ancient Near Easter law codes benefit the elite and place greater burdens on those in the lower strata of society.

V. Exploring Provisions: Various Accommodations for Servants in the OT

What provisions are made for servants in the Old Testament? Servitude typically came through poverty, and without poverty there would not be servitude. The poor and those in servitude—just like resident aliens, orphans, and widows—were easily marginalized; thus, Israel had to treat them with special concern.

What was Israel required to do to help those who could easily slip into poverty and become indentured servants? First, God's law contained provisions and controls to help prevent poverty and thus reduce indentured servanthood:

---

[11] Baker, *Tight Fists or Open Hands?*, 135.

(a) God mandated gleaning laws in Israel. Owners of olive or fig trees couldn't pick them clean, and the corners of their crops were to be left uncut so that the poor of the land could come and glean. Notice that this wasn't a "handout." Rather this provision required the poor to engage in working for their food.

(b) There were six-year service limits for servants—unless they desired to serve permanently (Ex 21.2–6). The prophet Jeremiah later raged against those who abused this law and took back Israelite servants after they had already worked their six-year term (Jer 34.14–17; cf. Amos 2.6, where Israel is condemned for selling those in poverty for a pair of sandals).

(c) There was the Year of Jubilee every fiftieth year, which brought relief to those encumbered with debt and who had had to lease their land to others.

(d) God routinely exhorted Israelites to look out for the stranger, the orphan, and the widow who were in their midst (Deut 16.11).

(e) We've seen that loans to fellow (impoverished) Israelites are to be interest-free so that they can be more easily stay out of debt and not feel pressed to sell themselves into servitude (Ex 22.25).

(f) Deuteronomy 15.7–8 urges Israelites to lend freely to the poor after their time of indentured service.

Second, another provision was Israel's anti-harm laws to protect servants. An employer ("master") could not do whatever he wanted with a servant—unlike both antebellum American slavery and other ancient Near Eastern cultures, where there was absolute rule and control over the servant or the slave. If one brought harm to his own Israelite servant—gouging out an eye, knocking out a tooth—the servant would go free (Ex 21.26–27). As we'll see, for an employer ("master") to kill his servant meant that his own life would be taken.

Third, Israel's law repudiated the "right of return"—unlike the antebellum South and ancient Near East, where a runaway slave was to be returned to his master because that was his property. Babylon's Code of

Hammurabi called for the death penalty for anyone harboring fugitive slaves.[12] The Egyptians, Hittites, and Amurru had extradition treaties to return fugitive slaves, and when slaves were returned, they were often brutalized by gouging out their eyes and so forth.[13] But in the Old Testament, foreign runaway slaves who came to Israel were not to be returned to their harsh masters but were to settle safely within any of Israel's cities; Israel was to be a haven of refuge (Deut 23.15–16).

Fourth, along with the rest of the ancient Near East, kidnapping was a capital offense in Israel: "He who kidnaps a man, whether he sells him or he is found in his possession, shall surely be put to death." (Ex 21.16; also Deut 24.7)

If these four Mosaic provisions had been heeded in the colonial West, we would not have had the slavery that marred this era. Old Testament scholar Christopher Wright says that "no other ancient Near Eastern law has been found that holds a master to account for the treatment of his own slaves … and the otherwise universal law regarding runaway slaves is that they must be sent back, with severe penalties for those who failed to comply."[14] So that's just a little bit of the backdrop that we have when it comes to certain servitude texts. Now we'll examine three important servitude texts.

VI. Inspecting Illustrations: Three Troubling Servitude Texts
A. Exodus 21.20–21

> If a man strikes his male servant or his female servant with a staff so that he or she dies as a result of the blow, he will surely be punished/avenged [*naqam*]. However, if the injured servant survives one or two days, the owner will not be punished [*naqam*], for he has suffered the loss [OR: "for he is his property" (NASB)]. (Ex 21.20–21, NET)

Notice the equality and the dignity of the male and female servant here. And if one of them, male or female, dies as a result of the blow, this death will be "avenged [*naqam*]"—a term used for capital punishment. The employer ("master") is held accountable for the brutal treatment of his servant.

---

[12] Code of Hammurabi, §§16 and 19.
[13] Baker, *Tight Fists or Open Hands*, 132.
[14] Wright, *Old Testament Ethics for the People of God*, 292.

Critics often latch on to the rest of the text: if the injured servant survives one or two days and then dies, he will not be avenged. They predictably say that a servant can be beaten to within an inch of his life, and so long as he doesn't die immediately, the one who struck him gets off scot-free. Actually, that is *not* the case. It doesn't tell us that there is no punishment—only that capital punishment is off the table. The implication is that there was no murderous intent.

The text says that the one who struck his servant "has suffered the loss." Now, one translation I like, the New American Standard Bible, has the unfortunate rendering here: "for he is his property." But the Hebrew is more literally "for he [or that] is his silver [*keseph*]." Let's work through this passage briefly.

As noted, the master is punished if the servant dies. There will be "vengeance," life for life, for this murderous act. But if the servant survives one or two days, the benefit of the doubt is given to the person who struck him *because no murderous intent was involved*. Judges would make these sorts of judgments, but keep in mind that any permanent injury would set the servant free (Ex 21.26–27). Notice that in this context, Exodus is addressing *accidental injuries*, which helps clarify the picture.

This brings us to the rendering "he is his silver" (v. 21). Now, the pronoun here (*hu*—translated *he*—can also be translated *that*) may not be referring to the *servant* but rather to the *medical fee* the master (employer) has had to pay in care for the injured servant ("*that* is his silver"). Harry Hoffner, the late Hittitologist (University of Chicago), held this "medical fee" view. The reason for this is twofold: (a) the context of accidental injuries and medical fees (Ex 21.18–19) immediately precedes this passage; that context mentions the medical bill owed for one injured in a quarrel; if a man is struck in a quarrel, doesn't die, but remains in bed and can walk on his staff, then the one who struck him won't be punished but will pay for "his loss of time, and shall take care of him until he is completely healed." (b) Hittite law offers an interesting parallel: If a medical payment is due for an injury, then the person who caused the injury should pay for the bill.

Even if we go with the rendering of *servant* as one's "silver," we know that the servant is *not* property; after all, if the servant who is struck dies, then the one who struck him will be put to death (and there is no death penalty for ruining property). Death after one or two days doesn't change the status of the rights-bearing, dignified servant. The point of the servant's being "his silver" would mean this: the employer stands to lose money if he mistreats his servant. Why hurt the help hired to work for you?

B. Exodus 21.2–6

> If you buy a Hebrew servant, he is to serve you for six years, but in the seventh year he will go out free without paying anything. If he came in by himself he will go out by himself; if he had a wife when he came in, then his wife will go out with him. If his master gave him a wife, and she bore sons or daughters, the wife and the children will belong to her master, and he will go out by himself. But if the servant should declare, "I love my master, my wife, and my children; I will not go out free," then his master must bring him to the judges, and he will bring him to the door or the doorposts, and his master will pierce his ear with an awl, and he shall serve him forever. (Ex 21.2–6, NET)

Critics or even honest questioners may wonder: "Isn't this a case of family separation—with the male being favored? The woman servant apparently has to stay behind if she's married during this contractual arrangement. The male can go free, but the female can't. And if there have been children during this time, the children can't go free either."

But as some scholars have noted, when you read the Hebrew law, it's not gender-specific. We could actually flip the scenario to focus on the female servant. As I discuss in *Is God a Moral Monster?*, Mosaic legislation can apply male and female interchangeably in most of the Law.[15] So we can just switch to the female and say: if you acquire a Hebrew servant, *she* is to serve you for six years, but in the seventh year, *she* will go out free; if *her* master gives *her* a husband and they have sons or daughters, the husband and the children will belong to her master, and *she* will go out by herself. Furthermore, Deuteronomy 15.12–13 makes this explicit: "If your

---

[15] See chapter 13 in Copan, *Is God a Moral Monster?*

kinsman, a Hebrew man or woman, is sold to you, then he shall serve you six years, but in the seventh year you shall set him free."

The point of the passage is that, regardless of whether one is male or female, the servant has to stick with the contract. If a male servant about to complete his seven-year term marries a female servant in the same household who is only two years into her term, she cannot leave just because she is now married. She must fulfill her obligations. It's like signing up for the Army. Getting married or having children does not cancel the military contract.

Now, basically, in this sort of scenario, the married servants who are about to be released have three options. Let's just assume the man goes out first and has to wait for his wife. First, he can *delay*; that is, he can leave the home where he served and then wait for his wife and children to finish their term. But that would usually be impractical. Second, he can *pay* to buy them out of their remaining years of service so that they are released. But given the constraints of poverty and the need to go into servitude in the first place, redeeming (buying out) is often impossible. The third option is to *stay*—that is, to work permanently in one's boss's household. This would be the more likely and often preferred option, assuming a good relationship between the servant and the boss exists.

C. Leviticus 25.44–48

Let me move on to probably the most difficult servitude text, which requires some patient unpacking.

> As for your male and female slaves whom you may have - you may acquire [*qanah*] male and female slaves from the pagan nations that are around you. Then, too, it is out of the sons of the sojourners [*toshabim*] who live as aliens [*garim*] among you that you may gain acquisition [*qanah*], and out of their families who are with you, whom they will have produced in your land; they also may become your possession. You may even bequeath them to your sons after you, to receive as a possession; you can use them as permanent slaves. But in respect to your countrymen, the sons of Israel, you shall not rule with severity over one another. Now if the means of a stranger [*toshab*] or of a sojourner [*ger*] with you becomes sufficient [*nasag*], and a countryman of yours becomes so poor with regard to him as to sell [*makar*] himself to a stranger

who is sojourning with you, or to the descendants of a stranger's family, then he shall have redemption right after he has been sold [*makar*]. One of his brothers may redeem him.

Leviticus 25 refers to the Year of Jubilee. It reminds us that only Israelites receive land from the Lord as a gift; foreigners cannot obtain land. Critics of this particular passage often stop reading partway through. They don't get to the part that says, "Now if the means of a stranger ... becomes sufficient" (v. 47). Up to this point, the critic assumes a stark distinction between the treatment of Israelite servants and foreign ones. But notice: the text mentions the potential prospering (*nasag*) of a *foreigner* or *sojourner*—the very one who could be "acquired [*qanah*]" by an Israelite (vv. 44–45)—who can then "acquire [*qanah*]" an impoverished Israelite as a servant. A relative may redeem or buy out this poor Israelite who has "sold [*makar*]" himself to a foreigner (v. 50).

Leviticus 25 ends with the historical note that God brought his servant Israel out of the land of Egypt (v. 55). In the Mosaic law, God regularly reminds Israel that they were once sojourners in Egypt, and they are likewise to care for and *love* the sojourners in their midst—something the Law mentions a few chapters earlier (19.34). We read elsewhere that Israel was not to mistreat foreigners in their midst: "the Levite, because he has no portion or inheritance among you, and the alien, the orphan and the widow who are in your town shall come and eat and be satisfied, in order that the LORD your God may bless you in all the work of your hand which you do" (Deut 14.29); again, "you shall not pervert the justice due an alien or an orphan, nor take a widow's garment in pledge." (Deut 24.17); once more, "cursed is he who distorts the justice due an alien, orphan and widow. And all the people shall say Amen." (Deut 27.19). As we've seen, foreign runaway slaves could find refuge in Israel rather than being returned to their harsh masters. It would be strange that, given all of Law's concern for the vulnerable and marginalized, mistreating the foreign servant is being condoned in Leviticus 25. Indeed, at the end of the prior chapter, both the *alien* and the *native* were to be under the same law (Lev 24.22; cf. Ex 12.49).

It might be helpful to see how foreigners fit into Israelite life. Plenty of foreigners who came to Israel acquired positions of influence and status, even though many of them were servants:

The Ethiopian Ebed-melech was a royal servant (Jer 38.7–15) whom God rewarded because acted courageously and trusted in the Lord (39.16–18).

Uriah the Hittite was a servant of king David and one of his "mighty men" (1 Chron 11.26, 41; cf. 2 Sam 11.11).

Jarha—an Egyptian servant—married one of Caleb's descendants (1 Chron 2.34–35).

One of Abraham's servants—and potential heir—was Eliezer of Damascus (Gen. 15.2).

Ittai the Gittite (Philistine) served in David's regiment (2 Sam 18.2).

Obed-Edom the Gittite (Philistine) was a gatekeeper of the ark of the covenant (1 Chron 15.24; cf. 2 Sam 6.10).

David gathered foreigners in Israel to do stone-cutting to build the house of God (1 Chron 22.2).

Foreigners in Judah joined in worship during the Feast of Unleavened Bread (2 Chron 30.25).

The Rechabite family in Judah was from the Kenite tribe, and God praised them for their steadfastness and dedication (1 Chron 2.55; Jer 35.19).

Clearly, foreigners—indeed, foreign servants in Israel—could have positions of status and influence within Israelite society.

Notice, too, that acquiring foreign servants is *permitted* but not *commanded*. And how were they acquired? Sometimes out of desperation, foreigners might "sell" family members to Israelites, since Israel would provide greater stability and brighter future prospects. Also, in the wake of war, Israelites might acquire foreign servants who could not own land but would have to attach themselves to Israelite households to sustain themselves. And when we look at other ancient Near Eastern nations and their practices, we see a noticeable difference with Israel. Conquering foreign nations would often enslave their captives, including turning virgins into cult prostitutes in their temples. And the alternative was simply to kill the members of the vanquished nation. Israel offered a superior option, even if it isn't ideal. Furthermore, we have already seen how specific foreigners—indeed foreign servants—ended up in Israel and found themselves in positions of influence, status, and prosperity. In these narratives, we do not see any kind of abuse or mistreatment of these foreigners.

If we follow the terms used in Leviticus 25, we see that foreigners could be acquired as servants in Israel, and this is the same language used of Israelites or prominent figures in Israel. Consider the word *qanah*—"acquire." That same term is used of Israelites or various prominent individuals, who are clearly not mere property. For example, God acquires or purchases (*qanah*) the people of Israel (Ex 15.18). Boaz acquires Ruth as his wife in this legal transaction (Ruth 4.5). Eve "acquires" (*qanah*) a child with the Lord's help. As I argue in my *Vindictive Bully* book, the terms related to foreign servants in Israel are the same terms used of Israelites in these kinds of contractual arrangements. Hence, Leviticus 25 doesn't turn foreign servants into property, but it uses the same transactional language as it does for Israelites themselves. The foreigner can *prosper* (25: 47), and the Israelite can *prosper* (v. 49). The foreigner may be *acquired* (vv. 44–45), and the Israelite may be *acquired* (v. 50). The parallels go on.

VII. Conclusion

Here I offer a few brief comments as we draw to a close.

First, consider that curious passage on tattoos. Some people have asked, "Does the Bible allow tattoos?" The common reply is that Leviticus 19.28 prohibits them—"You shall not make ... any tattoo marks on yourselves." But these are *not* the equivalent of modern-day tattoos. What did the tattoo refer to in the ancient world? There are three possibilities:

(a) tattoos might relate to *mourning practices*, as the text does include mention of cutting oneself for the dead (there isn't a lot of support for this view, though);

(b) tattoos are connected with *idolatry* or *paganism*—a view defended by ancient and medieval rabbis: the tattoo signified belonging to a pagan deity;

(c) the strongest alternative is that tattoos indicate *ownership of another person*—pure chattel slavery. Thus, Israel was prohibited from tattooing human beings because of the degradation involved in being owned or owning another human being as property.[16]

Second, the Old Testament law was intended to be *provisional*, not ideal. Even laws of servitude should not be seen as an ultimate, permanent arrangement for the people of God. The Law was like a booster rocket with a task to perform; once the booster rocket completes its function (once the Messiah and the new covenant come), the Mosaic law is no longer necessary. It was a custodian for Israel until the fulness of time had come (Gal 3.24–25; 4.4). As Paul says in Romans 7, the Law was good, spiritual, and holy—but not permanent. But even if what I've said about Leviticus 25 isn't a satisfactory solution, the distinction between Israelite and Gentile servants is not a rigid or absolute one. (And keep in mind that the Old Testament narratives certainly don't give any such indication, as we have seen.) God declares that eventually, all the families of the earth are going to be blessed through Abraham (Gen 12.3). Gentiles and Jews alike will come to the mountain of the Lord and obey God's law together (Is 2.2–4). God calls Assyria, Egypt, and Israel "My people," "the work of My hands," and "My inheritance" (Is 19.23–25). And so whatever Jew-Gentile distinction purportedly exists in Leviticus 25, all of this is going to give way in the new covenant, in which Jew-Gentile differences are leveled and rendered irrelevant, as the book of Galatians and Ephesians 2–3 make clear. Isaiah anticipates this when he writes:

---

[16] Huehnegard and Liebowitz, "The Biblical Prohibition Against Tattooing," 59–77.

> Let not the foreigner who has joined himself to the LORD say, "the LORD will surely separate me from his people." Nor let the eunuch say, "behold, I am a dry tree." ... Also the foreigners who join themselves to the LORD, to minister to him, and to love the name of the LORD, to be his servants, every one who keeps from profaning the Sabbath, and holds fast my covenant; even those I will bring to my holy mountain and make them joyful in my house of prayer. Their burnt offerings and their sacrifices will be acceptable on my altar; for my house will be called a house of prayer for all peoples. (Is 56.3, 6–7)

This is God's ultimate ideal, bringing Jew and Gentile alike through the Messiah.

Third, the Old Testament has within itself the undermining of any institutionalization of slavery or servitude. The late notable Old Testament scholar David Clines has pointed out that the extraordinary provision for foreign runaway slaves in Deuteronomy 23 ultimately undermines any possible institutionalization of servitude altogether. We could add that the same was true for oppressed Israelite servants within Israel. We read that Israelite servants would find ways of escaping from harsh Israelite "masters." For example, Abigail's husband, Nabal, answered David's servants who came to him pleading for food: "Who is David? And who is the son of Jesse? There are many servants today who are each breaking away from his master" (1 Sam 25.10). Generally speaking, Israelites weren't locked into oppressive servitude under fellow Israelites. They could go and find another place to take care of their debts in a more humane situation. This is true of both foreign and domestic servants. Clines observes:

> what is amazing about the law of the Fugitive Slave is that it enables the slave to inquire his or her own freedom—by the relatively simple expedient of runaway. A slave can choose not to be a slave. ... [and] if a slave can choose not to be a slave, then the concept of slavery does not exist as it was once thought to exist.[17]

Clines connects this to Exodus 21.6, where a servant loves his master and freely chooses to attach himself permanently to that household.

---

[17] Clines, "Ethics as Deconstruction, and, the Ethics of Deconstruction," 78–79.

"Slavery is in a sense, abolished when it ceases to be a state that a person is forced into against his will ... with this blurring of the lines between freedom and servant, [the institution has] lost its conceptual force."[18]

We really see the upshot of the attitude towards slavery or servitude in the Old Testament in Isaiah 58, where the "fast" of the Lord is "to loosen the bonds of wickedness, to undo the bands of the yoke, and to let the oppressed go free and break every yoke." (v. 6). *That* is the spirit and the vision of the Old Testament beyond. Hopefully this discussion gives a clearer glimpse of servitude in the Old Testament and the provisions God has made for servants in the land of Israel, whether domestic or foreign. They are indeed *men* and *brothers*.[19]

Bibliography

Baker, David L. *Tight Fists or Open Hands? Wealth and Poverty in Old Testament Law.* Grand Rapids, MI: Eerdmans, 2009.

Biggar, Nigel. *Colonialism: A Moral Reckoning.* London: William Collins, 2023.

Clines, D. J. A. "Ethics as Deconstruction, and, the Ethics of Deconstruction," in *The Bible in Ethics: The Second Sheffield Colloquium*, ed. J. W. Rogerson, Margaret Davies, and M. Daniel Carroll R., Journal for the Study of the Old Testament Supplement Series 207. Sheffield: Sheffield Academic Press, 1995.

Copan, Paul. *Is God a Moral Monster? Making Sense of the Old Testament God.* Grand Rapids, MI: Baker, 2011.

—————. *Is God a Vindictive Bully? Reconciling Portrayals of God in the Old and New Testaments.* Grand Rapids, MI: Baker Academic, 2022.

—————. "'Slavery' in the Old Testament," in *Christianity Contested: Replies to Critics' Toughest Questions.* Edited by Paul Copan and Stewart Kelly. Eugene, OR: Wipf & Stock, 2024.

Harris, Sam. *Letter to a Christian Nation.* New York: Knopf, 2006.

Huehnegard, John and Harold Liebowitz, "The Biblical Prohibition Against Tattooing." In *Vetus Testamentum* 63 (2013).

---

[18] Clines, 81.

[19] Thanks to Rhett Warner for his comments on an earlier version of this chapter.

Stowe, Harriet Beecher. *A Key to Uncle Tom's Cabin; presenting the Facts and Documents upon which the Story is Founded, together with Corroborative Statements verifying the Truth of the Work.* Boston: John P. Jewett, 1853.

Wright, Christopher J. H. *Old Testament Ethics for the People of God.* Downers Grove, IL: InterVarsity, 2004.

19

Straight to the Heart
Communicating the Gospel in an Emotionally Driven Culture

Mike Blackaby

I. Date Night at Disney

My wife Sarah and I recently traveled with our four young children from the west coast of Canada to Orlando, Florida, to enjoy a vacation at Disney World. Midway through our stay, Sarah informed me of Disney's extended evening hours for those staying in their resort hotels. So, on the evening of our visit to Epcot, we left the kids with grandpa and grandma and headed back to the park for two hours of child-free date night. What could go wrong?

Surrounding a giant lagoon, Epcot's famous "World Showcase" is sectioned off into various pavilions representing eleven different countries. Each country has restaurants and architecture that immerses you into their unique culture. By this point in our trip, I had blister bandages on almost all my toes, but planned to hobble around the park with the cheeriest disposition I could muster. We had purposefully skipped dinner in anticipation of dining our way through the culinary delights of several countries. When we arrived, the massive exodus of non-Disney-resort-people flowing through the exits only increased my excitement.

We looked at the app to select our first restaurant only to discover that almost none of them stay open for the later hours. All we could find was a small popcorn stand in ... Canada. I couldn't believe we had flown all the way *from* Canada so we could eat Canadian popcorn at the *World* Showcase! That bag of popcorn did little to satiate our ravenous hunger, but since we only had two hours, we quickly consulted the app to determine which ride to hit first. However, when everything *except* the rides is closed, the line at each ride becomes a 90-minute endurance test. Disappointed, but not wanting to waste our entire evening standing in line, we decided on an enjoyable sight-seeing walk instead. Halfway around the World Showcase we were met with a barricade, and an employee who informed us, "This section of the park is closed, you'll need to head back the way you came."

As we backtracked our steps on blistered feet, I was growing increasingly frustrated with "the most magical place on earth." Then I had an idea. The giant silver golf ball-looking structure that Epcot is famous for contains an attraction that my wife had never experienced. It's a leisurely indoor ride called Spaceship Earth that winds up and down the spherical building, taking you on a visual tour of world history, while a narrator explains the key events through speakers in your seat. The app informed us there was (mercifully) no line, so we hauled ourselves across the park, walked right in, and boarded our galactic time machine. There is a display screen in the front of each seat where you choose the language of your narrator. Sarah curiously began touching the screen, only to accidentally select "Mandarin" just as time ran out

to make our choice. So, for the next twenty minutes, our AI tour guide explained the history of the world in a language neither of us could understand. In exasperation, I declared: "This date night is the *worst!* Nothing is working out the way it was supposed to!" Sarah, who is significantly more mature emotionally and spiritually than I am, patiently replied, "I don't really mind what we do. I'm just happy to do it together."

In that encounter, my wife helped me see something important: There were countless distractions pulling my emotions away from the one person who mattered most that night. I was sitting on a ride at Disney World on a date night with my wife who loves me. My rational *head* could easily have told you that my reasons for being upset were foolish. My head *knew* that spending time with my wife was more important than all the minor inconveniences. However, the emotions of my *heart* were leading me in the opposite direction.

We humans navigate life primarily driven by our emotions, not our reason.[1] Much of what you may encounter in books on apologetics will focus on reason, evidence, and logic. These are significant and important topics. But let us not forget that people are a messy mixture of head *and* heart, reason *and* emotion, calculation *and* intuition, logic *and* aesthetics. There are a million things happening beneath the radar of our conscious awareness that shape the way we think, believe, and act. We may know something rationally in our head, but when push comes to shove, it is our *heart* that often chooses the path we follow. Modern culture, in many ways, has fully embraced this. People have elevated their emotions to the highest realm of authority. What they feel on the *inside* determines what is true on the *outside*. Their subjective internal experience defines their external reality.

II. The Interplay of Head and Heart

The heart also plays a major role in how we approach the gospel. People in our society don't just doubt that the "good news" is *true*. In an emotionally driven culture, peoples' hearts doubt that it is *good*. How many objections

---

[1] For a fuller exploration of the ideas in this chapter, see Mike and Daniel Blackaby, *Straight to the Heart: Communicating the Gospel in an Emotionally Driven Culture* (Colorado Springs, CO: David C. Cook, 2024).

to the Christian faith begin with, "I just don't understand how a loving God could…"? Blaise Pascal offered these thoughts on apologetics: "Men despise religion. They hate it and are afraid it may be true. The cure for this is first to show that religion is not contrary to reason, but worthy of reverence and respect. Next make it attractive, make good men wish it were true, and then show that it is. Worthy of reverence because it really understands human nature. Attractive because it promises true good."[2] Do you notice the language used? Words like "despise," "hate," and "afraid" are referring to an emotional response. He does not dismiss the rational side of the faith, but he does balance it with an appeal for us to "make it attractive." The gospel does make sense rationally, but it also promises something that we desire at an emotional level: goodness. Christianity is true for the head *and* the heart. Making people "wish it were true" is to speak to the desires of their hearts.

To be an effective apologist, we must come to understand how humans are wired and then speak to them holistically. When a lawyer asked Jesus what the most important law was, He replied, "You shall love the Lord your God with all your heart, with all your soul, and with all your mind. This is the great and first commandment. And the second is like it: you shall love your neighbor as yourself. On these two commands depend all the law and the prophets" (Mt 22.37–39). We are called to love God with our heart, soul, and mind. Our whole selves. Emotion *and* reason. Being a disciple of Jesus is not just about what someone *believes*, but about what someone *loves*. The world fundamentally has a love problem, not just a belief problem.

The apostle James famously said that even the demons believe in God (Jas 2.19). They do not, however, love Him. Jesus' ministry was not just about changing minds to accept a new set of facts *about* God but about changing peoples' hearts to restore a lost love *with* God. There are atheists today who have studied theology more than many Christians but have never come to love their Creator. They've encountered rational arguments, but the truth has never seeped into their souls. The desires of our hearts

---

[2] Pascal, *Pensées*, 4.

can lead us down destructive paths despite the urgent warnings of our rational mind. The apostle James wrote, "…each person is tempted when he is lured and enticed by his own desire. Then desire, when it has conceived, gives birth to sin, and sin when it is fully grown, brings forth death" (Jas 1.14–15). It is therefore not surprising that Proverbs 4.23 warns us: "Above all else, guard your heart, for everything you do flows from it." This helps make sense of many bewildering trends we see in our culture. People's hearts are unfulfilled, and their emotions are expressing this restlessness. Into such a culture we go as apologists. Not to people whose hearts are neutral. Our rational arguments may serve to turn "roadblocks" into "speedbumps," allowing people to slow down and proceed more carefully rather than abandoning the road completely. However, let us not forget that from the heart flows the gasoline to move forward at all.

The human brain operates on many levels, and in our common language we distinguish between what we call the head (rational, logical, evidential) and the heart (emotional, intuitive, aesthetic). The heart may more generally refer to what happens beneath our conscious awareness; those feelings and impressions that bubble up to the surface (or remain buried), largely unbidden or even unacknowledged by us. The head refers to our more focused, concentrated thinking. People commonly express this distinction with terms like "thinking" vs "feeling." For example, if I ask if you like this painting, you are going to have an immediate impression. If I ask you to explain *why* you feel that way, a different system in your brain kicks in. This is what psychologist Daniel Kahneman refers to as "thinking slow" as distinguished from the "thinking fast" of your immediate first

impression.³ We feel as though we owe a rational explanation for our opinion. However, the truth is that we don't really know why we felt what we felt. We didn't reason our way to our initial feelings. We feel first, and then we work backwards to try and rationalize *why* we felt that way. The head is downstream from the heart.

What if I tell you that this painting was the creation of an aspiring young German artist named Adolf Hitler? Now you're likely thinking, "Wait a second! No, I don't like the painting! I thought I did, but I don't!" Do you see what's happening? You're having an impression again. Your heart is pulling you in a different direction. What changed? Your heart did, at an emotional level. If you stop to think of an explanation, your "slow" system has kicked in to rationally justify what you've *already* felt.

We walk through life with this constant interplay between what Kahneman calls "system 1" (fast thinking) and "system 2" (slow thinking).⁴ For our purposes, let's consider it a union between the head and the heart. These two processes work together. David Brooks says it this way: "Reason and emotion are not separate and opposed. Reason is nestled upon emotion and dependent upon it. Emotion assigns value to things, and reason can only make choices on the basis of those valuations. The human mind can be pragmatic because deep down it is romantic."⁵ We primarily *feel* our way through the world. Our reason makes decisions based on what catches the attention of our heart.

III. The Rider and the Elephant

The psychologist Jonathan Haidt uses an interesting metaphor: he says our brains operate like a rider on an elephant. He explains, "The elephant includes the gut feelings, visceral reactions, emotions, and intuitions that comprise much of the automatic system," whereas the rider is "…conscious, controlled thought."⁶ Your elephant lumbers along, sniffing out things that it likes, and the rider is there to course-correct if the elephant

---

³ Kahneman, *Fast and Slow*, 20–21.
⁴ Ibid.
⁵ Brooks, *The Social Animal*, 21.
⁶ Haidt, *Happiness Hypothesis*, 17.

gets too far off the right path. In a direct battle of wills, the rider has little hope of overpowering the beast! Your rider tries in vain to tell you, "You must exercise! You made a New Year's resolution!" To which your elephant may respond, "Nah, I want to eat ice cream and binge Netflix instead." Can they work together in harmony? Haidt says, "An emotionally intelligent person has a skilled rider who knows how to distract and coax the elephant without having to engage in a direct contest of wills."[7] The rider may appeal to the desires of the elephant by promising to reward it with a smoothie (similar to ice cream!) *after* the exercise has been completed. Suddenly, the elephant's like, "OK, I'm listening…" and begins to wander back onto the healthier path.

The head and the heart, rider and elephant, can work together, or they can be in tension. It's easy to assume that the people we have apologetics conversations with are primarily driven by their rider. They aren't. They are mostly elephant, with a rider that acts more as an advisor or servant, rather than a king or president.[8] Does it mean that rational conversations are futile? No, but it is important to understand how much influence the Elephant (heart) has. People often operate in irrational ways and believe irrational things. We are not so much rational beings with emotions as we are emotional beings with the (occasional) capacity to reason. Because of this, we are easily tricked or distracted into acting irrationally.

One of these ways is called *priming*. Priming is when an idea is subtly put into your head that you aren't consciously aware of, and it impacts your actions. Psychologists have had fun experimenting with this phenomenon. One famous example involved a group of students from New York University. They were given five words and asked to form them into a short sentence. In one of these groups, they gave words that are typically associated with old, such as "grey," "bald," and "Florida." They gave different words to the control group. The participants were then sent down a hallway to another room. What they didn't realize was the actual experiment took place in the hallway. Do you know what they found? The people who were primed with thoughts of "old" walked measurably *slower* down

---

[7] Ibid., 18.
[8] Ibid., 17.

the hallway than the control group. They had no awareness of what was happening, but these subtle ideas manifested themselves in their actions.[9]

Our emotions give valuation to things so that our conscious self can make decisions. This is why when you go to the grocery store, you don't have to go to the cereal aisle and make a pros and cons list for each individual box. Instead, there are a few options that jump out at you immediately, and you choose based on what grabbed your attention. Advertisers know this. Their entire reason for existence is to try and get the attention of your elephant! I was visiting my brother recently and we went to a Target. As we walked in, we were met with evidence of somebody's rider having prevailed over their elephant because a box of Sour Patch Kids Oreos was sitting at the entrance alone, obviously not in its original aisle. Somebody had picked up those cookies in the cookie aisle and their rider had convinced their elephant to discard them before reaching the checkout. My brother and I were not so inclined. Our two internal elephants trumpeted their orders, and we almost knocked each other over trying to be the first to grab the object of our desire!

Psychologist Daniel Levitin notes, "In 1976, the average grocery store stocked 9,000 unique products; today, that number has ballooned to over 40,000 of them, yet the average person gets 80 to 85% of their needs in only 150 different supermarket items. That means that we need to ignore 39,850 items in the store."[10] Every one of those products is designed by professional advertisers to get the attention of your heart. Is it any wonder why we are tired all the time? Our hearts are constantly being pulled in different directions by endless stimuli from advertisers, social media, entertainment, etc.

Why does this matter? Because that is the world we navigate as apologists. We do not tread upon emotionally neutral ground. We should not expect easy rational conversations with rational people because people are very rarely acting rationally (including us). Now, we *do* have the capacity to reason, but each person we converse with is an internal conglomeration of emotions, impressions, and intuitions that influence their beliefs and

---

[9] Kahneman, *Fast and Slow*, 53.
[10] Levitin, *Organized Mind*, 5.

actions. This is why humans are more interesting than computers, but also why we are more frustrating.

IV. A Culture Primed for the Gospel

People are not emotionally neutral blank slates waiting to receive our rational arguments for the faith. They are not, as James K. A. Smith puts it, "mind-containers" waiting for the right ideas to be deposited.[11] It may be tempting to lament what we see as the emotional excess of our culture. Indeed, if we look for them, there are many examples of how our (not just "their") emotions drive us to foolishness. The heart has the capacity to greatly deceive (see Jer 17.9). Despite this, is there any room for optimism? In a culture that has elevated emotions and feelings to an authoritative status for determining truth, how might people be primed to receive the gospel at the level of the heart? Can we learn to speak the language of the heart in our apologetics?

The Scriptures present a holistic understanding of human nature. The word for heart appears over 800 times in the Bible. It's meaning usually refers to the core of who we are. It is probably better referred to as your "guts." Your guts are where you feel the strongest emotions. You get butterflies in your stomach when you are romantically attracted to someone. You feel an ache in your stomach when you are nervous about a situation.

The Bible contains appeals to the heart both in its message (*what* is communicated) as well as the medium (*how* it is communicated). God called his people to incorporate art and beauty in the tabernacle and the temple. Some of the architecture they were instructed to build within the tabernacle does not seem focused on practicality alone. It is also there for the sake of beauty (see 2 Chr 3.6–7 NKJV). This makes sense in a place of worship if we typically feel *before* we think. The first person in Scripture who is said to have been filled with the Holy Spirit was Bezalel (Ex 31.2–5). He was a craftsman and an artist. Bezalel was tasked to make the tabernacle *look good*, amidst other practical functions. Beauty, both in its natural manifestations and in our artistic expressions of it, matters to

---

[11] Smith, *What You Love*, 3.

God. Beauty speaks to our hearts. Yet, we often focus on "The Good" and "The True" of the classic transcendentals but forget about "The Beautiful." Beauty brings out a sense of awe which, in turn, leads us to worship. It is the fragrance of the True and the Good.

Jesus taught using stories, parables, and imagery. Stories are the language of the heart. Everybody loves (and remembers) stories. You may have already forgotten much of what I've written in this chapter, but you likely remember the opening story. Jesus, a master communicator, understood this and taught in a style that drew heavily on narrative. Even those who have lived their lives distanced from the church still have a basic recollection of stories like Noah's Ark, David and Goliath, Adam and Eve, and the Good Samaritan. Narrative is the most common genre found in the Bible. In fact, stories are so intrinsic to us, we provide our lives with a sense of unity, purpose, and meaning largely based on the internalized "narrative identity" we come to accept about ourselves.[12] We cannot help but synthesize the overwhelming amount of information coming into our brains as simplified stories. The Bible also contains metaphorical imagery, which is central to the Lord's Supper and baptism. In fact, metaphor is often necessary to try and understand an eternal God. It uses the familiar to simplify the unfamiliar. In addressing this very concept, God gave us a great example: "For as the heavens are higher than the earth, so My ways are higher than your ways and My thoughts than your thoughts" (Isa 55.9).

The Bible is also full of music. The first song in the Bible is sung by Moses and Miriam in Exodus 15. The last song in the Bible is Revelation 15.3, which references back to the first song. Songs and poetry fill many pages of our Scriptures in books like Psalms, Song of Songs, and Ecclesiastes. Has the church learned to speak the language of the heart in apologetics? What we say is important but so is *how we say it*. When the needs of the heart are met, the mind opens to accommodate and understand new truths.

Public intellectual Ayaan Hirsi Ali has an incredible story and has written powerful memoirs of her journey out of fundamentalist Islam.[13]

---

[12] McAdams, *Personality Development*, 250.
[13] See Ayaan Hirsi Ali, *Infidel* (New York: Free Press, 2007) and Ayaan Hirsi Ali, *Nomad* (New York: Free Press, 2010).

She eventually became the female representation of the New Atheism. Although she primarily criticized Islam, Ayaan was also openly skeptical of Christianity. Then, in 2023, she shocked everyone by writing an article entitled "Why I am Now a Christian" (a twist on Bertrand Russell's famous essay, "Why I Am Not a Christian"). She had much to say about the good of Christianity for society on a social and political level, seeing it as a bulwark holding back other destructive worldviews. But it was also personal for her. She wrote, "Yet I would not be truthful if I attributed my embrace of Christianity solely to the realization that atheism is too weak and divisive a doctrine to fortify us against our menacing foes. I have also turned to Christianity because I ultimately found life without any spiritual solace unendurable. Indeed, very nearly self-destructive. Atheism failed to answer a simple question: what is the meaning and purpose of life?"[14] The article landed like a bomb among her friends and allies in the New Atheist camp.

Famous atheist Richard Dawkins decided to debate Ayaan, with the purpose of convincing her that she was merely a "cultural Christian," much like himself. Near the beginning of their discussion, after she had told her story of crippling suicidal depression, and how she experienced God free her from it, Dawkins conceded that Ayaan was indeed a true believer. However, in exasperation, he challenged her to admit that much of what her vicar espouses is clearly "nonsense." Based on the foundation of the experience she had described earlier, she responded, "What has happened to me is, I think, I have accepted that there is something. And when you accept that there is something, there is a powerful entity (for me, the God that turned me around), I think what the vicar is saying no longer sounds nonsensical. I think it makes a great deal of sense."[15] Her head was now building a framework to understand what her heart knew to be true. She experienced something at an emotional level, and it had opened possibilities that her head had previously rejected. In a sense, her head was trying to catch up and understand what her heart had already accepted. Was she previously unaware of the rational arguments

---

[14] Ali, "Why I Am Now A Christian."
[15] Ali, "God Debate."

for God's existence? Not likely. However, an experience of the heart has a way of opening the mind.

V. Application to Apologetics

How might this understanding of the interplay between head and heart, reason and emotion, be applied to apologetics? I want to be careful not to limit the application only to those who consider themselves "creatives." I also don't want to give you a list of steps to closely follow. That's not what you do with creativity! What you can do is pray. Ask God to show you the many ways He has spoken to your heart. Was it through the beauty of nature? Art? Music? Poetry? Stories? What pulled you into the faith *at a heart level*, and how might God want to use similar (and new) ways to speak to hearts in our current culture? In our churches, do we encourage and deploy the artists, storytellers, and creatives who may not consider themselves apologists? It is easy to assume that apologetics is for the logical people, and those who are more creative are left to assume it is not their calling. The more I've come to understand how humans are wired, how the Bible reveals God to us, and what I see in my own experiences, I've become convinced that we are *all* emotional people deep down. We do apologetics (and everything else) within a world of emotional people. This is not a bad thing, even though it is often taken to excessive extremes. A culture that elevates the authority of the heart is primed to receive the gospel, which speaks to us at a heart level. James K. A. Smith notes, "It is not primarily our minds that are captivated but rather our *imaginations* that are captured, and when our imagination is hooked, *we're* hooked."[16] As Pascal reminded us at the beginning of this chapter, make them *wish* it were true...then *show* them that it is.

Why are people's beliefs so often shaped more by their media consumption than by our sermons and lectures? Do teenagers form their view of love based primarily on our church's deep-dive Bible studies into 1 Corinthians 13, or based on the Taylor Swift lyrics they have memorized? We cannot simply counteract the stories that culture aims at their hearts by

---

[16] Smith, *Desiring the Kingdom*, 54.

only filling their heads with more facts. In the times in which we live, the most effective apologists will be those who can converse with the head *and* the heart through stories, art, beauty, humor, music, poetry, hospitality, and any number of other ways that affect us at an emotional level. We must come to realize that the feelings of awe unleashed by the beauty of nature prime someone to discuss the transcendent more effectively than the four beige walls of a church basement. What we say is important but so is *how* and *where* we say it. Not all conversational contexts are created equal.

Do you practice hospitality? There are powerful examples of those who came to faith through conversations *in the context of relationships*, because apologists opened their homes and their lives to seekers and skeptics.[17] Are you an artist? Your ability to capture beauty and express it may just slip under the defenses of those who have a rational rebuttal to every logical argument. Are you a storyteller? A list of theological arguments may present true propositions to someone, but a well-told story can make them *feel* the truth. Indeed, we may not actively discuss the details of every movie we watch, but we are certainly being shaped by the stories we hear, see, and tell.

As we come to understand the desires of peoples' hearts, we'll know what is driving them through the world, and it will help us respond appropriately and effectively. The classic Scripture on apologetics (1 Pet 3.15) *first* tells us to honor Christ the Lord as holy in our "hearts." It then tells us to be ready to give a defense "…to anyone who *asks* you for a reason for the hope that is in you." It implies that we are listening to their questions, not just volunteering answers to the questions we *wish* they would ask. There is a big difference between having your finger on the pulse of culture and having your hands around the neck of culture. Apologetics takes place between humans who are driven by the desires and questions of their hearts. Beneath the surface of every atheist or agnostic is an elephant pulling a rider off the narrow path of Matthew 7.14. The seeker in 1 Peter 3.15 is not primarily working through logical conundrums; they are asking specifically about "hope." So was Ayaan Hirsi Ali. So is every

---

[17] For example, see Butterfield, *Secret Thoughts*.

one of us. All the rational arguments in the world are in vain unless the deepest questions of someone's heart are also addressed. It has never been either/or. It has always been both/and. Apologetics to the head without engaging the heart is like a movie script without a soundtrack; setting out the basic plot, but failing to ignite the imagination.

As I remember the World Showcase at Epcot, I think of the people in the world who are navigating through life with countless diversions pulling at their hearts, distracting them from that which is most important. God is there, and He desires for them to know His love and respond with all their heart, mind, soul, and strength. Let us show people that the gospel is not just *news*. It's also *good*. Jesus, quoting the book of Isaiah, said, "For this people's *hearts* have grown dull, and with their ears they can barely hear, and their eyes they have closed, lest they should see with their eyes, and hear with their ears, and *understand with their heart* and turn, and I would heal them" (Mt 13.15, emphasis added). May we seek to open minds by filling hearts.

Bibliography

Ali, Ayaan Hirsi. "Richard Dawkins vs. Ayaan Hirsi Ali: The God Debate." https://www.youtube.com/watch?v=DBsHdHMvucs&t=2s. Accessed January 27, 2025

Ali, Ayaan Hirsi. "Why I Am Now A Christian." https://unherd.com/2023/11/why-i-am-now-a-christian/. Accessed January 29, 2025.

Blackaby, Mike and Daniel. *Straight to the Heart: Communicating the Gospel in an Emotionally Driven Culture*. Colorado Springs, CO: David C. Cook, 2024.

Brooks, David. *The Social Animal: The Hidden Sources of Love, Character, and Achievement*. New York: Random House, 2012.

Butterfield, Rosaria Champaigne. *The Secret Thoughts of an Unlikely Convert: An English Professor's Journey Into The Christian Faith*. Pittsburgh, PA: Crown and Covenant Publications, 2014.

Haidt, Jonathan. *The Happiness Hypothesis: Finding Modern Truth in Ancient Widom*. New York: Basic Books, 2006.

Kahneman, Daniel. *Thinking Fast and Slow*. Toronto: Anchor Canada, 2013.

Levitin, Daniel J. *The Organized Mind: Thinking Straight in the Age of Information Overload*. New York: Penguin, 2014.

McAdams, Dan P. *The Art and Science of Personality Development*. New York: The Guilford Press, 2018.

Pascal, Blaise. *Pensées*. New York: Penguin, 1996.

Smith, James K. A. *Desiring the Kingdom: Worship, Worldview, and Cultural Formation*. Grand Rapids: Baker Academic, 2009.

Smith, James K. A. *You Are What You Love: The Spiritual Power of Habit*. Grand Rapids: Brazos Press, 2016.

20

Revelations of a Baptized Memory
Engaging Memory in Spiritual Development

Megan Rials

What is memory? Merriam Webster, that perennial fount of reliable definitions, supplies a number of meanings, two of which are as follows: "the power or process of reproducing or recalling what has been learned and retained especially through associative mechanisms," and "a particular act of recall or recollection."[1] The American Psychological Association, meanwhile, describes memory in this manner: "the ability to retain information or a representation of past experience, based on the mental processes of learning or encoding, retention across some interval of time, and retrieval or reactivation of the memory"; "specific information or a specific past experience that is recalled"; and "the hypothesized part of the brain where traces of information and past experiences are stored."[2]

As the breadth of these various definitions indicates, for a word used so often and so casually, memory remains a slippery concept to define, perhaps because its very essence is so difficult to pinpoint. For the Christian apologist, however, defining memory is essential, for memory plays a key role in spiritual development, and definition precedes understanding, which in turn precedes relying on it as an element of conversion and discipleship. The definitions above gravitate to one of two meanings: mem-

---
[1] Merriam-Webster, https://www.merriam-webster.com/dictionary/memory.
[2] American Psychological Assocation, https://dictionary.apa.org/memory.

ory as the faculty that equips us to recall past events and information, or memory as the specific events themselves that the faculty stores. In this chapter, I propose a definition of memory that encompasses both of these meanings, but drives home memory's spiritual significance: memory is the story we tell ourselves about our lives and our identity, which in turn shapes our view of ourselves and of God.

Defining the "Baptized Memory"

With that definition in place, let us address why memory holds such transcendence and importance. I will be working here with a concept I call the "baptized memory," which I have developed in conjunction with my research on C. S. Lewis. The term is a riff on another concept that, in his spiritual autobiography, Lewis calls the "baptized imagination," which he received when he read *Phantastes*, a novel by Scottish fantasy novelist and pastor George MacDonald that featured goodness and truth and caused him to long for heaven.[3] Although this chapter covers a broader range than Lewis's work, like most wisdom drawn from Lewis, the concept of the baptized memory holds far-reaching implications. I therefore discuss my findings from Lewis's corpus before moving into discussing the science on the mind-body connection with which God created us and how apologists can leverage it in their work.

In Lewis's essay "Myth Became Fact," he elaborates on the power of myth and points out that pagan mythology features many stories of so-called dying and rising gods, such as Osiris in Egyptian mythology and Balder in Norse mythology.[4] For Lewis, the power of myth lies in its combination of the abstraction of truth with the immediacy of direct experience.[5] He then argues the story of Jesus Christ is a true myth, the ultimate myth, because by living His life into history, He also brought the potent "dying and rising god" into historical existence.[6]

---

[3] Lewis, *Surprised by Joy*, 181.
[4] Lewis, "Myth Became Fact," in *God in the Dock*, 66–67.
[5] Lewis, "Myth Became Fact," in *God in the Dock*, 66.
[6] Lewis, "Myth Became Fact," in *God in the Dock*, 67.

The implication of this truth is that Jesus has sanctified and redeemed not only human nature, but also the narrative arc of storytelling itself. Because of time, history and life necessarily have a tripartite structure. Through Jesus's Incarnation, God Himself entered time, into history and life, and redeemed them as stories. Thus, each life is a story, and if chapters are ripped out, we cannot fully understand our story or continue to write it as God calls us in the present and into the future.

Let us now turn specifically to the "baptized memory" concept and its intrinsic connection to the power of story. Lewis calls memory the "polarised light" that brings the past into focus and helps us understand the events of the past more clearly.[7] His novel *Out of the Silent Planet* contains a wonderful illustration of how the baptized memory works in practice. There, one of Lewis's characters, Hyoi, says the following:

> A pleasure is full grown only when it is remembered. You are speaking, *Hman*, as if the pleasure were one thing and the memory another. It is all one thing... What you call remembering is the last part of the pleasure, as the *crah* is the last part of a poem. When you and I met, the meeting was over very shortly, it was nothing. Now it is growing something as we remember it. But still we know very little about it. What it will be when I remember it as I lie down to die, what it makes in me all my days till then—that is the real meeting.[8]

Hyoi's practice is reminiscent of Mary, who, using her own memory, after the Wise Men visited the baby Jesus, "treasured up all these things, pondering them in her heart" (Lk 2.19). For Lewis, experience and memory are intimately related because the pleasure, or the experience, reaches its fruition only once its effects can be later comprehended through memory. In other words, memory needs the context of an entire life to equip the individual to identify and recognize God's greatest blessings in his past. Memory thus derives its power to effect spiritual change from equipping the individual to understand the full ramifications of his past.

The capacities of Hyoi's memory, however, exceed those of a typical human memory, which raises the question: how can we similarly rely on

---

[7] Lewis, "Talking About Bicycles," 89.
[8] Lewis, *Out of the Silent Planet*, 74.

memory in spiritual development? The answer lies in Hyoi's status as the member of an unfallen race, which indicates that the remarkable powers Lewis ascribes to memory can be achieved only in an advanced spiritual state. Thus, for an individual in the fallen world, a serious maturation must occur for his memory to be purified and have the same effects.

That Lewis believed such a maturation was the result of Christian salvation becomes evident in his novel *The Great Divorce*. Therein, he casts George MacDonald, the author of *Phantastes*, as a character who acts as a Beatrice to Lewis's Dante in guiding Lewis around heaven. MacDonald explains that good and evil, in eternity, "become retrospective.... The good man's past begins to change so that his forgiven sins and remembered sorrows take on the quality of Heaven: the bad man's past already conforms to his badness and is filled only with dreariness."[9] He claims that "Heaven, once attained, will work backwards and turn even that agony [of suffering on earth] into a glory."[10]

In other words, the eternal destination of either hell or heaven influences the individual's memory and perception of his past. The dark lies of hell twist the damned individual's memory so that he falsely recalls his life as nothing but despair, whereas for the saved person, the light from heaven irradiates what he first believed were deserts and reveals them as oases. Salvation thus *baptizes* memory to allow it to act as the "polarised light" that allows us to see the past and God's hand in it clearly. As MacDonald's remarks reveal, though, for memory to possess this heavenly capability, we must first submit to salvation, which purifies the faculty of memory.

Lewis's best expression of this process lies in his character Orual, the narrator and main character of his last published novel, *Till We Have Faces*. Styled as the memoirs of a queen in a fictional pagan, pre-Christian nation who has spent her life rebelling against the divine and only at the end of her life experiences a conversion, the novel explores the salvation process and the role that memory plays. The writing of Orual's memoirs engages her memory and spurs her spiritual development. Although her stated purpose in writing her first book is to reveal the gods' supposed

---

[9] Lewis, *The Great Divorce*, 69.
[10] Lewis, The Great Divorce, 69.

injustices toward her, her memory causes it to have an unintended effect. Instead of bolstering her complaints, as she had intended, the writing of her book reveals her flaws, which awakens her realization of her sin.

Once Orual is saved, though, her memory undergoes the heavenly purification process described in *The Great Divorce*. Orual's mentor, the Fox, appears to her in a vision, and shows her a row of magical murals that depict her past in vivid detail. Through them, Orual discovers that where Orual believed her half-sister Psyche had suffered through various tasks, Psyche instead easily accomplished them—but, as the Fox explains, "Another bore nearly all the anguish," and Orual discovers that she bore the pain for Psyche.[11] This scene thus enacts Lewis's principle of the retroactivity of heaven and hell: Orual's memory has been baptized by the light of heaven so that she sees the truth of the past clearly. As the Fox remarks, "This age of ours will one day be the distant past. And the Divine Nature can change the past. Nothing is yet in its true form."[12] This "changing of the past" does not suggest the divine alters the events of the past; rather, it means that through her baptized memory, Orual sees the events of the past and their implications clearly, as the gods do. Because Orual finally understands the meaning of her life—specifically, that the god of love, not Orual herself, is the hero of her story—and can see how the gods used even her sin to accomplish the specific good of her, and her sister's Psyche's, salvation, she can write her second memoir about her conversion that reveals the goodness of the divine.

Orual's story demonstrates the importance of the baptized memory giving the proper perspective for viewing the past. Writing the story of her past awakens her to how she has used her memory in a self-deceptive way and prepares her to recognize her need for change, which puts her on the path to salvation. Thus, from Orual, apologists learn that memory can help individuals understand the story of their own lives and sort through the past to understand what direction they need to take in the present and the future.

The importance of the baptized memory as a framework that gives the proper perspective on life is closely connected to a perennial philosophical

---

[11] Lewis, *Till We Have Faces*, 300.
[12] Lewis, *Till We Have Faces*, 305.

and theological topic: what we behold shapes who we are and what we can see, and therefore who we become. As neuroscientist, philosopher, and literature scholar Iain McGilchrist writes, "Attention is a moral act: it creates, brings aspects of things into being."[13] Empirical research confirms this phenomenon. In a study, researchers asked participants to count how many times a basketball was passed around a group of people.[14] When asked about the person in a gorilla suit who had walked across the court in the middle of the exercise, however, many of the participants were unable to answer the question—because they had not even noticed it.[15] Their attention, focused as it was on counting the basketball passes, literally influenced what they did and did not see. To connect this concept explicitly to memory, additional research shows that our attention is specifically directed by memory. For example, one study showed that upon entering an apartment and scanning it to look for something, we know where to look based on our memory from prior visits.[16]

Memory thus literally shapes our vision. Far from being limited to the present, though, the baptized memory also equips believers to see their past with the particular kind of spiritual vision describes in *The Great Divorce*. According to the psychological concept called "affordances," our capabilities determine what we see: for example, a hunter with a gun will automatically see a wider range of where he can hunt than a hunter with a spear.[17] The same holds true for the believer's approach to the past. Understanding the past and God's work in his life determines how the believer sees the present and his perception of how God might work in it.

The Neuroscience of Memory

As we have seen, the stories we tell ourselves about our lives are of paramount importance, and apologists should help nonbelievers attend carefully to their memories to help them make sense of their past and how Christ has worked in them. In Curt Thompson's *Anatomy of the Soul*, he

---

[13] McGilchrist, *The Master and His Emissary*, 133.
[14] Brooks, *How to Know a Person*, 66.
[15] Brooks, *How to Know a Person*, 66.
[16] Ranganath, *Why We Remember*, 120.
[17] Brooks, *How to Know a Person*, 119.

explains the well-known theory that the brain is divided into the left hemisphere and the right hemisphere.[18] The left hemisphere focuses on logical, rational, linear thinking, and the right hemisphere focuses on understanding the world around us in a holistic manner based on the sensory inputs of the body and the mind.[19] The left hemisphere understands time and gives us a sense of the past and the future, whereas the right side focuses on the present because it is caught up in processing the information it is receiving in the present and therefore has no sense of time.[20]

The act of remembering one's past through telling it activates both the left brain, which remembers facts, and the right brain, which remembers impressions and sensations, such that it increases the chance of certain neurons activating simultaneously.[21] As the individual grows and matures, the part of the brain known as the hippocampus develops, which unites the memories of the left and right brain and thus helps the individual to develop his sense of self as he pays specific attention to his life.[22] Although remembering certainly involves the past, the act itself of remembering occurs in the present.[23] Because neurons that "fire together, wire together"—meaning that the brain learns to associate certain events with the emotions that accompany them—in recalling an event, the individual's present sensations and impressions influence his memories of past events.[24] Further, the same neural networks that assist in recalling the past are the same neurons and grooves that help us anticipate the future.[25] Thus, Thompson explains, when we remember the past, we are actually "remembering the future" as well, for how we recall the past directly affects how we view the future.[26]

This neuroscience is intimately connected with the power of storytelling. According to Thompson, the hippocampus and the prefrontal cortex

---

[18] Thompson, *Anatomy of the Soul*, 33–34.
[19] Thompson, *Anatomy of the Soul*, 33–36.
[20] Thompson, *Anatomy of the Soul*, 36–37.
[21] Thompson, *Anatomy of the Soul*, 79.
[22] Thompson, *Anatomy of the Soul*, 73–74.
[23] Thompson, *Anatomy of the Soul*, 76.
[24] Thompson, *Anatomy of the Soul*, 65, 76.
[25] Thompson, *Anatomy of the Soul*, 76.
[26] Thompson, *Anatomy of the Soul*, 63, 76.

in the brain, which are integral to the individual's capacity for memory, develop at the same time as the capacity for language and the recollection of facts (a left-hemisphere function), which in turn is intertwined with the individual's capacity for remembering sensations and feelings (a right hemisphere function).[27] Thus, this sequencing process becomes the narrative of the individual's life.[28] As Thompson explains,

> You construct your understanding of the world and your place in it through the lens of your own story. And the manner and context in which you reflect on your story (in your mind) or tell your story (to others) become part of the fabric of the narrative itself. In other words, the process of reflecting on and telling others your story, and the way you experience others hearing it, actually shapes the story and the very neural correlates, or networks, it represents.[29]

Thus, when the individual shares his memory by telling the story of his life, he activates both the left brain and the right brain, thus integrating them and uniting the linear, logical response and the perceptive, intuitive response to the events of his life.[30] Such sharing also rewires the individual's neural pathways in the brain, for when the individual recalls a painful experience, his listener's expressions of sympathy help him experience a different reaction to the event because the right hemisphere picks upon the listener's reactions to the story, and processing the memory in light of this compassionate reaction positively influences the individual's neural pathways involving his memory of the event..[31]

For Thompson, Scripture confirms the importance of having a listener in this process. Thompson believes David's petition in Psalm 86.11 for an "undivided heart" is indicative of David uniting his right and left hemispheres and further observes that David's request that God teach him His ways suggests this process is impossible without another mind listening and offering feedback.[32] Thus, Thompson explains, the spiritual and ther-

---

[27] Thompson, *Anatomy of the Soul*,
[28] Thompson, *Anatomy of the Soul*,
[29] Thompson, *Anatomy of the Soul*, 77.
[30] Thompson, *Anatomy of the Soul*, 79.
[31] Thompson, *Anatomy of the Soul*, 78.
[32] Thompson, *Anatomy of the Soul*, 168–169.

apeutic disciplines that involve individuals telling their stories to others directly give rise to neurological and spiritual healing, as minds meet and work together in the act of telling the stories of memory.[33]

This discussion demonstrates that the ability to create a cohesive narrative of our lives is essential to psychological and spiritual health. Although apologists certainly need not be professional therapists, understanding how memory works and addressing it with nonbelievers, either directly or indirectly, is crucial for apologists. Specifically, the apologist's goal when addressing memory is to equip the nonbeliever to undergo an experience similar to Orual's in writing her memoirs, a process that incorporated her life story as an integral component to her spiritual development and eventual salvation. Through asking for the nonbeliever's life story, apologists allow the nonbeliever's mind to undergo a different and healthier experience, as the very act of retelling the story gives the nonbeliever the opportunity to reframe that story and, in turn, the story he has internalized about himself. In this fashion, apologists can quite literally share the mind of Christ with nonbelievers (1 Cor. 2.16). Thus, in this way, apologists may help to transform nonbelievers' minds and memories and reshape the trajectory of their future—in other words, to help baptize their memory. Crafting an accurate story of our lives helps us form our sense of self, and as Lewis notes in *Mere Christianity*, it is when we seek Christ that He gives us our true personalities and selves.[34] Building a healthy memory thus prepares the groundwork for God to enter and heal believers and nonbelievers alike from the effects of sin in our fallen world. Specifically, for nonbelievers, the growth of a healthy memory ensures they have a strong sense of self to over to God for renewal and salvation. Apologists would do well to remember Thompson's concept of "remembering the future," which echoes Lewis's concept of the retroactivity of heaven and hell; thus, Romans 12.2's exhortation that believers be transformed by the renewing of their minds takes on a new meaning.

---

[33] Thompson, *Anatomy of the Soul*, 171.
[34] Lewis, *Mere Christianity*, 224–225.

Becoming Better Communicators

With this goal in place, what can apologists do to help shape the memory of nonbelievers? While not written for an apologetics or even a Christian audience per se, David Brooks's *How to Know a Person* offers insightful advice on communication and becoming a better listener that apologists can leverage. Brooks points out there are two different kinds of thinking: the paradigmatic mode, which is analytical and focuses on making an argument; and the narrative mode, which focuses on the life narrative of our interlocutor.[35] Apologists should note their training often focuses heavily on the paradigmatic mode, insofar as it frequently focuses on learning the strongest arguments and tactics to make the best case to sway nonbelievers to the side of Christianity. Although there is a time and a place for that mode, and it does indeed play a crucial role in apologetics, apologists must not lose sight of our real goal and who we are called to be. Jesus told the disciples He was calling them to be fishers of men, not winners of arguments or champion debaters (Matt. 4.19). If apologists win technical arguments, but lose the very people we say we want to convert, we have lost the heart of the Gospel. Here, the value of the narrative mode proves its worth, as it strengthens our relational skills so that we may imitate our Lord's example more fully.

Brooks's view of therapists as "story editors" confirms the value that the narrative mode holds for apologists.[36] Brooks points out that without the chance to tell his story, any given individual might never take stock of his life and thereby form his life's narrative.[37] He also emphasizes that editors are not passive: they actively point out problems, and if done in a loving way, this editing equips the author to see himself in a new light and afford him an opportunity to improve.[38] Brooks offers a powerful summary of how vital the creation of a life narrative is to the individual's identity, sense of self, and ability to grow:

> You can't know who you are unless you know how to tell your story. You can't have a stable identity unless you take the inchoate events of your life and give

---

[35] Brooks, *How to Know a Person*, 215.
[36] Brooks, *How to Know a Person*, 227.
[37] Brooks, *How to Know a Person*, 227.
[38] Brooks, *How to Know a Person*, 272.

your life meaning by turning the events into a coherent story. You can know what to do next only if you know what story you are a part of.[39]

This vision is one that apologists should also claim for themselves. In guiding nonbelievers to begin to see Jesus in their lives, apologists must necessarily attend to the power of narrative in the process and thereby act as "story editors" for nonbelievers as they gradually form life narratives that reveal Christ's work in their past—for, as Brooks writes, "wise people don't tell us what to do; they start by witnessing our story."[40]

The most effective way for the apologist to go about this task is to focus on being in the narrative mode when communicating with nonbelievers. By being attentive to others and their life stories—their sorrows, their struggles, their joys—we follow Jesus's lead in meeting the needs of others, as it helps facilitate at least in part the psychological healing from sin that fallen humankind desperately needs. To this end, Brooks offers practical tips on becoming a better listener and suggests specific things for which we should listen. One is "narrative flexibility": that is, the person's ability to update his life story so that it explains his current position in life and accurately reflects causation of events.[41] In so doing, apologists can watch in real time for the updating of the nonbeliever's memory, for as previously discussed, the telling of the story itself changes it. Further, listening for this receptivity in nonbelievers to updating their own story helps the apologist gauge the nonbeliever's openness to the good news we have to share.

Brooks suggests listening for two additional features of others' life stories that are helpful for apologists. First, he advocates paying attention to what roles into which they have cast themselves, such as a healer or a caregiver.[42] Second, we should attend to the type of narrative arc contained in others' life stories—for instance, if they have crafted a rags-to-riches or a quest narrative—so that we gain insight into how they view the trajectory of their lives.[43]

---

[39] Brooks, *How to Know a Person*, 217.
[40] Brooks, *How to Know a Person*, 248.
[41] Brooks, *How to Know a Person*, 225.
[42] Brooks, *How to Know a Person*, 221.
[43] Brooks, *How to Know a Person*, 223.

These features of others' life stories are important considerations for the apologist for two reasons. First, listening for the role in their life that others view themselves as inhabiting can show us their particular talents and giftings from God. It can also reveal their self-perception and its ripple effect on their approach to life. For example, perhaps they have cast themselves in the role of a victim or otherwise marginalized their role in their own life such that they have paralyzed themselves from taking action and are thereby missing the true role that God is calling them to play. Or perhaps, as Orual does, they have cast themselves in the role of their own savior, thereby displacing Christ and leaving no room for His salvific and purifying work. Closely attending to their stories allows us to understand and minister to their specific needs more precisely and intimately.

Regardless, Jesus Himself stands at the door and knocks, asking to enter into the nonbeliever's narrative to cleanse and guide it. As the closing of the Gospel of John tells us, we know Christ tells us each only our own stories, and we as apologists know that the role He calls each person to play in his own story and in the world is unique to that individual (Jn. 20–22). The apologist's role, then, is not only to guide nonbelievers to God, but also to act as midwife for their discovery of His will for their lives so that they can craft the unique narrative that Christ beckons them toward.

Listening, though, is only part of communication. Apologists can also learn to implement the narrative mode from Brooks's tips on how to speak to others. As Brooks puts it, when we ask good questions, we are "adopting a posture of humility . . . [and] also honoring a person."[44] Thus, learning this skill helps us assume a Christ-like character toward others. Based on his experience as a reporter, Brooks explains that individuals respond better to questions that call for a narrative, as they relax and become more comfortable to share when recounting a narrative.[45] For Brooks, factual questions, such as "Where did you go to college?", are evaluative in nature and do not help us know their deeper character and concerns.[46] He also warns against "closed" questions, such as "Were you

---

[44] Brooks, *How to Know a Person*, 84.
[45] Brooks, *How to Know a Person*, 84.
[46] Brooks, *How to Know a Person*, 88.

and your mom close?", that do not invite further detail and nuance, and from vague questions like "How's it going?" that tend to lead nowhere.[47]

Instead, we should ask more open-ended questions: "How did you…?", "What it's like…?", and "Tell me about…?"[48] He also recommends questions that reveal commonalities like a shared hobby or interest or profession, and "big questions" about a person's life such as "If you died tonight, what would you regret not doing?" and "If the next five years is a chapter in your life, what is that chapter about?"[49] Another way of asking these big questions is to focus on the more positive aspects of life as well, such as by asking, "Tell me about a time you adapted to change" and "What's working really well in your life?"[50]

In addition to developing our capacity to listen and converse well, Brooks offers further practical advice that can guide our actions to demonstrate the love of Christ to others. Although terms for virtue are often used without precise definition, Brooks carefully breaks down the precise behaviors that together compose the virtue of empathy. For Brooks, empathy consists of three skills: mirroring, mentalizing, and caring.[51] Mirroring is simply "the act of accurately catching the emotion of the person in front of you."[52] In other words, through mirroring, we can accurately read what another person is feeling and experience it ourselves: we smile when our interlocutor smiles, we yawn when he yawns, and so on.[53] The science of mirroring further drives home the significance of the strong mind-body connection with which God created us. Research shows that "mirror neurons" exist in the brain's cortex that allow us to perceive not only our conversation partners' physical movements, but their emotional states as well.[54] It also produces an effect of "co-regulation": that is, when two people are physically close and trust each other, a physical transfer

---

[47] Brooks, *How to Know a Person*, 88.
[48] Brooks, *How to Know a Person*, 88.
[49] Brooks, *How to Know a Person*, 89, 90–91.
[50] Brooks, *How to Know a Person*, 91.
[51] Brooks, *How to Know a Person*, 144.
[52] Brooks, *How to Know a Person*, 144.
[53] Brooks, *How to Know a Person*, 146.
[54] Thompson, *Anatomy of the Soul*, 42.

occurs.[55] Through this phenomenon, the two individuals regulate each other's heart rates and produce "higher vagal tone," that is, a whole-body state where one's "gut and innards feel secure and serene."[56] This research should encourage apologists that their mere physical presence is a witness to Jesus, as it allows us to share the peace of Christ even without speaking.

Turning now to "mentalizing," it is here that believers' baptized memories come to bear in apologetics in a significant practical sense. Mentalizing is understanding what others are experiencing, particularly their suffering, based on our own experiences.[57] Brooks explains that it is also what Adam Smith, the eighteenth-century philosopher and economist, called "projective empathy": that is, the process of projecting our own memories onto another person's situation.[58] This skill helps us understand complex emotional states; for instance, seeing someone nervous on the first day of a new job might remind us of all the contradictory emotions we ourselves had in the same or similar situation: fear, excitement, and nervousness all at once.[59] As Brooks notes, it also helps us sympathize with a friend's situation while also "detaching to make judgments about them."[60] In a humorous example, he explains mentalizing allows us to feel bad for someone whose brand-new Mercedes has been scratched, while also believing that feeling miserable about it is childish.[61] Thompson also further explains that mentalizing helps children understand themselves, for if an infant's parents are able to mentalize well, she will develop a healthy sense of self through their loving response; in other words, the infant "will see herself and come to understand herself primarily through what she witnesses in her mother's responses."[62] Although apologists cannot have the same fundamental effect on nonbelievers as parents do on their children, this example speaks volumes about the importance of mentalization and its effects on those around us.

---

[55] Brooks, *How to Know a Person*, 158.
[56] Brooks, *How to Know a Person*, 158.
[57] Brooks, *How to Know a Person*, 147.
[58] Brooks, *How to Know a Person*, 147.
[59] Brooks, *How to Know a Person*, 147.
[60] Brooks, *How to Know a Person*, 147.
[61] Brooks, *How to Know a Person*, 147.
[62] Thompson, *Anatomy of the Soul*, 117.

Brooks's commentary on the last element of empathy, caring, is a simple concept to summarize and needs little elaboration. For Brooks, caring constitutes being attentive to the fact that someone's needs in a certain situation might completely different from our own.[63] For instance, one person might need to process an embarrassing situation at work with a friend, whereas others will want a friend to distract them entirely from it.[64] Caring simply means recognizing our personality differences and acting accordingly to meet others' needs.

"All Tales May Come True"
Memory in the New Heavens and New Earth

In conclusion, in helping reshape memory as the story we tell ourselves about our lives, ourselves, and God, apologists fulfill an important task. Despite not addressing apologists, Brooks summarizes the transformative power of our calling well:

> Seeing someone well is a powerfully creative act. No one can fully appreciate their own beauty and strengths unless those things are mirrored back to them in the mind of another. There is something in being seen that brings forth growth.... In how you see me, I will learn to see myself.[65]

Brooks's thoughts accord with those of Lewis. As Lewis writes, God gives believers their true personalities, and when He looks at His sons and daughters, He sees us flowering to our full potential of who He created us to be, not only the flawed individuals we are on this side of heaven.[66] Thus, developing a strong sense of self, through cultivating the baptized memory that lets us see ourselves and God and the world truly and accurately, is an expression of God's love and desire that we inhabit His unique design and plan for each of us.

But the baptized memory's implications affect not just the present age. As Lewis's friend and *Lord of the Rings* author J. R. R. Tolkien writes, "All tales may come true," and this holds true even and especially for our mem-

---
[63] Brooks, *How to Know a Person*, 148–149.
[64] Brooks, *How to Know a Person*, 148–149.
[65] Brooks, *How to Know a Person*, 11.
[66] Lewis, *Mere Christianity*, 224–225; Lewis, *Problem of Pain*, 34–35.

ories.⁶⁷ At the close of *Letters to Malcolm*, Lewis discusses the resurrection of the body, writing that "memory as we now know it is a dim foretaste, a mirage even, of a power which the soul, or rather Christ in the soul ... will exercise hereafter," going so far as to say that the rosy hue memory casts on our perception of the past "is the beginning of the glorification."⁶⁸ In his essay "Transposition," meanwhile, Lewis discusses the seeming contradiction of certain spiritual events using natural rather than mystical means to manifest themselves, such as the celebration of the Lord's Supper through eating and drinking.⁶⁹ He explains that what is happening in the lower medium can be understood only when we know what is happening in the higher medium: in other words, to understand the glimpses of the higher spiritual life received through events like the Lord's Supper, one must first know the transcendence of that higher spiritual life.⁷⁰ Lewis sees such transposition occurring in the mind-body connection as well, for he observes that thought cannot be reduced to mere "movement in the brain."⁷¹ The implied role of memory is apparent, as memory is necessarily a function of the mind. He then further applies transposition to the resurrection of the body in the new heavens and the new earth, writing that transposition helps to connect "Spirit and Nature."⁷² This concept illuminates his thoughts at the close of *Letters to Malcolm*:

> Matter enters into our experience only by becoming sensation (when we perceive it) or conception (when we understand it). That is, by becoming soul. That element in the soul which it becomes will, in my view, be raised and glorified; the hills and valleys of Heaven will be those you now experience not as a copy is to an original, nor as a substitute is to the genuine article, but as the flower to the root, or the diamond to the coal. But in entering our soul as alone it can enter—that is, by being perceived and known—matter has turned into soul.⁷³

---

[67] Tolkien, "Leaf by Niggle," 73.
[68] Lewis, *Letters to Malcolm*, 122.
[69] Lewis, "Transposition," 100.
[70] Lewis, "Transposition," 100.
[71] Lewis, "Transposition," 103.
[72] Lewis, "Transposition," 115.
[73] Lewis, "Transposition," 123.

Thus, for Lewis, memory accomplishes the transposition of the mind-body connection through the "sensation" and "perception" of the physical world, and thereby ushers elements of our past into the new heavens and the new earth. This concept echoes the mysterious passage of 2 Timothy 2.11–13, which says that believers will reign with Christ in eternity. This chapter has shown that memory and the mind-body connection may well be part of that eternity. As believers, we know eternity begins now, with the stories, in the memories, that we create. Those tales of memory will certainly come true, for memory as the tale we tell ourselves about our lives, God, and our relationship to Him and with Him, bears directly not only on our present, but also on our future, either for good or for ill. Our role as apologists is to help those stories bear good fruit in eternity. May we use our own baptized memories well to guide nonbelievers to their own baptism in Christ.

Bibliography

Brooks, David. *How to Know a Person: The Art of Seeing Others Deeply and Being Deeply Seen.* New York: Random House, 2023.

Lewis, C.S. *The Great Divorce.* 1946. Reprint, New York: HarperCollins, 2001.

_____. *Letters to Malcolm.* 1963. Reprint, Orlando: Harcourt, 1991.

_____. *Mere Christianity.* 1952. Reprint, New York: HarperCollins, 2001.

_____. "Myth Became Fact." In *God in the Dock: Essays on Theology and Ethics,* 63–67. Edited by Walter Hooper. Grand Rapids: Eerdmans, 1970).

_____. *Out of the Silent Planet.* 1938. Reprint, New York: Scribner, 2003.

_____. *The Problem of Pain.* 1940. Reprint, New York: HarperCollins, 2001.

_____. "Talking About Bicycles." In *Present Concerns: Journalistic Essays,* 83–90. Edited by Walter Hooper. 1986. Reprint, New York: HarperCollins, 2017.

_____. *Till We Have Faces.* 1956. Reprint, Orlando: Harcourt, 1984.

_____. "Transposition." In *The Weight of Glory and Other Addresses,* 91–115. 1949. Reprint, New York: HarperCollins, 2001.

McGilchrist, Iain. *The Master and His Emissary: The Divided Brain and the Making of the Modern World*. New expanded edition. New Haven: Yale, 2019.

Ranganath, Charan. *Why We Remember: Unlocking Memory's Power To Hold On To What Matters*. New York: Doubleday, 2024.

Thompson, Curt. *Anatomy of the Soul: Surprising Connections between Neuroscience and Spiritual Practices That Can Transform Your Life and Relationships*. Carol Stream: Tyndale Momentum, 2010.

Tolkien, J. R. R. "On Fairy-Stories." In *Tree and Leaf*, 1–82. 1964. Reprint, London: HarperCollins, 2001.

Conclusion
A Truth Worth Defending

Tawa J. Anderson

Of the making of books there is no end. When it comes to the pursuit and proclamation of Christian truth, there is always need for more books which provide more tools for the Christ-follower to employ in our endeavor to share Jesus Christ with a broken and hurting world. Though many people today do not want to hear the truth, and may not even believe there is such a thing as truth, it is more necessary than ever to confidently *know* that our faith in Jesus Christ is true and to *show* to others the truth of the Christian worldview.

It is our sincere hope and prayer that the various chapters in this book, covering truth in epistemology, science, Scripture, and humanity, have stretched, challenged, and equipped you to be a more confident and courageous ambassador for the King of Kings. Truth is not meant to be hoarded and hidden under a basket. Truth is to be shared. Go, therefore, and present the truth of the Gospel to all who will listen.

Contributors

Tawa J. Anderson | New Orleans Baptist Theological Seminary
Raised in a non-Christian home, Tawa Anderson came to faith in high school. He was called to ministry, and served as English Pastor at Edmonton Chinese Baptist Church from 2001-2008. After completing his Ph.D., Dr. Anderson taught at Oklahoma Baptist University from 2011-2022 before joining the faculty at NOBTS. Tawa is the author of *Why Believe? Christian Apologetics for a Skeptical Age* (B&H Academic, 2021) and co-author of *An Introduction to Christian Worldview: Pursuing God's Perspective in a Pluralistic World* (IVP Academic, 2017).

Luke Barnes | Western Sydney University
Luke A. Barnes is a senior lecturer in physics at Western Sydney University, with a Ph.D. in astronomy from the University of Cambridge. The focus of his research has been the cosmic evolution of matter, and he has published papers in the field of galaxy formation and evolution, and on the fine-tuning of the universe for life. He is the co-author with Prof. Geraint Lewis of *A Fortunate Universe: Life in a Finely-Tuned Cosmos* and *The Cosmic Revolutionary's Handbook*, both published by Cambridge University Press.

Mike Blackaby | Blackaby Ministries International
Mike Blackaby is a pastor and church planter in Victoria, BC, Canada. He has a Ph.D. in Apologetics and Worldview from The Southern Baptist Theological Seminary and an M.Div. from Southeastern Baptist Theological Seminary. He has co-authored several books with his brother Daniel, including *God, Heroes, and Everyday Dragons: Finding Your Story in God's Story* and *Straight to the Heart: Communicating the Gospel in an Emotionally*

Driven Culture. He also contributed to the video teachings of the classic Bible study *Experience God*. Mike and his wife Sarah have 4 young children, 3 chickens, and 1 dog.

Robert M. Bowman Jr. | Institute for Religious Research
Dr. Bowman is an evangelical Christian apologist, biblical scholar, author, editor, and lecturer. He has lectured on biblical studies, religion, and apologetics at Biola University, Cornerstone University, and New Orleans Baptist Theological Seminary. Rob is the author of over sixty articles and the author or co-author of fifteen books including *Jesus' Resurrection and Joseph's Visions: Examining the Foundations of Christianity and Mormonism*. Dr. Bowman holds M.A. and Ph.D. degrees in biblical studies from Fuller Theological Seminary and South African Theological Seminary.

David H. Calhoun | Gonzaga University
Professor Calhoun's teaching and research focuses on topics in ancient Greek philosophy, human nature, the epistemology of belief and conversion, existentialism, Christianity and science, and Christianity and popular culture. In ancient philosophy, particular interests include Socratic method, Aristotelian virtue ethics, friendship, and Aristotle's theory of human nature. Regular teaching of Gonzaga's Philosophy of Human Nature course has fostered interest in questions about human and animal cognition, which led to exploration of the historical and conceptual relationships between philosophy, Christianity, and natural science. Much of his recent scholarship has been in philosophy and film, especially themes of religious faith and secularism.

Paul Copan | Palm Beach Atlantic
Dr. Paul Copan has a B.A. in biblical studies from Columbia International University; an M.A. in philosophy of religion and an M.Div., both from Trinity International University; and a Ph.D. in philosophy from Marquette University. He has been a visiting scholar at Oxford University. Dr. Copan is the author and editor of over forty books. For six years he served as the president of the Evangelical Philosophical Society, and he is currently chair of Tyndale Fellowship's Philosophy

of Religion Study Group (UK). He is part of the Worldview Bulletin team—an online Christian worldview resource.

Travis Dickinson | Dallas Baptist University

Travis Dickinson is Professor of Philosophy at Dallas Baptist University where he teaches all things philosophical and directs the philosophy program. He has a Ph.D. in philosophy from the University of Iowa, an M.A. in philosophy of religion and ethics, and an M.A. in Christian apologetics from Biola University. Travis is the author of *Wandering Toward God: Finding Faith amid Doubts and Big Questions*, *Logic and the Way of Jesus: Thinking Critically and Christianly* and the coauthor of *Stand Firm: Apologetics and the Brilliance of the Gospel*. He gets the privilege to regularly speak at churches and conferences and can be found online at www.travisdickinson.com.

Eric Hernandez | Texas Baptists

Eric Hernandez is a dynamic evangelist and apologist with a heart for proclaiming the gospel and defending the faith on theological and philosophical grounds. He's the author of the book, *The Lazy Approach to Evangelism: A Simple Guide for Conversing with Nonbelievers*, endorsed by J.P. Moreland, Mike Licona, J Warner Wallace, Frank Turek, and Lee Strobel. He's a licensed minister, a certified formation therapist, and the Apologetics Lead and Millennial Specialist for The Baptist General Convention of Texas. He holds an associate degree in social science, a bachelor's degree in theology, and a certificate in apologetics from Biola University.

Richard G. Howe | Southern Evangelical Seminary

Richard G. Howe is a writer as well as a public speaker and debater in churches, conferences, and university campuses on issues concerning Christian apologetics and philosophy. He is the Norman L. Geisler Chair of Christian Apologetics at Southern Evangelical Seminary in Charlotte, North Carolina, where he also serves as Professor of Philosophy and Apologetics and as the Provost. Dr. Howe is Past President of the International Society of Christian Apologetics. In their free time, Richard and his wife Rebekah enjoy international travel.

Brett Kunkle | Maven

Brett Kunkle is the founder and president of MAVEN (www.maventruth.com), a movement to equip the next generation to know truth, pursue goodness, and create beauty for the cause of Christ. Brett has 25+ years of experience working with youth and parents and is a Teaching Fellow at the Impact 360 Institute. He was an associate editor for *Apologetics Study Bible for Students* and co-authored *A Practical Guide to Culture: Helping the Next Generation Navigate Today's World* and *A Student's Guide to Culture*. He received his Master's degree in philosophy of religion and ethics from Talbot School of Theology.

Erin Kunkle | Maven

Erin Kunkle is the co-founder of MAVEN (www.maventruth.com). She is a regular speaker and has spoken to a wide range of audiences—parents, married couples, youth, moms, women, homeschooling groups and church audiences. Erin is also co-host of the MAVEN parent podcast, bringing the Christian worldview and practical application to bear on the challenging task of parenting in the 21st century. Erin received her bachelor's degree in social science with an emphasis in political science from Biola University. She is also a veteran homeschooling mom of 15 years and has been married to her husband, Brett, for 26 years.

Megan Rials | Society for Women of Letters

Megan Rials is a writer, literary scholar, and cultural apologist. She holds a Juris Doctor from the Louisiana State University Paul M. Hebert Law Center and a Master of Arts in cultural apologetics from Houston Christian University. She is a Senior Fellow at the Society for Women of Letters and serves on the core writing team for *Shadowlands Dispatch*, a magazine of cultural apologetics that she helped found and for which she served as its original Editor-in-Chief. Her main research interests include the role of memory in spiritual development, the power of language and narrative, and the Inklings. Her work has appeared in publications such as *Perichoresis*, *Christ and Pop Culture*, and *Mere Orthodoxy*.

Mary Jo Sharp | Confident Christianity
Mary Jo is the founder and director of Confident Christianity Apologetics Ministry. She serves on faculty with Summit Ministries Student Conferences, and is a published author with Kregel Publications, B&H Publications, and Zondervan. Her publications include *Why I Still Believe: A Former Atheist's Reckoning with the Bad Reputation Christians Give a Good God*, which recounts her own journey from atheism to the Christian faith, and *Why Do You Believe That?*, a study designed to instill confidence in conversations about faith.

Robert B. Stewart | New Orleans Baptist Theological Seminary
Robert Stewart is Professor Emeritus of Philosophy and Theology at New Orleans Baptist Theological Seminary. He has authored or edited several books including recent releases with Westminster John Knox, *What Did the Cross Accomplish: A conversation about Atonement* with N.T. Wright and Simon Gathercole, and *Can We Trust the Bible on the Historical Jesus?* with Craig Evans and Bart Ehrman. He has published numerous articles in books and in journals and has spoken in university settings in North America and Europe.

Michael G. Strauss | The University of Oklahoma
Dr. Michael G. Strauss (B.S., Biola University, Ph.D., University of California, Los Angeles) is a David Ross Boyd Professor of Physics at the University of Oklahoma. He conducts research in experimental particle physics at CERN laboratory in Geneva, Switzerland, where he studies the fundamental particles and forces in the universe. Dr. Strauss speaks about the intersection of science and Christianity at universities, schools, and churches throughout the world. He is the author of the book *The Creator Revealed: A Physicist Examines the Big Bang and the Bible*, and one of the general editors of Zondervan's *Dictionary of Christianity and Science*.

Matthew Tingblad | Josh McDowell Ministry
Matthew is a Christian writer and speaker with a passion for the church to be united, strengthened, and unleashed to spread the good news of Jesus to every corner of the world. With a focus on apologetics and spir-

itual growth, Matthew is a gifted public speaker who offers a fresh voice to a world full of tough questions and deep needs. He has spoken around the world on a variety of topics at the high-school and collegiate level. He also runs a YouTube channel discussing apologetic questions and is a regular contributor to the josh.org blog posts.

Melissa Cain Travis | Discovery Institute
Melissa Cain Travis earned a Ph.D. in Humanities with a Philosophy concentration from Faulkner University, where her dissertation research focused on the natural philosophy and natural theology of Johannes Kepler. She earned a Master of Arts degree in Science and Religion from Biola University and a Bachelor of Science in general biology from Campbell University. She serves as a Fellow at Discovery Institute's Center for Science and Culture and has taught university courses since 2014. She is the author of multiple books, including *Thinking God's Thoughts: Johannes Kepler and the Miracle of Cosmic Comprehensibility.*

James K. Walker | Watchman Fellowship
James Walker, the president of Watchman Fellowship, is a former fourth generation Mormon with over twenty years of ministry experience in the field of Christian counter-cult evangelism, apologetics, and discernment. He has been interviewed as an expert on new religious movements and cults on a variety of network television programs including *Nightline*, *ABC World News Tonight with Peter Jennings*, and *The News Hour with Jim Lehrer*. He has spoken at hundreds of churches, colleges, universities, and seminaries throughout the United States and internationally.

Nathan Ward | Florida College
Nathan Ward is Professor of Biblical Studies and Apologetics at Florida College and a minister of the word for the 58th Street Church in Tampa. He holds the D.Min. in theological exegesis (Knox Theological Seminary), master's degrees in biblical studies (Liberty) and Christian Apologetics (NOBTS), and bachelor's degrees in biblical studies (Florida College) and mass communications (USF). He has written and edited several books, including authoring *Our Eyes Are on You: A Study of Biblical*

Prayer and *God Unseen: A Theological Introduction to Esther*, and editing *From the Pen of Paul: An Introduction to the Pauline Epistles*. He lives in Thonotosassa, Fla. with his wife Brooke and sons, Silas and Judah.

Alycia Wood | Apologetics, Inc.
Growing up in church, Alycia always had questions. While studying for a degree in Criminal Justice and Sociology at Robert Wesleyan College, Alycia discovered Apologetics and learned that her quest for a deeper understanding of Christianity had a name. She earned her Master's in Social Justice from Marygrove College and spent a year studying apologetics in England. Before joining Apologetics, Inc., she spent 8 years as an Apologist with Ravi Zacharias International Ministries and has now spent over ten years in full-time apologetics ministry. You can find her on her podcast, "Hey Alycia!".

More Apologetics from DeWard

Faith Thinkers
For 2,000 years, Christians passionate to share the truth about Jesus with other people have thoughtfully done so through books. The technical term for such persons is apologists—meaning those who give a defense—but we could call them "faith thinkers." By profiling 30 "faith thinkers" from the first twenty centuries, you will get a clear overview of the history of Christian faith thinkers. Becoming familiar with the works of these 30 thinkers will prepare you to participate meaningfully in a 2,000-year-old conversation.

Jesus' Resurrection and Joseph's Visions
Just as the resurrection of Jesus is the foundation of Christianity, the visions of Joseph Smith are the foundation of Mormonism. In *Jesus' Resurrection and Joseph's Visions*, Robert Bowman compares the evidence for of these two alleged events, showing how the historical data confirm the truth of Jesus' resurrection, and that the accounts of Joseph Smith's visions are historically unreliable. For Mormons who have doubts about their religion, this study will help them find a more reliable basis for faith in Christ. For Christians, this study provides a fresh angle on the historical evidence for the truth of Christianity.

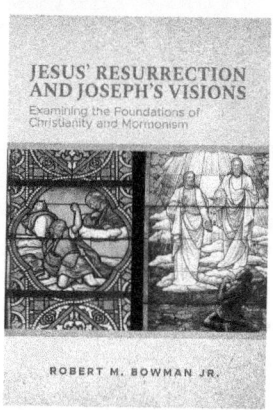

Too Good to be False
Skeptics say the Gospel is "only a story," a legend just like many other god-stories from ancient days. This book shows that although the skeptics' position is as far from truth as it could be. Jesus' character is unlike any other. No other hero—whether of history, myth, imagination, or legend—has loved as he loved, led as he led, cared as he cared, or understood himself as Jesus understood himself.

Testimonies to the Truth

With a heart for evangelism, equipping believers, and scholarship, McGrew brings together new arguments and old ones in a form that is readily accessible to laymen while being careful and rigorous. With these arguments in hand, you will never be stumped when someone asks, "Why should I believe what the Bible says about the life and teachings of Jesus?" Above all, McGrew points to Jesus himself, true God and true man, the One who teaches, loves, and suffers for us, described by the Gospels in vivid and credible detail.

Hidden in Plain View

An undesigned coincidence is an apparently casual, yet puzzle-like "fit" between two or more texts, and its best explanation is that the authors knew the truth about the events they describe or allude to. Connections of this kind among passages in the Gospels, as well as between Acts and the Pauline epistles, give us reason to believe that these documents came from honest eyewitness sources, people "in the know" about the events they relate. Supported by careful research yet accessibly written, *Hidden in Plain View* provides solid evidence that all Christians can use to defend the Scriptures and the truth of Christianity.

The Historical Tell

Bolstering the case for Luke's reliability, *The Historical Tell* investigates the significant claim Luke makes at the outset: that he relied on eyewitness testimony (Luke 1.1–4). It demonstrates that five patterns in Luke's Gospel are not only best explained by Luke's claim being true, but that these patterns fit together to form a corroborative evidence case. By following the evidence, we can gain new confidence in the claims Luke makes and in the eyewitnesses whose voices echo even today.

Mere Humanity

"Is Man a Myth?" asks the title of one of Mr. Tumnus's books. It was apparently an open question in Narnia during the Long Winter, and it has become so again for us. In *Mere Humanity*, Donald T. Williams plumbs the writings of three beloved Twentieth-Century authors to find answers that still resonate in the Twenty-First. Chesterton, Lewis, and Tolkien explain in their expositions and incarnate in their fiction a robust biblical doctrine of man that gives us a firm place to stand against the various forms of reductionism that dominate our thinking about human nature today.

Answers from Aslan

The world has changed radically in the eighty years since C.S. Lewis wrote his major apologetics works. His arguments are still valid, but that validity might not be as obvious as it used to be. It is not enough then for us just to parrot Lewis. We need to understand him so we can emulate him in a way nuanced to be effective with today's audience. We need to learn from Lewis's methods and approach and understand his proper role as a role model: to teach us how to do our own apologetic in our own voice for our own generation. The purpose of this book is to help him do just that.

The Case for Aslan

Did C.S. Lewis invent Aslan because he had lost confidence in Christ? Do the Chronicles of Narnia represent a retreat into a second childhood from a confident, rational Christianity? Or has Aslan grown even bigger since Lewis wrote these "simple children's stories?" Could Lucy's wardrobe door lead to a vision of Creation, Justice, the nature of evil, global faiths, the historical Jesus, miracles, and the Resurrection? Like the song of Aslan in an empty world, can it recreate our planet as well?

Evidences of Christianity

In this masterpiece of apologetics, J.W. McGarvey writes as a scholar who is thoroughly familiar with the most skeptical criticism of his day but at the same time completely persuaded that traditional views of the authorship, historical trustworthiness, and inspiration of Scripture are rationally defensible—a position more conservative than that held by most mainstream New Testament scholars today. But the change in the sociology of New Testament scholarship has been driven far more by philosophical fashion than by any change in the evidence itself. For just that reason, McGarvey's *Evidences of Christianity* affords a much-needed counterbalance for those whose study of apologetics has been filtered through the lens of modernism. Foreword by Timothy McGrew.

The Gospel of the Resurrection

In this classic work, B.F. Westcott offers not just a historical defense of the resurrection but also a wide-ranging exploration of the significance of the resurrection for the individual, for the church, for nations, for mankind, and at the widest reach, for creation itself. "The question at issue," he says, "is a view of the whole Universe, of all being and of all life, of man and of the world, and of God." New introduction by Timothy McGrew.

For a full listing of DeWard Publishing Company books, visit our website:

www.deward.com

www.ingramcontent.com/pod-product-compliance
Lightning Source LLC
Chambersburg PA
CBHW021140160426
43194CB00007B/641